TEUTONIC
TITANS

Reich President von Hindenburg (left, wielding blurred Marshal's baton) postwar wears a black mourning band on his left jacket sleeve in honor of Germany's war dead of 1914–18, followed by his son, Oskar, in steel helmet behind him. Note the cavalry officer at right in fur busby cap. In 1919, his postwar memoirs were ghostwritten by German Army Col. Hermann Mertz von Quirnheim. On October 1, 1919, Col. Mertz was named president of the Reich Archives, Potsdam—a post he held until October 31, 1931. (*HHA*)

TEUTONIC TITANS

HINDENBURG, LUDENDORFF, AND THE KAISER'S MARSHALS AND GENERALS, 1847-1955

BLAINE TAYLOR

FONTHILL

Dedication
*To Tom and Peggy Haderman of Middle River, MD, for their help
and friendship over twenty years—very much appreciated.*

Dearly Departed
*Jimmy Healy, career U.S. Postal employee, who died suddenly on
January 19, 2017, my sister's first husband. Gone, but not forgotten. RIP.*

Front cover image: From *Kaiser Bill*, 2014. One of the most famous pictures from the Great War. From left to right: Army Field Marshal Paul von Hindenburg, His Majesty the Kaiser and King, and Army Quartermaster-General Erich Ludendorff. (*Library of Congress*)

Rear cover image: Formal oil portrait of Field Marshal Paul von Beneckendorff und von Hindenburg with cloth cap and sword, by artist Franz Triebsch. (*U.S. Army Combat Art Collection*)

Fonthill Media Language Policy
Fonthill Media publishes in the international English language market. One language edition is published worldwide. As there are minor differences in spelling and presentation, especially with regard to American English and British English, a policy is necessary to define which form of English to use. The Fonthill Policy is to use the form of English native to the author. Blaine Taylor was born and educated in the U.S.; therefore American English has been adopted in this publication.

Fonthill Media Limited
Fonthill Media LLC
www.fonthillmedia.com
office@fonthillmedia.com

First published in the United Kingdom and the United States of America 2020

British Library Cataloguing in Publication Data:
A catalogue record for this book is available from the British Library

Copyright © Blaine Taylor 2020

ISBN 978-1-78155-773-0

Typeset in Minion Pro 10.5pt on 13.5pt
Printed and bound in England

Preface: Costs

World War II has tended to obscure the tremendous costs of World War I, known until 1939 as the Great War (indeed, it was), and the prewar continental Europe that existed before it never returned as a result.

An American postwar report on the vast struggle noted that the total lives lost by the Allies, or Entente Powers—as their enemies called them—was estimated at 6,422,738. For their Central Power foes, the death toll was 5 million. In all, 63,714,738 combatants served in all armies of both sides.

The total expenditure of monies by the Allies was $200 billion, while for the Central Powers, the toll was $110 billion. Just prior to the war, in the summer of 1914, a British banker had announced confidently that any such European war would have to conclude by the end of that year, because all the nations would go bankrupt; in the event, they simply borrowed more money.

The following biographical account—another in our series of fresh looks at the men and battles during the Great War's former centennial of 2014–18—presents the German emperor's field marshals and generals during the fighting; the revolution and civil war that resulted from it; and the republic and fascist dictatorship that evolved out of those, in most of which the very same men played major parts until their deaths—some as late as 1955.

In this expanded aspect, it is a largely untold story in such a comprehensive fashion as this, until now, a century later.

Blaine Taylor
Berkshires at Town Center
Towson, MD/USA
Centennial of the Great War
March 1, 2017

Acknowledgments

Thanks to Mrs. Erika Burke, Pearland, TX, and Hiltgunt Sherry Baker, Towson, MD—present and past translators; Photographic Consultant Stan Piet, Bel Air, MD; and to publisher Alan Sutton for making it possible. I am grateful to all of them and also to valued personal assistant Mrs. Doris Kropp of Towson, MD, as well as to Ms. Margaret Gers of the Enoch Pratt Free Library Periodicals Department and Mrs. Susannah Horrom of the Kelmscott Bookshop, both of Baltimore, MD/USA. Valued past typists on this overall project have included the former Joyce Gaston Taylor of Alabama and Shirley Hollifield of Middle River, MD/USA.

Contents

Timeline of Events

October 2, 1847:	Hindenburg is born at Posen, West Prussia.
December 6, 1849:	Mackensen is born.
1853:	Hindenburg at Cadet Academy, Wahlstadt, Silesia.
1863:	Hindenburg at Senior Cadet School, Berlin.
1865:	Hindenburg commissioned as a lieutenant in the 3rd Regiment Foot Guards, Prussian Army.
1866:	Hindenburg wins award for combat action at Battle of Königgrätz *versus* Austria.
October 1, 1869:	Mackensen volunteers a year for Hussar regiment and fights with it in the Franco-Prussian War, 1870–71, rising from the enlisted ranks.
1870:	Hindenburg fights in Battle of St Privat near Metz during the Franco-Prussian War.
1871:	Hindenburg attends proclamation of German Empire, rides into Paris; Berlin parade.
1873–76:	Hindenburg at War Academy, Berlin.
1877:	Hindenburg on the general staff, Berlin.
1879:	Hindenburg marries Gertrud Wilhelmine von Sperling, and Mackensen weds Doris von Horn.
1885:	Hindenburg's second tour of duty with the general staff, Berlin.
1889:	Hindenburg at War Ministry, Berlin.
1893–96:	Hindenburg commanding officer, 91st Infantry Regiment, Oldenburg.
1896–99:	Hindenburg chief of staff, 8th Army Corps, Koblenz.
1900–05:	Hindenburg commanding officer, 28th Division, Karlsruhe.
1905–11:	Hindenburg commanding officer, 4th Army Corps, Magdeburg.
January 9, 1911:	Hindenburg retires at Hanover.
June 28, 1914:	Austrian heir to throne assassinated at Sarajevo, Bosnia.
July 28, 1914:	Austria declares war on Serbia.
July 29, 1914:	Russia mobilizes its army.
August 1, 1914:	Germany declares war on Russia and France mobilizes its army.
August 2, 1914:	Germany invades Luxembourg.
August 3, 1914:	Germany declares war on France.
August 4, 1914:	Great Britain declares war on Germany as the latter invades Belgium.
August 5–17, 1914:	Battle of Fortress City of Liege; Belgium delays Schlieffen Plan.

August 6, 1914:	Austria-Hungary at war with Russia.
August 7, 1914:	British Expeditionary Force (BEF) lands in both France and Belgium, as promised; French invade German-occupied Alsace, with Joffre in command of the French Army; Montenegro at war with Germany.
August 8, 1914:	Serbia at war with Germany.
August 12, 1914:	France and the United Kingdom at war with Austria-Hungary, Montenegro at war with Germany.
August 15, 1914	Russian Army takes Königsberg, East Prussia
August 17, 1914:	Belgian fortress city of Liege surrenders to Ludendorff; Belgian capital moved from Brussels to Antwerp; von François wins Battle of Stallupönen in east.
August 17–23, 1914:	Russians defeat Mackensen at Battle of Gumbinnen.
August 20, 1914:	Brussels taken by German Army.
August 21, 1914:	Battle of Charleroi between French and Germans.
August 22, 1914:	Hindenburg and Ludendorff named to command of German 8th Army.
August 23–26, 1914:	First modern combat ever between Germans and British at Battle of Mons, followed by a second Reich victory over the BEF at Battle of Le Cateau; Crown Prince Wilhelm wins the Battle of the Frontiers against the French as the "Hero of Longwy."
August 24, 1914:	Germans invade France at Lille.
August 26, 1914:	German Army sacks and burns Louvain, Belgium.
August 28, 1914:	Austria-Hungary declares war on Belgium.
August 30, 1914:	Germans take Amiens, France.
August 26–31, 1914:	Hindenburg defeats Russian 2nd Army at Battle of Tannenberg.
September 3, 1914:	French government leaves Paris for Bordeaux on coast.
September 4, 1914:	Germans take Reims, France.
September 6–10, 1914:	German 1st Army of von Kluck defeated by Joffre's French Army and the BEF at the First Battle of the Marne River, with general retreat of the western German armies to the Soissons–Reims Line.
September 7–14, 1914:	Hindenburg wins First Battle of the Masurian Lakes.
September 14, 1914:	French Army retakes Amiens and Reims; von Moltke tells the Kaiser that the Schlieffen Plan has failed and that Germany has thereby already lost the war in the west.
September 20, 1914:	Reims Cathedral shelled by German Army.
September 28 to November 1, 1914:	Battle of Łódź in east.
September 29, 1914:	Germans bombard Antwerp, Belgium.
October 2, 1914:	British Royal Navy mines North Sea, starting naval blockade of Germany, 1914–20.
October 9, 1914:	Antwerp surrenders, with Belgian government retreating to Ostend; Mackensen fights Russian Army C-in-C Grand Duke Nicholas Nikolaevich at Battle of Lötzen Gap, and the latter falls back on Łódź.
October 13, 1914:	BEF wins First Battle of Ypres.
October 14, 1914:	Canadian Expeditionary Force (CEF) lands 32,000 men at Plymouth, UK; First Battle of Champagne, France.
October 15, 1914:	Germans take Ostend, with Belgian government moving to Le Havre, France.
October 24, 1914:	Allies occupy Péronne.

November 1914:	Turkey joins the Central Powers of Germany and Austria-Hungary *versus* the Entente Powers of Russia, France, and the UK.
November 1, 1914:	Mackensen named commander of German 9th Army in east by the Kaiser, with Grünert as chief of staff.
November 2, 1914:	The Kaiser promotes Hindenburg to general field marshal.
November 10, 1914:	Battle of Langemarck, Belgium; young Germans massacred.
November 11, 1914:	Mackensen advances on Łódź.
Mid-September to December 1914:	War of movement morphs into one of opposing trench systems 400 miles long, from the English Channel to the Swiss frontier, where they remain for the next four years.
December 24–25, 1914:	Christmas Truce between armies of both sides.
February 7–22, 1915:	Second Battle of the Masurian Lakes, another German victory.
February 18, 1915:	German Navy declares blockade of British Isles.
February 19–20, 1915:	First German Zeppelin airship raid on England.
March 10, 1915:	BEF takes Neuve Chapelle in Flanders, Belgium.
April 22, 1915:	At Second Battle of Ypres, Germans use poison gas to attack CEF.
May 2, 1915:	Gorlice–Tarnów Offensive, Germans *vs.* Russians.
May 7, 1915:	German Navy U-boat submarine sinks passenger liner *Lusitania* off Ireland.
May 23, 1915:	Savoyard Italy declares war on Austria on a 60-mile front, and on Germany three months later, both former allies since 1882.
May 31, 1915:	Zeppelin *LZ 38* bombs London.
June 4–6, 1915:	German aircraft bombs English towns.
June 15, 1915:	Allied planes bomb Karlsruhe, Germany.
June 22, 1915:	Mackensen awarded his field marshal's baton by the Kaiser after the capture of Lemberg.
July 31, 1915:	French Air Force bombs Baden, Germany.
August 5, 1915:	Germans take Warsaw.
September 25, 1915:	Allies take Lens in Second Battle of Artois.
October 12, 1915:	English Nurse Edith Cavell shot by Germans for helping British POWs escape from Belgium.
October 13, 1915:	Zeppelins bomb London, with fifty-five dead and 114 wounded.
October 14, 1915:	Bulgaria joins Central Powers of Germany, Austria-Hungary, and Turkey; invades Serbia.
October 15, 1915:	Great Britain declares war on Bulgaria.
October 17, 1915:	France declares war on Bulgaria.
November 17, 1915:	Anglo-French Allied war council holds its first meeting at Paris.
January 29–31, 1916:	Zeppelins bomb Paris and also English towns.
February 21, 1916:	Battle of Verdun begins in France.
February 25, 1916:	Verdun's Ft. Douaumont taken by Germans.
March 9, 1916:	Germany declares war on longtime British ally Portugal.
March 15, 1916:	Austria-Hungary declares war on Portugal.
March 31, 1916:	Melancourt at Verdun taken by Germans.
April 14, 1916:	British Royal Naval Air Service bombs both Constantinople and Adrianople in Turkey.
April 20, 1916:	Russian troops land at Marseilles for service on Western Front.
May 2–6, 1916:	German Gorlice–Tarnów Offensive.
May 15, 1916:	BEF takes Vimy Ridge.
May 31, 1916:	Naval Battle of Jutland (Skagerrak) fought between German and British Navies with heavy losses on both sides; Germans

	win a narrow victory, but never sortie out in strength again, to preserve "fleet in being" stance.
June 4, 1916:	Russian Army Brusilov Offensive begins against Austro-Hungarian Army.
June 6, 1916:	Germans take Ft. Vaux at Verdun.
July 1, 1916:	BEF and French attack north and south of Somme River in First Battle of the Somme, and RFC gains air control.
July 14, 1916:	BEF cavalry breaches German lines.
July 15, 1916:	BEF takes Longueval.
July 25, 1916:	BEF takes Pozières.
July 30, 1916:	BEF and French advance between Delville Wood and Somme River; British RFC and French Army of the Air conduct first joint aerial operations against the Imperial German Flying Corps.
August 3, 1916:	French Army recaptures Fleury.
August 27, 1916:	Romania declares war on Austria-Hungary.
August 28, 1916:	Italy declares war on Germany, and the latter on Romania.
August 29, 1916:	Hindenburg succeeds von Falkenhayn as chief of the German general staff with Ludendorff as first quartermaster general.
August 31, 1916:	Bulgaria and Turkey declare war on Romania.
September 2–3, 1916:	First Zeppelin shot down over U.K.
September 4, 1916:	Mackensen invades Romania with German & Bulgarian armies.
September 15, 1916:	BEF takes Flers–Courcelette and other positions on Western Front using tanks directed by aircraft.
September 26, 1916:	BEF and French take Combles and Thiepval.
October 24, 1916:	Verdun's Ft. Douaumont retaken by French.
November 2, 1916:	Germans evacuate Verdun's Ft. Vaux.
November 13, 1916:	BEF advances along Ancre River.
November 29, 1916:	Kaiser Franz Josef I of Austria-Hungary dies and is succeeded by Kaiser Karl.
November 23, 1916:	German Navy bombards English coast.
November 28, 1916:	First German daylight air raid on London.
December 6, 1916:	Mackensen links up with von Falkenhayn, and the field marshal enters fallen Bucharest on a white horse on his sixty-seventh birthday.
December 15, 1916:	French Army wins attrition Battle of Verdun.
December 18, 1916:	U.S. President Woodrow Wilson issues first offer of peace mediation to both sides; rejected.
December 26, 1916:	Germany suggests a peace conference.
January 22, 1917:	Wilson suggests a "peace without victory."
February 1, 1917:	Germans resume unrestricted submarine warfare against both Allied and neutral shipping.
February 3, 1917:	U.S. breaks diplomatic relations with Germany, and the German ambassador returns home.
February 17, 1917:	BEF wins Battle of Ancre River.
February 28, 1917:	Zimmermann telegram published, in which Germany secretly offers both Japan and Mexico a wartime alliance against the U.S. with American territory to be ceded in Far West, including New Mexico and Arizona.
March 3, 1917:	BEF advances on Bapaume.
March 4, 1917:	Germans withdraw to defensive positions of Siegfried/Hindenburg Line, thus shortening their Western Front by 75 miles.

March 14, 1917:	China breaks with Germany.
March 15, 1917:	Abdication of Tsar Nicholas and Tsesarevich Alexei in Russia, that stays in the war.
March 17, 1917:	BEF takes Bapaume as French capture Roye and Lassigny.
March 18, 1917:	Germans retreat, giving up Péronne, Chaulnes, Nesle, and Noyon.
March 26–31, 1917:	Battle of Cambrai between BEF and Germans.
April 6, 1917:	U.S. declares war on Germany.
April 7, 1917:	Cuba and Panama declare war on Germany.
April 8, 1917:	Austria-Hungary breaks diplomatic relations with U.S.
April 9, 1917:	BEF defeats Germans at Battle of Arras, as Bolivia severs diplomatic relations with Germany.
April 1917:	Germans smuggle Lenin into Russia by rail.
April 13, 1917:	Canadians take Vimy, Givenchy, Bailleul, and Lens from the Germans.
April 20, 1917:	Turkey breaks diplomatic relations with the U.S.
May 7, 1917:	German Gotha bombers make first night raid on London.
May 9, 1917:	Liberia breaks with Germany.
May 16, 1917:	BEF takes Bullecourt during aftermath of Battle of Arras.
May 17, 1917:	Honduras breaks with Germany.
May 19, 1917:	Nicaragua breaks with Germany.
May 25, 1917:	Twenty-one heavy German Gotha bombers make first mass daylight attack on U.K.
June 7, 1917:	BEF takes Messines–Wytschaete Ridge.
June 13, 1917:	First mass daylight Gotha bomber raid (fourteen) on London with 588 casualties.
June 18, 1917:	Haiti breaks with Germany.
July 1, 1917:	Kerensky Offensive by Russian Army starts in Galicia.
July 3, 1917:	First American Expeditionary Force (AEF) arrives in France.
July 12, 1917:	Pro-German King Constantine of Greece abdicates in favor of his son.
July 19, 1917:	Bethmann-Hollweg fired as imperial chancellor, succeeded by Dr Michaelis.
July 16–23, 1917:	Russian Army beaten by Germans and retreats on a 155-mile-long front.
July 22, 1917:	Siam declares war on Germany and Austria-Hungary.
August 7, 1917:	Liberia declares war on Germany.
August 14, 1917:	China declares war on Germany and Austria-Hungary.
August 15, 1917:	CEF takes Hill 70 overlooking Lens; St Quentin Cathedral destroyed by German Army.
August 22, 1917:	Final German aerial daylight bombing of U.K.
September 5, 1917:	New American Army begins assembly.
September 16, 1917:	Kerensky proclaims Russian Republic.
September 20, 1917:	Costa Rica breaks with Germany.
September 26, 1917:	During Battle of Ypres, BEF takes Zonnebeke, Polygon Wood, and Tower Hamlets.
October 6, 1917:	Peru and Uruguay break with Reich.
October 9, 1917:	BEF and French take Poelcapelle.
October 23, 1917:	AEF fires its first shots in trench warfare, as French Army advances northeast of Soissons.
October 26, 1917:	Brazil declares war on Germany.

November 1, 1917:	German Army abandons Chemin des Dames position.
November 6, 1917:	Canadians take Passchendaele.
November 7, 1917:	Lenin's Bolsheviks depose Kerensky.
November 9, 1917:	Italian Army retreats to Piave River during Battle of Caporetto.
November 15, 1917:	Clemenceau becomes premier of France.
November 20, 1917:	Second Battle of Cambrai.
November 21, 1917:	BEF takes Ribécourt, Flesquières, Havrincourt, and Marcoing.
November 23, 1917:	Italians repulse Germans from Asiago Plateau to Breneta River, with aid of eleven French and British divisions.
November 24, 1917:	During Battle of Cambrai, BEF tanks capture Bourlon Wood.
December 1, 1917:	German East Africa falls to Allies; Allied Supreme War Council meets for first time at Versailles representing top four European Entente powers; US, UK, France, and Italy.
December 3, 1917:	Russians ask Germans for an armistice.
December 5, 1917:	BEF retreats from Bourlon Wood and Graincourt west of Cambrai
December 7, 1917:	Finland declares independence from Russia under German aegis.
December 8, 1917:	Jerusalem lost by Turks after 673 years to British Army, and Ecuador breaks with Germany.
December 10, 1917:	Panama declares war on Austria-Hungary.
December 11, 1917:	U.S. declares war on Austria-Hungary.
January 8, 1918:	Wilson proclaims his Fourteen Points for peace.
January 19, 1918:	AEF takes over sector NE of Toul, France.
February 1, 1918:	Argentina recalls military attaches from Berlin.
February 18, 1918:	AEF in Chemin des Dames sector.
March 1, 1918:	AEF wins victory in salient north of Toul.
March 3, 1918:	Russia and Germany sign peace Treaty of Brest-Litovsk.
March 4, 1918:	Treaty signed between Reich and Finland.
March 5, 1918:	Preliminary peace treaty signed between defeated Romania and Central Powers.
March 9, 1918:	Lenin moves Russian capital from Petrograd to Moscow.
March 21, 1918:	Germans launch Kaiser's Battle/Michael Offensive against Allies on the Western Front to win the war on a 50-mile front from Arras to La Fère, including a bombardment of Paris from a long-range gun 76 miles distant.
March 24, 1918:	German Army takes Péronne, Ham, and Chauny.
March 25, 1918:	Bapaume and Nesle fall again to Germans.
April 9, 1918:	Germans start second drive in Flanders, Belgium.
April 10, 1918:	First German drive halted at Amiens after an advance of 35 miles.
April 15, 1918:	Second German drive stopped at Ypres after a 10-mile advance.
April 21, 1918:	Guatemala declares war on Germany; German air ace Baron Manfred von Richthofen killed in combat.
April 23, 1918:	Royal Navy raids German submarine base at Zeebrugge, Belgium, blocking its access channel.
May 7, 1918:	Nicaragua declares war on all Central Powers.
May 19–20, 1918:	Final German bomber raid on U.K. in which there are casulties.
May 24, 1918:	Costa Rica declares war on Central Powers.
May 27, 1918:	Third German drive starts on Aisne-Marne River front of 30 miles between Soissons and Reims, France in Second Battle of the Marne.

May 28, 1918:	Germans sweep past Chemin des Dames, crossing the Vesle River at Fismes, while AEF takes Cantigny.
May 29, 1918:	French Army gives up Soissons.
May 31, 1918:	Germans cross Marne River, reaching Château-Thierry, 40 miles from Paris, but lose the Second Battle of the Marne.
June 3–6, 1918:	U.S. Marines and Army halt German advance at Château-Thierry and Neuilly after an advance of 32 miles, as U.S. cooperation with Allies begins on a large scale.
June 5, 1918:	Strategic bombing of Germany by British bombers starts.
June 9–14, 1918:	German Army halted on Western Front.
June 15–24, 1918:	Austrians defeated by Italian Army.
June 30, 1918:	AEF numbers 1,019,115 soldiers in France; U.S. Marines engage the German Army at Belleau Wood, and recognized as having saved Paris.
July 1, 1918:	AEF takes Vaux.
July 3, 1918:	Turkish Sultan Mohammed V dies.
July 15, 1918:	Haiti declares war on Germany, and AEF halts renewed German drive on Paris.
July 18, 1918:	French Army and AEF launch joint offensive on Marne-Aisne River front.
July 23, 1918:	French seize Oulchy-le-Château, driving the Germans back 10 miles between Aisne and Marne Rivers.
July 30, 1918:	Allies on the Ourcq River, with Germans in full retreat to the Vesle River.
August 2, 1918:	French army retakes Soissons.
August 3, 1918:	Wilson agrees to joint Allied Expeditionary Force with U.K., Japan, and France to Murmansk, Archangel, and Vladivostok; Allies push past Reims and Soissons, capturing German Fismes base as well as the entire Aisne-Vesle River front.
August 5, 1918:	Final Zeppelin air raid on England.
August 7, 1918:	French and AEF cross the Vesle River.
August 8, 1918:	BEF drive starts in Picardy, advancing 14 miles; "Black Day of the German Army," according to Ludendorff, as Allies break through German lines.
August 11, 1918:	Allies retake Montdidier.
August 12, 1918:	Mt. Lassigny taken by French.
August 13, 1918:	Hindenburg and Ludendorff tell Kaiser Wilhelm that the war cannot be won, and must be ended.
August 15, 1918:	CEF captures Damery and Parvillers northwest of Roye.
August 21, 1918:	Battle of Bapaume.
August 26, 1918:	Battle of the Scarpe.
August 28, 1918:	Renewed Battle of the Somme River.
August 29, 1918:	Allies retake Noyon and Bapaume.
September 1, 1918:	Australian Army takes Péronne; AEF fights in Belgium for the first time, capturing Voormezeele.
September 11, 1918:	German Army driven back to the Hindenburg Line of November 1917.
September 14, 1918:	AEF starts St Mihiel offensive on a 40-mile front.
September 15, 1918:	St Mihiel recaptured from Germans, with 150 square miles of France liberated from German occupation since 1914.
September 19–20, 1918:	British RAF destroys Turkish 7th Army in Palestine from the air.

September 21, 1918:	Turkish Army loses 40,000 prisoners to the British in Palestine.
September 27, 1918:	French and AEF take 30,000 POWs in drive from Reims to Verdun, attacking the Hindenburg Line.
September 28, 1918:	Belgian Army assaults Germans from Ypres to the North Sea, advancing 4 miles.
September 29, 1918:	Bulgaria surrenders to the Allied Army of French Gen. Franchet d'Espèrey.
September 30, 1918:	British-Belgian Army advance reaches Roulers.
October 1918:	U.S. Marines defeat Germans at Battle of Blanc Mont/White Mountain.
October 1, 1918:	Allies capture Hindenburg Line cornerstone of St Quentin; Damascus taken by British Army during Palestine campaign.
October 2, 1918:	Germans retreat from Lens.
October 3, 1918:	Italians clear Austrian Army from Albania.
October 4, 1918:	Tsar Ferdinand of Bulgaria abdicates, succeeded by son, Crown Prince Boris.
October 5, 1918:	German Imperial Chancellor Prince Max of Baden asks for Allied Armistice terms from President Wilson.
October 7, 1918:	French Army takes Berry-au-Bac.
October 9, 1918:	Allies take Cambrai.
October 11, 1918:	AEF advances in Meuse-Argonne Forest.
October 12, 1918:	German Foreign Minister Solf states that Germany will give up all occupied territory.
October 13, 1918:	Germans retreat from Laon and La Fère; AEF takes Grandpré after four-day battle.
October 14, 1918:	Wilson refers Germans to French Marshal Foch for Armistice terms.
October 16, 1918:	BEF enters Lille.
October 17, 1918:	German submarine base at Ostend, Belgium, taken by Allied amphibious attack; Allies take Douai, former GAF base.
October 19, 1918:	Belgian cities Bruges and Zeebrugge fall to Belgian Army and BEF.
October 25, 1918:	First five days of Italian Army offensive gains 50,000 POWs.
October 26, 1918:	Kaiser fires Ludendorff as first quartermaster general, replacing him with Gen. Wilhelm Groener; Hindenburg remains as chief of the general staff.
October 30, 1918:	Austria-Hungary and Turkey desert Germany by leaving the war.
October 31, 1918:	Turkey surrenders, and Dardanelles Straits open to shipping.
November 1, 1918:	U.S. 1st Army takes Cléry-le-Grand.
November 3, 1918:	AEF sweeps ahead on 50-mile front above Verdun, with Germans in full retreat.
November 4, 1918:	AEF strikes at Sedan; Italians win Battle of Vittorio Veneto.
November 7, 1918:	AEF enters Sedan.
November 8, 1918:	Sedan heights taken by AEF.
November 9, 1918:	Allies take Maubeuge; Kaiser Wilhelm II decides to leave for neutral Holland.
November 10, 1918:	CEF takes Mons; Kaiser flees German General Headquarters at Spa, Belgium and crosses Dutch frontier at Eijsden, Holland.
November 11, 1918:	Germans and Allies sign Armistice, effectively ending World War I; Kaiser receives shelter at Amerongen, Holland.

November 29, 1918:	Kaiser abdicates officially as German Emperor and King of Prussia.
December 1, 1918:	Imperial German Crown Prince Wilhelm abdicates his offices, from Holland also.
February 11, 1919:	Friedrich Ebert elected first German civilian Reich president.
June 21, 1919:	German High Seas Fleet scuttles itself at Scapa Flow, Scotland.
June 28, 1919:	Versailles Peace Treaty signed by Weimar Republican Germany.
July 4, 1919:	Hindenburg retires from German Army for Second time.
March 4, 1920:	Kapp–Lüttwitz uprising at Berlin fails; Ludendorff escapes prosecution for treason.
1922:	Hindenburg and Ludendorff stage triumphal visit to Munich.
January 1923:	French and Belgian armies occupy the German industrial Ruhr Valley, runaway German inflation results.
November 9–10, 1923:	Hitler-Ludendorff Beer Hall Putsch at Munich fails.
April 1924:	Ludendorff acquitted at Munich trial, with Hitler sentenced to five years' fortress detention; serves but nine months, and is released.
April 26, 1925:	Hindenburg elected second Reich president of Weimar Republic; final break between him and Ludendorff later.
October 29, 1929:	Great Depression worldwide starts.
April 1932:	Hindenburg defeats Hitler for reelection to the presidency—twice.
January 30, 1933:	Hindenburg appoints Hitler Reich chancellor.
June 30 to July 3, 1934:	Goering has former Reich chancellor and Army Gen. Kurt von Schleicher murdered during the Nazi Blood Purge.
August 2, 1934:	Hindenburg dies at the age of eighty-seven at country estate Neudeck, with Hitler merging the two offices of Reich president and chancellor into one: Führer and Reich chancellor, with armed forces taking a personal oath of allegiance to him alone.
August 7, 1934:	Hindenburg buried at Tannenberg Memorial alongside his late wife.
December 22, 1937:	State funeral for Ludendorff at Munich, after his having refused Hitler's offer to name him a field marshal.
June 5, 1941:	Death of Kaiser Wilhelm II at the age of eighty-two.
January 1945:	Hindenburg coffins removed from Tannenberg from path of Red Army.
August 1945:	Their coffins, regimental colors, and Hitlerian wreath reburied at the Elizabeth Church at Marburg an der Lahn, after being found by U.S. Army.

1

Stage, 1847–1914

The Kaiser Creates His Great War Marshalate, 1914–17

The very first marshal created by the Kaiser was Paul von Beneckendorff und von Hindenburg (1847–1934) on November 2, 1914; followed by Karl von Bülow (1846–1921) on January 27, 1915; and then joined by a pair on June 22, 1915: the German August von Mackensen (1849–1945) and the Austrian Army Royal Habsburg Commander Archduke Frederick, Duke of Teschen (1856–1936).

On June 26, 1915, there came the venerable King Ludwig III of Bavaria (1845–1921) and another royal the following January 18, 1916, Tsar Ferdinand I of Bulgaria (1861–1948). Another monarch followed on July 23, 1916, King Wilhelm II of Württemberg (1848–1921).

A royal triad received their coveted baton staffs on August 1, 1916 simultaneously: Prince Leopold of Bavaria (1846–1930), Duke Albrecht of Württemberg (1865–1939), and Crown Prince Rupprecht of Bavaria (1869–1955). Another imperial head to receive a German GFM's baton was Austria-Hungary's last Kaiser and King, Emperor Karl (1887–1922).

Two more marshal's staffs were awarded by the Kaiser on December 18, 1917 to Remus von Woyrsch (1847–1920) and Hermann von Eichhorn (1848–1918), the only one of the overall stellar cast to be killed as the result of enemy action—in his case at the hands of a Russian assassin.

The next Austrian was the chief of the Austrian army's general staff, Franz Conrad von Hötzendorf (1852–1925), in 1916; he was blamed by some modern historians as being one of the five or six men responsible for the outbreak of World War I in 1914.

Beneckendorff

Characterized as "A giant rock of a man," the silent Prussian field marshal bridged an era from Hohenzollern Kaiser to Nazi Führer.

His name was Paul von Beneckendorff und von Hindenburg, which in English meant, "Paul, of the families of Hindenburg and Beneckendorff." He was born in 1847 and he died in 1934, and during that eighty-seven-year expanse of time, he witnessed the rise and fall of an empire and then its rebirth as the Third Reich of one of his former enlisted soldiers.

He was only the second man in history to be awarded the Star to the Grand Cross, the great Marshal Blücher being the first.

Traditionally, the Kaiser was the father symbol of his people, as had been Kaiser Wilhelm I. With the advent of Hindenburg, however, all this changed. A few months after the shattering German victory at Tannenberg, Hindenburg had already replaced the Kaiser in the hearts of his people. Wilhelm II realized this and hated Hindenburg for it. He envied the popularity of his chief field marshal—a popularity that he was never to regain.

Successively serving as Prussian officer, German field marshal, and Republic president, Hindenburg fought for two Kaisers and later occupied their former position as Supreme Head of the State as well.

"A great battle was fought for him, and for 20 years the legend of his having been the victor of it carried him far beyond the normal duties of an army officer. His very name became a burning symbol to his people, and in his time of service, he lent it to almost every cause that came his way," noted one period commentator. These causes included imperialism, democracy, and, lastly, the German form of Italian fascism in Germanic raiments: Nazism. In 1918, a German official joyously chortled, "Hindenburg belongs to the German nation!" and he was right, in many ways in which he had not imagined.

By the time of his death, the veteran field marshal had shaken hands with almost everyone, of every class and creed: the Hohenzollern Kaiser Wilhelm II, the Republican president and one-time saddler socialist Friedrich Ebert—both of whom he succeeded—and the upstart Austrian Nazi Hitler, who ran against him twice, losing both times.

To the world, Hindenburg was a field marshal and the elected president of the German Reich in his own right; an "Almost ideal type of single-minded patriot who had twice emerged from a well-earned retirement to answer his country's call to further service;" a mighty rock of a man in the view of his legion of admirers who had won the fabulous martial Battle of Tannenberg in August 1914; and, for the two decades following, his nation's chief statesman.

A soldier, statesman, man of honor, reputed patriotic giant, he was, seemingly, one of the great men of his day, no less, but the inevitable critics of his own time later carped, "Or was he?" They answered no.

They rather saw and see him instead as a "wooden titan," a figurehead used by men stronger than he for purposes of which he had little understanding, a man of no ambition who was himself a pawn used by and for other ambitious men.

These allegedly included his Great War chief of staff, Ludendorff; his governmental state secretary, Meissner; the intriguer, von Schleicher; and, of course, Hitler.

The eminent English historian and biographer Sir John W. Wheeler-Bennett once attended a dinner in Berlin during the later years of Hindenburg's tenure of office as Reich president when a retired German naval officer made the following comment on the "Old Gentleman," noted in Wheeler-Bennett's *Wooden Titan*:

Hindenburg's record is a bad one! Ludendorff won his battles for him, and he betrayed Ludendorff. The Kaiser made him a field marshal, and he betrayed the Kaiser! The Right elected him in 1925, he betrayed the Right [in 1932–33]. The Left elected him in 1932, and he betrayed the Left [during 1933–34].

Another of the field marshal's more famous biographers, Emil Ludwig Cohn, described him thusly in *Wilhelm Hohenzollern*:

> [He was] A Junker and field marshal and President who was driven into dictatorship—first by environment—and then by longstanding authoritarian instincts, until, most tragically at last, he surrendered power to a group of gangsters, to die profoundly embittered.…
>
> People will tell one another tales about the old German giant who—after many adventures—was appointed watchman on a dam. One day—in a moment of mental confusion—he opened the sluices to inundate the surrounding country.
>
> And there came a flood that destroyed all that had been dear to him, in whose waters he himself at last perished.

Was this, then, the real saga of Hindenburg? I think maybe not, but we shall see.

In the Days of Frederick the Great
Hindenburg came from a clan that had its origins in the union of two august houses, each of which traced its military record back to the thirteenth century, when their ancestors had been knights of the famed Teutonic Order.

The name Hindenburg had been in that family for sixty years upon the birth of the future field marshal, having become extinct in 1789. The last holder of that name had been a colonel on the staff of Prussia's famous King Frederick II the Great and, during the latter's Seven Years' War, had ridden beside *Der alte Fritz* (The Old Fritz) when a cannonball shattered his leg.

In return for this combat wound, Frederick gratefully gave him the East Prussian estates of Neudeck and Limbsee. The latter was sold after the 1813 German War of Liberation, but Neudeck was retained until the demise of the widow of one of the marshal's younger brothers after the Great War in 1918.

When this noble ancestor died, he bequeathed the twin estates "To his great-nephew Beneckendorff," with the stipulation that the heir was to join the name and arms of the Hindenburg family to that of Beneckendorff.

The Prussian monarch of 1789, Frederick Wilhelm II, gave his royal assent to the dying soldier.

The Grenadier
The later marshal had not only military and landowner blood in his line, but also that of several tradesmen, among them masons, nappers, shearmen, ropemakers, fishermen, and clergymen parsons.

It was from his great-grandfather—Grenadier Schickhardt—that Hindenburg received his own impressive height of 6 feet 2 inches. He served for almost four decades among the tall grenadiers of Frederick the Great, the famed unit having been founded by his eccentric father, King Frederick Wilhelm I.

The future marshal would have been astounded to know that after his own death, he himself would be buried near these two famed Prussian soldier kings in 1945–50.

There was, though, another soldier from his past who cast a shadow across Hindenburg's career, and a namesake at that: Maj. Paul von Hindenburg, who was shot in 1806 during the first Prussian campaign against the Emperor Napoleon I for surrendering to the French army the great stone Spandau Fortress outside the capital of Berlin.

The marshal's early "official" biographers called his maternal grandfather "a surgeon general" and his mother "a soldier's daughter." Paul's own father served a short stint in the military before managing the Neudeck estate in his retiring years.

Birth and Youth

The field marshal and Reich president was born on October 2, 1847 at Posen, in what was then East Prussia (today known as West Poland). The family was of the aristocratic "von"—the landowning, but financially poor ruling class of Prussia.

In their joint distant past, the kings of Prussia and their *Junker* servants developed a relationship that served them all well. The monarch protected the *Junker* class and awarded them special privileges in his state.

In turn, the *Junkers* provided Their Majesties with soldiers officered by themselves for the royal army, pledged to protect his throne with their lives and those of their men as well. The agreement held until the *Junkers* abandoned their Kaiser on November 9, 1918, led by his own field marshal.

In 1858, eleven-year-old Hindenburg joined the elite Prussian corps of cadets at Wahlstadt in Silesia, where he lived a typical Spartan martial life, subject for the next several years to the gruff bark of a drill sergeant on the parade ground, complete with all the usual drill, harassment, and harsh discipline.

In 1860, Cadet Paul von Hindenburg wrote home to his parents (noted in Hindenburg's *The Great War*):

> I want to arrange my knickknack shelf as follows: at the back—against the wall—a big Prussian eagle; in the middle, Old Fritz on a pedestal surrounded by his generals, with a group of Black Hussars below; right in front, a chain stretched from side to side, behind which are to be two sentry boxes occupied by two of Frederick the Great's grenadiers. So far, I have not the materials to carry out my schemes: I set my hopes on Christmas!

Despite his boyish enthusiasm, during a short leave home, he was reluctant to return, due to the school's harsh *milieu* that personally repelled him. Duty and service, however, made him comply in the end, and these twin forces continued to rule his life until his death.

Decades later, when asked to cite his life's greatest day, Hindenburg said nothing about Tannenberg, but, rather, "The day when I was allowed to eat as much cake and whipped cream as anyone else!"

He also wrote home of a visit of the crown prince of Prussia to his cadet school: "For nearly all of us, this was the first time we had seen a member of our Royal House! Never had we raised our legs so high in the goose step as when we paraded that day!"

At the age of sixteen, in 1863, Cadet von Hindenburg was transferred to Berlin's central school, being appointed as honorary page to the widowed Queen Elizabeth of Prussia, receiving from her the personal gift of a watch that he wore proudly for the rest of his long life.

But even greater excitements awaited: "At the spring review—and later at the autumn review—I was at length permitted to have a glance of my most gracious Master, King Wilhelm I."

Commissioned Second Lieutenant, 1864

Commissioned a second lieutenant in 1864, the new Lt von Hindenburg was duly presented to His Majesty in the era of Prussia's Royal Chancellor Otto von Bismarck, the engineer of a series of three wars to achieve the long-delayed German national unification with Prussia at its core.

The first—with tiny Denmark in 1864—came too soon for the not yet graduated Hindenburg to see combat, but he was eighteen years old and commissioned two years later for the Seven Weeks' War of 1866 against Austria, longtime foe and ally of Royal Prussia since 1740.

Prior to the decisive battle of that war—Königgrätz in June 1866—Hindenburg took his cherished oath of allegiance to his king, one that every Prussian officer considered sacred, binding for life. Noted in *The Great* War, he intoned:

> I—Paul Ludwig Hans Anton von Beneckendorff und von Hindenburg—hereby swear to God the Omniscient and Almighty that I will faithfully and loyally serve His Majesty the King of Prussia, my most gracious Sovereign, on every occasion on land or at sea in war and in peace and at every place, whatsoever.
>
> That I will further the All-Highest's best advantage, while averting from him injury and disadvantage; that I will closely abide by the Articles of War that have been read to me, and precisely obey the orders I receive, and that I will so conduct myself as becomes an upright, fearless, dutiful, and honorable soldier, so help me God, through Jesus Christ and His Holy Gospel!

The 1866 War with Austria

Receiving his baptism of fire before the Austrian Army at the Battle of Soor in 1866, von Hindenburg later fought also at the famed Battle of Königgrätz that effectively won both the campaign and the war. He recalled in *The Great War*:

> The only coordinating impulse was the resolution to get to close quarters with the enemy … murderous hand-to-hand fighting took place in the streets between the thatched cottages on fire.

> All idea of fighting in regular units was lost. Everyone shot and stabbed at random to the best of his ability.... With drums beating, we all stormed forward once more against the enemy.

Storming an enemy artillery battery, the unit he led took the five guns, he being slightly wounded thereby (taken from Hindenburg's *The Great War*):

> A bullet went clean through the eagle on my helmet, grazed my head without causing any serious damage, and passed out behind....
>
> The doctor wanted to send me to hospital on account of my head wound, but ... I contented myself with poultices and a light bandage, and for the rest of the march, had to wear a cap instead of my helmet.

Until life's end, the proud soldier retained this combat souvenir of the shattered helmet on his office desk and was also awarded at the campaign's end the Prussian Order of the Red Eagle from the king personally.

The Franco-Prussian War, 1870–71

In the final and largest of the Bismarckian Wars of Unification—that with the Imperial France of Emperor Napoleon III—he fought in the Battle of Sedan, for which he was awarded the coveted Iron Cross for bravery against the enemy.

At the earlier fighting at the Battle of St Privat, he remembered decades later and noted in *The Great War*:

> Stray bullets from enemy riflemen ... fell here and there among our formations in close order ... the compact columns formed a front against the enemy lines, and in open order stormed forward.
>
> On the morning 2 September 1870, we had a visit from the Crown Prince [the future Kaiser Frederick III] who brought us the first news of the capture of Napoleon and his army, and in the afternoon it was followed by that of our King and military leaders.
>
> It is impossible to form any conception of the unexampled enthusiasm with which the monarch was received! The men simply could not be kept in ranks! They swarmed round their dearly loved master and kissed his hands and feet.
>
> His Majesty saw his Guards for the first time, and thanked us for all we had done at St Privat.

More than that, Lt von Hindenburg was picked from the officers of his regiment to represent them at the proclamation of His Majesty the King as the newly elected German emperor in the Hall of Mirrors at the French Palace of Versailles in January 1871.

Of this event, he proudly wrote to his family: "At the Coronation of the Emperor at a one o'clock court reception, and proclamation of Emperor and Empire, after which we were invited to dinner."

After Paris fell, on March 2, 1871, von Hindenburg took his one and only ride in the captured French capital to the *Arc de Triomphe*, built to celebrate the great Napoleon's victories, many of them against Beneckendorff's own Prussian forebears.

"Throughout my ride, I let the historical monuments of the past of a great enemy produce their full effect on me." Four decades later—in the next century—he would lead armies that would try, vainly, to retake the City of Light once again.

Like most soldiers, von Hindenburg was fond of telling "war stories," and he loved to recall anecdotes about the aged Field Marshal Helmuth von Moltke the Elder from his early career.

Legendary as "the man who was silent in seven languages," von Moltke was renowned for not talking much. As von Hindenburg remembered in 1919 in *The Great War*:

> The gentlemen asserted that von Moltke's toast of the Kaiser would not contain more than 10 words, including the speech and the first *Hoch!*
>
> Bets were laid; I did not take any part. The gentleman who took the bet lost, for the field marshal merely said, "*Meine Herrn, der Kaiser Hoch!*"

He remembered also calling on the veteran chief of staff once when the latter forgot to don his famous wig.

Later, he was proud to have been selected twice again to stand as an honor guard at the deathbed of the famous Dane in 1890, as well as at the funeral bier of the late Kaiser Wilhelm I in 1888. He met the old emperor's impulsive successor and grandson, Kaiser Wilhelm II, for the first time in 1886, while the crown prince was twenty-eight years old.

Von Hindenburg had a far more serious side, was very religious, and deeply devoted to both his own parents and family, including his wife, two daughters, and only son, Oskar, who resembled him both facially and physically a great deal, judging from their photographs both together and apart.

By the time his later famous subordinate Ludendorff was born in 1865, Beneckendorff was already an eighteen-year-old commissioned second lieutenant in the Prussian Army.

Forty Years from Captain to Lieutenant General in the Imperial German Army, 1871–1911

During this period, Hindenburg rose to command larger military units, taught at the Prussian War Academy, and served on the general staff himself. His early German biographer Niemann wrote of those four decades that his services "Were valuable, though not decisive," with but twenty pages devoted to them by Hindenburg himself in his post-Great War memoirs after his name had made global martial history.

During those four decades, the professional career soldier made his way steadily upward from captain to lieutenant general, a successful run by any military standard, and in 1904, he received command of the 4th Army Corps headquartered at Magdeburg.

Reportedly, at the annual fall military maneuvers at Mecklenburg in 1908, Gen. von Hindenburg defeated the forces commanded by His Imperial Majesty Kaiser Wilhelm

II. Legend had it that this earned him the ire of the miffed German supreme warlord, leading in 1911 to an enforced early retirement from the army. The retiree himself denied this, writing: "My military career had carried me much farther than I had ever dared to hope! There was no prospect of war, and—as I recognized that it was my duty to make way for younger men—I applied … to be allowed to retire [at the age of sixty-four following fifty-three years of service]."

Thus, he hung up his sword scabbard for good—or so he thought. Three years later, in August 1914, the outbreak of the Great War thrust him suddenly and forever into world military history: the legend of von Hindenburg was about to be born.

Above left: Iconic Great War symbol of Imperial German Eagle of the ruling dynastic House of Hohenzollern (top half) and 1870 Franco-Prussian War Iron Cross with the monogram letter "W" of King Wilhelm I of Prussia at center and *Gott mit Uns* (God with Us) motto surrounding. Note the crown of Royal Prussia surmounting the eagle's head. (*Library of Congress, Washington, D.C., USA—hereafter LC*)

Above right: Imperial Germany's foremost field marshal when the Great War broke out in August 1914 was Kaiser Wilhelm II (fourth from right), seen here in the black-and-white-trimmed cavalry busby and uniform of the famed Death's Head Lifeguard Hussars. The Kaiser brandishes his own bejeweled, ornate baton, self-awarded in 1900. From left to right are also seen his empress, Kaiserin Auguste Viktoria; his only daughter and youngest child, Princess Viktoria Luise of Prussia; and her husband of 1913, Grand Duke Ernst of Schleswig-Holstein, also sporting hussar cap and kit. The other men are imperial court officials in their colorful period uniforms. Regarding the *Totenkopf* (Death's Head) on the facade of the Kaiser's head wear, one account explains, "The skull continued to be used throughout the Prussian and Brunswick armed forces until 1918" and "in Germany throughout the interwar period, most prominently by the Free Corps. In 1933, it was in use by the regimental staff of the 1st, 5th, and 11th squadrons of the Reichswehr's 5th Cavalry Regiment as a continuation of a tradition from the *Kaiserreich*." The French Army referred to them as the Hussars of Death. (*Viktoria Luise Albums, Doorn House, Holland*)

A youthful-looking Prince Wilhelm wears the prewar Prussian Army blue uniform, complete with shoulder boards. (*LC*)

I believe that the Kaiser was a bipolar manic depressive. Adds Jarvis in *Did You Know?* "To most of the world, Germany's Kaiser Wilhelm II was a scoundrel, but to his countrymen, he was great. They prospered under his leadership. He was blamed for World War I, but historians think others were equally guilty. He fought against his cousins: George V of England and Russia's Nicholas II."

Following the death of Queen Victoria—and his own accession to the British throne as King Edward VII—the former Prince of Wales Bertie, the younger Kaiser's maternal uncle, bestowed upon his nephew the baton and red uniform jacket of a British Army field marshal as well, returned to Great Britain in August 1914 upon the British declaration of war against Germany. On June 2, 2017, the Kaiser became an international movie star once again, as played by Canadian actor Christopher Plummer in the World War II-era spy film *The Exception*, the locale of which was centered on a Belgian manor house standing in for his actual exile site of Doorn House, the Netherlands, in an excellent portrayal in my view.

According to Jack Sweetman in 1973, in 1914, Wilhelm's *Junker* nobility class had control over Prussia and Germany, with their members including seven of eleven Prussian State ministers, eight of twelve provincial governors, 270 of 490 *Landrate* councilors, six of seven Great War field marshals, and eleven of fifteen full generals in the Imperial Army as well. Recognizing the power of this class after World War II, on February 25, 1947, the victorious Allies simply dissolved Prussia as a political entity, thus wiping it off the historical, geographical map.

Prussian and German Army Field Marshal Count von Haessler, the Kaiser's oldest bearer of the award at the commencement of the Great War in 1914. Note here his older style uniform jacket of Prussian blue—replaced by German field gray later—as well as the Iron Cross on his left chest, *Pour le Mérite* award at the throat, and twin crossed batons on the shoulder boards. (*LC*)

Sporting colorful and ornate Uhlan's cavalry helmet, the aging and dour field marshal glares at the camera's lens. (*LC*)

According to von der Goltz, even in 1918, Germany had but ten serviceable tanks in action *versus* the 800 of the Western Allies—Ludendorff's fault, assert others.

Graf v. Haeseler
Generalfeldmarschall.

Above left: Marshal von Häßler wearing Uhlan helmet and long cavalry cape. (*LC*)

On November 9, 1918, Hindenburg told the Kaiser flat out that it was militarily impossible for the defeated German Army to win a civil war at home afterwards.

Above right: Graf von Häßler as a young man: Gottlieb Ferdinand Albert Alexis Graf von Häßler (1836–1919). (*Alan Sutton Archive—hereafter ASA*)

Had the Kaiser opted for a last, fatal personal cavalry charge against the Allies on the Western front on November 9, 1918, reportedly, Hindenburg was ready to saddle up and ride with Wilhelm II to their joint ends.

Above left: Two female German Royals in the uniforms of their very own honorary regiments: at left, His Majesty's only daughter, Princess Viktoria Luise, Duchess of Brunswick, and at right, her sister-in-law and the wife of her eldest brother, Crown Princess Cecilie. (*Doorn House Albums, Holland—hereafter DH*)

On September 9, 1912 at the annual Fall military maneuvers, His Majesty met with his first Great War chief of the imperial great German general staff, Helmuth Count von Moltke the Younger— commander of the opening summer–fall phase of the German armies in World War I, 1914. They were visiting the right column of the 3rd Cavalry Division site of the maneuvers. Initially, Moltke pleaded not to take the general staff posting, telling the Kaiser that he was not suited for it, but relented when the Kaiser told him not to worry: "In war, I shall be my own Chief of General Staff anyway!" but was not in the actual event, as it turned out.

Above right: The wartime Kaiser (*right*) on a hot day in the field in 1915 at Magura Odobeti, cap in hand, as his field baton is carried for him at left by the commandant of all the Kaiser's field headquarters in both peace and war, Colonel General Hans von Plessen, appearing here in the famed Prussian spiked helmet that was so designed to ward off head blows from enemy cavalry saber attack in battle. Note also that the Kaiser wears a protective holstered pistol sidearm on his right hip. This swagger stick baton was "an undress or service version of the field marshal's baton known as an *Interimstab*." (*DH*)

Prewar, the Kaiser (*right*) wears the high cap and white uniform jacket of the Austro–Hungarian Army of his ally, Kaiser Franz Josef I of the House of Habsburg. The two armies were foes during 1740–86 and again in 1866, then allies afterwards until November 1918. According to *Baltimore Sun* newspaper columnist Fred Rasmussen to the author on June 26, 2015, "In the 1920s, [H. L.] Mencken visited the Kaiser in exile, and asked for a souvenir of their meeting, and he gave HLM a gray, felt-covered pocket cigarette case with his Royal insignia." Years ago—when I was doing research in the Mencken Room at [the Baltimore Enoch] Pratt [Free Library], I found it inside written on a carefully folded piece of *Sun* copy paper in pencil in Mencken's hand the following: "The Kaiser gave this to me." (*LC*)

COMFORT IN EXILE.

Imperial Brother-in-Law. "AFTER ALL, MY DEAR TINO, YOU ARE SOMETHING BETTER THAN A KING; YOU ARE A FIELD-MARSHAL IN MY ARMY! YOU SHALL PRESENTLY HAVE A COMMAND ON THE WESTERN FRONT."
Tino (*without enthusiasm*). "THANK YOU VERY MUCH."

A Bernard Partridge cartoon in *Punch*, published June 16, 1917. One German field marshal (*left*) lectures another—and both royals! (*ASA*)

In the middle of the Great War, then-neutral Greece joined the Allies against the Kaiser's Central Powers, after the overthrow of the Greek King Constantine shown here by his own prime minister. The Greek monarch was married to one of the Kaiser's sisters.

His Highness Prince Leopold of Bavaria (1846–1930), later made a field marshal. (*ASA*)

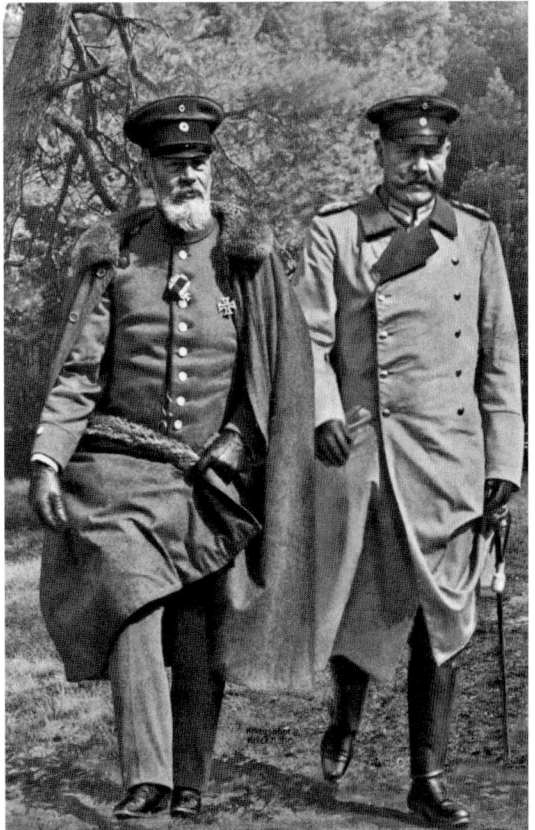

HRH Prince Leopold of Bavaria (*left*) with a genial von Hindenburg (*right*). (*ASA*)

When he took the oath as Reich president in 1925, reportedly, Hindenburg had himself "become a monarch," but also, "The sentry in front of the Royal fortress in order to open the gates for the King's return" that never came in either of their lifetimes.

"Our Emperor in the Field" is the title of this wartime picture postcard of Wilhelm II, sufficiently bundled up against the harsh cold of the outdoor battlements in winter. Note also the wartime camouflage covering on his gleaming spiked helmet. (*LC*)

Field Marshal von Hindenburg was almost always "the tallest man wherever he appeared, the Blücher Star on his breast." Later, as president, he "read the [Federal] Constitution in large text."

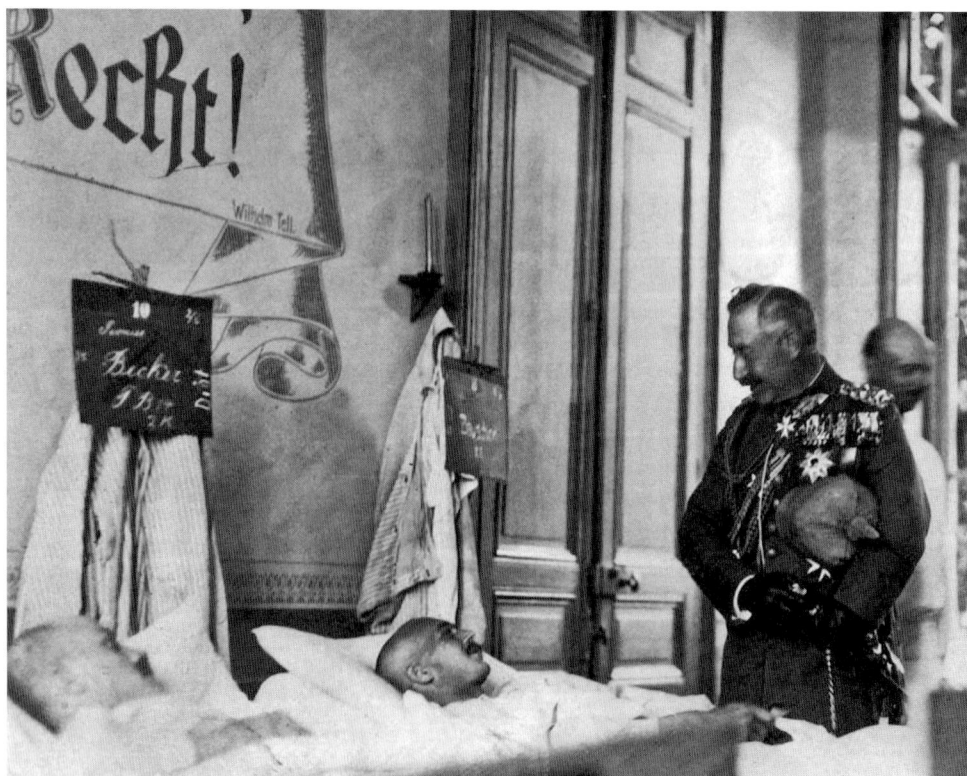

The Kaiser (*right*) cracking jokes while visiting wounded soldiers in a wartime field hospital, his helmet crooked in the corner of his left arm, damaged at birth. (*DH*)

Famed British military writer Liddell-Hart referred to Ludendorff as "the robot Napoleon."

The field marshal (*center*) comforts a wheel-chair bound wounded soldier. Later, his son, Colonel Oskar von Hindenburg, boasted, correctly, that "History shall not say that I have been nothing more than my father's son!" He was right: he helped pave the way for Hitler, and, with him, world war and holocaust. (*ASA*)

His Majesty the German Emperor William II (*left*) smiling wished Marshal von Hindenburg (*right*) a happy 70th birthday, October 2, 1917. (*ASA*)

2

East, 1914–18

The Great War in the East Opens, August 1914

In the west, Imperial Germany launched the still debated Schlieffen Plan invasion of Belgium, Luxembourg, and France, a blueprint for a rapid victory on which all the hopes of the German general staff rested.

This encompassed a vast turning movement through Belgium that was to strike France in a "great right wheel" to concentrate all German forces in the west. This left the German east less well defended, in hopes of a quick victory against the western Allied armies that included a British Expeditionary Force that the Kaiser unwisely, but infamously, denigrated as "A contemptible army!"

The generals of this same staff had duly calculated upon East Prussia being invaded by the Russians, but they did not foresee at all the swiftness and massive strength with which it was done.

The German defensive forces in East Prussia that had already long been deployed to meet this expected Russian thrust was the 8th Army of fourteen divisions commanded by Gen. Maximilian von Prittwitz, who, as fate would have it, was a first cousin of von Hindenburg. Opposed to him were two full-sized and vaster Russian armies, both numerically stronger than his. Thus was East Prussia laid bare on August 15, 1914 to the advancing legions of the Tsar of All the Russias, the Kaiser's own royal cousin, Nicholas II. Noted one military affairs commentator somewhat dramatically: "All Germany was bewailing the fire and sword that was sweeping East Prussia, and Wilhelm II's pride was deeply stung."

Although the Kaiser well knew that the Schlieffen Plan demanded utter concentration on the far more martially important Western Front, he nevertheless complained indignantly of the violation "Of our lovely Masurian Lakes!"

In the face of this great challenge, von Prittwitz hesitated in his immediate response, while his senior staff officer, Lt Col. Max Hoffmann, and two of his own corps commanders, Gens. August von Mackensen and Hermann von François, were champing at the bit to close with their eastern enemy in combat, but the nervous von Prittwitz held back.

On August 20, 1914, he telephoned von Moltke—with the suggestion of himself and his own staff chief—that, perhaps, the 8th Army should retreat *en masse* away from the oncoming Russian armies that might destroy his smaller command. This angered the Kaiser, and it put the count in a quandary as well. Both agreed that their two reluctant soldiers in the east would be replaced, but who by? That was the question.

Meanwhile, unknown to all of them, the Russian High Command had its own problems simultaneously.

Unquiet Allies! Gens. Rennenkampf and Samsonov

General of Cavalry Pavel (Paul) Karlovich Rennenkampf (April 17, 1854 to April 1, 1918)
Ever since Tannenberg, historians generally have seen him as that epic battle's real loser and not the man blamed for it, Samsonov; the reason is that the former did not aid his colleague in need, thus allowing him to lose. Reportedly, the bad blood between them began during the earlier lost Russo-Japanese War of 1904–05, when there occurred a similar incident following the Battle of Mukden. The slight rankled, unforgotten, almost a decade later.

Because he was a favorite of the Tsar, the errant Gen. Rennenkampf managed to survive both martial blunders, however, continuing to lead his army well into 1915 no less.

Having beaten von Mackensen at the Battle of Gumbinnen, stumbling badly during Tannenberg, and being beaten himself at the First Battle of the Masurian Lakes and at Łódź also—all in the summer of 1914—Rennenkampf was fired on October 6, 1915, over a year after the events.

Arrested and imprisoned after the February 1917 Revolution that overthrew his patron, the Tsar, Gen. Rennenkampf was charged with both embezzlement and mismanagement. His luck held again, however, and he was freed after the October 1917 Revolution that brought Lenin to office.

Then his luck ran out for good when he was executed on April 1, 1918 by the Reds for refusing to fight for the Bolsheviks during the Russian Civil War.

General of Cavalry Alexander Vasilyevich Samsonov (November 14, 1859 to August 30, 1914)
A veteran horse commander during both the Boxer Rebellion in China and then the Imperial Japanese Army in Manchuria afterwards, Gen. Samsonov suffered the greatest defeat of any C.O. of any armed force of the Great War right at its very outset.

By August 29, 1914, his Russian 2nd Army was surrounded by the Germans in a forest situated between Allenstein and Willenberg in East Prussia, and the next day, he shot himself near the latter, his body—pistol in hand and bullet in head—being found later by a German patrol.

The International Red Cross arranged for his body to be returned to his widow in 1916.

General of Infantry Hermann von François, *Disobeyer of Orders*

Gen. Hermann Karl Bruno von François (January 31, 1856 to May 15, 1933) stands out in the early history of the Great War as the premiere disobeyer of orders of several superior commanders running. As such, he was staying true to one of the cardinal rules of all German officers: use your initiative at all times. This he did, in the very first triad of major battles on the Eastern Front: Stallupönen, Gumbinnen, and the all-important Tannenberg/Christmas Mountain.

Born in Luxembourg a Huguenot, von François began the war as commanding officer of the German 8th Army's 1st Corps, tasked with defending the East Prussian frontier against any Russian Army invasion headed for the provincial capital of Königsberg, site in 1861 of the coronation of King Wilhelm I of Prussia, the last such ever held anywhere.

On August 15, 1914, East Prussia was suddenly and surprisingly invaded by the right wing of a double-pronged thrust of Russian Gen. Pavel Rennenkampf's 1st Army. As von François dealt with this, his 8th Army commander, Gen. von Prittwitz, two days later ordered him to retreat in front of the Russian advance.

Col. Gen. Maximilian von Prittwitz und Gaffron: First Fired!

Maximilian Wilhelm Gustav von Prittwitz und Gaffron (November 27, 1848 to March 29, 1917) has the distinction of being the very first commanding general of any army on either side of the Great War to be fired from his post; in this case, for being willing to abandon East Prussia to the invading Russian Army via a speedy retreat west of the Vistula River. Neither the Kaiser nor von Moltke accepted this, so von Prittwitz was replaced by the later-styled von Hindenburg, then Beneckendorff.

Prittwitz, like his cousin, had also fought in both the Austro-Prussian War of 1866 and the Franco-Prussian War of 1870–71, and, unlike the then-retired von Hindenburg, in 1913 was both promoted full general at four stars as well as CO of the 16th Army Corps at Metz, opposite the French Army.

He commanded the German 8th Army defending East Prussia a mere three weeks to the day—August 2–23, 1914—but allowed himself to be spooked by the rapid invasion of his charge by a pair of Russian armies under veteran generals on August 15, 1914.

Alarmed by the near defeat at Stallupönen and the actual rout of von Mackensen at Gumbinnen, von Prittwitz decided on a complete withdrawal but was stopped in his tracks by the Kaiser and his CGS.

The cast-down commander lived in retirement at Berlin in the vast, dark, cold shadow of Tannenberg, dying of a heart attack at the age of sixty-nine, nicknamed "Fatty" by his detractors. His martial reputation has not yet recovered.

German 8th Army East Prussian Headquarters: Castle Marienburg at Malbork

Gen. von Prittwitz's former military headquarters in East Prussia was in the famous Malbork red brick Castle Marienburg, built in the thirteenth century by the Knights of the Teutonic Order as their command center in what later evolved into Royal Prussia, completely abolished by the Allies in 1945.

Known as Marienburg in German when founded in 1274, the town was named for the order's patron saint, the Virgin Mary, and remains today Europe's largest Gothic-style fortress. The town and the fort were destroyed by the Red Army on March 9, 1945, and that June became part of today's Poland as Malbork.

Von François Wins the Battle of Stallupönen, August 17, 1914

Overall, the Russians fielded ten full armies *versus* the Germans' lesser eight for their projected march on Königsberg, the capital of East Prussia, which they duly invaded in force on August 15, 1914.

Stallupönen (today's Nesterov in Russia) was the very first conflict fought by the armies of Imperial Germany and Tsarist Russia on the newly opened Eastern Front on August 17, 1914, just two days later.

Von François pluckily and successfully waged an attack with his German 1st Corps against four full Russian infantry divisions, even creating a gap between two of them in what proved to be a minor victory, but one that made no dent in the enemy's advance afterwards. Ordered by his superior, von Prittwitz, to break off this fight, François told his adjutant to reply thus: "Report to Gen. Prittwitz that Gen. von François will withdraw when he has defeated the Russians!"

True to his boast, the plucky François then withdrew 15 miles westward, and three days later, he engaged Rennenkampf again at the Battle of Gumbinnen that was a rout for German Hussar Gen. August von Mackensen—his first and only.

The Battle of Gumbinnen, August 17–23, 1914

Gen. von Prittwitz—emboldened by von François's pluck at Stallupönen—attacked too soon at Gumbinnen, however, causing it to instead become a Russian victory, their first over the hated and arrogant German Army at what is now Gusev, Russia. Samsonov's Russians defeated Mackensen's Germans, despite the fact that the victors suffered 18,839 losses in all to the "beaten" foe's 14,607 according to 2016 statistics. The German 8th Army numbered 148,000 men *versus* their enemy's superior force of 192,000 soldiers.

Still fuming that von François had disobeyed his orders in engaging the Russians at Stallupönen just days before, now von Prittwitz disobeyed his own orders from Moltke not to give battle until the campaign in the west was won. He rashly decided to follow up his subordinate's successful fight with one of his own at Gumbinnen, where Russian cavalry encountered German infantry on August 19, 2014.

This time, von François was given an order to advance against the Russians that night, his cavalry backing up the German infantry, but the resulting battle stalemated when the Russians ran out of artillery ammunition. Until that happened, though, their gunfire halted Mackensen's advance against Rennenkampf and led to the German's flank being turned, thus precipitating a rout to their own lines at Insterburg–Angerburg to the rear, with 6,000 POWs being bagged by the victorious Russians.

According to Brownell in *First Nazi*: "The uncharacteristic sight of defeated German soldiers streaming moblike to the rear really unnerved von Prittwitz," who feared that his own army would be completely sandwiched, and thus destroyed between those of Rennenkampf and Samsonov: "Prittwitz panicked and—with a decision out of all proportion to the severity of the situation—ordered a general retreat to the Vistula River, leaving East Prussia to the Russians."

Back at KHQ Koblenz, both His Majesty and von Moltke had visions of Russian Cossack horses trotting down the boulevards of Berlin itself, as had occurred during the Seven Years' War that Frederick the Great almost lost to the Russian Army. Their solution had been to send the duo east, but they also wrongly detached a trio of infantry corps plus a cavalry division from the marching wing of the German Army in the west to march eastward, where they arrived too late to have any effect whatever on the Battle of Tannenberg, thus being useless on fronts both east and west simultaneously.

Despite his surprise victory against both Mackensen and von François, Gumbinnen caused Gen. Rennenkampf himself to pause and take stock of the aggressive German commanders to his front. By then, von Moltke had replaced the retreating von Prittwitz, and von François was on his way via rail to take on yet another Russian force. This was the 2nd Army of Gen. Samsonov, and, despite his disobedience at Gumbinnen, the new commander Beneckendorff entrusted the scrappy von François with the decisive aspect of the approaching Battle of Tannenberg as well.

How Tannenberg Evolved from the German Defeat at Gumbinnen

By now, the duo had reached their new command and jelled with the savvy Hoffmann as well. Meanwhile, a note had been found on the body of a dead Russian officer that changed the entire strategic picture overall.

Recalled Hindenburg in his postwar memoirs: "It told us that Rennenkampf's army was to pass the Masurian Lakes on the north, and advance against the Insterburg–Angerburg line … to attack the German forces presumed to be behind the Angerapp, while Samsonov's Narew Army was to cross the Lötzen–Ortelsburg line to take the Germans in flank."

Thus forewarned, the duo stopped the German retreat, reversed course, and decided to attack instead their Russian foes, thus setting the stage for the Battle of Tannenberg, acknowledged by all martial historians as "One of Germany's greatest victories."

This saw von François as the spear point of the attack against Samsonov on August 27, 1914, plunging deep into the penetrated Russian rear. This led the new Chief of Staff Ludendorff to fear a counterattack from Rennenkampf to aid Gen. Samsonov, so von François was ordered to halt his advance. This the latter again refused to do, thus breaking orders for the second important time within days, continuing his own encirclement of a much larger force, that of Samsonov.

The new commander and his chief of staff got the majority glory for the victory, but they never forgot who had really earned it: Hermann von François.

Erich Ludendorff Arrives!

Erich Frederick Wilhelm Ludendorff (September 4, 1865 to December 20, 1937) was the first officer to come to the minds of both von Moltke and his Kaiser, and not Hindenburg—still known on the retired list of officers alphabetically under "B" as Beneckendorff.

Brig. Gen. Ludendorff was a commoner born in 1865, when the future field marshal was already eighteen years old and a commissioned officer soon to fight their future allies, the Austrians. Oddly, both had been born at Posen, however. Both had also attended the same military schools and also served, but not met, on the same general staff, but Ludendorff lacked any combat experience whatsoever when World War I erupted.

A strenuous workhorse by reputation and an able specialist, Ludendorff was regarded as one of the general staff's best minds, but he was also disliked for his cold and haughty personality. Due to a prewar clash with a minister of war, he was deployed away from Berlin to a regimental command, which he needed on his service record anyway to progress upwards.

In 1918, Ludendorff became one of the five awardees of the Grand Cross of the Iron Cross. Born as the third of six offspring to reserve cavalry Capt. August Wilhelm Ludendorff and Clara von Rempelhoff Ludendorff, young Ludendorff grew up on the farming estate that his father managed, Kruzewnia (near modern Poland's Poznan or Posen).

He traced his lineage not only to Prussia but also had strains of Polish, Swedish, and even Finnish blood. Like Kaiser Wilhelm II's sons, Ludendorff entered the Royal Cadet School at Plon in Schleswig-Holstein at the age of twelve, and he was known for being both studious and fanatically disciplined.

At this early date, he was a rather handsome young man, that being belied in middle age as he put on weight in both face and girth. At the age of fourteen, Cadet Ludendorff moved on to the Prussian Military Academy at Groß-Lichterfelde, Berlin, where his later Nazi Party political ally Hermann Goering studied after him.

In 1882—the year of the birth of Imperial Crown Prince Wilhelm—Cadet Ludendorff was commissioned as an infantry junior lieutenant at seventeen years old, his first posting for the next five years being in the 8th Westphalian Regiment.

During 1887–90, he had the rather unusual assignment of serving at the great German sea base at Wilhelmshaven with an elite naval infantry unit. In that capacity, he even sailed aboard a trio of German warships—the *Niobe*, *Baden*, and *Kaiser*—into both Scandinavian waters and around the British Isles, his future enemy.

Promoted Senior Lt Ludendorff at Frankfurt-an-der-Oder River attached to Lifeguard Grenadier Regiment No. 8, his next posting was at the prestigious Army War College at Berlin, assigned as his main subject the difficult Russian language for three years.

Upon graduation in 1894, the new Russian linguist was sent to Russia as a military *attaché*, being promoted to captain on his return. He was stationed on the great general staff at Berlin, thus having gained some unique insight into the affairs of his future foe, the Imperial Russian Army, in the meantime.

Capt. Ludendorff in 1896 was transferred to the German 6th Army Corps headquartered at Magdeburg, and two years later, he performed the obligatory line command duty as a company commander in Infantry Regiment No. 61, 8th Pomeranian.

In 1901, Ludendorff became a staff officer at Glogau's 9th Infantry Division, commanded by a future German field marshal, then Gen. von Eichhorn, who was also one of Ludendorff's own subordinates during the Great War.

After three years, Maj. Ludendorff in 1904 was returned to the general staff under then-Chief Gen. Alfred Count von Schlieffen in the 2nd Department, Mobilization—one of the most important posts in the entire Army.

Ludendorff became the departmental chief when Count von Moltke the Younger succeeded the great Schlieffen, and he immediately became a passionate proponent of better field communications, the usage of aircraft for reconnaissance, and the deployment of heavier artillery.

Physically, Ludendorff presented as a stern-looking man: a short, rather dumpy, dour figure with clear, penetrating blue eyes, double chin, straight medium nose, close-cut hair, bushy moustache, and thin lips.

Considered difficult with whom to get along, many have then and since rated Ludendorff a military genius—brilliant and incisive—but also as extremely nervous, high-strung, and overly ambitious. His constant intrigues to get ahead and his avoidance of the normal chain of command thereby earned Ludendorff many enemies on the CGS at Berlin, winning him fewer friends. Worse than that, however, his military career could have been entirely derailed by his affair with a then-married woman whom he persuaded to leave her husband so that they could marry. This was Margarethe Schmidt Pernet Ludendorff (1875–1936), born the daughter of a wealthy industrialist. Her first husband was Karl Maria Anton Pernet, with whom she had a daughter, Margot, and a trio of sons, all of them later officers in the German Army: Franz, Heinz Otto, Kurt, and Erich, Pernets all four.

Amazingly, Ludendorff's career survived the scandal, but he was transferred to a lower post as a colonel in command of Infantry Regiment No. 39 at Düsseldorf. Possibly a demotion, it can also be seen as the normal posting of a staff officer to a command position to keep his military service record up to par with his rivals and compatriots.

This was followed by promotion to major general in command of an infantry brigade at Strasbourg, but when the Great War broke out in August 1914, instead of being returned to the CGS at Berlin, he was named second quartermaster general under Gen. Karl von Bülow, thus earmarked for the all-important invasion of Belgium that he himself had helped plan.

A Sword Hilt for a Belgian Gate, August 7, 1914

In the first days of the fighting in the west, Ludendorff soon covered himself with martial glory and renown by almost single-handedly taking the Belgian Fortress Liege at the head of the 14th Infantry Brigade, whose command he assumed under fire upon the death in action of its CO, Gen. von Wussow.

According to one 2016 account, "Ludendorff quickly took the initiative, and led the 14th as it fought its way through the village of Queue-du-Bois in the early morning hours of 7 August 1914, dispatching a colonel into Liege itself to demand the city's surrender. Ludendorff later arrived at the Citadel and pounded on the door, falsely believing it to be in German hands." Legend has it that he was first on its ramparts, after having somewhat theatrically banged on the city gates with his sword pommel demanding its surrender—and getting it.

For this gallant exploit that thrilled the German home front, Gen. Ludendorff was personally awarded by the Kaiser the famed *Pour le Mérite* (For Your Merit or Blue

Max) medal, the very first thus presented in the entire war. "More importantly, the German Supreme Command" of the Kaiser and Count von Moltke the Younger "now saw Ludendorff as a proven, decisive leader and strategist."

Thus, on August 22, 1914, at Wavre, Ludendorff received the news of his sudden appointment as the new chief of staff of German 8th Army East Prussia. Indeed, his former boss, Count von Moltke, wrote him: "A difficult task is being entrusted to you, one more difficult perhaps than the capture of Liege! I know of no other person whom I trust as implicitly as yourself! Perhaps you may succeed in saving the position in the east." In this same letter, Ludendorff learned the name of his new commanding officer, one Gen. Paul von Beneckendorff und von Hindenburg.

Once arrived in East Prussia, Ludendorff won the respect of the man who was to be both his trusted subordinate and rival, Col. Max Hoffmann, his own deputy chief of staff, who said of him: "Gen. Ludendorff is a first-class man to work for. He is also the right man for this job: cold and ruthless."

One who did not like Ludendorff was his supreme warlord, German Emperor Wilhelm II, who told his Imperial Chancellor Theodor von Bethmann-Hollweg in January 1915, "I will never allow Ludendorff to become Chief of General Staff! He is a dubious character, fired by personal ambition!" He was right.

Nevertheless, Wilhelm II showered his difficult subordinate with both medals and promotions, including naming him general of infantry on August 29, 1916, in tandem with his being named Hindenburg's first quartermaster general at KHQ Castle Pless in 1916.

Another who met him in August 1917 was the German-American *Baltimore Sun* newspaper man and famed columnist Henry Louis Mencken: "He is chilly, reserved, remote, and almost wholly without charm! He seems devoid of any social instinct … a man of mystery."

Yet, he had his softer side, as revealed in the oddly titled book by his later divorced first wife, Margarethe, *My Marriage to Ludendorff*: "My children warmed to their new father from the very beginning! Their love and admiration for him grew even deeper as the war progressed."

He truly loved his stepchildren as well, grieving especially for two of the Pernet sons who died as pilots during the war—Franz in September 1917 and Erich in March 1918. The remaining son became his personal military aide after the war.

A Letter in Search of a Command

How had Hindenburg come to receive the top job over Ludendorff, and what had he been doing in the early days of August 1914? Both His Majesty and the count wanted a steadier hand at the helm of 8th Army than that of the excitable, choleric tempered Ludendorff.

A few days before the momentous appointment, Gen. Hermann von Stein on the count's staff received a letter from a retired general officer at Hanover:

One request: do not forget me if—as things develop—a commanding officer is needed anywhere!

Both in body and mind, I am robust, and was therefore considered for active employment last autumn, although I am on the Retired List. You can imagine for yourself what my feelings were when I saw men of my own age going to the front, while I had to sit at home twiddling my thumbs! I am ashamed to show my face in the street! Von Beneckendorff und Hindenburg.

Both the Kaiser and his general staff chief read this letter, and its writer seemed to them to be the perfect choice for commanding general of 8th Army. Ludendorff would be the real head of the army, with the older man as the figurehead by some accounts, but in reality, this copied the time-honored tradition of the usual working relationship between commander and his chief of staff—no more, no less.

But if he was to be a figurehead, he was also to be a responsible one. Although Ludendorff might be the source of victory or defeat, Hindenburg alone would bear the ultimate responsibility for the outcome of his able subordinate's schemes. His fine aristocratic name would make up for his subordinate's middle-class deficiencies in the socially conscious *milieu* of the Wilhelmine Second Reich of 1914.

Despite this, however, the man still known as Beneckendorff had had well enough of sitting at home in Hanover and reading about the battlefronts in his daily newspapers, sticking pins into a wall map, and marking both the advances and retreats of his country's armies both east and west. Now he was ready for action! Years before, while playing with his only son, Oskar (Hindenburg had married Gertrude Wilhelmine von Sperling, the boy's mother, in 1879), Hindenburg even then dreamed of them both sitting around a future wartime campfire as fellow soldiers at war with the Russians.

In his memoirs, the elder von Hindenburg also recalled holding up the then five-year-old boy in a crowd to see Kaiser Wilhelm I, telling his son in his rather simple, unaffected way, "If you never forget this moment as long as you live, you will always do right!"

During World War I, Oskar served as an army officer on the general staff, the pinnacle of Prussian militarism, and also as his father's aide both during the war and later for the entirety of his presidency of the Reich (1925–34).

A series of telegrams from Imperial General Headquarters in West Germany arrived in rapid succession summoning him back into active service and command, with a train being duly sent to fetch him away from Hanover to East Prussia in company with his new chief of staff for the next four years and more: Erich Ludendorff.

He was to command an entire army in his native East Prussia. Ludendorff had received his own new orders at KHQ Koblenz on August 22, 1914 direct from Count von Moltke, and even before meeting his new CO early the next morning at Hanover railway station, Ludendorff had already issued what he felt to be the necessary orders to their new joint command, the German 8th Army, by wire.

Col. Max Hoffmann

Hundreds of miles away—and also on that historic August 22, 1914—Col. Max Hoffmann of 8th Army staff was issuing exactly the same, as-yet unknown orders that Ludendorff was busy formulating, two minds thinking in tandem, but separately.

Both men realized that Samsonov's army was then their greatest menace, and both laid down basically the same directives to combat it. Later, both men would claim the same credit for the victory that history, by an odd quirk of fate, awarded to neither of them, but, rather, to their chief, Beneckendorff, instead.

Karl Adolf Maximilian Hoffmann (January 25, 1869 to July 8, 1927) had yet another claim to martial fame than winning both the Battles of Tannenberg and First Masurian Lakes, and that was in playing a major role in knocking Russia out of the Great War altogether during 1917–18. This was proven by his successful negotiations ending the fighting via the Treaty of Brest-Litovsk, signed by Imperial Germany and the Russian Red regime on March 3, 1918.

Born at Homberg, Upper Hesse, Hoffmann graduated from the elite Prussian Military Academy before being posted as a commissioned officer in 1887 in the 4th Thuringian Infantry Regiment. After graduation from the Berlin War College in 1889, he, like Ludendorff, was appointed to the general staff in its Russian section, also spending six months in Russia as an interpreter.

During his service as a military observer with the Japanese 1st Army in Manchuria during the Russo-Japanese War, Hoffmann met an American counterpart who would later command all U.S. forces in Europe against the German armies during the Great War: John J. Pershing.

Beginning World War I as a lieutenant colonel, by its end, Hoffmann would be a major general and an awardee of the Blue Max and the Iron Cross 1st Class, along with both of his more famous chiefs.

When the duo moved west in August 1916, Hoffmann remained behind in the east as the chief of staff to Hindenburg's successor as commander-in-chief of all German forces on the Eastern Front: Prince Leopold of Bavaria.

After the February 1917 Russian Revolution ushered in the July/Kerensky Offensive, Hoffmann received from Ludendorff six full divisions to organize a counterattack and was thus enabled to take Riga on the Baltic Sea. His own attack thus stymied, Kerensky was overthrown by the Reds, and this in turn led to the Bolshevik exit from the war altogether so that Lenin and Trotsky would be free to win their Civil War at home against the pro-Tsarist White forces, thereby establishing the world's first communist state.

Postwar, Maj. Gen. Hoffmann published his memoirs—*The War of Lost Opportunities*—dying at fifty-eight years old at Bad Reichenhall, Bavaria. In retrospect, his military reputation outshines those of his two jealous superiors—the toxic duo—as they lost their war, while he won his.

Hoffmann's famous cutting remark about Hindenburg has also survived in most martial histories of the period, reportedly made to a group of army cadets: "This is where Hindenburg slept before the battle [of Tannenberg,] this where he slept after the battle, and this is where he slept during the battle!" as he conducted a postwar tour of the famous site.

Fischer took this a step further in 1961, asserting that Col. Hoffmann "Had an extraordinarily low opinion of Hindenburg—'A wretched fellow … this great military genius and idol of the people…. No one in history ever became so famous at the cost of so little intellectual and physical exertion!'"

The Duo Forged!

That was all still in the future, though, when Beneckendorff's new subordinate reported to him on the bare station platform at Hanover: "Maj. Gen. Ludendorff, Your Excellency, by order of 21 August, of the All-Highest's Military Cabinet, appointed chief of staff of the 8th Army!" Thus was forged one of military history's most renowned teams. They conferred on their train, agreed, and turned in for the night.

Train Passenger Mrs. Margarete Ludendorff's Recollections (*My Married Life*)

Here the two generals met for the first time…. It was said that on receiving the summons, Hindenburg had exclaimed, "I can only do it with Ludendorff!" Many maintained that it had been the other way round….

It was about nine o'clock that we went into the saloon to have breakfast with … Hindenburg. He came to greet me with a touch of real friendliness, and greeted me kindly….

He … made a deep impression on me…. From the first moment I saw him, my heart went out to him in confidence and admiration … "Look," he finished by saying, "my uniform and boots are not according to the regulations, and I have to go to the front with my old *Litewka* from the 3rd Guards Regiment!" …

The special train at a tearing speed passed a chain of munition trucks and transports … all going eastwards. The carriages were decked with flowers, and from every window the fresh smiling faces of our soldiers looked out…. I heard the sounds of clear laughter and cheerful singing…. There was a lively satisfaction at being able to take part…. The whole thing seemed a dream.

When we reached Kustrin, I had to take my leave … handed over to the care of the station commandant…

Beneckendorff Physically

In 1914, Beneckendorff was an imposing figure physically: over 6 feet tall; of massive bulk; with a large square head with clear blue eyes; a long fleshy nose; "the largest moustache in Germany," it was later asserted; short, gray hair in a Prussian crewcut; and large, sunken jowls.

A veritable giant of a man, in this regard, his forebear Grenadier Schwickart had served him well. To most, his very appearance seemed calm and stability personified, displaying at all times a classic, peaceful demeanor, and nerves that inspired the utmost confidence in all who encountered him. In moments of stress, trial, or crisis, this man never seemed to get rattled by events, but simply went his way, unperturbed. Good-natured and kindly to his subordinates, Beneckendorff was what he seemed to be: completely devoted to both duty and service as he understood them to be in all cases.

The Duo Compared

The commander modest and retiring, his staff chief arrogant and egotistical; the first using "we," the second "I;" the former a man of slow, but always accurate judgment, the latter more brilliant and having a quicker grasp of the overall situation, but prone to moments of panic when things seemed to go awry.

Noted one observer of them both, Hindenburg "Possessed great insight, and his mature and considered judgments often restrained Ludendorff's unstable and less perfectly balanced temper."

Previous biographers note Hindenburg's "character" and Ludendorff's "intelligence," rarely, if ever, transposing the two, one for the other. No one thought Hindenburg a "genius," but neither did they see any cordial or friendly traits in his dour chief of staff.

Their longtime French opponent, Marshal Ferdinand Foch of France, wrote of them thus: "Ludendorff, a general; Hindenburg, a patriot!" Next to the towering, broad Herculean figure of Beneckendorff, Ludendorff was shorter and stockier.

The boss was relaxed in manner, his subordinate always tense. Hindenburg never lost his temper, while no one ever recalled Ludendorff laughing—or even smiling. The first had qualities, the second talents; the former constancy, the latter knowledge. Both of them had staying power, sense of duty, and purpose, and each was incorruptible, at least until 1927, at any rate.

In his postwar memoirs, Hindenburg wrote: "One of my most noteworthy tasks was … to leave as free a scope as possible to the brilliant thoughts of my chief of staff, to his almost superhuman powers of work, and to his unwearied energies. I had to be to him a loyal comrade in war." Noted Ludendorff in *Ludendorff's Own Story*:

> After talking things over with my colleague, I frankly told the [future] field marshal my ideas as to the best conduct of operations, and laid definite proposals before him.
>
> It was a great gratification to me---invariably from Tannenberg to the time of my retirement---that he agreed with my ideas…I honored him highly, served him faithfully, esteeming his lofty sense of honor no less than his loyalty to his King and his joyful sense of responsibility.

The Battle of Tannenberg, August 26–29, 1914

Hoffmann, the 8th Army's operations officer, noted on August 23, 1914: "There has never been—and no doubt will never be again—such a war as this, fought with such bestial fury. The Russians are burning everything down!"

The Germans faced two Russian armies, each equal to their sole 8th Army, but 30 miles apart. If they linked up, Ludendorff later admitted, "We would have been beaten." The war might have ended in 1914 with a single Russian victory in the east and a comparable French triumph in the west at the Marne.

Had the war ended with the Hohenzollern monarchy retained intact—with no future Hitler or Lenin, and neither a Nazi nor a Red state—there might not have been a World War II, but who can say? A retained, defeated Hohenzollern regime might have rebounded for renewed war in 1939, just as it had in 1813 in the War of Liberation, following the catastrophic Napoleonic defeats of the Prussian Army in 1806 at the Battles of Jena-Auerstedt. In any case, it was not to be—1914 occurred as it did.

Noted another period chronicler: "Few battles in history have given rise to so many myths as Tannenberg! According to one popular legend, Beneckendorff worked out his plans for it 25 years earlier, when—as a captain—he was General Staff Officer to the 1st Division," even then planning in future to drive the hapless Russians to their deaths by drowning in the area's many swamps and quicksand in the vast Tannenberg forests. But there were no swamps in the Tannenberg forests, Ludendorff later asserted.

Beneckendorff himself downplayed his own mythical fable thus: "Before this day of 24 August 1914, I had never seen the battlefield." Indeed, the new martial duo arrived at 8th Army headquarters on the 23rd, being informed to their joint amazement that their new subordinate, Col. Hoffmann, had already issued "their" orders.

Reportedly, both men were silently irritated with Col. Hoffmann. Hindenburg never mentioned the former colonel in his own memoirs, while Ludendorff cast him a scant mention only.

Publicly, in his own memoirs, then-Lt Gen. Hoffmann gamely credited his higher ups, privately asserting himself as the unheralded author of the great battlefield success, the only clear-cut German victory during the Great War. He did later note sourly, however, that if Hindenburg had won the Battle of Tannenberg, one could cease believing in Hannibal and Caesar—sour grapes as this tart comment was.

The Immediate Pre-Battle Military Situation, August 22–25, 1914
As of August 24, 1914, Gen. Samsonov was driving swiftly though East Prussia towards them at Marienburg. Gen. Rennenkampf had been fiercely attacked and temporarily halted by Gen. von François at Gumbinnen a few days prior to Tannenberg.

The overall triad plan of the two generals and their colonel was to surround and then annihilate Samsonov's army before Rennenkampf could come to his aid. Having achieved that initial ambitious goal, the 8th Army would then focus on Rennenkampf and destroy him next.

Samsonov was to be surrounded and utterly smashed by a force smaller than his, while Rennenkampf was to be kept checkmated before Königsberg—today's Red Kaliningrad—by a lighter covering force of both infantry and cavalry.

Due to an alleged intense 1905 rift between the two Russian commanders during the Russo-Japanese War in the Far East (information supplied by then German military *attaché* and eyewitness Hoffmann in person), it was believed possible to keep their armies separated.

The plan worked excellently; the period of August 24–25, 1914 was spent in preparations and final dispositions of German troops. Von François commanded the right wing, with Gens. von Bülow and Mackensen jointly commanding the left.

The center was left weak as a bait to tempt Gen. Samsonov's ill-considered attack.

On the evening of the 25th, Beneckendorff told his assembled staff: "Gentlemen, our preparations are so well in hand that we can sleep soundly tonight." The next day, August 26, 1914, the epic and epochal Battle of Tannenberg began.

Samsonov fell for the offered bait of the German 20th Corps, and the fighting was soon underway, as tension mounted at 8th Army headquarters as to what Rennenkampf might do in response. Only Hoffmann, reportedly, remained undisturbed, confident of victory.

Once he realized the full scope of the imminent disaster facing him, Gen. Samsonov duly wired Rennenkampf for help, but the latter sat tight, not moving. On the evening of August 26, 1914, a moment of tense crisis came at German headquarters at Marienburg, as Russian cavalry and one of Rennenkampf's own corps were wrongly reported to be in the rear of Gen. von François' forces.

Ludendorff's First Panic

At this point, allegedly, Ludendorff lost his nerve, wanting to recall François, breaking off the battle with Samsonov, but Hindenburg refused, and herein lies his own chief claim to having "won" Tannenberg.

So it was that—each in his own way—the overall quartet of Hindenburg-Ludendorff-Hoffmann-François "won" the Battle of Tannenberg. The reports of Rennenkampf's advance were wrong, and thus the battle continued on through August 27–29, 1914.

On the night of the 29th, there occurred a lineup of the forces of Mackensen on the left and von François on the right, thus completing the pincer movement of encirclement around Samsonov's men.

This accomplished, the destruction of his army proceeded apace. That night, the Russian Army had sustained the greatest defeat of any throughout the entire course of the Great War, with 100,000 dead, including Samsonov himself—a suicide by pistol shot.

There were, reportedly, a further 100,000 POWs taken by the Germans, plus thousands of captured guns, three entire army corps destroyed, and the scattered survivors fleeing in broken disorder toward the Russo-German frontier whence they had invaded East Prussia but two weeks earlier.

Thus had been won the most smashing martial triumph in the annals of both Prussia and Germany to date. To the Kaiser and von Moltke at KHQ Koblenz engaged in their Western Front crisis, the stunning news from Tannenberg came as a much-needed saving grace, indeed: their brain child of teaming Beneckendorff with Ludendorff had worked.

Enter Hindenburg!

His Majesty awarded "Hindenburg"—and not "Beneckendorff" in the news releases—the Blue Max, while both Ludendorff and Hoffmann received from him the Iron Cross.

Faced with uncertain news from the Western Front, the German home front went wild with joy over that of the clear-cut victory of Tannenberg, it overshadowing all else about the war for the next four years and beyond.

Church bells rang out across the Second Reich in celebration, schools applauded, and captured Russian artillery rolled under the Brandenburg Gate at Berlin: it seemed to be 1870 all over again.

Adds Brownell in *First Nazi*: "Although the battle actually took place near Allenstein [now Olsztyn, Poland], Hindenburg named it after Tannenberg [now Stębark, Poland], 30 kms to the west, to avenge the defeat of the Teutonic Knights at the earlier Battle of Grunwald of 1410 having the same name."

Ever since, the two battles—1410 and 1914—have been referred to as first and second Tannenberg to differentiate them. The German 8th Army fielded 150,000 men *versus* the Russian 2nd Army's 230,000, with an estimated 13,873 German casualties against 170,000 Russian, in 2016 figures.

"Hindenburg [Beneckendorff] had been thinking about that [earlier] battle since the evening before, when he strolled near the ruins of the castle of the Teutonic Order. In 1910, the Slavs had commemorated their triumph on the old battlefield," thus celebrating its 500th anniversary.

At one point, allegedly, "Ludendorff screamed at him until François finally agreed to attack, but with the proviso that—because his ammunition column was still on the road—his men must charge with bayonets."

As the Russians fled, the Germans "Had endured long marches in sweltering weather, but some men still had the energy to pursue on bicycles requisitioned from civilians." Bicycles again would see combat service with another German Army a generation later against the children of these fleeing Russians.

Ludendorff's Second Panic

Ludendorff [had earlier] announced that the attack on the 2nd Army must be broken off. Beneckendorff led him behind a nearby hedge; when they emerged the latter said that operations would continue as planned....

The noose was in place. The Russians who had been attacking were surrounded.... The Russians who tried to break through by dashing across open fields heavy with crops were mown down. They were in a cauldron near Frogenau, east of Tannenberg....

Many surrendered—long columns of prisoners jammed the roads away from the battleground. The Duo watched from a hilltop, with only a single field telephone line; thereafter, they stayed closer to the telephone network.

Beneckendorff met one captured Russian corps commander that day, and another on the day following.... On 31 August 1914, Beneckendorff formally reported to the Kaiser that three Russian Army Corps—13th, 15th, and 23rd—had been destroyed....

He requested that the battle be named Tannenberg, an imaginative touch that both Ludendorff *and* Hoffmann claimed as their own.

Notes Brownell in *First Nazi*:

> Samsonov's 2nd Army had been almost annihilated: 92,000 captured; 78,000 killed or wounded, and only 10,000—mostly from retreating flanks—escaping.
>
> The Russians had lost 350 big guns. The Germans suffered just 12,000 casualties out of 150,000 men committed to the battle; 60 trains were required to take captured Russian equipment to Germany.
>
> Other historians give smaller numbers for Russian killed and wounded, that were never properly recorded. For instance, 30,000 Russians killed or wounded, with 13 generals and 500 guns captured.…
>
> The Russian 1st Army was still in East Prussia [but Tannenberg] set the stage for the First Battle of the Masurian Lakes a week later, when the reinforced German 8th Army confronted the Russian 1st Army. Rennenkampf retreated hastily back over the prewar border before *they* could be encircled…

Hindenburg's 1934 Admission

Military historian Walter Elze wrote that, a few months before his death, "Hindenburg finally acknowledged that Ludendorff had been in a funk that evening."

He also remarked: "After all, I know something about the business! I was the instructor in tactics at the War Academy for six years!" the closest he ever came to actively claiming credit for winning the battle.

In 1925, Ludendorff named his personal political movement the *Tannenbergbund*.

Comes the Mighty Hero!

Overnight, the formerly unknown Beneckendorff morphed into the universally acclaimed Hindenburg in every German newspaper and in newsreels in all German movie theaters, with mail being delivered to 8th Army HQ Marienburg addressed simply to "The Most Popular Man in Germany." In short, Hindenburg had arrived.

Next came the wartime merchandizing of his now exalted name, with Hindenburg cigars, ties, boots, and restaurant dishes—more would follow postwar. That Christmas, 1914, he was deluged with over 600 gifts of wine, pipes, and tobacco alone, plus thousands of other presents. Young women sent him pillows stuffed with their own hair, and older ones galoshes to keep his feet dry.

Back at Hanover, the city fathers named him as their number one resident, and thousands of picture postcards of his stolid face flooded the shops and kiosks of the Second Reich, making him—along with his Kaiser and his own later and last Reich Chancellor Hitler—the most photographed and painted man in German history.

Affectionately called "*Unser* [Our] Hindenburg," he soon became known as well as the "Wooden Titan," as huge wooden statues of him appeared nationally, into which people drove iron nails for a patriotic financial donation to the cause of winning the war. His portrait soon graced most German homes, too, and busts proliferated as well.

Over the past century, the reasons for this sudden fame have been pondered and debated. Noted Wheeler-Bennett's *Wooden Titan*:

> His monumental stature, great head, up-turned moustaches, and quiet manners all endeared him to the average German.
>
> Moreover, he had no flaw of genius, as had Goethe, Bismarck, Frederick the Great, Schiller—and Ludendorff. He was a simple, uncomplicated man, and his people loved him for it. Although they respected Ludendorff's abilities and talents, he was not so well esteemed.

Another reason for Hindenburg's spectacular and sudden rise to instant fame was that it was officially promoted by the emperor's Army and government, Tannenberg being offered as the replacement success for what had not occurred on the Western Front, where the failure of the Battle of First Marne was quietly shunted aside.

"Hindenburg became not only a hero, but the living symbol of embattled Germany, a star to which his country could now look with hope and certainty to guide them through war to victory." Thus was established for the next two decades and beyond the Hindenburg Legend, not losing its luster until after the end of his long life.

Mrs. Ludendorff Witnesses Their Fame at Vienna (*My Married Life*)

> When Hindenburg arrived with all his staff of officers, the Hotel Metropole filled up in a trice…Outside in the streets stood a dense crowd of cheering and enthusiastic people. The national hymn was sung.…
>
> Again and again, Hindenburg and Ludendorff were called for. They could not show themselves often enough, and were made a perfect target for flowers!

Mrs. Ludendorff and the "Wooden Titan"

She recalled her personal experience with one of these famous likenesses:

> A platform was erected in front of the statue, and in the foreground was placed a seat of honor, and on this throne I was expected to mount.
>
> Then—when I had hammered in my golden nail—a photograph was to be taken.… Later, I found my name under the photograph of Princess Wedel.

Meanwhile, in the West

"Majesty, the war is lost!" von Moltke had frankly told Wilhelm II to his face after the loss of First Marne, and so, indeed, it was. Although great victories would continue to be won in the east, the decisive theater of war was in the west.

After the initial German failure there, the war of movement ceased, with that of trench warfare and attrition replacing it for the next four years.

The First Battle of the Masurian Lakes, September 7–14, 1914
Thus, as the victors of Tannenberg left for Russian Poland to lead their new command of the German 9th Army, Gen. von François stayed behind with his victorious 1st Corps in East Prussia, but he was soon in action again and winning once more.

The smashing success at Tannenberg was followed up by the First Battle of the Masurian Lakes, in which a great victory was won over the surviving forces of Gen. Rennenkampf himself, resulting in East Prussia being entirely freed of the enemy presence.

For the third time, von François refused to obey orders. This occurred when the new 8th Army CO Gen. Richard von Schubert directed him once more to retreat, which von François simply cancelled out by a telegram of refusal.

Reportedly, the man who intercepted it was a famous sender of telegrams himself: the German emperor. Firing Gen. von Schubert, the Kaiser thereby promoted von François to his own 8th Army command on October 3, 1914.

This First Battle of the Masurian Lakes resulted in the Russian 1st Army being forced back all along its wide front, ultimately ejecting it from East Prussia and Germany altogether.

Its success was halted, though, when the Russian 10th Army suddenly appeared on the Germans' left flank. Once more, Russian superiority in mass numbers trumped German strategic brilliance, as it would time and again on the Eastern Front until March 1918.

At the outset of First Masurian Lakes, Rennenkampf's 1st Army of the Niemen River numbered 490,000 men to the Germans' 215,000, with the German 8th Army comprising sixteen infantry and a pair of cavalry divisions against the Russians' twenty-two infantry and 20,000 cavalrymen in five mounted divisions overall.

In the First Lakes battle that resulted, the Germans lost but 10,000 men killed in action to the Russian's stunning 125,000, plus an estimated 45,000 POWs. Still, a decisive second Tannenberg-like mammoth victory eluded the Germans when the Russians were able to successfully retreat to the safety of their own frontier forts.

Overall German casualties were reported to be about 70,000, inclusive of killed, missing in action, and wounded.

Thus was the overall German East Prussian campaign of August–September a resounding success, with fully three invading armies—including the follow-up Russian 10th—completely thrown out of the country, but Russia remained in the war.

The First Lakes victory was short-lived, though, as the Russians rebounded during September 25–28, regaining much of the lost territory, a pattern established by them that carried on throughout most of the war in the east. Not only that, but the Russians also badly defeated the Germans' ally, the Austro-Hungarian Army, in time driving the latter out of both Galicia and from Russian Poland.

Von François Plunges On!
Von François got away with disobeying orders three times, but came a-cropper the fourth, when his superiors fired him for sending them the wrong unit requested. Thus, in November 1914, von François was succeeded as CO 8th Army by Gen. Otto von Below.

On December 24, 1914, the rebellious general received from Wilhelm II yet another gift command; however, that of the 41st Reserve Corps, was sent west, then transferred back east in April 1915 just in time to help conquer Russian Poland.

He was awarded the Blue Max by the emperor on May 14, 1915 for his role in von Mackensen's Gorlice–Tarnów Offensive breakthrough.

That was not all, either. In July 1915, von François commanded a Westphalian Corps in France, as well as Meuse Group West during the Battle of Verdun in July 1916, for which the following July 1917, the Kaiser awarded him the Oak Leaves to his Max.

Unused during the March–June 1918 Kaiser's Battle in the West, von François gave up his command and was placed in reserve to October 1918, taking retirement. He became the postwar author of the 1920 memoir *Marne Battle & Tannenberg*.

The general died at the age of seventy-seven at Berlin on May 15, 1933, during the early phase of the Nazi Third Reich.

Field Marshal August von Mackensen (1849–1945)

"He was bold in front of the enemy, and only feared God," it was said of August von Mackensen, the Kaiser's favorite soldier and the House of Hohenzollern's last appointed general field marshal (GFM). So asserted the official 1938 work *Prussian-German Field Marshals & Grand Admirals*, published postwar in Berlin. As for the former sergeant of the Franco-Prussian War Battle of Sedan himself, when Kaiser Wilhelm II—his admiring patron—raised him to the nobility in 1899, the newly created August von Mackensen chose as his familial motto the simpler theme of "*Memini initii*" ("Remember the Beginning"), recalling his humble origins.

Indeed, his British critic Cyril Falls called him "One of the most over-advertised generals of the war," after reviewing how, in August 1914, the advancing Russians had taken 6,000 of his men prisoners, before he was able to halt in his personal command car their 15-mile-long rout to the rear, at Gumbinnen.

In addition, Falls asserted: "He used to boast of his descent from a Highland chieftain, a Mackenzie. When this became unsuitable, it was given out that his name was derived from the village of Mackenhausen."

The 1938 *Prussian-German Field Marshals & Grand Admirals* stated: "The Mackensens were farm people from Solling in Niedersachsen, where the Village of Mackensen was probably the birthplace of the Mackensen lineage. His father Ludwig was a farmer who worked hard, and went from leasing a parcel of land to owning an estate. His mother—Marie Rink Mackensen—gave birth to her eldest son Anton Ludwig Friedrich August on 6 December 1849 in Leipnitz, Sachsen."

The future Saxon warrior against Russians, Serbs, and Romanians in the Great War as—earlier, against the French—played with toy soldiers as a boy and dreamed of a military career, just like his later superior, rival, and ally, Hindenburg.

Since his father could not afford to send him to a military academy for officer training, young August instead took a one-year enlistment as a volunteer on October 1, 1869 with the 2nd Lifeguard Hussars.

When war broke out with Imperial France in July 1870, Mackensen fought at Sedan and led a reconnaissance patrol that resulted in his division commander personally nominating him for the Iron Cross.

That December 4, he took several French prisoners, and on the 12th, he was promoted from the ranks to lieutenant in the Royal Prussian Army Reserves, a single step up. In 1873, Mackensen was named lieutenant of the Lifeguard Hussars, three years later as adjutant to 1st Cavalry, and promoted first lieutenant in 1878, being chosen two years later for the prestigious German general staff as well.

Promoted captain in 1882, he was named to the general staff of the 14th Division in 1885, and two years later as Chief of Dragoons for Regiment No. 9. That same year, his friends gave him a plaque with the inscription "For Capt. Mackensen: who will advance with lightning speed and become a General Field Marshal"; prophetic words, indeed, for one who would later also assert that he wore the same uniform size throughout his entire military career.

Named major in 1888, three years later, Mackensen was adjutant to the influential Chief of the German General Staff Field Marshal Alfred Graf von Schlieffen. This brought him into the regular circle of the Kaiser, with whom his career, fate, and destiny would forever be linked through two world wars. Mackensen angered his contemporaries by kissing the Kaiser's hand.

Mackensen was promoted lieutenant colonel in 1894 as commander of the 1st Lifeguard Hussar Regiment, and in 1897, he was jumped to full colonel. The following year witnessed his promotion to the post of senior adjutant to the Kaiser, and after his ennoblement, his children were entitled to inherit his "von," as the male members did. He had three sons and a daughter.

The future field marshal was married twice. After the death of his first wife, Doris von Horn, he married Leonie von der Osten, twenty-eight years his junior.

After having accompanied the Kaiser to Palestine in 1898, Mackensen was promoted to major general in 1900, and the next year received the plum Lifeguard Hussars Brigade appointment at Danzig, where he remained until the war began in 1914.

In 1903, von Mackensen had been named lieutenant general as commander of the 36th Cavalry Division, and five years later, he was again promoted to general of cavalry and commander of the 17th Army Corps.

On July 17, 1914—at the age of sixty-five and seemingly on the verge of retirement after a most successful military career, the majority of it in peacetime—fate intervened, and August von Mackensen took his place on the martial stage as a great captain in the most stupendous conflict in all recorded history to that date.

The 17th Corps that he had already commanded for six years prior to the outbreak of World War I encompassed a pair of divisions of eight infantry regiments, one battalion of *Jägers* (Sharpshooters), three regiments of cavalry Hussars, the 4th Regiment of Mounted Rifles, two brigades of field artillery, Corps heavy artillery reinforced with pioneer/engineer troops, and the aerial 17th Detachment for reconnaissance.

The corps commander's headquarters was located at Deutsch-Eylau, later relocated to Darkehmen.

On August 15, 1914, it was the Tsarist Imperial Army that surprised the world by launching an offensive into the Kaiser's own backyard in Prussia, winning the Battle of Gumbinnen on August 20, 1914 against none other than 17th Corps Commander Gen. von Mackensen, defeating the German emperor's favorite horseman, thereby knocking his units into a headlong retreat.

Noted *Ludendorff's Own Story*:

> The infantry lost 200 officers and 8,900 men in combat, as well as 1,000 prisoners-of-war [to the victorious Russians]. Two batteries daringly advanced very far forward to help the infantry, but were annihilated, losing 13 officers and 150 men.
>
> The headquarters itself with its park of cars and horses of the escort was taken under Russian artillery fire.... The infantry lost more than a third of its strength killed and injured.... The Russians were content to pursue the retreating Prussians with their artillery fire.

It was this loss that caused his superior—German 8th Army C.O. Gen. Prittwitz und Gaffron—to consider abandoning East Prussia altogether to the two invading Russian armies, via a pell-mell retreat behind the Vistula River instead.

Still, the beaten but determined von Mackensen promised to tell the Kaiser in person of the bravery of the many soldiers who had stood and fought during the mêlée, closing his oration with the exhortation, "Whatever the future can bring us—for His Majesty the Emperor and King, hurray!" Still, the very first German defeat of the war in the east had been his. Von Mackensen's role at Tannenberg was to attack the Russian right wing at Bischofsburg and Sensburg in what today is Poland.

Expunging somewhat his humiliating defeat at Gumbinnen a few days before, he both broke and pursued it in his characteristically aggressive fashion.

At the follow-up First Battle of the Masurian Lakes of September 9–14, 1914, southeast of Königsberg in East Prussia, the redeployed German 8th Army of his superiors pursued Rennenkampf's twelve divisions, resulting in a second German victory, with 10,000 German killed to the Russians' 45,000 lost and 150 guns taken. Still, though, this 1st Russian Army escaped annihilation by retreating back into European Russia from whence it had so unexpectedly come.

Mackensen led from the front, and thus often higher headquarters did not always know exactly where his 17th Corps was, as he rejected orders that countermanded his own desires to keep pursuing the retreating enemy and—as at the Lötzen Gap—assaulted the Russians morning, noon, and night of the same day.

On October 9, 1914, the overall Russian commander, Grand Duke Nicholas (aged fifty-seven), threw fourteen Russian and Siberian divisions against Mackensen's five, necessitating a fallback upon Łódź.

On November 1, 1914, von Mackensen was named commander of the 9th Army before Warsaw, with his 250,000 men facing double that number of the resilient enemy.

That December, von Mackensen's forces retook Łódź and then Lvov in Poland, preparing for the Gorlice–Tarnów Offensive breakthrough of May 2, 1915 before Warsaw.

That April, he had been named commander of the 11th Army, as well as being promoted to the grade of colonel general.

Asserted Asprey in *The German High Command*: "Mackensen handled his forces well, relying as earlier on powerful artillery support against a confused enemy short of reserves. Though progress was slower at Gorlice because of limited roads, Mackensen continued to employ tactics built around a strong center of heavy guns." He had learned from his mistakes at Gumbinnen the year before. With the brilliant Gen. Hans von Seeckt as his chief of staff, von Mackensen stormed the Russian positions and won a victory on May 2, 1915.

On the following June 22, when Lemberg (Lviv) fell to his Austrian troops as well—the Kaiser promoted him at Castle Pless to the rank of general field marshal, thus reaching the pinnacle of his storied martial career.

On August 26, 1915, the newly minted general field marshal also took the embattled Russian Fortress of Brest-Litovsk that would assume a diplomatic role during 1917–18. He was honored as well with the command of the Austro-Hungarian Army Hussar Regiment No. 10, backdated to June 11, 1915.

Three days later—on August 29, 1915—Prince Leopold of Austria succeeded Hindenburg as Supreme Commander of All German Forces on the Eastern Front, with Gen. Hoffmann as his chief of staff. Reportedly, His Bavarian Majesty retained this command until the end of the war and was also a potential German candidate for the throne of the puppet Kingdom of Poland that never materialized. Prince Leopold ended his military career with more success, therefore, than did some other GFMs of the period; he died on September 28, 1930 and is buried at the Columbarium of St Michael's Church at Munich.

When it was announced that there would be a combined German-Austrian-Bulgarian invasion of Serbia under von Mackensen—the Serbs had already beaten the hapless Austrians twice—Hoffmann noted sourly, "Now that all available honors, titles, and orders have been showered in so short a time on this one devoted head, there will be nothing left for him after the capture of Belgrade but to be re-christened Prince Eugene!" after the famous Austrian commander of yore.

Explained Asprey, "Field Marshal Prince Eugene of Savoy (1663–1736) was Austria's 'noble cavalier,' a heavily decorated (and richly rewarded) military and political genius, gray eminence to Kaiser Karl VI, and builder of Vienna's beautiful Castle Belvedere."

Mackensen's combined force had as its core nine German Army divisions, as of September 16, 1915. The Serb capital of Belgrade duly fell to his forces on October 9, 1915, and both he and von Seeckt wanted to push on to Salonika in Greece, but the now so-called Palatine of the Balkans was overruled by Supreme Headquarters in favor of a joint attack into Romania with Gen. Erich von Falkenhayn in September 1916 instead.

Mackensen crossed into enemy Dobrudja on September 4, 1916, destroying Fortress Tutracaia on the Danube River, even though his force was smaller than its garrison. Next, he took forced marches on to Fortress Silistria, 70 miles southeast of Romania's capital city of Bucharest.

Linking up with von Falkenhayn, Mackensen managed to enter the next captured enemy capital ahead of his co-warrior—riding in on a white steed like the showoff cavalryman that he had always been—on December 6, 1916, the acclaimed hero of the Central Powers once more, and, as always, the cherished martial darling of the Kaiser.

Indeed, the startled Kaiser declared that he would name the next German naval battle cruiser after his battlefield pet, but this never occurred. The glorious commander had been awarded the Blue Max on November 27, 1914, its ninth awardee of the Great War, and also held both the Iron Cross 1st and 2nd Classes.

In January 1917, the black-clad soldier in the Death's Head fur busby was also granted the Grand Cross of the Iron Cross, its other distinguished holders being Hindenburg, Ludendorff, and Field Marshal Prince Leopold of Bavaria.

Naturally—as in all armies from time immemorial—all this notoriety only increased the professional jealousy of von Mackensen's successes, even on May 26, 1917 by his former subordinate and supposed admirer, Imperial German Crown Prince Wilhelm, who believed he was "Quoted far too often."

The other strains of the long war were already being felt, however, as noted by Navy Adml. Karl von Müller in his wartime diary entry for September 22, 1917: "Mackensen's deputy … reports that the tension between the Bulgarian troops and our own in the Dobrudja is very serious, and that hostilities can start at any moment. King Ferdinand's warning to Mackensen should not be dismissed lightly."

When an armistice was announced with Romania on March 2, 1918, the admiral further recorded this entry: "The Dobrudja will not be ceded to Bulgaria, but to the Central Powers, who will come to a decision on its future at a later date. We—Germany—want to retain the use of the Cernavodă-Constanța Railway…. Thank God Mackensen was there, or else things would not have been dealt with so summarily."

In his multiple successful martial operations, the Black Marshal was quick to acknowledge in his postwar 1938 memoirs the services of his triad of talented Chiefs of Staff: Col. Hans von Seeckt in his Serbian campaign, the transitional Lt Col. Richard Hentsch, followed by his permanent Romanian Campaign C of S, Lt Gen. Gerhard Tappen.

Lt Gen. Gerhard Tappen

Dietrich Gerhard Emil Theodor Tappen (July 3, 1866 to May 28, 1953) survived the *Kaiserreich* (Imperial Reach), Weimar Republic, Third Reich, and the start-up of the Allied West German Republic at Bonn before his demise in 1953.

At the start of the Great War, then Col. Tappen served at Imperial Headquarters at Koblenz when, in September 1914, von Moltke sent him on one of the most important secret missions of the war. This was to visit the First Marne battle commanders to determine for him, the CGS, if they and Col. Tappen believed the fighting should continue, or if defeat would be accepted instead. Col. Tappen advised the latter, and so it occurred.

Named chief of staff the following March 1915 to former War Minister Gen. Josiah von Heeringen in his capacity as commanding officer of the 7th Army, Tappen was promoted to major general on June 26, 1915.

Awarded the Blue Max by the Kaiser on September 11, 1915—near the anniversary of the lost First Marne—Gen. Tappen received as well its second Oak Leaves awarding the following January 1916.

On August 31, 1916, he was transferred to the Balkan Theater of Operations as the chief of staff to the new Romanian Front's CO of Army Group Mackensen. That December, he was granted his own field command of the 5th Ersatz Division, and during September 1917 to November 11, 1918, Gen. Tappen led the 15th Infantry Division.

He retired from the Army in 1919, apparently seeing no further service at all until his death at the age of eighty-six on May 28, 1953 at Goslar, Germany.

Gen. Karl Litzmann

Revered in German martial history during 1914–18, Karl Ludwig Wilhelm Hermann Litzmann (1850–1936) later joined the Nazi pantheon of Great War heroes as well.

Born on January 22, 1850 at Neuglobsow, Stechlin, in the ancient Mark of Brandenburg, Litzmann was awarded the Blue Max by the Kaiser on November 29, 1914, followed by the second award of the coveted Oak Leaves the following August 18, 1915.

A general of infantry from December 24, 1914, his army service career spanned 1867–1918, winning the Iron Cross 2nd Class during his 1870–71 combat tour against the French.

Litzmann held numerous troop commands, among them being the 49th (6th Pomeranian) Infantry, the 74th Infantry Brigade, 39th Division, and his most famous combat unit, the 3rd Guards Division, with which he won its part of the overall Battle of Łódź against the Russians.

The Battle of Łódź, November 11 to December 6, 1914

The Battle of Łódź, in which Gen. Litzmann emerged as one of its main heroes, took place in bitter wintry Poland during November–December 1914, pitting the German 9th Army against a trio of combined Russian armies—the 1st, 2nd, and 5th—in twenty-six days of fierce combat overall.

Hindenburg, Ludendorff, and von Mackensen were the overall German commanders, opposed again by Rennenkampf and a trio of lesser Russian Army generals. Again, the Germans were outnumbered, this time by two to one, with 500,000 Russians *versus* 250,000 German soldiers.

The strategic situation was that the Russians had beaten the Austro-Hungarians in the Battle of Galicia, with the latter retreating from their surrounded Fortress Przemyśl, then under siege by the enemy's own 8th Army.

The Germans themselves had lost the Battle of the Vistula River, their incursion thereby being ejected from Russian Poland. To rectify this, the Kaiser had named Hindenburg as the commanding officer of two combined German armies on the embattled Eastern Front, one—the 8th—still defending East Prussia from a possible renewed enemy invasion.

The duo's new 9th Army was commanded by von Mackensen, deployed on the Polish–Silesian frontier, shadowing whatever Russian move might come next. This was revealed once more by an intercepted enemy wireless message asserting that Silesia would be invaded by the Russians on November 14, 1914.

The duo decided to forestall this by attacking the Russian right flank via moving 9th Army north by rail over ten days on eighty trains daily. This gambit took the stunned Russians completely by surprise on November 11, 1914 as the Battle of Łódź opened, with Mackensen's 9th Army assaulting Rennenkampf's 1st Army's 5th Siberian Corps.

Badly routed, the shocked Siberians left 12,000 POWs behind in their wake. Later, it was the Germans themselves who were almost taken in a pocket at Łódź, but Mackensen correctly assured Hindenburg that such would not occur.

When the duo learned from yet another intercepted wireless message that the Russians were going to evacuate Łódź, they ordered it occupied on December 6, 1914, thus taking an industrial city of more than 500,000 in population.

The resulting German victory saw but 35,000 Reich casualties to double that for the Russians, with seventy-nine guns taken and 25,000 POWs going into the Aryan bag. It was this stellar win that convinced the eastern duo more than ever that, with enough reinforcements, they could knock the Russians completely out of the war.

This was a goal reached not by them, Mackensen, or von François, however, but instead by Hoffmann, via negotiation, and not by more inconclusive ground victories such as theirs had been.

Gen. Litzmann's Later Career Path

During December 24, 1914 through August 6, 1918, Gen. Litzmann was commanding officer of the 49th Reserve Corps; he retired for health reasons, being succeeded by Lt Gen. Paul Grünert.

Born the son of a wealthy estate owner in Mark Brandenburg, Litzmann began his career at the age of seventeen, seeing his first combat action as a lieutenant during the Franco-Prussian War in the Guards Pioneer/Engineer Battalion, but he was mainly an infantryman throughout his long career.

In 1883, he became a teacher at the Metz War School, and during 1902–05, he served as head of Prussia's prestigious War Academy at Berlin, when he established the German Defense Union. This was followed in 1911 by his foundation of the Young Germany League as well.

At the age of fifty-five, and already a lieutenant general, Litzmann was placed on inactive reserve status, but recalled to the colors in 1914 on the Eastern Front for renewed active combat duty at sixty-four years old.

According to *Ludendorff's Own Story*, Gen. Litzmann was reactivated to head the Line of Communications Inspectorate at Gen. Max von Hausen's 3rd Army Headquarters at Dresden, but then he was transferred to succeed Gen. Max von Gallwitz as commanding officer of the elite 3rd Guards Division, with the latter then becoming his corps command superior.

Fighting in support of Gen. Reinhard von Scheffer-Boyadel during the Battle of Łódź in November 1914, Litzmann's divisional troops were such a key factor in the German victory.

During the 1915 campaign season, Litzmann led his corps into the Second Battle of the Masurian Lakes, which included the taking of Fortress Kovno, and supposedly rejected an offer from Kaiser Wilhelm II to elevate him to the "von" nobility status, accepted before him by Mackensen.

Continuing his advance along the Nieme River, Litzmann led his corps to success again with the taking of Vilnius from the Russians in September 1915. The following July 1916, he led his command southward to Ukraine's Volhynia, in which it achieved a successful frontal defense against superior forces near Korytnica-Szelvov.

Fighting the Russians again in the rugged Apuseni area in the Carpathian Mountains in Hungary, the following August 1917, the doughty commander led Group Stanislav in Eastern Galicia also. His corps was transferred to the Western Front in January 1918 as part of Group Souchez to support the German 6th Army. Having retired due to ill health, Gen. Litzmann declined the Kaiser's command that he take charge of Berlin's security forces in the closing days of the war, there being a dearth of the necessary forces to command in action.

The venerable general published his two-volume war memoirs during 1926–28, and in 1929, he joined Hitler's Nazis after having become an SA member. He declined to serve as an elected N.S. Deputy to the Reichstag in 1932 due to already having such duties in the Prussian State Parliament as its most senior member, known as *Alterspräsident* ("Father of the House").

After 1933, Litzmann became the most prominent former member of the Kaiser's Army—after von Mackensen—to back Hitler's new regime publicly, being paraded by the Nazis as often as possible.

Named an honorary Reichstag president under Goering during 1932–36, Gen. Litzmann held this title until his death at the age of eighty-six on May 28, 1936, when both Goering and Hitler attended his state funeral.

According to his *New York Times* obituary of May 29, 1936:

Gen. Karl Litzmann—a Nazi general since 1929—his devotion to Hitler brought him into conflict with President von Hindenburg, and in January 1933, just before the Nazis came into power, the German Retired Officers Association issued a declaration condemning him for his attacks on the Reich President....

Hitler made him the gift of a new [Mercedes-Benz] car on his 85th birthday as a token of his gratitude for the service Litzmann rendered the Nazi cause.... In his speech opening the newly elected Reichstag on 6 December 1932, Gen. Litzmann rebuked Hindenburg for having denied Hitler [being appointed Reich Chancellor already].

"Millions of Germans revere Hitler as the outstanding German of his day, and as the man who—after 14 years of study—alone knows how Germany can be saved!"...

Gen. Litzmann further contended that his infantry brigade had carried the day in the Battle of Łódź, and that Hindenburg admitted owing his marshal's baton to the valor of the Litzmann troops.

Named an honorary citizen of Neuruppin, this was withdrawn in 2007, however. Passau, Germany, named a street after him also. On April 11, 1940, the Nazis officially renamed Łódź in Poland after him, as Litzmannstadt and later Brzeziny as Löwenstadt, but with the German loss of the war in 1945, they both reverted back to their original Polish names.

Second Battle of the Masurian Lakes, February 7–22, 1915

This Second Battle of the Masurian Lakes (a.k.a. the Winter Battle of the Masurian Lakes) took place over February 7–22, 1915 and was the northern segment of the overall Central Powers' combined offensive designed—as had been all the earlier ones—to knock Russia out of the Great War. Like them, it, too, failed to achieve that always over-ambitious goal.

Taking place in then-East Prussia (today's modern Poland), it pitted the duo, Hoffmann, and Gen. Hermann von Eichhorn all against a trio of Russian commanders, with a pair of German armies *versus* two Russian.

As always, the Germans were vastly outnumbered, this time by more than two to one—220,000 Russians opposed to 100,000 German soldiers. Significantly, and again as usual, the Russian losses were hugely out of all proportion to their Teutonic foes: 200,000 Slavic casualties of all kinds *versus* 16,200 German killed, wounded, and missing.

This time, the duo had little to complain about regarding von Falkenhayn supporting them, as he deployed four more army corps to their aid. Thus, by February 1915, fully 36 percent of the total German field army was fighting on the Eastern Front under the duo.

In this new winter campaign of 1915, the duo's 8th Army was led by Gen. Otto von Below, while the German 10th was skippered by von Eichhorn, both against the Russian 10th and 12th Armies.

On February 7, 1915, in a blinding blizzard snowstorm, the Russians were again surprised by an assault from von Below, followed by the German 10th Army the next day as well. In a single week, the German Army advanced 75 miles, causing terrific casualties among the embattled Russians, whose rout led to many POWs being taken. The climax of the battle came on February 18, 1915, when an entire Russian corps was encircled in the massive Augustov Forest; three days later, it surrendered.

Their stand until then, though, allowed the rest of the Russian 10th Army to escape capture, even launching a counterattack via the Russian 12th Army on the 22nd, thus ending the German advance.

Statistics vary as to Russian gun losses (185–300), as well as POWs (anywhere from 56,000–92,000 men taken). Reportedly, the Germans lost fourteen guns and 7,500 men. The Germans failed to take the besieged Russian Ft. Osowiec, though, thus marring the completeness of a Teutonic win once again.

Second Lakes was also offset by the failure of Gen. Alexander von Linsingen's attack with heavy losses, with the Austrian Ft. Przemyśl falling as well to the Russians. Once more, despite all their best efforts, the Germans simply could not close the deal against the Russians in the east. They remained in the war despite all their defeats.

The Central Powers' Gorlice–Tarnów Offensive, May 2 to June 1915

The combined Central Powers' Gorlice–Tarnów Offensive was their major attack for that year, resulting in the complete destruction of the Russian lines leading to their retreat far into Russia itself; it was thus a major victory for the two allied Kaisers, Wilhelm II and Franz Josef.

Subsequent attacks ended the campaign season that autumn in October 1915, with all Russian forces having been thrown out of the entire Masurian Lakes region of today's northeastern Poland, encompassing the loss of nearly 200,000 dead or captured soldiers.

This was yet another victory for the team of von Mackensen and his most talented staff chief, Gen. Hans von Seeckt, resulting in 250,000 POWs being taken during May–June 1915, balanced against 87,000 German casualties overall: killed, wounded, and missing in action.

This second duo was ably aided by their commander of heavy artillery, Maj. Gen. Alfred Ziethen, in their joint efforts of combating the Russian 3rd Army of eighteen and a half infantry and five and a half cavalry divisions.

Mackensen fielded ten infantry and a single cavalry division that included 126,000 soldiers, 457 light field pieces, 159 heavier guns, and ninety-six mortars, cementing his growing reputation as an artillery-centered commander facing in one combat alone five Russian divisions of 60,000 men armed with 141 light and four heavy guns.

For once, therefore, the Germans enjoyed a superiority of all kinds, and Mackensen's forces moved forward in unison against weak Russian defensive lines. Still, however, "When driven back, the Russians almost invariably counterattacked in thick masses, only adding to their losses," according to Brownell in *First Nazi*.

Meanwhile, at a top-level Castle Pless conference, CGS von Falkenhayn on May 12, 1915 ordered Army Group Mackensen to establish bridgeheads across the eastern bank of the San River in Poland to await the coming online of rebuilt railway lines. These would take AGM to the forty-four forts surrounding Russian-held Fortress Przemyśl. On May 30, 1915, Mackensen's guns of all calibers began blasting the Russian fortress complex, with the initial trio falling on June 1, 1915, and the combined Austro-German forces entering the city in triumph on the 4th.

Galicia's capital city of Lemberg (Lviv) became the next Central Powers' objective, with the Russians in full retreat from it after an attack launched on June 13, 1915, and all of Galicia being evacuated by the Russians on June 21.

The next day, Mackensen's combined Central Power forces occupied Lemberg itself, with the captured Galician oilfields thereafter supplying the Imperial German Navy with 480,000 tons of oil daily.

In its headlong retreat back into European Russia, the Russian Army left behind 140,000 POWs, the rout becoming known as "The Great Retreat of 1915" thereafter in military annals.

Warsaw Taken!

As a result, Warsaw finally fell as well to the German 12th Army on August 5, 1915, and by the end of that month, all of formerly Russian Poland was occupied jointly by the Central Powers.

The victory of the Black Hussar Marshal August von Mackensen was complete and also led to the firing of the Grand Duke Nicholas as Russian C-in-C, his replacement being none other than Tsar Nicholas II in person.

Von Woyrsch, Opponent of the Brusilov Offensive, 1916

Martin Wilhelm Remus von Woyrsch (February 4, 1847 to August 6, 1920) held a variety of important field commands during the Great War. These included *Landwehr* (Militia Reserve, August 2, 1914 to September 23, 1916); Assault Army Woyrsch (October 14, 1914 to December 15, 1917); and Army Group Woyrsch (August 29, 1916 to December 15, 1917), during which latter year he was promoted GFM by the German emperor.

His first combat task in August 1914 was to reinforce the Kaiser's embattled Austro-Hungarian Army Central Powers ally under Gen. Viktor Dankl von Krasnik, covering the latter's retreat from the pursuing Russian Army.

In *The German High Command*, Asprey noted that an enemy newspaper from the Russian capital stated, "Only the activity of the small Prussian *Landwehr* troops in this battle prevented the complete destruction of the Austrian Army!"

As part of Hindenburg's 1915 9th Army, von Woyrsch that July helped win the break-through Battle of Sienno near Wągrowiec, and in 1916 helped stave off as well the Russian summer steamroller Brusilov Offensive that badly defeated the Austrians yet again.

For all of the above, he was awarded his GFM staff the following year. Remaining in the service after the war, Field Marshal von Woyrsch retired in 1920 to his Castle Pilsnitz near Breslau, where after his death a famous statue was sculpted in his martial honor, clad in the traditional knight's garb of chain mail and grasping a sword.

Von Eichhorn: The Assassinated Marshal

Hermann Emil Gottfried von Eichhorn (February 13, 1828 to July 30, 1918) began his Great War service as a field commander on the Western Front at the Battle of Soissons, and he commanded the German 10th Army during January 21, 1915 to March 5, 1918, including at the Second Battle of the Masurian Lakes in February 1915.

His forces took Kovno on the Eastern Front as well, and then both the Grodno and Olita Forts, he being award the Blue Max by his grateful Kaiser on August 18, 1915, followed by the Second Oak Leaves award on September 28, 1915.

Named commanding officer of Army Group Eichhorn on July 30, 1916 simultaneously still leading the 10th Army, he led both until March 31, 1918. Having been raised to the rank of GFM the previous December 1917, von Eichhorn was promoted yet again to supreme commander of Army Group Kiev in the former Russian Ukraine, where he also served as military governor.

It was at Kiev that Field Marshal von Eichhorn was assassinated by Red terrorist B. M. Donskoy. His stricken German emperor, Wilhelm II, honored the slain GFM doubly: first with a state funeral and burial at Berlin's Invaliden Cemetery, and second by naming one of the eight towers of Castle Marienburg for him.

General of Cavalry Georg von der Marwitz, Leader of Prussian Horse

Johannes Georg von der Marwitz (July 7, 1856 to October 27, 1929) was a noted leader like von Mackensen of Prussian horse, plus an army commander on fronts both east and west during World War I, who began it by leading a cavalry corps in action. As such, von der Marwitz commanded his 2nd Cavalry Corps at the Battle of Haelen on the Western Front, then he was sent east as C.O. of the just established 38th Reserve Corps, which he led to victory in the Second Battle of the Masurian Lakes in the winter of 1915.

He was next moved south, where his command fought alongside their Austro-Hungarian Army allies, again against the Russians. For this, the Kaiser awarded von der Marwitz his Blue Max medal on March 7, 1915. This was followed by a surprise posting on October 6, 1916 as personal adjutant to the Kaiser himself, which he left less than two months later for another field command; his new command was as C.O. of the German 2nd Army back on the Western Front, a command that lasted from December 17, 1916 to September 22, 1918.

Gen. Alexander von Linsingen and the Army of the Bug

Gen. Alexander Adolf August von Linsingen (February 10, 1850 to June 5, 1935) commanded the oddly named Army of the Bug (River) in the Russian east in 1915. Prior to that, he had been a corps commander at First Marne and then was transferred to Austrian Galicia as C.O. of the German South Army, beating the Russians and taking 60,000 POWs.

Awarded the Blue Max on May 14, 1915, he also received its Second Oak Leaves honor that July. Then came his "Bug" command, simultaneously with that of Army Group Linsingen, with which he faced the Russian Brusilov Offensive of June 1916.

Reversing a retreat, Gen. von Linsingen halted the Russian surge at the Battle of Kowel, for which he was promoted colonel general with four stars. Following the signing of the Treaty of Brest-Litovsk in March 1918, the general spearheaded the steamroller German advance into Ukraine. On the 31st, however, his AGL component was stood down, and that June, he was named military governor of Berlin. Postwar, Gen. Linsingen died at the age of eighty-five on June 5, 1935 during the Third Reich.

The Two Generals von Below, Otto and Fritz

General of Infantry Otto von Below

Otto Ernst Vincent Leo von Below (January 18, 1857 to March 15, 1944) was the co-commander of the stellar Central Powers' victory of the German and Austro-Hungarian Armies over the Royal Savoyard Army at the decisive Battle of Caporetto in 1917 on the Italian Front. His colleague therein was Austro-Hungarian Gen. Svetozar Boroević, and a then obscure German junior officer who also won personal battlefield laurels, Erwin Rommel.

This von Below began his Great War as a corps C.O. in the momentous Battles of Gumbinnen, Tannenberg, and the First Masurian Lakes, thus seeing him promoted as general of infantry early in the summer of 1914, gaining the command of the duo's own 8th Army that November. This he led to victory in the Second Battle of the Masurian Lakes in

February 1915 and again with it as the renamed Niemen River Army in the May Kurland Offensive, which saw German troops on the southern shores of the Lithuanian Drina River.

An interim posting took place in the ancient Macedonia of Philip of Macedon and Alexander the Great in October 1916 in joint command of the German 11th Army and its new allies, the 1st and 2nd Royal Bulgarian Armies, following a brief assignment at Lille on the Western Front to command 6th Army in April 1917.

From there, von Below was off to the rugged frontier mountain ranges of Italy that September, in which his forces completely routed the Royal Savoyard Italian Army with German Storm Troops and the infiltration tactics partially developed by Gen. Oskar von Hutier earlier.

As on the Western Front, German poison gas helped scatter the Italian 2nd Army at Caporetto, while lack of supplies at last halted the German advance on the shores of the Piave River, with trench warfare returning thereafter.

Fresh from this remarkable martial win, Gen. Otto von Below was another of Ludendorff's handpicked veteran combat commanders for the upcoming March 1918 Kaiser's Battle. He was unable to overrun the Western Allies at Arras as he had done the Italians before, though, and thus the Somme position remained untaken. He fought two British armies this time, the 3rd and 5th.

Prior to Michael, von Below approached Ludendorff with a radical idea that was to remain an unachieved goal in January 1918: "Forget about the offensive! Shorten the front lines as much as necessary, then construct tanks all through the rest of 1918, and with them, break all the way to the Channel Coast in the spring of 1919!" an occurrence that would not be seen until twenty-two years later.

Before the Armistice, von Below prepared a top secret plan for a last fight, but on German soil—Home Defense Forces West—that also did not occur until decades later, in 1945.

Retired in 1919, von Below found himself in March 1944 at Danzig in East Prussia, in the path of another eventual Russian steamroller—that of the Red Army—but he died at eighty-seven years old, the year before this crashed on through. His cousin was Gen. Fritz von Below.

The Other Gen. von Below, Fritz
General of Infantry Fritz Theodor Karl von Below (September 23, 1853 to November 23, 1918) was a prominent Western Front commander in the Battles of Somme, Second Aisne River, and Michael.

He began his wartime service, however, in the winter Second Battle of the Masurian Lakes in 1915, and he was awarded the Blue Max for all of these fights combined. In the west later on, he fought under a former artillery colleague from the east, Gen. Max von Gallwitz, the latter as C.O. of Army Group Gallwitz-Somme.

For his successful cooperation on the Somme, this von Below received a second awarding of the Max, via its prized Oak Leaves. His contraction of pneumonia in June 1918, however, ended his combat command career, and he died at Weimar on November 23, 1918, aged sixty-five, decades before his cousin and fellow Gen. von Below, Otto.

Above left: The Kaiser's most famous serving wartime field marshal was Paul von Beneckendorff und von Hindenburg, seen in this signed portrait by artist Hugo Vogel on April 10, 1915 as "von Hindenburg." (*LC*)

Hindenburg asserted, "I want thus to be represented to posterity!" signing the work personally with a piece of chalk as a personal memento." As a colonel, Oskar von Hindenburg married a *Baronin,* thus outdoing his more famous father at least in that respect.

Above right: Hindenburg at work at his map table during the Great War, wearing crossed baton shoulder boards, Iron Crosses, and Blue Max at the throat, an image meant to inspire confidence in both Imperial Germany and her allies; it did. (*LC*)

"Hindenburg's entry into Breslau was like a triumphant procession," the first Mrs Ludendorff recalled. In 1893, Hindenburg commanded an infantry regiment at Oldenburg, a division in 1900 at Karlsruhe, the 4th Army Corps in 1905, and took his first retirement in 1911, three full years before the Great War began.

The great man's autograph. (*LC*)

"When the Russians surprised the Germans by their quick mobilization and invasion of East Prussia in August 1914, the German emperor summoned General von Hindenburg from retirement and gave him command in the region of which he had made a life study. He concentrated most of his forces about the Russian Warsaw Army in the region he knew so well. Having drawn a net about his victims, he massed his heavy artillery, and practically annihilated the Russian Army, that lost about 100,000 troops with guns and flags innumerable. This was the victory of Tannenberg that made Hindenburg the idol of the German people," noted a period history published after the end of the Great War.

A formal portrait of Field Marshal von Hindenburg festooned in all his prewar and wartime medals, awards, and decorations, complete with crown-topped *interimstab* (informal stick) baton at lower left of this frame. (*LC*)

He was only the second man in history to win the Star to the Grand Cross of the 1914 Iron Cross. Today, the *Hindenburgstern* is in the former Communist Eastern Europe.

Also mourning the death of the late Austrian Kaiser Franz Josef in November 1916, Hindenburg here wears the uniform and rank collar tabs of the Austro-Hungarian Army, complete with black band affixed to left sleeve. (*LC*)

In the spring of 1932, the former imperial crown prince correctly told Reich Chancellor Dr Heinrich Brüning: "The field marshal [President von Hindenburg] does not wish to vacate his throne!" if he failed to run for and win his post anew.

Above left: Prussian Infantry officer Lt Paul von Beneckendorff in the Austro-Prussian Six Weeks' War of 1866, complete with blanket roll, ammunition pouch, dispatch case, binoculars case at left, and sword in scabbard at right. (*LC*)

During the Great War, even later Nazi architect and minister Dr Albert Speer pounded a nail into Hindenburg's wooden statue for the cost of a mark.

Above right: Young Paul as a skirted lad at home. (*LC*)

"Ida von Hindenburg was meticulous about not exploiting her brother's position. Only very rarely did she travel to Berlin to visit him. The last time I saw her, she had been to the Presidential Palace only once.… She told me: 'The good, good brother comes out to Potsdam to visit me as frequently as he can. When I … celebrated my birthday, he personally brought me an immense basket of good things to eat. I always know when he comes by hearing his firm, even tread,'" recalled Lochner decades later of the marshal's sister.

Military Academy cadet days, the latter in 1860, the year before the outbreak of the American Civil War in North America, one that later greatly influenced the Prussian and German Armies. (*LC*)

"When we are together," continued his sister, Ida, "I try to make him forget the worries of partisan political strife, and we devote our time to reminiscences of our childhood days. We laugh heartily over our merry pranks and over the little squabbles that children do have. The field marshal's expansive, contagious laugh always delights me!"

On the next page:

Above left: In parade dress, complete with riding crop tucked under left armpit, as lieutenant and unit adjutant, 1870–71. (*LC*)

Ida von Hindenburg: "Even when he is very busy, he does not forget me! During the last days of December he was hard at work composing the speech he was to deliver to the diplomatic corps on New Year's Day. The lights had gone out in the Presidential Palace because of a defect at the Berlin electric light plant, and my brother had to work by candlelight! Nevertheless, he wrote me a personal note of good wishes for the new year, adding that he would come to see me as soon as he possibly could tear himself away from his official duties."

Above right: Regimental colonel, 1878. (*LC*)

"My acquaintance with Ida von Hindenburg proved of decisive help. I was able to secure an exclusive interview with her brother, thanks to a letter she had given to me. The field marshal denied being a partisan candidate of the conservative nationalists. 'I am enough of a man to shoulder responsibility myself and make my own decisions. This is what I used to do as a soldier!'" added Lochner.

Right: Major general, 1897. (*LC*)

"One day Hilde and I were invited to a Presidential garden party. [Zeppelin executive Dr Hugo] Eckener was then on a cruise around the world [1929]. When our turn came in the receiving line, we were rather surprised to find him addressing us in these words: 'I am so happy to note what a wonderful reception you Americans are giving our Dr Eckener! Those "confetti parades" in New York and Chicago must have been something unforgettable! The Zeppelin is proving to be a tie for binding the nations together.' Nobody prompted him to tell us who we were; merely our names were mentioned. If he was briefed before he met his many guests, his memory must have been exceptional," added Lochner of Hindenburg's time as Reich president.

Der Kaiser
im Gespräch mit dem
Kronprinzen Rupprecht v. Bayern

7115
Verlag von
GUSTAV LIERSCH & Cⁱ
BERLIN S.W.

It reads, "The Kaiser speaks with Crown Prince Rupprecht of Bavaria," in this prewar view. (*ASA*)

Hindenburg was the most celebrated officer in the German Army. Recollected Lochner of him decades on: "Another occasion that I remember vividly was a dinner given in honor of Egyptian King Fuad. When Hindenburg wore his spiked helmet, one was not quite sure whether his natural height or the elongated headgear made him look so enormous and bulky.… On (another) evening, however, he wore tails. There was no doubt about it: he was a modern Goliath in his own right!" Indeed, when he met the man he had just twice defeated for the Reich presidency, Adolf Hitler, on August 13, 1932, Hindenburg was the tallest of the seven men present. The very day before, Hitler's alleged Bavarian mistress had tried to kill herself.

The handsome young officer. (*LC*)

"My funny bone was tickled … when I saw this gargantuan east Prussian—whose ancestors might well have served with the tall Teutonic Knights— reach not for a big long, black cigar, as one might expect of a man of his proportions, but for a wee little cigarette that disappeared completely from view when it reached his mouth, where it was lost between his bushy mustache and large hands." In 1932, the elite *Herrenklub* at Berlin concocted a scheme whereby Crown Prince Wilhelm would become Reich chancellor with Hitler as president of Prussia. Neither event occurred.

The von Beneckendorff family. *From left to right*: wife and mother, Gertrude; son, Oskar; and husband and father, Paul, during their garrison post years. (*LC*)

"If a tiny cigarette seemed incongruous … how much more to the point was this descriptive adjective when applied to a phrase that the venerable field marshal was wont to use when talking to his lady guests! A cavalier of the old school, after dinner President von Hindenburg would insist—as his guests stood around in groups, sipping their coffee and liqueurs—upon saying a few personal words to every guest. To the ladies, this enormous, ponderous, heavy-set giant loved to remark—as he excused himself to proceed to the next group—'I am like a butterfly. I must flutter from flower to flower!'"

During the four years of the Great War, the husband wrote his wife more than 1,500 letters. Noted Lochner of Mexican Ambassador to Berlin Sánchez-Mejorada: "[he was] Every bit as tall, though not as broad-shouldered, as President von Hindenburg."

Rather more at ease, Mrs. von Hindenburg cracks a smile at right during a walk. (*LC*)

"President von Hindenburg and I surveyed the world situation from a higher plane!" After the speeches in the Potsdam Garrison Church on March 21, 1933, according to Emil Ludwig Cohn two years later: "His chancellor [Hitler] seemed to vanish. [Hindenburg], Gigantic, grizzled, helmeted and be-starred—looking like a knight from earlier centuries—stood there with deep-set eyes, bluish-white complexion, and vacant gaze, hand on sword hilt, a monumental figure from the distant days of chivalry." This was the man whom his wife had married, decades before this actual event, as afterwards the Mexican diplomat told American reporter Lochner.

Above: The living room at their Hanover home, complete with framed oil portrait on display. (*LC*)

Ironically, Churchill was rather a surprising personal fan of his former war adversary, the German field marshal: "Hindenburg! The name itself is massive. It harmonizes with the tall, thick-set personage with beetling brows, strong features, and heavy jowl, familiar to the modern world."

Noted Churchill in 1937 on the late German Reich president: "It is a face that you could magnify tenfold—a hundredfold!—a thousandfold, and it would gain in dignity, nay, even in majesty, a face most impressive when gigantic."

Left: The little boy has grown up! Paul (*left*) with son, Oskar, (*right*) during their joint service together in the office of the Reich presidency at Berlin, 1926–34. (*LC*)

In 1914, 1.7 million German soldiers faced 2.3 million Allies. By 1916, these relative numbers ramped up to 2.3 million Germans *versus* 3.5 million Allies, and with the Americans coming into the war during 1917–18, the statistics grew even more daunting against the Second Reich.

Kossaken Kommen (Cossacks Coming)! (*LC*)

The dreaded cry announcing the unexpected Russian Imperial Army invasion of German East Prussia in August to September 1914 that formed the platform for the launch of the first duo's meteoric success and global fame. By June 1915, the Allies outnumbered the Germans on the Western Front alone by more than 500,000 men reportedly.

A prewar visit of the Kaiser (*sixth from left*, wearing Russian Army uniform) to the Imperial Russian High Command, seen here at a military review, complete with brass band at right. Striding at center is the Kaiser's imperial cousin, Nicholas II, Tsar of All the Russias, and at right the tallest man saluting is his cousin and commander-in-chief of the Russian Army in 1914–15, Grand Duke Nicholas Nikolaevich, nicknamed "Nikolasha" within the imperial family.

In the summer of 1915, the tsar suddenly reassigned his uncle to command Russian forces in the Caucasus against the Turks, assuming supreme command at *Stavka* (headquarters) himself personally. In this photo, the Kaiser's headquarters' commandant, Colonel General von Plessen, appears in Russian Army kit at the far left. (*LC*)

Above left: As his own chief of staff, the tsar chose talented Russian Army General Mikhail Alexiev (1857–1918), who served in that post during 1915–17, when Nicholas II abdicated. From *Stavka*, General Alexiev was promoted commander-in-chief of the entire Russian Army under the new Provisional Government of Alexander Kerensky during March to May 1917, and later helped established the new Volunteer Army to fight the Reds in the Russian Civil War, during which he died of a heart attack. (*LC*)

Above right: Army General Pavel von Rennenkampf, a Russian commander with a Germanized name. (*LC*)

"What good does it do if *we* take Paris or Brussels, but the Cossacks take Berlin?" wailed one exasperated German. In fact, during the Seven Years' War of Frederick the Great, the Russians had taken Berlin, as they would again in 1945.

Rennenkampf's Russian rival—but also fellow commander-in-arms—was his 1904 Russo-Japanese War irritant, General Alexander Samsonov, seen here in 1913. Between them, the entire campaign in East Prussia and the Masurian Lakes was lost during 1914–15. The latter also committed suicide during the Tannenberg disaster. (*LC*)

The best compact overall map of the German–Russian Front in the East, also Russia's West, displaying main railways, forts, roads, and "The strategic significance of Warsaw." (*LC, The War Illustrated,* London, 1915)

A popular wartime picture postcard of the German subordinate who seemingly made a successful career disobeying orders: General Hermann von Francois, thus endearing himself to the Kaiser, who protected him politically from the wrath of his superiors. (*LC*)

The walled and moat red-brick Teutonic fortress of Marienburg in East Prussia that both von Prittwitz and the duo used as their main headquarters during the summer and fall 1914 campaign. The town of 21,000 in 1914 was located about 30 miles southeast of Danzig (now Gdańsk) and 50 miles northwest of Tannenberg. (*LC*)

Above left: Prussian Army General Maximilian von Prittwitz—nicknamed "Fatty" by his detractors—wearing his prewar blue uniform jacket with red collar. Ironically, he was successor Beneckendorff's own first cousin. (*LC*)

"The egotistical Kaiser did not like Hindenburg. During the annual maneuvers in 1908 … Hindenburg had refused to let the Kaiser win a particular encounter. Hindenburg—with dangerous candor—had quipped, 'If this were war, you would be my prisoner!' Kaiser Wilhelm II had been humiliated. From that moment, he shunned Hindenburg at court," according to the Brownells.

Above right: Another handsome young officer in Prussian blue in 1892 was Erich Ludendorff (1865–1937) later general of infantry and during 1916–18 first quartermaster general to Hindenburg, who referred to him consistently as "my assistant," much to his stifled annoyance, allegedly. (*LC*)

Above left: In middle age and still donning royal Prussian blue at left is an older Ludendorff with his mother at right. Note also the glimpse of a smile on the general's far more usually serious visage as we have come to know it in the century plus since 1914. (*LC*)

In 1918, Ludendorff's greatest technological failure was to allow the German Army's tanks to be outnumbered by those of the Allies at the astonishing number of 4,000 to but 20!

Above right: Ludendorff, aged forty-four, stole this attractive married woman—Margarethe Schmidt Pernet Ludendorff (1875–1936)—away from her first husband, a businessman, in August 1909 in order to marry her. Remarkably, he was not kicked out of the German Army in utter disgrace thereby. She died on August 13, 1936 at the age of sixty-one after he had divorced her a decade earlier. (*LC*)

"Since Tannenberg, Ludendorff suffered from megalomania!" noted the Kaiser's Chief of Naval Cabinet Admiral Georg von Muller.

Ludendorff sporting the upturned waxed mustache of the man he came to despise: his own ruler, Kaiser Wilhelm II. Also ironically, this photo from his postwar memoirs mistakenly listed him as von Ludendorff, but the Kaiser never ennobled this arrogant subordinate. (*LC*)

In one single month—at Tannenberg and again at the Masurian Lakes—he demonstrated his skill in organizing the rapid maneuver of large-scale forces. The Gorlice–Tarnów Offensive in Poland in 1915 contrasted starkly with the stalemate on the Western Front."

Above left: The Kaiser look is gone. (*LC*)

Although there were German naval warships named after Field Marshal von Hindenburg, there would never be a Ludendorff, since the Kaiser despised this most prickly of troublesome subordinates. Hitler followed suit under the Third Reich as well. Upon the by then pagan Ludendorff's death in 1937, the Kaiser told Sigurd von Ilsemann in their joint Dutch exile: "At any rate, one must be glad that the Christian Church is freed from such an enemy!"

Above right: The more familiar stern gaze has arrived. (*LC*)

"As his exhausted armies fell back in the face of counterattacks from July 1918, Ludendorff's nerves broke. By September, he was insisting that Germany must make peace immediately, and was forced to resign in October 1918." Reportedly, it was Ludendorff who coined the term *totale krieg* (total war) of whole societies fighting one another. Ludendorf's wartime psychiatrist noted of his illustrious patient that "He had never seen a flower bloom, never heard a bird sing, never watched the sun set. I used to treat him for his soul.

The first quartermaster general's most enduring look before history is this one, seen postwar in 1923 during his ill-fated political flirtation with Nazi Revolution. (*LC*)

His most recent biography labels him as the "First Nazi." At his firing by the Kaiser on October 26, 1918, the Kaiser astonished Ludendorff by blurting out—in response to his offered resignation— "I thank you! You are thereby making my position much easier! I shall endeavor—with the help of the Social Democrats—to build a new Reich for myself!" and this regarding the emperor's sworn political enemies since 1890!

Above left: Maj. General Max Hoffmann, the enduring military genius of Germany's Eastern Front from start to finish all during its entirety of 1914–18. Indeed, it was he—and not the departed duo—that brought final victory in the east via the signed Treaty of Brest–Litovsk of March 3, 1918 between victorious Imperial Germany and beaten Red Russia, an achievement that vanished altogether but eight months later. In 1925, General Hoffmann published his book, *The War of Lost Opportunities*, dying two years later. (*LC*)

Above right: World War I, Battle of Tannenberg (East Prussia): German Field Marshal Paul von Hindenburg (*center*) and his staff. Right of him General Erich Ludendorff, left of him Lieutenant Colonel Max Hoffmann, in the German military headquarters, August 1914.

By 1918, Ludendorff found the following states ranged against both him and Imperial Germany: the U.S., the U.K., France, Russia, Canada, Australia, much of Latin America, Rhodesia, New Zealand, India, and the French colonial empire overseas, with a combined Allied population of 100 million people.

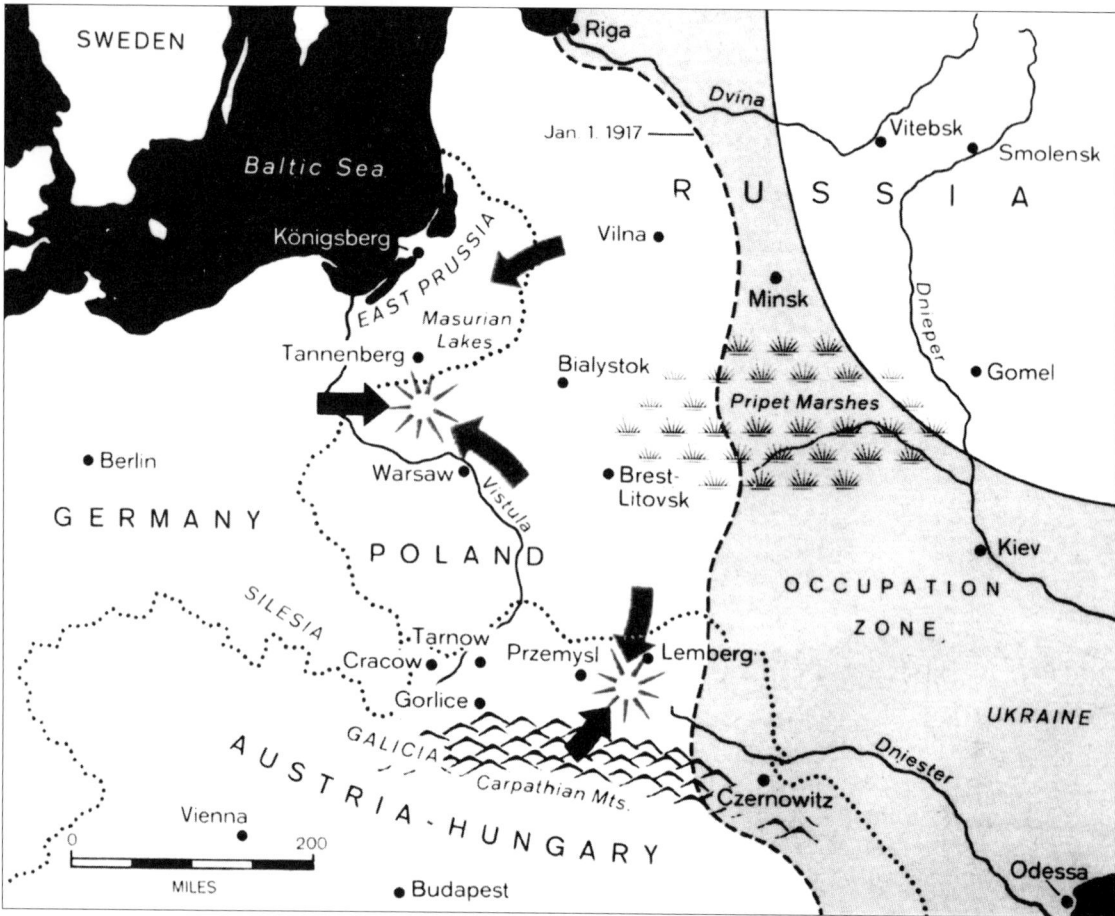

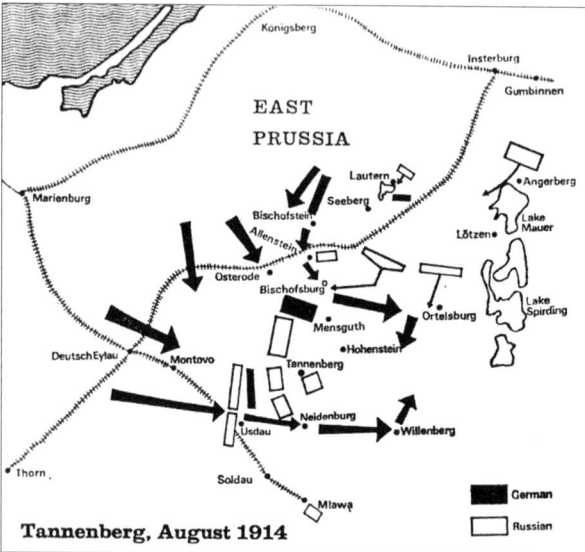

Tannenberg, August 1914

■ German
□ Russian

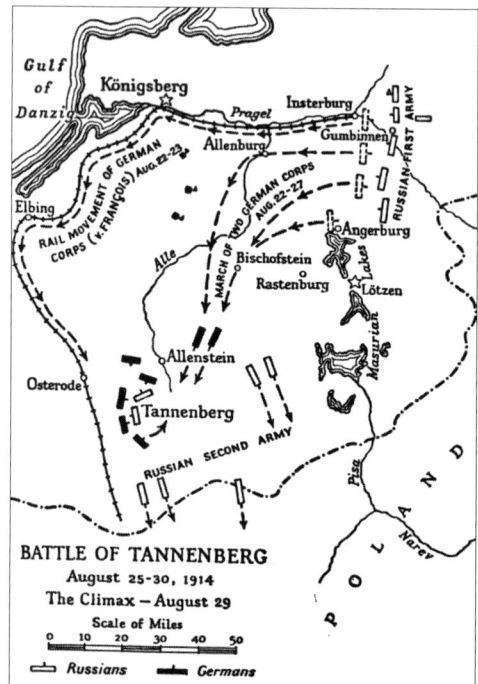

BATTLE OF TANNENBERG
August 25-30, 1914
The Climax — August 29
Scale of Miles
0 10 20 30 40 50
▭ *Russians* ▬ *Germans*

General von Morgen.

On the previous page: A trio of excellent Tannenberg battle campaign maps. Noted the American magazine *Life* in 1964: "On the Eastern Front—shown on this map—fighting raged over Poland, East Prussia, and part of the Austrian Empire. Arrow shows Russia's two-pronged offensive in East Prussia in 1914, that was stopped at the Battle of Tannenberg, and the Russian counteroffensive in the south that drove the Austrian Army against the Carpathian Mountains. Broken line at right shows the front at the end of 1916; gray area shows German occupation zone after the Russian armistice a year later." (*LC*)

Above: A wartime artistic rendering of the duo's Battle of Tannenberg command post hilltop scene, in which Ludendorff displays the map, while below at far right, interested Russian POWs trudge by the scene. Note also the Austrian Army liaison officer in his higher cap, with Hoffmann manning the periscope, as well as the sole field telephone at the bottom left-hand corner of this Hugo Vogel canvas. Entitled *The Battle of Tannenberg,* his work measured 5½ yards long. (*LC*)

Right: General Kurt von Morgen, also at Tannenberg. He was at one point 1st Reserve Corps commanding officer. (*The Times History of the War,* London, 1917–19)

When the Kaiser fired Ludendorff on October 26, 1918, so overjoyed was he that he chortled aloud, "I have separated the Siamese Twins!" meaning Ludendorff from his superior, Hindenburg.

General von Morgen.

Verlag von
Bernhard Nöhring

After hours at GHQ Marienburg, 1914, with a glass of lemonade being poured at center for the reclining victor, fifth from left. A chagrined-looking Ludendorff peers up from his book at table, while Hoffmann stands behind him. At right is seated the command's medical officer in German Red Cross armband, with the Austrian liaison officer standing among the ferns at far right in this wartime painting by artist Hugo Vogel, Hindenburg's favorite right into the start of his Reich presidency term in 1926, more than a decade later. (*LC*)

Die Heerführer von Tannenberg am 24. August 1924 in Königsberg i. Pr.

Heye v. Schmidtseck v. Conta Hell v. Morgen Franz v. Staabs v. Schmettau
v. Duncker v. Mackensen v. François v. Hindenburg v Scholtz

A seated group of Tannenberg surviving commanders postwar. *From left to right, seated*: unknown, Mackensen, Francois, Hindenburg, and unknown. (*LC*)

On November 1, 1914, the Kaiser named Hindenburg commander-in-chief of the Eastern Front. This is a special 1914 silver medallion struck to commemorate the victory of Tannenberg, with his head on one side and his full naked body on the other killing the Russian bear with a double-bladed Germanic sword. (*LC*)

HINDENBURGITIS; OR, THE PRUSSIAN HOME MADE BEAUTIFUL

British wartime *Punch* cartoon on the merchandising of Hindenburg imagery within the common German home: flower pots, beer steins, lamps, portraits, busts, and even throw pillows! Do not forget the bottom trim on the tablecloth, either! (*LC*)

Propaganda film *Tannenberg*, 1932, with Ludendorff at left, Hindenburg (actor Karl Korner) at center, and possibly Hoffmann at right, directed by Heinz Paul.

The marble bust that the Kaiser once gave Hindenburg was displayed at the latter's study in his East Prussian home, Neudeck, as seen when he died in 1934.

Above: The 1915 Iron Hindenburg medallion with ribbon. The inscription reads "For the Iron Hindenburg, from the German People." Notes one account: "The medal measured 18 mm in diameter, was manufactured variously in iron, zinc, and aluminum by the Nuremberg firm Munz–Prague Anstalt Ludwig Christian Lauer. The *Eiserne* [Iron] *Hindenburg-Denkmünze* [Memorial Coin] was worn suspended from a small bow about 28 mm wide." (*LC*)

Right: On parade on August 18, 1918, Hindenburg was greeted by a fellow but retired veteran of both the 1866 war and also the Franco–Prussian War of 1870–71, Maj. von Seel, his company chief, on the anniversary of the Battle of St-Privat in France. (*LC*)

In 1918, the German Army had on the Western Front 36,000 trucks, but still, this was but a third of what the Allies deployed there.

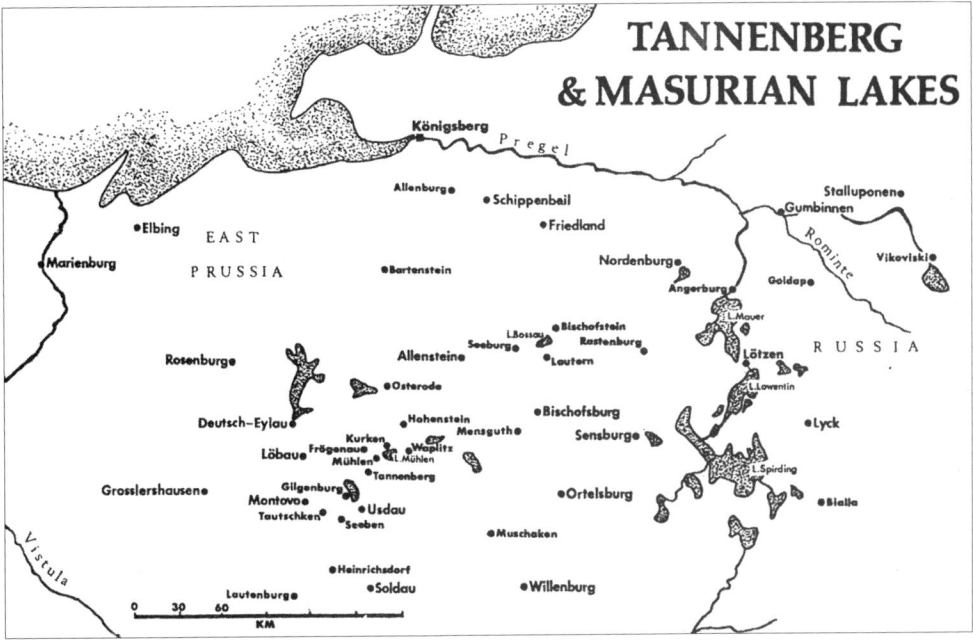

TANNENBERG & MASURIAN LAKES

Königsberg

Pregel

EAST PRUSSIA

RUSSIA

Elbing
Marienburg
Allenburg
Schippenbeil
Friedland
Stalluponen
Gumbinnen
Vikovlski
Rominte
Nordenburg
Bartenstein
Angerburg
Goldape
L.Mauer
L.Bossau
Bischofstein
Seeburg
Rastenburg
Lautern
Lötzen
L.Lowentin
Rosenburge
Allensteine
Osterode
Bischofsburg
Hohenstein
Mensguth
Sensburge
Lyck
Deutsch-Eylau
Kurken
Frögenau
Waplitz
L.Spirding
Löbau
Mühlen
Kl.Mühlen
Tannenberg
Grosslershausen
Gilgenburg
Montovo
Usdau
Ortelsburg
Bialla
Tautschken
Seeben
Muschaken
Vistula
Heinrichsdorf
Soldau
Willenburg
Lautenburge

0   30   60
KM

Campaign map of Tannenberg and Masurian Lakes in East Prussia and European Russia, 1914–15. (*LC*)

Regarding geography and topography, the later Field Marshal August von Mackensen "Astonished his subordinates by his detailed knowledge of the territory of his command—including West Prussia and a part of Pomerania—and not only of localities, but also of people, thanks to an excellent memory of places and people, that greatly contributed to his popularity."

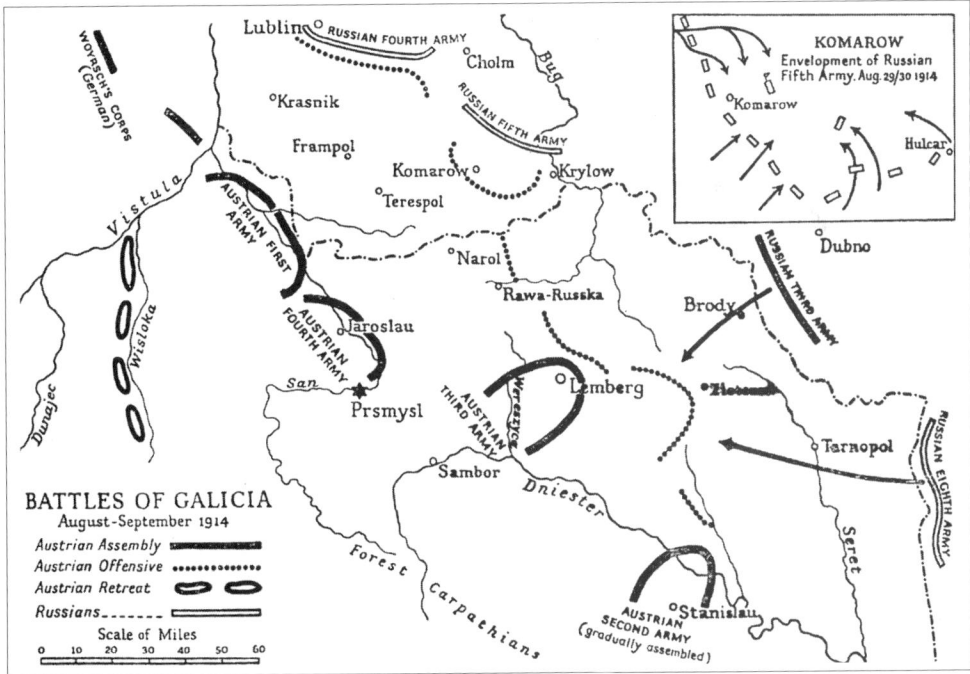

BATTLES OF GALICIA
August-September 1914

Austrian Assembly
Austrian Offensive
Austrian Retreat
Russians

Scale of Miles
0   10   20   30   40   50   60

WOYRSCH'S CORPS (German)
Lublin
RUSSIAN FOURTH ARMY
Cholm
Bug
Krasnik
RUSSIAN FIFTH ARMY
Frampol
Vistula
AUSTRIAN FIRST ARMY
Komarow
Krylow
Terespol
Wisloka
Narol
AUSTRIAN FOURTH ARMY
Rawa-Russka
Brody
RUSSIAN THIRD ARMY
Dubno
San
Jaroslau
Prsmysl
AUSTRIAN THIRD ARMY
WERESZYCA
Lemberg
Dwajiec
Sambor
Dniester
Tarnopol
RUSSIAN EIGHTH ARMY
Forest
Carpathians
Seret
AUSTRIAN SECOND ARMY (gradually assembled)
Stanislau

KOMAROW
Envelopment of Russian Fifth Army. Aug. 29/30 1914

Komarow
Hulcar

Campaign map of the Battles of Galicia, August–September 1914, between the rival Austrian and Russian armies. (*LC*)

Regarding von Mackensen during his later life: "Still slender and vigorous, every day he rode on horseback for hours to inspect troops, judge maneuvers, and hunt. In England, one said, 'Hunting three times a week is the best practice for a chief of cavalry.'"

Regarding the still famed Potsdam Garrison Church, Roy notes: "The famous Potsdam bells rang from the belfry, each named after an illustrious general or an individual battle." In 1945, they were all that was left of the devastated former structure.

DEUTSCHLANDS STOLZ!

"Germany's Pride!" proclaims this wartime composite view of Wilhelm II (*left*) and Marshal von Hindenburg (*right*). (*LC*)

"On the evenings of 14–15 April 1945, wave after wave of British bombers demolished the Garrison Church along with entire blocks in all directions around it. Combing through the debris, 'rubble women' of the reconstruction era found the bells, but little else," continued Roy, as depicted later on in this very narrative.

At the fighting fronts, Germany's men-at-arms made their own celebrations of their heroes—the Kaiser at left and the marshal at right, busts surrounded with pine tree leaves. (*LC*)

By 1999, alas, historian-tourist Roy recalled sadly: "I present my old map, and ask where the site of Potsdam's Garrison Church had once been—and no one has ever heard of it!" During July 18 to November 11, 1918, the Germans lost 420,000 killed in action and also 340,000 wounded or lost to the Allies as POWs, reportedly.

Der Befreier des Ostens.

Twin variations on the same theme: Hindenburg (*center*) as "The Liberator of the East," flanked in both cases by the civilian emperors of Germany (*left*) and Austria–Hungary (*right*). Above, soldiers stand at attention, while below, they break into cheers. In both, a Russian bear appears: alive above and almost slain below, with the same five fortress cities also being depicted in each, while in both, eagles, a dirigible, and an airplane soar overhead. The landscape above is at peace, while that below flames, smokes, and burns. (*LC*)

Der Befreier des Ostens.

In this postcard view, Hindenburg appears in prewar Prussian blue uniform outer coat at left. (*LC*)

Wilhelm II did not intentionally abandon his wife, the Kaiserin, to her fate at Berlin prior to his flight to Dutch exile in 1918: "From Spa, the emperor sent his wife a letter dated 7 November 1918, but it never reached Potsdam, as the Postal stations nearby were in the hands of the revolutionaries. A second letter was written the next day.... Their sons would take over the task of defending her in the event of disturbances until he and the troops could come to her aid. If it was no longer safe for her in Potsdam, she would have to go with the children to Königsberg, or Rominten if necessary," reported Van der Kiste.

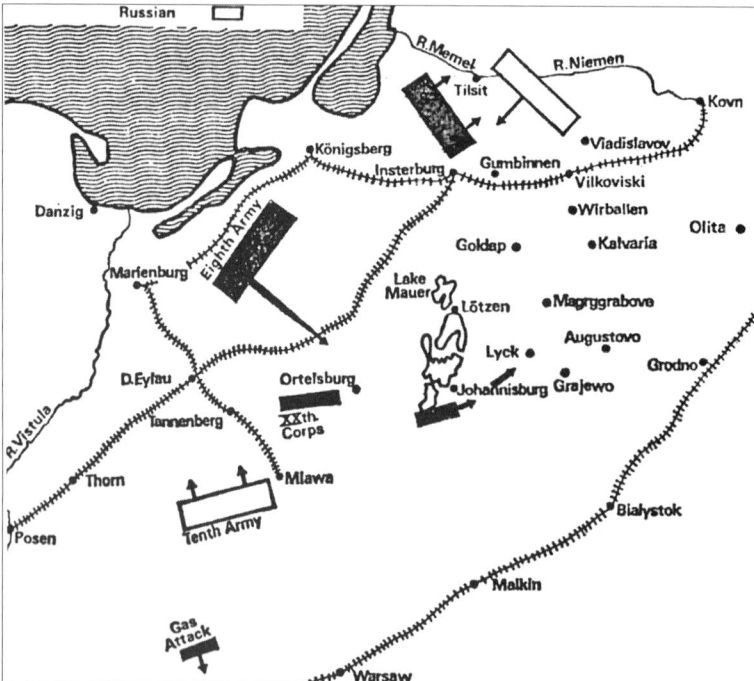

Wartime campaign map of the Winter Battle of Masuria, 1915. (*LC*)

In the actual event, the Kaiserin personally faced the rebel troops, but was completely unharmed by them, as the revered "Mother of the Country."

In this fanciful view, a giant Hindenburg—not yet a field marshal!—gathers up an entire army of hapless Russian Army foes on February 17, 1915 during the Second Battle of the Masurian Lakes. (*LC*)

During French Marshal Foch's July 18, 1918 counteroffensive in the West against the German Army, he turned the tide at the Marne River salient with 350 tanks that "chewed up" ten German divisions.

A 1916 scene of German Army trench work life, minus the rats, water, filth, and inevitable disease that followed in their wake. (*LC*)

One later anti-Hindenburg/Ludendorff joke was that the august duo "Rose in the east but set in the west."

A period woodcut scene of all manner of German Army headgear worn in the trenches: 1914–16 spiked helmets, the later 1916–18 steel helms, and also cloth garrison caps. At top right, a wounded soldier is evacuated via stretcher, a dead one is buried at bottom left, water canteens are filled at center, and construction is underway at mid-right. (*U.S. Army Combat Art Collection*)

"By 1917 ... line upon line of trenches—8–12 feet [2.5–3.7 meters] deep—stretched from Switzerland to the Atlantic Ocean. The sides of these trenches were supported by sandbags and a basket weave of poles and sticks or boards, with loopholes and openings along the top facing the enemy," noted *Life in WWI Trenches* in 1979.

The Maxim machine gun was "king of the battlefield," as were machine guns in all of Great War armies on every fighting front almost from the very start of the fighting. Belted ammunition was fed through the deadly weapon from metal boxes underneath it. (*ASA*)

The front side had a fire step on which soldiers stood to shoot. In well-constructed trenches, the bottom was covered by board walkways, although these were of little use when it rained. In wet weather—that seemed to be the rule rather than the exception—the men were often waist-deep in water."

A heavier infantry indirect fire weapon was the versatile 7.6-cm light trench mortar mounted on a circular base plate about to be fired here by the gunner at right, 1916. (*Friedrich Hermann Memorial Collection*)

"The soldiers in these front line trenches slept in dugouts cut from the earth and covered with heavy sandbagged roofs as protection against shell explosions. Few trenches were lit by electricity, so candles provided most of the light. Beds consisted of crude bunks, folding cots made of canvas, chairs, tables, and ammunition boxes."

Above left: A pair of field marshals in command: von Hindenburg of Germany at left and Conrad von Hötzendorf (1852–1925) of Austria-Hungary at right. The difference between them was that the former had the wherewithal to carry out his designs, while his counterpart never really did. During 1906–17, Field Marshal von Hötzendorf was chief of staff of both the Austrian Army and Navy. He and Hindenburg got along well, reportedly. (*LC*)

Above right: When the Kaiser ennobled his very favorite soldier even before the war, August von Mackensen chose as his new crest one whose mantra at bottom was "I Remember the Beginning," and he never forgot his origins, either. (*LC*)

"Von Mackensen was born on 6 December 1849 at *Haus Leipnitz* in Saxony. His father [Ludwig Mackensen] was a well-to-do estate agent. The future field marshal was educated at the Gymnasium/high school at Torgau and the University of Halle. On 1 October 1869, he entered the 2nd Guards Hussar regiment, and went to war against the French in 1870 as a non-commissioned officer. He was promoted to lieutenant and was placed on the reserve list after the Franco-Prussian War," according to his *New York Times* obituary in November 1945.

A trio of views of handsome young von Mackensen across the early stages of his celebrated career martial, as—from left to right—"The one-year volunteer in Lissa," at Melun, France during 1870–71, and as the newly-promoted second lieutenant postwar with cap and riding crop. (*LC*)

Mackensen's proudest boast in 1945 was that he had worn the same size uniform throughout his entire military progression upward. He was engaged to marry on May 24, 1879 to Doris von Horn, and they wed on November 21, 1879 at Königsberg Castle Church, East Prussia. They had a daughter, Else, and three sons, Hans-Georg, Manfred, and Eberhard. Later, his fellow officers in the Rhineland gave Mackensen a vase decorated with a little monkey climbing up its side. Its inscription read: "To the captain who climbs with monkey-like speed to become Field Marshal Mackensen"—an accurate prediction, as it turned out.

Right: General Karl von Litzmann wearing prewar royal Prussian blue military kit. (*LC*)

"The dank moisture of the trenches probably caused more casualties than the bayonets of the enemy. Trench foot, fever, and mouth were all a result of this condition, and thousands of men died from drowning in flooded shell holes, dugouts, and trenches. These same pools of water became natural breeding grounds for flies and other insects, causing deadly malaria and other diseases."

Below left: A 1916 portrait of General Litzmann wearing the later field gray uniform and red-and-gold collar tabs of the overall German Army, autographed at bottom. (*Litzmann Collection*)

"While trenches offered some protection, they could also be death traps. Being fixed, they were easy targets for heavy artillery. Sometimes the enemy dug mine tunnels under them and blew them up. Even worse, most poison gases were heavier than air and thus settled in the trenches. Defenders who were choking on chlorine gas or burning from mustard gas were helpless before an advancing enemy."

Above right: General Litzmann's wartime chief of staff, Lt Colonel Mengelbier, on October 12, 1915. (*Litzmann Collection*)

Rats also infested the trenches of all the combatant armies. According to Astore and Showalter: "From 1904–24, he [Hindenburg] shot 104 wild boar, 76 roebuck, 27 red deer, 24 does, six black cock, six chamois, and assorted minor game."

General Litzmann and mount. (*Litzmann Collection*)

In addition to German, Hindenburg also spoke Polish. Of the dangerous situation he faced in East Prussia in late August 1914, Hindenburg recalled in his postwar memoirs: "At first, the Russians were hot on our heels, but then the distance between us began to increase," stated Messenger. In a similar situation in 1945 with another Russian Army, Heinrich Himmler gained no such life-saving reprieve, however.

General Litzmann's own combat art rendition of *The Burning of Karwarja, 30 April 1915*, complete with his monogram, "KL." In the lower right part of the frame are seen Austrian and German observers. (*Litzmann Collection*)

By the terms of the Treaty of Brest–Litovsk that ended the Russian Front war in the east in a massive German victory, the Second Reich gained an estimated 89 percent of all Russian coal!

A 1917 Litzmann combat art drawing of a battle for a contended peak. (*Litzmann Collection*)

Before his assassination, German Field Marshal von Eichhorn reportedly was called "The Uncrowned King of Ukraine." At one point, the Kaiser pictured himself as "Duke of Kurland," a title he never acquired, alas, because the Second Reich lost the war in the west.

The war that did not end by Christmas 1914 as predicted dragged on into 1915, as depicted in this period postcard. Shown, from left to right, are Mackensen, Kluck, Bavarian Crown Prince Rupprecht, their overall commander-in-chief the Kaiser, Imperial German Crown Prince Wilhelm, Ludendorff, Hindenburg, and General Erich von Falkenhayn. German chief of general staff during 1914–16. The exhortation below asserts "Hail Victory!" (*LC*)

A Uhlan cavalryman of Franz von Grafenstein's King's Bavarian Uhlan Regiment Kaiser Wilhelm 2 King of Prussia. Note the drinking cup affixed below underneath his leather ammo pouches. (*ASA*)

German General von Mackensen proudly presented the fallen Fortress Przemyśl to Kaiser Franz Josef I after its fall.

His Majesty Wilhelm II, the last reigning King of Wurtemberg (1848–1921), who ruled from October 6, 1891 to his overthrow on November 30, 1918. (*ASA*)

A wooden statue of Hindenburg was erected in 1915 on Berlin's Königsplatz (King's Plaza) called the "Iron Hindenburg" that stood 42 feet high and 7 feet across. Notes one former biographer: "Thousands of loyal subjects daily stood in line to buy iron brass or nails to pound into it." Added another account: "To raise funds" for the war effort, "the public were encouraged to buy nails, and hammer them in. A total of some 5.9 tons of iron, silver, and gilt nails were sold."

The Berlin version of the gigantic Hindenburg statue was built from Russian alder wood and iron at 12 meters tall. The causes befitting from the nail sale included "Wounded soldiers and also widows and orphans." The Berlin statue was located near both the 1870 *Siegessäule* (Victory Column) that still stands today and the latter Reichstag Building. Known as the *Eisener* Hindenburg, it was claimed by two sculptors Georg Marschall (1871–1956) and Oswald Schimmelpfennig (1872–1944), the construction of which was supervised by engineer Kohlrausch.

The "Iron Hindenburg" wooden statue was but the largest of more than 700 *Nagelmänner* (Nail Men) that appeared all across the Second Reich during the war years as patriotic fundraising devices. Also, it was claimed that the Berlin statue was the tallest such across the entire globe with a height of 13 meters, a diameter of 3.14 meters, and circumference of 9 meters at "its greatest extent, around the greatcoat skirts" below. An estimated 7–7.3 tons of iron were reportedly used to build its internal composition. (*ASA*)

Der eiserne Hindenburg zu Berlin.

Höhe: 13 Mtr. — Kopfhöhe: 1,35 Mtr. — Durchm.: 3,14 Mtr. — Größter Umfang: 9 Mtr. — Gewicht: 20000 Kg. Erlenholz und 7000 Kg. Eisen für die innere Konstruktion. — Zur Benagelung sind 6000 Kg. goldene, silberne u. eiserne Nägel bereitgestellt, zum Preise von 100, 5 u. 1 M. Man beachte unsere Feldgrauen bei der Nagelung, sie erscheinen wie übermütige Jungen im Arm des Vaters.

Surrounded by access scaffolding, the Wooden Titan Hindenburg structure's internal iron was covered with an estimated 20 tons of Russian alder wood. Martial airs were played in good weather by regimental military bands to serenade Berliners out for a stroll, and these in turn drew them to the imposing figure as well. In addition, four captured Russian army field artillery pieces taken at the now mythic Tannenberg were located in front of its pedestal.

"German communities as far east as Romania's Vampire War Transylvania, where both Mackensen and Falkenhayn were fighting in 1916 also built warrior statues. The iron nails used at the Berlin Hindenburg structure alone amounted to just under 6 tons, "Although the individual pieces themselves were of various finishes," notes one 2017 source, "that dictated their price to the public."

At Berlin, cast-iron nails cost a single mark each, with silvered versions raised to five, and the most costly were gold-cast at 100 Reichsmarks each, all then hammered into the wooden effigy of the field marshal. To aid in this, "A four-tiered wooden gallery was erected round the pedestal of the "Iron Hindenburg", allowing Berliners to reach the upper portion of the figure, and hammer their chosen nail at a height of several meters." It debuted on September 4, 1915 before thousands of onlookers, dedicated by Princess of Prussia Alexandra Viktoria (April 24, 1887 to April 15, 1957), the wife of Prince August Wilhelm, "Auwi," fourth son of the Kaiser. As two giant German airships drifted overhead, both Imperial Chancellor Theobald von Bethmann-Hollweg (1856–1921) and Lord Mayor of Berlin Adolf Wermuth (1855–1937) delivered addresses. Both the princess and the chancellor each hammered one such golden nail into the name "HINDENBURG" at the base of the huge structure: she the "H" and he the "B." After five hours of public hammering, fully 20,000 nails had been driven home. (*ASA*)

Above left: German Crown Prince Wilhelm seen prewar in picturesque cuirassier's kit. (*ASA*)

Above right: Future German Army Field Marshal Remus von Woyrsch, one of the lesser-known holders of the coveted batons, seen here outfitted in prewar Prussian blue with red collar, the famous M1903 Litewka coat worn by officers. From 1915–18, the simpler *Einheitsmantal* were worn instead, a single-breasted jacket with six buttons down the front. (*LC*)

Regarding Hindenburg's Berlin wooden statue, "By August 1918 5,600 golden, 75,000 silvered, and 780,000 cast-iron nails had been hammered in, with only a part of the field marshal's greatcoat left uncovered, eventually realizing a total profit of 1.15 million Reichsmarks."

A year later came the British imitation in September 1916 by two British nurses: "By the residents of Stepney … a three-meter-high wooden monster purporting to be the German field marshal … to raise money for wounded and disabled British troops," as covered in *The Illustrated War News* of September 27, 1916. (*ASA*)

March 1917—German Field Marshal Remus von Woyrsch inspecting captured Russian machine guns on the Eastern Front. (*ASA*)

Wilhelm II was welcomed to von Woyrsch's wartime headquarters at Baranavichy on November 11, 1915 during a formal Front Visit as troops presented arms. International newspaper coverage attended the events at Berlin regarding the 30-foot-high Iron Hindenburg statue, such as the September 5, 1915 edition of *The New York Times*.

Above: Von Eichhorn (right, with baton in right hand) troops the line at a wartime troop review. (*ASA*)

Left: German Army Field Marshal Hermann von Eichhorn, the only one of the Kaiser's marshals killed during the war.

Colonel General Georg von der Marwitz with leather binocular case and strap held in left hand. Reportedly, he "turned the Battle of Cambrai from defeat into victory." (*LC*)

It was not followed through, however, as Ludendorff neglected to build more tanks for the coming 1918 campaigns, thus losing the ground war for certain well in advance of the Armistice. "In October 1918, a revolutionary mob of soldiers tried to burn the "Iron Hindenburg" to the ground, it only being saved by … the police. In 1919, the Military Inter-Allied Control Commission demanded that the colossus be dismantled … it being put into storage in a north Berlin warehouse."

"A newspaper report in 1920 stated that the German government sold the statue to a private company, that resold it to American entrepreneurs to exhibit in the US, though in the end this fate for the field marshal seems *not* to have come to pass."

"The real fate for the statue was only slightly less ignominious … eventually broken in Berlin for firewood, a casualty of Germany's harsh economic climate during the years of the Weimar Republic. Although the head of the statue—some 1.35 m high—did initially remain intact [from 1938 being exhibited in the Aviation Museum at the Lehrte train station, Berlin], even this unique piece was ultimately lost, destroyed by Allied bombing during the closing stages of World War II."

"Hindenburg was not the only German warlord whose likeness appeared in the form of a 'Nail Man.' Thus we find Grand Admiral Alfred von Tirpitz [1849–1930], Field Marshal Crown Prince Rupprecht of Bavaria, General of Infantry Otto von Emmich, and even Captain Karl von Müller [1873–1923]—commanding officer of the light cruiser SMS *Emden*—all recreated in wooden effigy."

"Some *Nagelmänner* were figures from German history…. Others included knights, soldiers, heroes from German mythology, shields, coats of arms, Iron Crosses, animals, flowers, ships, and submarines."

Twin views of Colonel General Alexander von Linsingen in both undress uniform (*below*) and more formal parade ground kit, complete with plumed helmet (*right*). Reportedly, he had little use for his Austro–Hungarian compatriots. (*LC*)

A pair of uniformed views of General Otto von Below, in wartime field gray (*left*) and prewar blue (*right*). (*LC*)

An infantry officer, von Below initially commanded the 1st Reserve Corps on the Eastern Front in 1914, and then the 14th Army in Italy in the fall of 1917. Utilizing the new *Sturmtruppen* tactics of infiltration against the inferior Royal Savoyard Italian Army, von Below defeated it massively at the great Central Powers' victory at the Battle of Caporetto. In March 1918, he led as well the 17th Army in Ludendorff's Kaiser's Battle that it was hoped would secure final victory over the Allies, but did not. The Kaiser had already awarded von Below the Blue Max for taking part as 8th Army commander in February 1915 of the Second Battle of the Masurian Lakes. According to his most recent previous biographer, von Below was "widely regarded as one of Germany's best field commanders," and "was named colonel-in-chief of the 9th Jäger Battalion on November 18, 1916; in 1917, he was decorated with the [Prussian] Order of the Black Eagle, and on 29 March 1917, with the Oak Leaves to his *Pour le Mérite*.… After the Armistice, von Below was sent to Kassel when he was given command of the Western Front [by Hindenburg], avoiding a revolution. From January–June 1919, he would hold his last command … at Danzig. He was dismissed in late June 1919 after threatening that he would lead an uprising against Germany's acceptance of the Versailles Treaty, and died at Bogenhausen near Gottingen."

General Fritz von Below.

3

Middle East, 1914–18

Ottoman Turkey Joins the Central Powers, 1914

At Istanbul on July 30, 1914, the Ottoman Turkish Empire decided to join the anti-Russian Central Powers of Imperial Germany and Austria-Hungary in waging the Great War, officially joining them on October 31, 1914, after the German Army had already lost at First Marne, thus keeping nonetheless its pledged word.

The Entente Powers allied to Tsarist Russia—Great Britain and France—declared war against Turkey on November 5, 1914, leading the Turks to call for a Muslim *jihad* (holy war) against the triad of Christian states of the west on the part of all its own Arab and other dominions that same month.

Gen. Otto Liman von Sanders

Advising the Turks at Istanbul as head of the official German Military Mission was General of Cavalry Otto Viktor Karl Liman von Sanders (February 17, 1855 to August 22, 1929); he, in 1918, also led a field command Turkish Army against the British Empire Dominion armies in the climactic Sinai-Palestinian Campaign.

During the earlier Gallipoli Campaign in the spring of 1915, Liman faced a strong British Army following a seaborne landing as commander of the very best Ottoman Army then fielded (the 5th) that encompassed 84,000 troops in six divisions.

One of his best decisions had been to name Mustafa Kemal (Ataturk) as the C.O. of the 19th Division therein, with the all-important heights above the landing site being held for more than five months. Another such landing was made at Suva Bay—also defeated by the Turks—and at least part of the credit for that victory has come down to Liman von Sanders.

In 1918, Liman succeeded Gen. Erich von Falkenhayn as commander of the fighting in the Sinai-Palestine Campaign after the latter had been defeated by British Gen. Sir Edmund Allenby the previous year.

In Allenby's smashing final victory at the Battle of Megiddo, "The entire Ottoman Army was destroyed in a week of fighting," according to one 2016 account, with Liman himself very nearly having been captured in the rout. Thus, his military career concluded with him having the dubious honor of having been the last German advisor trying unsuccessfully to "modernize" the Turkish Army after a record of four decades of Germans having failed.

Arrested on British Malta in February 1919 as an accused war criminal, Liman was released six months afterwards, retiring from the German Army that same year after forty-four years of service.

In 1927, the United States Naval Institute Press published his postwar memoirs, *Five Years in Turkey,* while an August 25, 1929 *New York Times* obituary referred to him as "Field Marshal" of the beaten Ottoman Army—he having died at Munich at the age of seventy-four.

His major wartime command had been of the Turkish Yıldırım Army Group (from von Falkenhayn), in which he was in turn succeeded by his former protégé, Mustafa Kemal.

Liman's Man: Kress von Kressenstein

Gen. Frederick Baron Kress von Kressenstein (April 24, 1870 to October 16, 1948) was an important member of the Liman Military Mission to Istanbul that providentially arrived in Turkey just before the outbreak of World War I.

An artilleryman initially, Kressenstein in January 1915 served as both a military engineer and chief of staff to Djemal Pasha's Ottoman Army in the daring First Suez Offensive designed to take the vital British Suez Canal in occupied Egypt.

Notes Faulkner in *Great War in the Mideast*: "Kress was responsible for creating special pontoon boats for crossing the Canal, as well as organizing the crossing of the Sinai Desert," the latter accomplished with few casualties. The British defenders were well aware of the coming assault on the Canal, however, and defeated it in two days of combat, with the Kressenstein pontoon craft never deployed in action.

The Second Battle of the Suez Canal saw Kressenstein leading an even larger force across the burning Sinai Desert, waging the Battle of Romani on August 3, 1916 against a strong British Army defensive position about 40 km. east of Suez. It, too, was defeated, with the Turks retreating once more into occupied Palestine.

Now it was the British turn to attack, as they did in the First Battle of Gaza in March 1917 when they failed to take Fort Gaza. A second attempt that April was also beaten by the hardy Turkish troops under the able generalship of Kress von Kressenstein. The Turks, meanwhile, brought in von Falkenhayn—fresh from his Romanian victories in the Balkans—to take command of the Ottoman 8th Army with Kressenstein as his chief of staff to retain control of Gaza, but they were beaten by Allenby.

Gen. Allenby was again victorious in November 1917 at the Battles of Beersheba and Third Gaza, with Kressenstein nonetheless able to execute a skillful retreat to new northern defensive posts.

Next, Kressenstein was redeployed to Soviet Georgia in mid-1918 to halt the Red Army assault on Abkazia, which he did. He retired from the German Army in 1929, died at Munich in 1948, and thus did not live to see his postwar memoirs, *My Mission in Caucasus*, published in 2001 at Tbilisi, Georgia, after the fall of both his own empire and that of the Soviet Union.

Colmar Baron von der Goltz: The Kaiser's Middle Eastern Marshal
Wilhelm Leopold Colmar Baron von der Goltz (August 12, 1843 to April 19, 1916) was
the Kaiser's most renowned GFM to die during World War I, possibly also by assassination like von Eichhorn. Revered among Imperial Germany's Ottoman Turkish Middle
Eastern allies as Goltz Pasha, he began the war with a long career both as a practical
soldier and a martial affairs author behind him, his works being read worldwide.

Like Hindenburg, recalled to active duty in 1914 after an earlier retirement, Goltz
began the Great War as the ruthless military governor of German-occupied Belgium.
Indeed, in *Hindenburg* it is noted that on October 5, 1914 Goltz ordered the following:

> In future, villages … in places where railway and telegraph lines are destroyed, will be
> punished without pity, whether they are guilty or not of the acts in question.…
>
> Hostages have been taken in all villages near the railway lines that are threatened by
> such attacks, upon the first attempt to destroy lines of railway, telegraph, or telephone,
> they will immediately be shot!

During 1915–16, Goltz returned to his prior posting in Ottoman Turkey as military
aide to Sultan Mehmed, where he clashed with both the real civil and military power
at Istanbul—Enver Pasha—but also with the then current head of the German Military
Mission to Turkey, Gen. Otto Liman von Sanders.

Despite their dislike for each other, Enver named Goltz in October 1915 to command his own 5th Army to face a British Army advancing on Baghdad in today's Iraq.
The resultant Battle of Ctesiphon ended in a tie, with both armies leaving the field
unconquered.

Then Goltz surprised his British opponent by pursuing him downriver to start the
Siege of Kut. A series of three major battles by the British Army to relieve the siege took
place, all failing, costing the English 23,000 casualties, all at the hands of the Turkish
6th Army under the command of Goltz's colleague, Halil Kut Pasha.

Although he had initially authorized the Turkish assault on the Armenian population
of Russia, once he realized the full, apparent genocidal scope of the operation, Goltz in
December 1915 ordered it halted, threatening to resign, then did not.

At Kut—a mere two weeks before the British surrender—on April 19, 1916, Goltz
died of typhus officially, although murder by poisoning was suspected as well. He was
buried on the grounds of Istanbul's German Consulate overlooking the Bosporus, a
foreign ally among his longtime Turkish military students and colleagues.

He remains today as the author of fourteen published books, among the varied
topics being the Franco-Prussian War of 1870–71, the earlier Battles of Rossbach under
Frederick the Great, and the twin 1806 defeats by Napoleon I at Jena and Auerstedt,
plus the 1813 War of Liberation struggle between Bonaparte and Prussian Field Marshal
von Blücher, the latter published by Goltz as a fellow marshal during the centennial of
that war in 1913.

Campaign map of the Turko–German War in the Middle East, 1914–18.

Diplomatically, the Kaiser managed to both get and keep Turkey in the war until almost the very end in the fall of 1918, mainly by personal visits such as this one to Istanbul, with him at left, the Turkish Sultan at center, and the real power in Turkey at right, Enver Pasha, killed in action postwar still fighting. (*LC*)

Also visiting Enver (*left*) during the war was the popular August von Mackensen, seen here smiling at center among Turkish Army fez caps, as well as an Austrian officer at far left and a German spiked helmet appearing also at center rear during a wartime visit to a railway yard. The two armies enjoyed good fighting relations right up to the end of the war, in the main. Noted his *New York Times* obituary in November 1945, after the Great War: "There were those who accused him of having demonstrated a ruthless disregard of life, when the hue and cry went up for the heads of the 'criminal warlords,'" but he was never brought to trial by anyone. (*LC*)

ALSO RAN.

WILHELM. "ARE YOU LURING THEM ON, LIKE ME?"   MEHMED. "I'M AFRAID I AM!"

A *Punch* cartoon by Bernard Partridge, published July 3, 1917.

A view of the dilemma faced by the two Central Powers' partners in the Middle East—Kaiser and Sultan.

8754.

Ein Vierverband, doch nicht von Englands Gnaden,
Kein heimlich Machwerk brit'scher Mühlerei;
Ein freier Bund von Waffenkameraden
Zu brechen Englands Völkertyrannei.

Ein Vierverband, doch nicht von Englands Gnaden.
Kein Heimlich Machwerg brit'icher Mühlerie;
Ein frier Bund von Waffenkameraden
Zu brechen Englands Völkerthrannei

A Band of Four
But not by the Grace of England.
No secretly heavyweight British Grinding;
A Free Union of Comrades-in-Arms
To Break England's Empire of Nations

In true union: a trio of wartime Central Powers' banners. *From left to right*: Austria-Hungary, Imperial Germany, and Turkey. In 1916, they would be joined by one other: that of Bulgaria. The laurel victors' wreath below would drop away by the fall of 1918.

Recalled Ludendorff of his frustration during the war in his memoirs: "I felt I was in another world!… People did not realize the seriousness of our position in the war" at Berlin. (*LC*)

On the following page:

Above: The last unsuccessful wartime command held by General von Falkenhayn was in the Middle East, where he was made a Turkish Army field marshal, as seen here (tallest figure). (*ASA*)

The duo reigned over all at supreme HQ during August 29, 1916 to October 26, 1918, when the Kaiser suddenly dumped Ludendorff, who recalled, from the outset in 1916, "My position was a thankless one.… The task was perfectly enormous.… Never has Fate before suddenly placed so heavy a burden on human shoulders!" as his.

Below left: The German Army Middle East Theater Commander was Lt-General Otto Viktor Karl Liman von Sanders, also defeated in the end, however. (*LC*)

Below right: Von Sanders's subordinate was General Friedrich Baron Kress von Kressenstein, adorned with fur cap. (*LC*)

Continued Ludendorff in his postwar memoirs: "It has been my destiny to hold various high appointments … now the German people fought as men have never fought before!" as written at Hessleholmsgard, Sweden, during November 18, 1918 to February 1919, and then completed at Berlin on June 23, 1919, "The day on which we accepted the peace."

Ger. Consul.   Gen. Falk'n   Jamal P. I.   Abd el Kerim Bey.

Austr. Consul.   Abd el Karim P.   Fuad Bey (chief of Staff to Jamal P.)

Left: Another powerful German Army presence in the Middle Eastern theater of war was Field Marshal Colmar von der Goltz, seen here in prewar dress uniform. The eminent German military scholar-author Walter Gorlitz published *The Memoirs of Field Marshal Colmar von der Goltz.* (*LC*)

Below: Goltz (*right*) as seen with Death's Head Hussar staffers during prewar military maneuvers in the Second Reich. Renowned as "a very great chief well-known for his character, originality, knowledge, and demands," Goltz was "Historian, theoretician and appreciated instructor, and as re-organizer of the Turkish Army, was awarded by the Sultan with the title of *Pasha*" in his own right. (*DH*)

After the 1908 annual fall maneuvers of the German Army, this eminent martial figure assessed the commander of the 17th Army Corps thus: "Mackensen drove it well. He has very great, quick qualities, a wide memory of localities, and clear look and good vision, so that I think he will be capable of important actions as an Army commander." Despite this high praise, in the actual first event of August 1914, Mackensen was "Just an elderly man swept away by a gray tide," his own retreating army at the lost Battle of Gumbinnen against the Russians. Like Napoleon and Lee before him, however, the Black Hussar was able to rebound after defeat and go on to win many stunning triumphs martial thereafter, never suffering another defeat in the field.

4

Balkan States, 1916–18

Serbian Field Marshal Radomir Putnik Fights Mackensen from a Sickbed

First Serbian Army Field Marshal Radomir Putnik (January 24, 1847 to May 17, 1917) had two rather unique distinctions, among many. First, he fought in all of Serbia's wars during 1867–1917—a span of five decades—that included the Serbo-Turkish, Serbo-Bulgarian, First and Second Balkan, and World War I. Second, as the Serbian Army initial Great War C-in-C, Marshal Putnik also waged his struggle from both a sickbed and heated hospital room far from the front, in combat removed from one of the German Army's most forward ranging commanders, fellow Marshal von Mackensen.

As World War I opened in August 1914 with an outright invasion of Serbia by the Austro-Hungarian Army shelling the capital city of Belgrade, Serbian King Peter I refused to accept his marshal's resignation on grounds of ill health, well founded though they were. Instead, the Serbian marshal organized the successful defense of his invaded land from a well-heated hospital room, even beating the Austrian Army in the Battles of Cer and Kolubara during August–September, completing the rout of the enemy from the land that December 1914, a martial feat that stunned the world. In the fall of 1915, however, came a new, more skillful, and better prepared foe—the newly created Marshal August von Mackensen, leading a combined German-Austrian force of 300,000 troops.

Bulgaria was also massing its armies on the Serbs' eastern frontier, but had not yet declared war against Belgrade. Notes Brownell in 2009's *First Nazi*, this more than doubled the size of the vast force with which the Black Hussar invaded Serbia in 1915, to fully "682,000 soldiers!"

The Serb marshal set his forces retreating toward the famous national battlefield of Kosovo during October 31 to November 1915. Having already occupied most of Serbia, including the capital Belgrade, his opponent von Mackensen declined to follow the fleeing Serbian columns into the deadly mountain passes of Albania.

Following their declaration of war against the Serbs, the now also victorious Bulgars were satisfied with the territory they had occupied in northern Macedonia and north-west Serbia. Perhaps fittingly, considering the Serbs' past history, the major fight of the campaign took place at the Battle of Kosovo's Field of the Blackbirds during November 19–24, 1915, with the Serbian Army also stricken with a typhus outbreak.

Thus, on November 25, 1915, Marshal Putnik duly ordered a full retreat via Montenegro into Albania, with 155,000 soldiers out of an initial starting force of 250,000 reaching the Adriatic Sea Coast, where they were taken aboard Allied ships bound for safety on the Greek Island of Corfu and others.

True to form, invalid commander Marshal Putnik was carried through the snow-clad Albanian peaks in a chair, deathly ill with bronchitis, influenza, and pneumonia, being evacuated as well to Corfu along with his men.

Still, his defeated government fired him in January 1916, while the French honored him with both martial honors and a villa at sunny Nice to help him recover, but he died of lung emphysema on May 17, 1917, his body returned to Belgrade and buried with military honors in 1926. His tombstone reads "Grateful Homeland to Radomir Putnik." As for the winning Marshal von Mackensen, he died shooing away Red Army soldiers from pigs on his German farm in 1945.

Still, the huge effect of von Mackensen's ultimate victory over conquered Serbia is not to be ignored, despite how the two men ended their lives. Notes Asprey in *The German High Command*:

> The Kingdom of Serbia lost one million inhabitants during the war, both Army and civilian losses.
>
> Of 4.5 million people, 275,000 were military deaths, while 450,000 were civilian, mostly due to food shortages, epidemics, and the [1918] Spanish flu, and there were 133,148 wounded) that represented over 15% of its overall population.…
>
> According to the [successive] Yugoslav government in 1924, Serbia lost 365,164 soldiers—or 26%—of all mobilized personnel, while France suffered 16.8%, Germany 15.4%, Russia 11.5%, and Italy 10.3%.
>
> At the end of the war, there were 114,000 disabled soldiers and 500,000 orphaned children.

Thus were the results of the Austro-Hungarian inflicted casualties of 1914, and the German-Austro tolls during 1915–18.

Added the *New York Times* in 2009: "The total number of casualties is placed around one million—25% of Serbia's prewar size—and an absolute majority (57%) of its overall male population."

Gen. Hans von Seeckt Helped Make Possible the Mackensen Victory Parade

The brilliant staff chief who helped make the Black Hussar Marshal von Mackensen's many victories possible was Col. Gen. Johannes Frederick Hans von Seeckt (April 22, 1866 to December 27, 1936), one of the most able organizers in all of German martial annals.

Known as "The Sphinx," Seeckt was born in Kaiserin Dona's Grand Duchy of Schleswig-Holstein on the German–Danish frontier, serving in the German Army during 1885–1935. Dying at the age of seventy in 1936, he closed out his career as an important military advisor to Nationalist China's Generalissimo Chiang Kai-shek, then fighting the Imperial Japanese Army.

Born an aristocrat, von Seeckt began his service aged eighteen following that of his father, then the military governor of Posen, birthplace of both members of the first duo. Joining Mackensen, von Seeckt thus formed the second duo that brought such luster to Germanic arms during the Great War.

After service with the elite Kaiser Alexander Guard Grenadiers, von Seeckt was posted to the Prussian General Staff in 1897, becoming in 1913 staff chief of the German Army's 3rd Corps, headquartered at Berlin as a lieutenant colonel in August 1914.

The 3rd Corps took part in the 1914 French campaign, with Seeckt being promoted to colonel on January 27, 1915. That March, he was redeployed east to become Mackensen's chief of staff for the German 11th Army, and together they made Teutonic military history alongside the first duo of Hindenburg and Ludendorff.

The first Mackensen-Seeckt success was in the Gorlice–Tarnów Offensive of May–June 1915, which witnessed the stunning breakthrough that split apart the pair of Russian armies opposite them, and that June, Seeckt was promoted major general thereby. Their newly formed Army Group Mackensen encompassed the German 11th Army, Austria-Hungary's 3rd, and Bulgaria's 1st, and together they won the stunning campaign victory over Serbia of October 6 to November 24, 1915.

This lightning campaign spawned among their victorious troops the mantra, "Where Mackensen is, Seeckt is; where Seeckt is, victory is!" And so it was. Awarded the Blue Max by the Kaiser in June 1916, von Seeckt switched armies to aid the Central Powers' weak sister—the failing Austro-Hungarian Army—as chief of staff to its 7th Army in Galicia.

The following year, 1917, von Seeckt was redeployed once again on a similar detached service, this time to help the ailing army of "The Sick Man of Europe"—that of the Ottoman Turks. Therein, he succeeded Col. Friedrich Bronsart von Schellendorf as chief of staff, but he was far less effective with Johnny Turk than he had been in his earlier postings.

Returned to the defeated Germany at the war's end, in spring 1919, von Seeckt found himself as part of the German Peace Delegation at Paris. Postwar, it fell to him to implement the Treaty of Versailles' mandated downgrading of the Weimar Republican German Army, as successor commander-in-chief in effect to both Hindenburg and Groener.

Von Seeckt's able reforms set the stage in time for the Hitlerian expansion and rearmament that ushered in World War II in 1939, three years after his death. Truly, few soldiers of any army or historical period have been as successful or influential in their careers as was Col. Gen. Hans von Seeckt.

A pre-Great War campaign map of the 1912–13 Balkan Wars that covered the very same ground there during 1914–18 as well. (*LC*)

CONQUEST OF SERBIA, 1915, AND RUMANIA, 1916

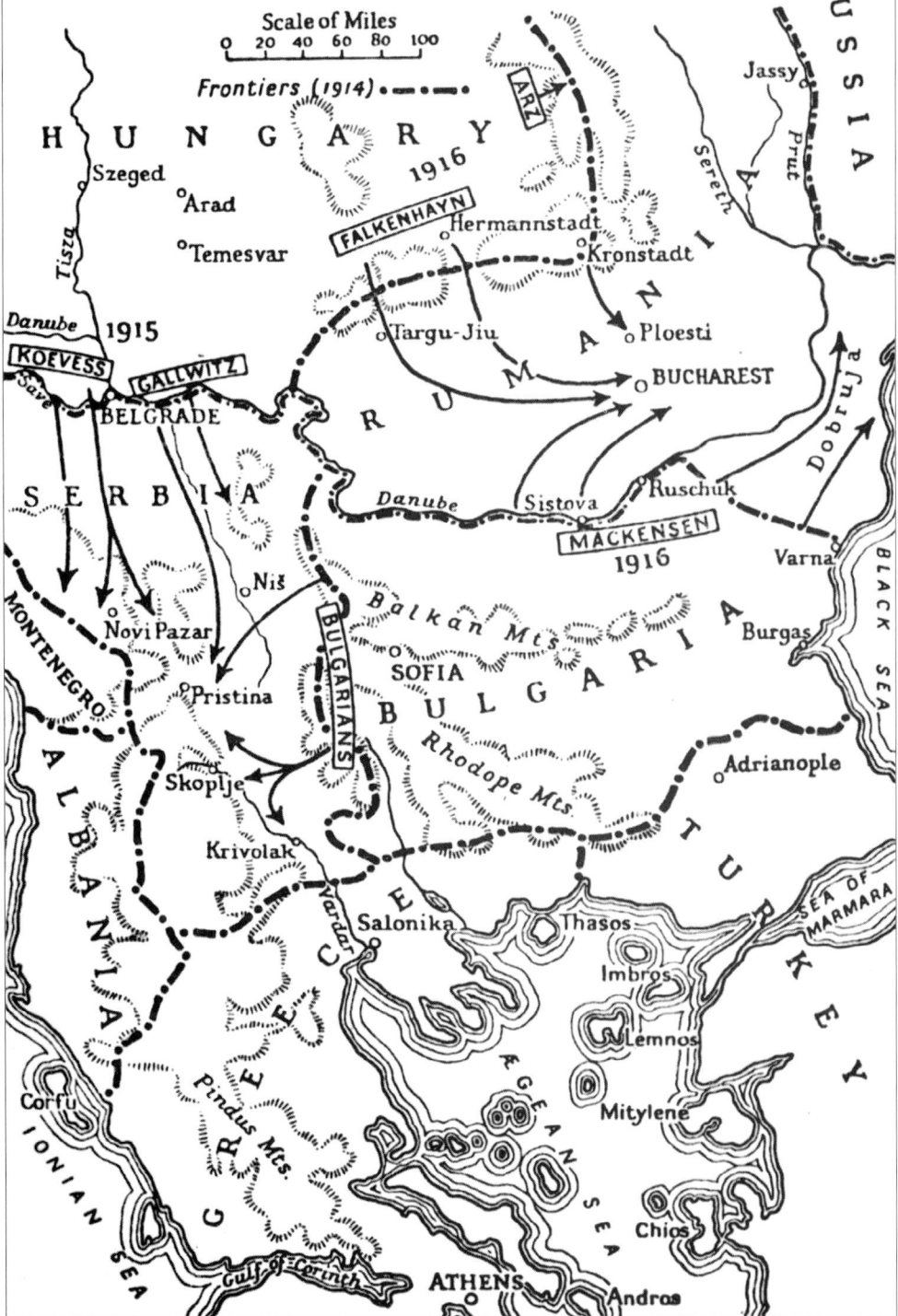

Scale of Miles

0 20 40 60 80 100

Frontiers (1914) .—.—.

RUSSIA

Jassy

HUNGARY

Szeged

Arad

Temesvar

1916

ARZ

FALKENHAYN

Hermannstadt

Kronstadt

Sereth

Prut

Tisza

Danube 1915

KOEVESS

GALLWITZ

BELGRADE

Save

Targu-Jiu

Ploesti

RUMANIA

BUCHAREST

SERBIA

MONTENEGRO

Novi Pazar

Pristina

Skoplje

Krivolak

Niš

Danube

Sistova

Ruschuk

MACKENSEN
1916

Dobrudja

Varna

BLACK SEA

Balkan Mts.

BULGARIANS

SOFIA

BULGARIA

Burgas

Rhodope Mts.

Adrianople

TURKEY

ALBANIA

Vardar

Salonika

Thasos

SEA OF MARMARA

GREECE

Imbros

Lemnos

Corfu

IONIAN SEA

Pindus Mts.

AEGEAN SEA

Mitylene

Chios

Gulf of Corinth

ATHENS

Andros

How the Germans and Bulgarians beat Serbia in 1915 and Romania in 1916 in coordinated campaigns. (*LC*)

Mackensen's Serbian Army counterpart was the resourceful Marshal Radomir Putnik, a worthy opponent as chief of its general staff during 1914–15. Living in exile in France, Marshal Putnik died there in 1916. (*LC*)

"I was astonished at the optimism I found that prevailed in Berlin at the end of October 1914! There seemed to be no realization of the tremendous gravity of our situation in view of the numerical superiority [against us], and that Germany was surrounded by enemies," recalled Ludendorff in 1919.

States David Edkins in *The Prussian Orden Pour le Mérite/History of the Blue Max*: "Field Marshal von Mackensen was one of Germany's most successful and most decorated military leaders. A master of organization and a recognized strategist, Mackensen did not attend the War College, but worked his way up from the lowest of ranks and was highly regarded by the military High Command as well as the soldiers under him.... Mackensen was 64 years old at the start of World War I. In 1914, he was appointed second-in-command to Hindenburg on the Eastern Front, where he first emerged as a national military figure at the Battle of Lodz, when he saved his army from annihilation by rallying his men and breaking through the surrounding Russian forces with a bold and shattering bayonet charge. For this he was granted the *Pour le Mérite* on November 27, 1914, the ninth award of the war."

Mackensen was also an Austro–Hungarian field marshal. He was one of only five recipients of the Grand Cross of the Iron Cross of 1914, the others being Hindenburg, Ludendorff, Field Marshal Prince Leopold of Bavaria, and the Kaiser himself. He took four major enemy cities, three of them national capitals no less: Lviv, Warsaw, Belgrade, and Bucharest. (*ASA*)

Mackensen took as his mantra this motto: "Do what you are supposed to, come what may." Others composed about him the descriptive phrase, "When he sits on his white horse, his eyes flash! It is certain he has a plan."

Mackensen wearing large fur busby cap with skull-and-crossbones emblem. (*ASA*)

Period commanders of Central Powers' forces delighted in both these prewar and wartime crossover appointments in each other's armies. According to Lamar Cecil: "Next to Hindenburg, he was the most beloved officer of the Imperial Army." Still, despite all their joint mighty martial victories over the tsar's armies during 1914–15, Imperial Russia was not knocked out of the war, rather fighting on into the winter of 1918. Noted one period biographer of von Mackensen: "His stately appearance assured him a glowing career. Mackensen became a model hussar."

Talented Mackensen chief of staff was Colonel General Hans von Seeckt, seen here in the later dress uniform of the German Army of the Weimar Republic. During 1920–26, General von Seeckt had replaced Groener as C-in-C of the new German Army, only to be fired in 1926 by President von Hindenburg after allowing Prince Wilhelm of Prussia—first-born son of Crown Prince Wilhelm—to attend its annual maneuvers. (*ASA*)

Another successful Mackensen chief of staff was General Gerhard Tappen, outfitted here in prewar Prussian blue with red collar and Iron Cross medal and ribbon. (*ASA*)

The Serbian capital of Belgrade fell to Mackensen's troops on October 9, 1915, and he led the joint German-Bulgarian invasion of Allied Romania in September 1916 also.

5

Baltic States, 1916–18

Wilhelm II's "Wallenstein Freebooter:" Rüdiger Graf von der Goltz
Gustav Adolf Joachim Rüdiger Graf von der Goltz (December 8, 1865 to November 4, 1946) became perhaps the very closest commander the Kaiser had in the vein of the swashbuckling "Wallenstein-like" freebooter of the former 30 Years' War era.

A major general commanding the Foot Guards in France, Count von der Goltz was suddenly transferred to embattled Finland in March 1918 to help local Gen. Baron Karl Mannerheim—formerly of the Russian Tsarist Army—defeat an invasion by Lenin's Red Army.

Goltz's elite Baltic Sea Division made a rare successful Great War amphibious landing at Hanko, Finland, during April 3–5, 1918, taking the "Red" Finnish capital at Helsinki on the 13th; by May, he and the forces of Baron Mannerheim had almost completely ejected the beaten Red Army from Finland.

Realizing that Goltz meant to stay permanently as commander of a German Army of Occupation until a Hessian prince could ascend the Finnish "throne," Mannerheim did all he could to effect a German evacuation of Finland. This was aided by the Allies allowing a German armed force to help halt the Red Army in the neighboring Baltic Sea states as well.

This Goltz was happy to do, and during November 1918 to May 1919, he duly commanded a sizable, combined mixed force of the Iron Division, the German Baltic Landwehr, and various, assorted Free Korps units devoted not only to beating the Reds, but also to as much plunder and mayhem as they could achieve.

Latvia was cleared and Riga taken on May 22–23, 1918 after the Allies had reneged and ordered Goltz not to. Previously, he had taken Kurland's major port of Ventspils. As the occupying power in Latvia—as he had earlier been in Finland—Goltz overthrew the local Latvian government and installed his own. This enabled a Latvian-Estonian military alliance to be forged against Goltz, and on June 19, 1919—six months after the Great War had ended—he attacked the Estonians at the Battle of Cēsis, but lost to Ernest Podder's 3rd Estonian Division, retreating back to Riga on the 23rd.

Using their small Royal Navy Baltic Squadron to blockade the coastline to deny Goltz the sea-borne supplies vital to his forces, the Allies forced his command to exit Latvia. To spite the Entente Powers, he turned them over to the West Russian Volunteer Army instead.

In his postwar 1920 memoirs, Gen. von der Goltz asserted that his goal in taking Riga had been but to prepare the way to seize Red Petrograd (later Leningrad) as a future means of overthrowing the then-embryonic USSR altogether, just as the Allies were then trying to do as well.

All failed, but Goltz's attempt to establish a pro-German puppet regime at Petrograd might very well have succeeded had the Allies supported it. During 1924–30, the count ran the military education department of the German Socialist government for young potential future recruits, reporting on it on July 17, 1931 to then-Reich President von Hindenburg.

That October, Goltz resurfaced yet again, this time as a right-wing German politician backing the Nazi-Nationalist Harzburg Front. When Hitler came to invade the Baltics in June 1941, he did not avail himself of such independent talents as those the count had displayed in 1919, and thus the latter died peacefully at his Kinsegg country estate at Bernbeuren, Germany, in 1946.

Gen. Oskar von Hutier, Amphibious Conqueror

Oskar Emil von Hutier (August 27, 1857 to December 5, 1934) held a quartet of high German commands during the Great War: 21st Corps (April 4, 1915 to January 2, 1917), Army Detachment "D" (January 2 to April 22, 1917), 8th Army (April 22 to December 12, 1917), and 18th Army (December 22, 1917 to January 2, 1919), his service extending into the postwar era as well.

Gen. Hutier spent 1914–15 leading the 1st Guards Infantry Division on the Western Front until April, when he was transferred to the east, where he was awarded command of von Hindenburg's own former 8th Army. Von Hutier was also promoted to general of infantry.

Prior to the later Gen. Rüdiger Graf von der Goltz in Latvia, Hutier had taken its capital of Riga—but from the Russians—on September 3, 1917 following a siege of two years, after both a heavy bombardment coupled with a surprise Drina River crossing. This was followed by his unique amphibious achievement via the waterborne capture of Russian Islands in the Gulf of Riga in the daring Operation Albion that proved to be the only such successful mission of the entire war by any army or navy in a joint action.

The delighted Kaiser awarded him the Blue Max, while Ludendorff brought Gen. Hutier back west to take part in Operation Michael in March 1918. Employing the German Army's shock troop tactics—that von Hutier did not invent, however—the scrappy commander pounded the British 5th Army toward Amiens over fifteen days, moving steadily forward some 40 miles.

His victorious forces took some 50,000 BEF POWs, followed by a June 1918 attack that was finally halted by a heavy Allied artillery defense, stopping von Hutier's men in the early autumn of 1918.

As one of Hindenburg's homeward-bound commanders leading his troops back into the Reich, von Hutier received a hero's welcome, retiring from the army postwar. Both he and his cousin, Ludendorff, asserted postwar that their men had been betrayed by traitors on the German home front. Postwar, Gen. von Hutier served during 1919–34 to the age of seventy-seven as president of the German Officers' League.

Baltic Wallenstein General Rüdiger Graf von der Goltz (center, rendering hand salute to helmet) is seen here with his Finnish Army ally at far right, General Karl Gustav Baron von Mannerheim, hero of two armies and four wars, as well as a celebrated Asian explorer in his own right. Together, he and Goltz drove out the Reds. (*ASA*)

Above left: Influential General Oskar von Hutier. In April 1918—as part of Ludendorff's overall Michael offensive battles—Hutier commanded the German 18th Army at Villers-Bretonneux, but failed to prevent the French Army from successfully reinforcing the BEF. (*ASA*)

Above right: Perhaps the most talented Russian tsarist commander was General Alexsei Brusilov, whose summer 1916 offensive in the east gave the Central Powers an unaccustomed and nasty shock. Later, he served as well commanding Red Bolshevik troops. (*ASA*)

6

West, 1914–18

His Majesty's Prussian War Ministers, 1913–18

Col. Gen. Josias von Heeringen
Gen. Josias von Heeringen (March 9, 1850 to October 9, 1926) was the Kaiser's Prussian War Minister during 1913–14. Prior to the war's outbreak that August, he commanded the reported "decoy" 7th Army (August 2, 1914 to August 28, 1916) for the supposed German invasion of France, beating the French Army in the Battle of Mulhouse in Alsace.

Therein, young infantry Lt Goering planned a harebrained horseback kidnapping of that force's commanding officer, Gen. Paul Castelnau, which never happened. Gen. von Heeringen, however, was awarded the Blue Max by the Kaiser, an award that Goering would also receive from the Kaiser in June 1918.

Gen. von Heeringen was next transferred as commander, High Command Coastal Defense (August 29, 1916 to September 19, 1918), retiring as a decorated colonel general. During 1918–26, the general served as president of the Kyffhäuserbund, dying at Berlin that latter year.

Col. Gen. Erich von Falkenhayn, Turkish Field Marshal
Perhaps one of the most truly versatile German generals of the entire war, Erich Georg Anton von Falkenhayn (September 11, 1861 to April 8, 1922) was the serving Prussian War Minister when the Great War erupted in late July 1914, a post he held during 1913–15 as well.

In this, he was succeeded by Gens. Adolf Wild von Hohenborn, Hermann von Stein, and Walther Reinhardt, 1918–21, each playing an important role in keeping the Prussian war machine running smoothly.

It fell to Falkenhayn, however, to retain this post while also quietly, firmly, and effectively taking on the additional and unexpected job of simultaneously being chief of the German general staff in the light of the firing of von Moltke.

Thus, these two overlapped at perhaps the greatest early crisis of the Great War: War Minister (June 7, 1913 to January 21, 1915) and CGS (September 14, 1914 to August 29, 1916).

Falkenhayn took over the latter in the very wake of the loss of the First Battle of the Marne River that completely unhinged the entire, long-planned German plan of attack in the West. He also lost his own "Race to the Sea" against the Allied armies that fall, blundered into one of the worst overall casualty campaigns in German military history in the Battle of Verdun in 1916, took a beating in the initial Franco-British Somme River Offensive, and politically incorrectly forecast the entry into the war of Romania on the Entente side to boot!

His sprint toward the North Sea coast to beat the Allies to it failed when the vital Entente resupply ports were safeguarded by the Germans being halted at the First Battle of Ypres of October–November 1914, the CGS's own initial defeat.

At Verdun—wherein von Falkenhayn was lambasted by his own men as "The Blood Miller"—more than 250,000 German soldiers perished for no good military reason, and both he and Imperial Crown Prince Wilhelm found themselves beaten.

In the east, the inexperienced CGS was surprised by the steamroller Russian Army Brusilov Offensive that routed the Germans' feckless Central Power ally, Austria-Hungary, in 1916. Still, the Kaiser preferred the suave, urbane, and trim von Falkenhayn to the duo that he realized from the start would lead to the loss of his thrones via a won or lost war. This explained von Falkenhayn's remarkable dexterity in regaining his slippery footwork time after time.

When he dropped the ball on the Romanian entry, however, even the Kaiser had to let him go, but if he was down, he was never out. In that very country, von Falkenhayn managed to co-launch a joint attack alongside a former subordinate—Mackensen, the Black Hussar—that knocked the Romanian Army out of the fighting altogether. This was achieved, basically, via a strong drive into the country from Transylvania, through the South Carpathian Mountain passes, and then by smashing his shattered foe in Moldavia.

Falkenhayn proceeded as the Kaiser's second favorite warrior on to the Middle East, as C.O. of Ottoman Palestine, where he again faced his old nemesis, the tough British Army Tommy Atkins. Now he found himself jumped up to the exalted rank of *Mushir* (field marshal) in charge of the Turkish Yıldırım Army Group "F."

Beaten by Allenby outside Jerusalem in December 1917, von Falkenhayn's luck ran out yet again, but once more his patron, Wilhelm, ensured that he received another field command, of the 10th Army in Soviet Belarus, personally fighting those old foes of his rivals the duo, the Russians. Indeed, the formal list of his appointments reads like a veritable laundry sheet of some of the top, and also most varied, command billets on most fronts: commanding officer 9th Army (September 6, 1916 to May 1, 1917), CO Army Group "F" (July 20, 1917 to February 6, 1918), and of 10th Army (March 5, 1918 to January 1919).

In all these latter, "lesser" posts, Falkenhayn shone, especially in the important field commands in both Romania and Syria, grudgingly parceled out to him by the spiteful duo in order to keep Wilhelm II happy.

What rankled the duo most was that, despite his other glaring errors, he was right about the cardinal salient point of the entire struggle: it could be won nowhere but on the Western Front, and not, therefore, in the east.

Postwar, from his estate Castle Lindstedt near Potsdam outside Berlin, Falkenhayn published in 1919 his memoirs, *The German General Staff and Its Critical Decisions, 1914–16*, and died there in 1922, aged sixty.

Reportedly, both Churchill and military theorist Dupuy graded von Falkenhayn in the top tier of his rivals—near the hated duo. Noted Faulkner in *The Great War in the Mideast*: "All sources portray Falkenhayn as a loyal, honest, and punctilious friend and superior." That is far more than either of the duo ever got.

Gen. Adolf Wild von Hohenborn

"Wild" (July 8, 1860 to October 25, 1925) served as Prussian Minister of War during January 21, 1915 to October 29, 1916, thus overlapping two successive chiefs of German general staff—that of both von Falkenhayn and Hindenburg. In his succession post, Wild was still an ally of von Falkenhayn.

His tenure under Hindenburg was cut short because the duo had the Kaiser fire him for being critical of their Hindenburg Program to ramp up the Second Reich's overall domestic war economy, which even then they perceived to be skidding toward an eventual defeat, as occurred. Two months to the day of the HL posting, Wild was gone.

Gen. Walther Reinhardt: Overthrow the Traitor Government!

Maj. Gen. Walther Gustav Reinhardt (March 24, 1872 to August 8, 1930) turned out to be the very last Prussian Minister of War, the only one under a Soci government, and the very first so styled Head of the Army Command within the newly created Reichswehr Ministry, 1918–19.

From taking the position of being willing to lead an actual anti-government revolt at the start of this tenure, he ended it in being one of the very few former Imperial Army officers ready to defend it—and all based on his own, changing, personal convictions.

Maj. Reinhardt began the Great War on staff on the Western Front during 1916–17 at corps level, then became chief of staff for 1916–17 of the Macedonian Front's 11th Army, and finally to France on staff of the 7th Army in 1917–18. Thus, his entire wartime career was spent as a staff officer with no field troop commands whatsoever, a most unusual martial service record then for any officer in any army, then to now.

As a colonel in November 1918, Reinhardt was posted at Berlin's War Ministry as the all-important Head of Demobilization, to reverse all that had been done in 1914 in getting the army out to the fighting fronts.

He was also onsite, however, to deploy troops to protect the Reich Chancellery of Soci political leader Friedrich Ebert when the latter took over from Prince Max of Baden. This won him Reich Chancellor Ebert's trust, as well as the surprise appointment as Prussian War Minister on January 12, 1919.

Now Maj. Gen. Reinhardt accepted the post on the condition that the Soci Cabinet would back the officer corps over the authority of the Red Soldiers' and Workers' Councils. In return, he had to pay homage to the new order of things by agreeing to shed the traditional shoulder board epaulettes in favor of plain blue sleeve stripes, the latter drawing a rebuke of the new War Minister by Capt. Goering at a public meeting of officers in a Berlin hall postwar.

While the general agreed to the switch, another who did not, along with Goering, was Marshal von Hindenburg, who vowed that he would let no one strip him of his epaulettes; they remained.

Under Minister Reinhardt's regime, the OHL team of Hindenburg-Groener was dissolved as well, with the marshal resigning from the German Army altogether for the second time on June 29, 1919, the day after Soci President Ebert's Cabinet authorized the signing of the Treaty of Versailles.

That August 1919 with the coming into effect of the newly voted upon Weimar Republican Constitution, Gen. Reinhardt was replaced as Defense Minister by a Soci civilian appointee, Gustav Noske, who also became in effect commander-in-chief of the army.

Simultaneously, the war ministries of the Federated States of Bavaria, Saxony, and Württemberg were abolished along with that of Prussia, absorbed into Minister Noske's new Reichswehr Ministry Berlin on September 13, 1919.

On October 1, 1919, the former Minister Reinhardt morphed into the new chief of the army command, his major task being reducing the then standing German Army of about 350,000 men down to the 100,000 mandated by the Treaty of Versailles.

With the collapse of the Kapp–Lüttwitz Putsch of March 13–18, 1920, the general resigned his post along with Minister Noske on March 22, 1920 in solidarity, being replaced as chief of army command by Gen. Hans von Seeckt.

During 1920–24, Gen. Reinhardt remained in the Army, however, as commanding officer of the new Military District 5 at Stuttgart, and in 1923, he led the suppression of a Red revolt in Thuringia. Promoted general of infantry in 1925, Reinhardt took charge of Group Command 2 at Kassel, retiring in 1927, later teaching military courses at Berlin University. The general died on the anniversary of Ludendorff's Black Day of the German Army, August 8, 1930, at Groß-Lichterfelde.

The Marshal Blamed for the First Marne Battle Loss: Karl von Bülow

Karl Wilhelm Paul von Bülow (March 24, 1846 to August 31, 1921) was the commander of the German 2nd Army that invaded Belgium during the opening gambit of the Great War, his force credited with taking Fortress Liege (by Ludendorff) on August 7, 1914, and also with the fall of Fortress Namur during August 22–23, 1914.

Reportedly, Gen. von Bülow also defeated French Army Gen. Charles Lanrezac twice, first at the Battle of Charleroi on August 23–24, 1914, and again at St Quentin on the 29–30th. Then his record took a turn for the worse, according to Brownell in *First Nazi*:

> As the 2nd Army and Gen. Alexander von Kluck's 1st Army neared Paris during 31 August–2 September 1914, Bülow—concerned about the growing gap between the two armies—ordered Kluck to turn the 1st Army on his right, towards him.
>
> This decision, however, resulted in Kluck's advancing south and east of Paris, instead of south and west, as specified in the Schlieffen Plan. Bülow crossed the Marne River

on 4 September 1914, but was ordered to retreat to the Aisne River, after the successful counterattack by combined British and French forces against Kluck's 1st Army at the First Battle of the Marne during 5–10 September 1914.

Bülow was believed by the German public to be responsible for the German failure to capture Paris.

Nevertheless—perhaps as a way of shielding this—the Kaiser promoted him to field marshal in January 1915. The following March, the new GFM had a heart attack, and retired in early 1916.

His formal command of the German 2nd Army included August 2, 1914 to April 4, 1915, in which post he was succeeded by General of Infantry Fritz von Below. The field marshal was the brother of the former Imperial German Chancellor Prince Bernhard von Bülow.

Imperial Crown Prince Wilhelm (1882–1951)

The First Battle of the Marne had recently been won by the French Army when, in the first half of November 1914, American Hearst Corporation journalist Karl von Wiegand paid a visit to the commander of the German 5th Army at Stenay in occupied France.

He was stunned to hear its commander—Imperial Crown Prince Wilhelm himself of the reigning House of Hohenzollern—assert in a private aside, "We have lost the war! It will go on for a long time, but lost it is already!"

This accurate analysis was not published until 1961 by German author Klaus Jonas in his groundbreaking, and still singular today, biography of the man his enemies both foreign and domestic derided as Little Willy, to denote him from his father the Kaiser.

Crown Prince Wilhelm's offhand remark was seen as all the more surprising in that it had been said three and a half years before the bloody struggle ground to a halt following the also lost Second Battle of the Marne in 1918.

The other surprise was that it had been correctly foreseen by a man many considered to be a failed soldier, and also a morally discredited heir to the throne who was long thought to be an ineffectual fool supremely interested in chasing women, racing cars and horses, playing tennis, and hunting stags.

Ironically, this supposed intellectual lightweight had foreseen what the learned gentle-men of the German general staff at supreme headquarters had failed to admit—even to themselves—that the former, much-touted Schlieffen Plan to defeat the combined Allied armies of France, Great Britain, and Belgium on the Western Front had been stillborn. Thus, their expected war of movement was abruptly over, that of the stalemated trenches begun, and the vaunted victories in the east ultimately made meaningless thereby.

Beyond that, His Royal Highness also grasped simultaneously that Imperial Germany and his own ruling dynasty—caught in the maw of war—had thus doomed itself, and this at the very start of the conflict it had worked a generation to win.

Not so ironically, this very same young prince—aged thirty-two at its outset—had been a trained soldier for most of his life: in childhood, adolescence, and on into adulthood, as had also previously been the case with all the male members of his family, commissioned lieutenant at the age of ten. Oddly, the 1914 celebrated "Hero of Longwy" soon emerged early on in the conflict as one of the most cruelly maligned figures of the entire Great War.

Noted Horne: "The leptic, unfinished-looking figure—with the narrow, sloping shoulders and almost deformed Modigliani neck in its high collar, and the elongated features of an amiable greyhound—was a boon to the caricaturists."

Added Tuchman, "The cartoonists' pet was the Crown Prince, whom they delighted to draw as an exaggerated fop with pinched waist, high tight collar, rakish cap, and an expression of fatuous vacuity" that, often enough, unfortunately for him, was not very far from being the truth.

Yet German and foreign women the world over found the prim, prudish Kaiser's eldest son and offspring wildly sexy and attractive, an attribute that, in the end, helped materially in losing him his 300-year-old rightful crown as his father's legal successor. In studied contrast to his father—who himself had served as crown prince for a mere ninety-nine days—Little Willy was fated to be the long-suffering heir for sixty-nine years, one of the longest such stints on record.

As a six-year-old at his father's 1888 accession, from then on, Willy's most personal dealings with his august, austere father had to occur through the latter's formal chief of the military cabinet, as a younger officer to his army superior.

He became a corporal in the Prussian Army at the age of seven, having been placed within the daily regimen of a series of martial tutors. Indeed, in full Prussian dress kit and regalia, "the pathetic little boy" saluted on a parade ground his own father on the latter's thirtieth birthday in 1889 during the first year of the latter's three-decade-long reign.

One of his thousands of ardent female admirers was his own younger and only sister, Princess Viktoria Luise of Prussia, who gushed that "He looked brilliant, and—because of his natural, unaffected manner—won a lot of sympathy," but rarely from his Imperial father, however.

Tuchman described Little Willy in rather less fulsome terms. In 1914, "The Imperial scion was a narrow chested, willowy creature with the face of a fox," who was known as an avowed militarist who had already glorified war in a book he had edited for children entitled, *Germany in Arms*, which celebrated the centennial of the War of Liberation against the hated, but feared, Napoleon Bonaparte that had been led by his own earlier dynasty, no less, and won. Postwar, the imperial author published a pair of autobiographical works that I have found useful here, both in 1922, while he was in his Dutch exile: *The Memoirs of the Crown Prince of Germany* and *My War Experiences*.

In the latter, young Wilhelm recalled watching with glee his invading, "Joyous German soldiers with sparkling eyes," as they launched the later famed Battle of the Frontiers of August–September 1914 against the French. During the heady general mobilization days of August 1914, as all Europe went to war, it seemed, Albrecht Duke of Württemberg (1865–1939) and *Kronprinz* Rupprecht (1869–1955) of Bavaria of the ruling House of Wittelsbach each received Army commands from their imperial master the Kaiser. Thus it was both politically and dynastically essential that the German Imperial Crown Prince Wilhelm as his own heir receive one as well.

Then, as Little Willy looked forward to the "happy, cheerful war," as he initially called it, German general headquarters—where sat his own father as Supreme Warlord, no less—created the imperial crown prince an army commander as well, complete with his own first chief of staff, Gen. Konstantin Schmidt von Knobelsdorf (1860–1936.)

The crown prince's father-*cum*-military superior sternly admonished his oldest—and by then, well wayward—son as he left for the Western Front: "Whatever he advises you, you must do!"

Thus did Little Willy enter upon a four-year-long top combat command with but a prior colonelcy of the famed Death's Head Hussars under his belt, that and a year on the general staff at Berlin, but no experience as either a divisional or a corps commander—and more was to come, too.

Nevertheless, the steeple-chasing imperial crown prince had faith in himself, as he later wrote, and believed as well that what he had, "Gave [him] the theoretical groundwork for command of large units." Indeed, von Moltke told HRH personally that he had "a good military outlook and a healthy common sense." He would both need and display them before the Great War played itself out, four years and more later.

Indeed, to almost everyone's astonishment, on both sides, his 5th Army won the Battle of the Frontiers, making him instantly renowned as the "Hero of the Battle of Longwy" of August 23, 1914, and this on the very day that far to the east the Hindenburg-Ludendorff team was being forged in steel as well.

That day, his 5th Army bypassed the Longwy Fortress itself, leaving it to be taken later by follow-up siege troops and engineers. Thus freed of this obstacle now to his rear, the intrepid imperial crown prince won laurels in the media for advancing, impressing for the very first time even his stern papa. Flush with this victory that reflected well on their dynasty jointly, the Kaiser joyously awarded him, as well as Rupprecht, the coveted Iron Cross, both First and Second Class, simultaneously.

"Deeply moved," the proud crown prince handed his father's telegram around for all his personal staff to see as well. Soon, the handsome young prince would be awarding combat medals for battlefield bravery himself, clad in "A dazzling white tunic, walking between two lines of soldiers distributing Iron Crosses from a basket carried by an aide," thus aping his father's own front visit style.

The coveted telegram trumpeted, "Well done! Am proud of you!" In fact, the incident even made the famous American *New York Times* edition August 26, 1914 thus:

Kaiser Decorates 2 Sons for Bravery
Berlin, via Copenhagen & London—Emperor William has conferred the decoration of the Iron Cross of the 2nd and 1st Class on Crown Prince Frederick William and Duke Albrecht of Württemberg.

He has conferred also the Iron Cross decoration of the 2nd Class on his son Prince Oskar.

His Majesty also sent the following telegram to the Crown Princess: "I thank thee with all my heart, dear child; I rejoice with thee over the first victory of Wilhelm!"

"God has been on his side, and has most brilliantly supported him! To Him be thanks and honor! I remit to Wilhelm the Iron Cross of the 2nd and 1st Class. Oskar also fought brilliantly with his grenadiers!

"He has achieved the Iron Cross of the 2nd Class. Repeat that to Ina and Marie! Also in the future, God be with thee and all wives! Papa Wilhelm."

The younger son again made the *New York Times* on February 8, 1916:

Kaiser's Son Oskar is Wounded Again. Hit in the Head and Thigh by Shell Splinters on the Russian Front

Amsterdam—Prince Oskar of Prussia—fifth son of Emperor William—has been slightly wounded in the head and on the upper part of the thigh by shell splinters during the fighting in the eastern war theater, according to a Berlin official report received here.

Prince Oskar was wounded at Virton, Belgium in September 1914. He was ill for a long time, and was declared to be suffering also from an affection of the heart. He returned to duty in the field in November 1914, and narrowly escaped capture the following month during the fighting in Poland.

In Klaus Jonas's *The Life of Crown Prince Wilhelm*, it was written that in that same early spirit of wartime magnanimity, the crown prince's own 5th Army Chamberlain Elard von Oldenburg-Januschau (1855–1937) recalled in his postwar memoirs of 1936:

I shall never forget how the Crown Prince with a noble gesture returned the sword to the brave French commander, and gave him the choice of returning to France if he would give his word of honor not to fight any longer against Germany.

However, the officer frankly refused the offer, and accepted the hard fate of imprisonment.

Following the sudden and totally unexpected loss of First Marne—for the remainder of 1914 and all of 1915—Imperial Crown Prince Wilhelm remained at his Stenay Field headquarters while the interminable trench warfare dragged on.

By the end of 1915, he had concluded that Germany simply could not win a two-front war, and, therefore, must seek to conclude a peace in either the east or the west. He even floated the controversial idea himself of returning to the French their famous lost Fortress Metz of 1870 as an olive branch toward a peace settlement with at least the Gauls, if not yet the English.

The Battle of Verdun, February–December 1916

Then came the idea of "bleeding white" the French Army opposite the crown prince's own 5th German Army command at the former's Verdun fortress system, which was proposed by the Kaiser's favorite chief of general staff, Gen. von Falkenhayn. He was the Kaiser's antidote to the politically feared duo of the Eastern Front—Hindenburg and Ludendorff. Here, then, was how the bogged down war in the west would be won, via a brutal wastage slugfest, but it never was.

Asserted Perrett: "The German intention was to impose a ruinous battle of attrition on the French Army, thereby destroying its limited manpower reserves at this fortified city on the upper Meuse River in eastern France."

The overall main battle lasted from February 21 to December 18, 1916, with Gen. Henri Philippe Pétain and then Gen. Robert Nivelle facing the imperial crown prince of the German Reich.

The epic bloodletting was an inconclusive standoff between Gallic defender and Teutonic attacker, with severe casualties on both sides—overall French Army commander Gen. Joseph "Papa" Joffre lost 362,000 killed to the German toll of 337,000 slain and wounded. Begun under von Falkenhayn's aegis, it took the succeeding duo partnership another four months to wind down the slaughter, even after they assumed the supreme command on August 29, 1916. This abrupt change-of-command was one that the political intriguer Crown Prince Wilhelm had worked for mightily behind the scenes, proving that he had some powerful domestic chops as well.

The blame on the German side of the ledger for the Verdun debacle—for, indeed, such it was, with very little actually accomplished—has been debated by military historians ever since. Again, proposed by von Falkenhayn at the start, it had nonetheless been warmly endorsed by both the crown prince and his respected chief of staff, von Knobelsdorf. As the grim death toll mounted, however, young Wilhelm began more and more to have his own serious doubts as to the operation's actual worth.

The story is told that—at the other end of the world—the great British explorer Sir Ernest Shackleton reached South Georgia Island in 1916 after two years' isolation in Antarctica and asked when the war had ended. He was told, "The war is not over! Millions are being killed. Europe is mad. The world is mad!" according to Horne. Indeed, thought one German writer of the struggle at Verdun, there would be no end, "Until the last German and the last Frenchman hobbled out of the trenches on crutches to exterminate each other with pocket knives, or teeth and finger nails."

The overall battle statistics were truly staggering: German artillery alone shot about 22 million rounds, with the French guns also accounting for an estimated 15 million. The French Army in 1916 boasted ninety-six divisions stationed on the Western Front, and of these, seventy had been deployed to Verdun, with the Germans throwing in a little over forty-six of their divisional-sized units.

All that either side ever gained territorially was about that of the size of the Royal Parks of London combined, leading the later crestfallen Little Willy—once so fond of glorious wartime exploits—to note postwar that "The Mill on the Meuse ground to powder the hearts as well as the bodies of the troops."

Nevertheless, both he and his staff learned well the lessons that the sturdy French had so bloodily taught the German 5th Army at Verdun, and they employed them well the following year, as he later admitted: "Had we held to such defenses that had hitherto been the rule, I am convinced that we should not have come through the great defensive battles of 1917."

By now, Gen. Friedrich von der Schulenburg had replaced Schmidt von Knobelsdorf as the crown prince's new and final chief of staff, and the former leather *pickelhaube* (spiked helmet) was superseded by the 1916–35 "coal scuttle" helmet as well. Some things remained grimly the same as always, however, such as the men shitting their pants as they went "over the top" from both ends of the battlefields to their deaths.

By then, the crown prince had joined the scheming duo of the east in their behind-the-scenes political maneuvering at the Kaiser's court, which helped overthrow the 1914 era's Imperial Chancellor Theobald von Bethmann-Hollweg (1856–1921).

The crown prince went further by backing Hindenburg's abrupt First Quartermaster General Ludendorff against the interests of his father by campaigning, successfully, to have certain high members of the Kaiser's various personal cabinets removed as well, especially that of the Civil Cabinet, Rudolf von Valentini.

Indeed, it must have seemed like a long time ago, as Crown Prince Wilhelm later recalled in his postwar memoirs: "The moment when I was standing in the old chapel of the Berlin Castle and took my military oath in front of my father the Kaiser, and stands out in my mind as my most cherished memory."

Countered Jonas, however, of the crown prince in *The Life of Crown Prince Wilhelm*:

He had often—without wanting to—shocked soldiers returning from the front lines when he greeted them in his extravagant clothing, with a narrow riding whip in his hand, surrounded by his Indian whippets.

If now and then in his white uniform he threw them cigarettes, many of them indignantly thought that he had just come back from playing tennis. Whenever young French girls waved to him, he made his bright red car stop in the street, picked them up, and listened with a great deal of interest to their worries about the fate of their husbands or sweethearts.

Often, he promised to make inquiries for them in Supreme Headquarters, and by doing so, completely ruined his reputation at the German High Command.

Battle of the Somme, July 1 to November 18, 1916

Overlapping both the Battle of Verdun and the twin CGS tenures of Falkenhayn and Hindenburg was the epic, mammoth Battle of the Somme River in France, mainly notable for a triad of martial firsts: the usage of armored tanks, concentrated airpower, and for being the worst single day in the history of the British Army.

Its very first day earned that grim distinction, with the BEF suffering 57,470 casualties. Notes Gessner in 2017's *Tannenberg*: "More than one million men were wounded or killed, making it one of the bloodiest battles in human history."

Also known as the Somme Offensive, it encompassed 420,000 British, 200,000 French, and 430,000–500,000 German casualties overall.

By the battle's end in November 1916, fifty-one British and forty-eight French divisions fought fifty German divisions. The British divisions included troops from all of the

British Empire's far-flung Commonwealth of Nations' Imperial Dominions: Australia, Bermuda, Canada, India, Newfoundland, New Zealand, South Africa, Southern Rhodesia, and the United Kingdom of England, Scotland, and Wales proper.

The major Allied commanders were Field Marshal Sir Douglas Haig and later Marshal of France and Allied Generalissimo Ferdinand Foch *versus* German commanders Gens. Max von Gallwitz and Fritz von Below under Field Marshal Crown Prince Rupprecht of Bavaria.

The Duo Achieves the Supreme Command, August 29, 1916

The Kaiser finally gave way to popular demand, firing Falkenhayn and replacing him as chief of the general staff with von Hindenburg on August 29, 1916—the highest post after that of the emperor himself in the Imperial Army—with trusty Ludendorff as first quartermaster general, the latter's chosen title, as opposed to deputy chief of general staff.

Would the war have turned out any differently had the appointment been made two years earlier, after Tannenberg? We can only speculate, as historians have done ever since. As it was, calls for Hindenburg to take over the supreme command had begun as early as March 1915, when German Navy Grand Adml. Alfred von Tirpitz wrote to a friend:

> I see only one way out!
>
> The Kaiser must give out that he is on the sick list for eight weeks or more, Hindenburg must come and take Bethmann[-Hollweg]'s place [as Reich Chancellor], and take control of everything—including the Army and Navy! Oh, blessed Hindenburg—save us!

Now, Hindenburg was, indeed, on the scene, and in total command at last, the virtual dictator—with Ludendorff—of Germany's entire war effort, but already it was too late for the Second Reich to win World War I by a purely military victory in the field. A negotiated peace was still possible, but the proud twin brethren were having none of that.

There now developed an uneasy relationship between the erratic Kaiser and his two generals. Wilhelm II seemed "Almost slight compared to the tall, broad-shouldered field marshal, whose harsh tones and short, clipped sentences reminded him of his dead grandfather's Royal paladins" of yesteryear, von Moltke and Roon, then Prussian war minister under Bismarck:

> For the first time in his Reign, he had a man at his side who reminded him of that great man from the Sachsenwald, Bismarck.... In soldier-like fashion, he "most humbly took his leave of his Imperial Master"....
>
> Before leaving the Kaiser's presence, he would look at him steadily, as though wishing to encourage and reassure him, "I am here! You can trust me! With God's help, we shall surely bring it off!"

But in the end they did not.

It was precisely because von Hindenburg reminded him of the crafty old iron chancellor whom he had fired in 1890 that the Kaiser now also feared his towering field marshal. He had dismissed Prince Bismarck because he felt that the House of Bismarck was overshadowing that of his own in the public mind: "He has planted his chair outside my door!" the younger Kaiser had wailed back then to his aides.

Now, this was happening anew in the case of Hindenburg's rising popularity in contrast to that of his own sinking reputation. Jealous of his own field marshal, paradoxically, the Kaiser was forced to rely upon that same stalwart warrior nevertheless to save both his throne and his dynasty for him.

For his part, the field marshal handled his high-strung Kaiser with considerable tact, always being very respectful, and in the main preserving the outward façade of Wilhelm's being supreme warlord, a role he was himself taking over more and more as time went on.

That October 1916, the Kaiser told the chief of his naval cabinet, Adml. Müller, "That he, the Supreme Warlord, was not for the moment the ruler. During the war, he had to take a back seat! Hindenburg had said that politics had no place at Headquarters!"

As the duo's power grew, however, the pair became increasingly more remote from their emperor. In time, Ludendorff would inform the Kaiser on their visits to Berlin that Field Marshal von Hindenburg would not be able to spare the time to make daily trips to Potsdam to report to him anymore.

When the emperor suggested that Ludendorff come instead, the latter replied that he, also, was "too busy." In future, a lower-ranking staff officer would make the trip in their place. In the main, Wilhelm II swallowed this impertinence as well, but not forever.

Ludendorff *versus* the Kaiser, 1916–18

Ludendorff's attitude to the emperor had been completely different from Hindenburg's almost from the start. Himself a reputed "man of genius," he looked upon the Kaiser as a fool, not worthy of the exalted position to which he had been born, and he was far from being alone in that view.

Ludendorff hated his meetings with the Kaiser and could not wait to leave. Recalled one observer: "If the Kaiser asked a question, Ludendorff would clap his monocle in his eye, bend over his map, mark off distances with the compasses that the Kaiser would follow with his beringed finger…"

Ludendorff would then "Hurriedly roll up the maps and await the hint to withdraw.… There was a click of spurs, an effortless about face—no walking backward for him!—and the Quartermaster-General returned to work."

The Alleged Silent Dictatorship, 1916–18

As soon as the two took over at great general headquarters at Castle Pless in Upper Silesia, a great many things changed, both for better and worse. The duo branched out into all phases of German national domestic life as well as their former purely military sphere, thus controlling the economy, media, and politics, in addition to all things martial.

Thus, it became a silent—as opposed to a more visible outright—military takeover of the civilian state, with the Kaiser still in nominal control overall, however.

Ludendorff's September 1917 Train Wreck

Ludendorff recalled in his postwar memoirs the closest he ever came to death since his August 1914 derring-do at the Liege gate, the train wreck of September 1917: "On a journey to the west, I met with a railway accident. Another train ran into the coach in which I was dining with my officers, and overturned it, but that caused only a momentary fright."

In her splendid own postwar memoirs, his first wife, Margarethe, provided better details of this unique event:

> In the most serious time, a railway accident occurred. The officers of the Supreme Command were traveling from Avesnes to the front.
>
> The night was dark. The driver of the engine observed with some difficulty that the signal given at one of the switchboxes was of an uncertain character. What could that mean? Pull up? All clear?
>
> He went on through the darkness with extreme caution. Suddenly, there was a frightful crash—a collision had ensued! A heavy munition train had struck the train of the Supreme Command broadside on, [and] derailed the latter by its mighty weight and turned it into a heap of ruins.
>
> As though by a miracle, no one was injured! No harm came to any officers in whose hands lay the conduct of the war at that time, and even the plans and maps that they had with them were undamaged.

Apparently, Hindenburg himself was not aboard.

Ludendorff as the German Cromwell

Despite this, though, almost all the military men—Mackensen, Seeckt, the crown prince, and many others—pressed for a complete and actual coup-like, outright takeover, while members of the Reichstag were also supportive.

Noted one scribe: "Parliamentarians like Gustav Stresemann—a later Chancellor of the Weimar Republic—were becoming increasingly convinced that a military dictatorship was the only hope of salvation, and were toasting Ludendorff as the German Cromwell," the former dictator after the overthrown Stuart dynasty of the executed King Charles I in England centuries before.

The duo's rash support of all-out submarine warfare against neutral shipping brought United States entry into the war on the side of the Allies, at a time when that was badly needed as their last saving hope. Nor did those very same U-boats ever sink a single U.S. troopship bound from America for France, in either world war, no less!

This came at the precise moment when German armies freed from further deployment on the Eastern Front were heading west to win the war, hopefully, before the American masses decamped on the European continent for the expected campaigns of 1918–20, and maybe beyond.

The political fall of Imperial Chancellor von Bethmann-Hollweg (1909–17) was entirely engineered by the duo and their political allies, such as the crown prince and his mother, Kaiserin Augusta Viktoria. This was done in hopes of a more vigorous prosecution of the domestic war effort overall, while their future spring 1918 grand offensive was their last throw of the iron martial dice of war to break the trench warfare system deadlock on the former 1914 war of movement.

The Kaiser Enraged!

To overthrow the imperial chancellor, the duo traveled to Berlin to confront the Kaiser with their joint demand of threatening to resign themselves if the monarch did not comply. Shocked, the Kaiser agreed because they were simply too valuable for him to lose politically at that juncture of the Great War.

Privately, however, he was indignant, telling Adml. Georg von Müller, "This behavior on the part of Prussian generals had never before been heard of in the history of Prussia!" The subsequent chancellors were not of Bethmann-Hollweg's quality, and thus the real issues were decided upon instead by the two soldiers.

The Battle of Passchendaele, July 31 to November 10, 1917

Aside from waging the already in-progress Battles of Verdun and the Somme River in 1916, a year later, the duo fought the Battle of Passchendaele Belgian Campaign from July 31 to November 10, 1917 against the same foes as at the Somme, as well as the added enemy of the Royal Belgian Army. It was also known as the Third Battle of Ypres, or Wipers as the Brit Tommy Atkins pronounced it, over the course of three bloody months and six days.

Waged for control of ridges south and east of the embattled Belgian city of Ypres in West Flanders, the Passchendaele Campaign was fought by British Field Marshal Haig *versus* Ludendorff, the Bavarian crown prince, and Gen. Friedrich Sixt von Arnim, pitting fifty BEF and six French Army divisions against seventy-seven to eighty-three German ones at differing times. The casualties are still disputed, with a 2017 estimate being 200,000–448,614 for the Entente Powers, as opposed to 217,000–410,000 for the Germans, the latter figure including 24,065 POWs.

The ridges were located near key German railway supply junctions and lines that the Allies sought to take. In November 1917, the Canadian Corps ended the campaign by taking Passchendaele itself.

In 1918, the Entente forces succeeded in reaching the Dutch frontier and seizing the Belgian coastal ports, following the Battles of Lys and the Fifth Battle of Ypres. The "Battle" of Passchendaele was really an overall campaign of several smaller, composite battles at Pilckem Ridge, Westhoek, Hill 70, Langemarck, Menin Road Ridge, Polygon Wood, Broodseinde, Poelcappelle, First and Second Passchendaele, and La Malmaison.

Haig's political opponent, British wartime Prime Minister David Lloyd George, asserted in his 1938 memoirs that "Passchendaele was, indeed, one of the greatest disasters of the war.... No soldier of any intelligence now defends this senseless campaign!" The debate continues 100 years later as I write these words.

Von Marwitz Surprised by British Tanks at Cambrai, November 20, 1917
On November 20, 1917, German 2nd Army C.O. Gen. Georg von der Marwitz was part of Crown Prince Rupprecht's forces in France when he was taken by surprise by a massed BEF tank assault in the Battle of Cambrai. This was despite positive intelligence being reported of their actual presence opposite him. This usage of armor by Haig was the most extensive tank deployment to date, more than double the numbers used previously, in fact.

This British armored thrust led the crown prince and Marwitz to launch their first attack against Tommy Atkins since April 1915. Despite having already destroyed hundreds of Allied tanks in this battle alone, the Germans found themselves confronted by thousands, making their shock all the greater.

Thus was vividly exposed one of Ludendorff's most glaring weaknesses: his lack of taking the new armored warfare seriously. Fortunately for von der Marwitz, the attack eventually slowed, halted by a severe blizzard on December 7, 1917 with 50,000 German casualties, of which more than 10,000 were POWs.

Unknown to the Allies, as their tanks were coming to a halt in the bitter snowbound fighting, the Germans were running out of ammunition. Von der Marwitz was not so lucky on August 11, 1918 following the end of Ludendorff's last great attack, though, when a renewed massive Allied tank force overwhelmed his men yet again.

Beaten badly by Australian British Commonwealth troops, Marwitz' dilemma was ably shown when on August 24, 1918 he decorated a single officer who had alone destroyed fourteen Allied tanks.

Noted Brownell in *First Nazi*: "Tanks generally struck terror in the ranks, who bound grenades together in anticipation; rifles were abandoned for heavy machineguns, leaving artillery unprotected in the rearguard." Tanks became an ever growing problem for Ludendorff throughout the final year of the Great War—November to November—a fact that did not augur well for the fate of his coming last throw of the dice in March 1918.

As for von der Marwitz, he was relieved of command of the 2nd Army on September 22, 1918 via promotion "upstairs" to lead the 5th Army, which ended the war with nine divisions only. This final command for von der Marwitz ended on January 30, 1919, and he died a decade later at the age of seventy-three at Wundichow, a commander undone by one of Winston Churchill's most effective wartime inventions ever, the tank.

Kaiserschlacht (The Kaiser's Battle!)—Operation Michael Launches Five Offensives
As the fateful year 1918 opened, there was hope that Imperial Germany might yet win, especially since Russia, Romania, and Serbia had all been knocked out in the east, and the Americans had not so far proven their effectiveness on the Western Front.

At the outset in 1918, when the Kaiser still fervently believed in the ultimate Teutonic victory's certainty—he chortled, "If a British Parliamentarian comes to sue for peace, he must first *kneel* before the Imperial standard, for this is a victory of monarchy over democracy!" That having been said, in 1932, then-Reich President von Hindenburg admitted to his Great War combat veteran machine-gun company commander, Chancellor (former captain) Heinrich Brüning: "I knew that the war was lost in February 1918, but I decided to let Ludendorff have his fling!" And what a mad dervish whirl that turned out to be.

How casually, therefore, he referred in retrospect to the great offensive that was launched in March 1918. Although it almost smashed through the Allied lines and reached Paris, it was later stopped cold in its tracks by the fresh American troop reserves from across the Atlantic Ocean, brought there by the sinking of such neutral passenger liners as the *Lusitania*.

Before this occurred, however, Little Willy's Count von der Schulenburg argued that the German armies must first defeat the French and take Paris, then the British, prior to the American presence making itself fully felt in any meaningful way. The Supreme Command agreed regarding the latter, and here is what Ludendorff planned for what his boss the field marshal later so glibly passed off as his "fling."

The first attack: Plan Michael, named for the patron saint of Germany, St Michael the Archangel, was set for March 21, 1918, and encompassed two full army groups, those of the two crown princes, between them including seventy-one divisions. The assault force would comprise thirty-two divisions, supported by thirty-nine reserve divisions, all attacking across a 49-mile-wide front between Arras and La Fère, themselves backed up by 7,000 guns firing a four-day supply of 9 million rounds.

When and if this faltered, the next gambit—Blücher-Yorck—called for the triad of armies of Crown Prince Wilhelm's 5th Army Group (the 1st, 7th, and 18th, comprising forty-one divisions) to attack at Chemin des Dames on May 27, 1918, on a 22-mile-long "rest" front where they could face four British and seven French divisions along the line Anizy–Berry-au-Bac. By the end of May, the Germans had taken Château-Thierry and were set to cross the Marne River, a mere 50 miles from the French capital, until this stalled also.

Under Plan Gneisenau—named for one of Field Marshal Blücher's Napoleonic Wars staff chiefs—the Teutonic drive on Paris continued, and a replay of 1871 seemed to be at hand, with the German armies within 39 miles of the French capital.

Indeed, by June 1, 1918, over 65,000 Allied POWs were "in the bag," when a totally unexpected event occurred that stopped the offensive cold in its tracks: widespread German looting and drunkenness broke out. This reflected a weariness at the front that had long been felt on the domestic scene meanwhile. By June 3, the exasperated Ludendorff was forced to call off the attack. By August 1918, the entire Imperial Army was on the verge of total collapse, with an imminent Allied invasion of the Reich itself expected either for the autumn of 1918 or the spring of 1919.

The deadly trench life resumed, with some officers issuing opium to retard or even halt bowel movements so that deadly runs to the latrine under enemy sniper fire would be less frequent. Other soldiers let fly on their spades covered with dirt, throwing the mess over the side afterwards.

Prince Eitel Frederick told his older brother, Imperial Crown Prince Wilhelm, that the American artillery greatly exceeded "In intensity and heaviness anything we had known at Verdun or on the Somme [against the BEF]."

The Allies Strike Back with the 100 Days' Offensive, July 18 to November 11, 1918
On July 18, 1918, the Allies themselves launched their own mighty counteroffensive, which smashed through the German lines, coming right up against the vaunted Hindenburg Line itself—the last major defensive position of the Fatherland on foreign soil.

On August 8, 1918—called by Ludendorff "The Black Day of the German Army"—when German lines were badly breached, the first quartermaster general also recognized that the war was, indeed, irretrievably lost. The next Entente assault would see their armies fighting on the scared soil of the Imperial Reich anew, just as in August 1914.

Wilson: The Kaiser Must Go!
Two days later, on August 10, 1918, Hindenburg informed the Kaiser that the war could not be won, and peace feelers were then immediately extended to the west. Back came the rejected answer: the Kaiser must go, declared new belligerent U.S. President Woodrow Wilson.

The Kaiser Fires Ludendorff, October 26, 1918
Stung at last into action to personally protect his throne, the Kaiser angrily demanded that his top two soldiers appear before him in imperial audience at Castle Bellevue, Berlin, on October 26, 1918 to demand Ludendorff's resignation, which was immediately tendered and accepted; the first quartermaster general had been fired.

"You stay!" the Kaiser barked at the stunned field marshal, and the latter said not a word in defense of his former "happy marriage" partner, Ludendorff, the man to whom he owed so much, including his field marshal's baton.

Now, at last, Ludendorff got his well-deserved comeuppance for his prior disdain of the Kaiser. The field marshal neither divested himself of the credit nor accepted the blame for what had happened during the war. In the words of Wheeler-Bennett in 1936, "He remained the Wooden Titan, into which the worms of decay had already entered."

Ludwig Cohn's Account, 1935 (*Wilhelm Hohenzollern*)
When William now summoned both the commanders to Schloss Bellevue, Ludendorff referred on the journey to the probability of his dismissal. Hindenburg rejoined that—in that case—he would himself resign.

To the Emperor, Ludendorff began by abusing the new government on the ground that it was not backing up the High Command. The Emperor declared that the General Staff had made a mess of things.

Ludendorff begged permission to resign. William replied: "I thank you for expressing that wish, as it makes things easier for me! I shall try to rebuild my Empire with the aid of the Social Democrats!"

These were the very same Socis with whom he had been at political war since the lost Reichstag election of 1890, before which the young Wilhelm II had avowed an intention of becoming the "Soci Kaiser," but later still urged his troops to shoot them down, even if they were their own parents, brothers, and sisters. Wilhelm II was flexibility itself when occasion seemed to him to demand it.

> Next, William suggested various military measures, which Ludendorff rejected as impractical. Then Ludendorff took his leave. When Hindenburg expressed a wish to resign—saying he did not care to separate from his collaborator—the Emperor replied: "You are the palladium of the German people! You must not desert it in its utmost need!" "My appeal was successful," related the Emperor subsequently. "The field marshal agreed, after a severe struggle with his feelings." One wonders!
>
> Concerning Hindenburg's alleged struggle with his feelings … we know Ludendorff's impression. "My husband considered," writes Ludendorff's wife, "that he had been left in the lurch by Hindenburg, with whom he had shared the joys and sorrows of all these years, and who now allowed him to resign, while himself remaining in the Emperor's service." "Ludendorff won his battles for him, and he betrayed Ludendorff."

My Personal View
My own view is this: a military chief of staff had been dismissed, nothing more and nothing less—life martial went on for the survivors, and so did the Great War.

Toland's Account, 1980
Toland stated in *No Man's Land*:

> Col. von Haeften burst in with news overheard in the lobby of the Chancellery: at the insistence of Prince Max, the Kaiser was proposing to dismiss Ludendorff.
>
> He had hurried over to warn the Quartermaster General, "So that the final scene might be played in as dignified a form as possible." Before Ludendorff could recover from the shock, official word came that he and Hindenburg were to report at once to Bellevue Castle.
>
> Ludendorff's hands shook so that he had difficulty buttoning his uniform, and he was still virtually beside himself as he reported to His Majesty. In a manner wholly changed from yesterday, the Kaiser complained about the Army order of the 24th calling on all troops to fight rather than bow to Wilson's demands.
>
> "There followed," wrote Ludendorff, "some of the bitterest moments of my life. I said respectfully to His Majesty that I had gained the painful impression that I no longer enjoyed his confidence, and that I accordingly begged most humbly to be relieved of my office."
>
> According to Hindenburg, the scene was tempestuous. Ludendorff responded to the Kaiser's complaint of abrupt changes in the OHL position with vehement accusations against Prince Max for not siding with the General Staff when it was unfairly attacked.
>
> His tone became so sharp that the Kaiser said, "You seem to forget that you are addressing your monarch!" Ludendorff retorted with a demand to be relieved, and—upon being offered command of an army group [*à la* Falkenhayn in 1916, no less] brusquely refused it.

This infuriated the Kaiser, who said it was to himself as Supreme Warlord to decide when and whether Ludendorff was to go! Once more Ludendorff offered his resignation, and this time it was accepted.

Thus did Ludendorff himself bring to an end his own military career, foolishly rejecting the offer of a major command that would have at least left him in a position of some influence.

The bitterest blow to Ludendorff was Hindenburg's silence. He never came to his subordinate's support; and only, at the end, offered his own resignation. "You will stay," said the Kaiser tartly, and the field marshal bowed from the waist.

After the two officers left, the Kaiser remarked with satisfaction, "The operation is over. I have separated the Siamese twins!"

The later BBC television series *Fall of Eagles* put an even more dramatic spin on these events, as when Ludendorff balked, the Kaiser turned to a nearby sentry and immediately commanded, "Arrest that man!" Choking back his fear, Ludendorff backed down.

Outside the castle, Ludendorff accused Hindenburg of treachery, and refused to ride in the same car. Margarethe Ludendorff was standing in the window as her husband's car arrived.... Pale as death, he came into the room and sat down heavily in a chair....

"The Kaiser has sacked me! I have been dismissed!"

"Who is to be your successor?" I asked.

"I have suggested Kuhl."

"Why not Seeckt?" I said.

"I never thought of him," he replied. Then he jumped up and said abruptly: "In a fortnight, we shall have no Empire, and no Emperor left, you will see!"

Neither man got the nod, however. "Gen. Groener was appointed Hindenburg's new chief of staff.... Gen. von Loßberg was given the responsible task of withdrawing the Army—that had already retired to the Siegfried/Hindenburg Line—with as little loss as possible to Germany," following the signature of the Armistice, under the new duo of Hindenburg and Groener from GHQ Kassel on the Rhine River in West Germany. Meanwhile, Prince Max was meeting with his own advisors, when Col. von Haeften again burst in with the latest news: "'Gen. Ludendorff is dismissed!' 'And Hindenburg?' 'He is to stay.' 'Thank God!' everyone chorused," asserted Toland.

Ludendorff's Regrets

The fired first quartermaster general's divorced wife recalled after the war: "He often used to say afterwards, 'I ought never to have let myself be dismissed! It would have been better if—while the war was still in progress—I had snatched the Dictatorship for myself!'"

The Duo's Interpersonal Sundering, 1918–25

Despite the acrimony of their October 26, 1918 parting, the duo did manage to patch things up until after the marshal became Reich president in 1925. Indeed, Ludendorff's cast-aside first wife vividly recalled the "Old Gentleman's" visits during this period in *My Married Life*:

> Every year, Hindenburg used to come to us from Dietramzell. His visits were always days of rejoicing in which all our neighbors in Ludwigshöhe took part.… The arrival of the field marshal was ardently awaited.
>
> Along the whole road, flowers were thrown into his car so that only his head projected from the green mountain of blossom. A storm of cheers met him as he stepped out, and he had a kind word, a nod, or a friendly smile for all.
>
> It is impossible to give any idea of the pleasure his presence gave us, and he was always ready with the same good nature to put his signature at the foot of those cards and photographs that were pushed in front of him…

Wheeler-Bennett noted in *Wooden Titan* that, after his election as Reich president, however, the following occurred:

> The field marshal was no longer a private person.… The Chancellor … Dr Luther … protested against Hindenburg's visit at Ludwigshöhe, and demanded its cancellation on political grounds.
>
> Ludendorff foamed with rage: he felt himself deeply wounded. I had seldom seen him in such a state! He had always insisted: "Come what may, in the eyes of the world, Hindenburg and I must always stand together, and be and remain the pattern of German loyalty and unity!"
>
> Now that ideal, too, was shattered.… Only a small circle was aware of the breach between them. The anniversary of Tannenberg came round, and with it the dedication of the Great War memorial.
>
> Then it became clear to all how matters stood between them. Ludendorff publicly refused to stand side by side with Hindenburg, and made his own appearance dependent on this condition.
>
> It was like a blow from a club, well aimed and delivered with full force—brutal, and with consequences that were duly taken into account.

KHQ Spa, Belgium, 1918

General H.Q. had previously been moved to the Hotel Brittanique in the Belgian resort town of Spa, to which the Kaiser now left Berlin for good on the evening of October 29, 1918, never to see his imperial capital again, much to the distress of his last noble-born chancellor and first cousin, Prince Maximilian von Baden.

President Wilson had issued his famous Fourteen Points for peace in the world, and one of their major tenets was the overthrow of the Kaiser himself personally, preferably by the German people themselves. To these war-weary people late in 1918, Wilhelm II seemed to be the only obstacle in their way to a just peace in the world and the ending of the incessant fighting that had consumed thousands of German lives, both on the fighting fronts and at home. In this, Hindenburg stood alone, without the fired Ludendorff to blame.

Revolution at Kiel! October 29, 1918

The very night that the Kaiser left Reich Capital Berlin for Spa, his beloved Imperial Navy—created by him personally three decades before—mutinied at the great naval station at Kiel, following their Russian counterparts at Kronstadt Naval Base, St Petersburg, the year before. Indeed, after the 1917 Russian Revolution had deposed Nicholas II, Russian soldiers in the trenches on the Eastern Front taunted the weary German soldiers there to, "Get rid of your Tsar!"

Now the German naval revolt continued into the 30th across all the Second Reich's other major port cities that were Imperial naval bases also. By November 5, 1918, Hamburg, Lubeck, Bremen, and Wilhelmshaven were all in the hands of Communist Soldiers' and Workers' Councils, something previously unheard of in the German Reich, or Royal Prussia before it.

By the 7th, virtually all German cities were in their hands as well, and the Reichstag issued an ultimatum to Prince Max: unless the Kaiser himself abdicated his throne peacefully by noon the next day, "They would walk out of the government and organize the revolutionaries." The event most dreaded by Wilhelm II for the past three decades had now, indeed, come to pass. Prince Max telegraphed the grim news to the Kaiser at Spa, but the latter refused to go.

The German Revolution Spreads

At midday, the Socialists—long the Kaiser's sworn enemies—left the government in unison, while the Bavarian monarchy of the Wittelsbach dynasty was overthrown as well. To this, the Kaiser proclaimed to his generals at Spa that he would personally lead his troops back to Berlin from the Western Front to restore order at home.

A crown council conference was called, which included the Kaiser, the field marshal, Ludendorff's successor as first quartermaster general Wilhelm Groener, H.Q. Commandant Gen. Hans von Plessen, Count von der Schulenburg, the imperial crown prince's chief of staff, Baron von Grünau, and Lt Col. Niemann.

Once more—this time in tears—Hindenburg remained silent, and thus it remained for Gen. Groener to tell the Kaiser that he must in the end abdicate. Meanwhile, voices were growing louder and more both in Berlin and in the Allied capitals for the abdication from the throne and trial as war criminals of the Kaiser and of his designated successor, a fact that remained fully un-grasped as late as early November 1918, in the very last weeks of the Great War.

In the end, the Hohenzollern Dynasty could have been saved to still rule Germany today as a democratic, constitutional monarchy on the British model, if both the Kaiser and the crown prince had resigned together in favor of one of his brothers, or for a regency for one of his own sons, and/or another of the Kaiser's grandsons.

They did not, however, and thus the German Majority Social Democratic Party at Berlin proclaimed their joint ouster, with the establishment of an illegal republic. To their credit, none of the crown prince's five brothers tried to usurp his right of succession, nor their father's throne either.

The final blow came from von Hindenburg himself to the Kaiser thus: "I cannot accept the responsibility of seeing the Kaiser hauled to Berlin by insurgent troops and delivered over as a prisoner to the Revolutionary government! I must advise Your Majesty to abdicate, and proceed to Holland!"

The emperor shot back at him: "Do you think that I am afraid to remain with my troops?"

To which Hindenburg replied: "The Army and the troops are no longer behind Your Majesty! There are no loyal troops left! Would to God, Your Majesty, that it were otherwise!" Taking his leave of Wilhelm II, Hindenburg would never see his Kaiser again, not bothering once to visit him in exile over the course of the next fifteen years, it should be noted.

The Kaiser repaired in exile for good on November 10, 1918 to nearby neutral Holland, while his eldest son and now deposed heir spent five lonely years of exile as well on the barren Dutch Isle of Wieringen in the Zuider Zee before being allowed to return home in 1923.

At Amerongen in Holland, the Kaiser signed his Act of Abdication, thus ending 217 years of continuous Hohenzollern rule, the dynasty passing into history. Hindenburg was in large measure responsible for it: "The Kaiser made him a field marshal, and he betrayed the Kaiser!"

Ludendorff's Unachieved Vow

Continued the first Mrs. Ludendorff's postwar recollections: "After the Revolution, Ludendorff repeatedly declared, 'The greatest blunder of the Revolutionaries was to leave *us* all alive! If I once get back to power, there will be no quarter! I should hang up Ebert, Scheidemann, and the comrades with a clear conscience, and watch them dangle!'" It never happened, not even under the also bellicose Nazis later on: the "November Criminals" mostly survived.

Ludendorff as Fugitive, 1918–19

"Ludendorff decided to escape, and left the house under cover of night with a false beard and blue spectacles, after having formally acquainted Ebert with his intention"—the very man he had vowed to hang.

"The next few days he spent in Potsdam—near his brother—since much had to be settled before the general could leave for Denmark," the same destination later taken by Capt. Goering after him: "In spite of his disguise, he was recognized during the crossing when already on the steamer, by a naval officer who communicated his discovery to the captain."

"Consequently, he did not succeed in reaching Copenhagen unobserved, and found himself after a few days the target of all eyes…. He decided to retire to Sweden," again, just like Goering later.

From there, the gruff Ludendorff sent his wife a letter, revealing another side of this bluff soldier: "My Dear Wife: My heart was torn at leaving you, and having to leave you alone, and what made me saddest of all was the memory of my hard words to you shortly before I left. My own wife, we shall see each other again, and I will be different to you! I love you, and there seems no end to my misery.... I love you! Your own husband."

Crown Prince Rupprecht of Bavaria

"In his hand, the marshal's staff was more than just an ornament!" it was said of Bavaria's heir to the throne, Crown Prince Rupprecht, who both served a Kaiser and frightened a future Nazi Führer.

The noted German author Blohm referred to Rupprecht as "A man of simple tastes who was a great soldier and a powerful leader." Even his testy battlefield superior and later critic Ludendorff said of Rupprecht that "He is a man who takes his rank and his military task very seriously. With the help of his General Staff, he was able to master its demands the way a great leader should."

Bongard described Rupprecht as "A man of imposing features and presence ... without doubt the ablest and most professional of the three German Princely army group commanders..."

Nor was Rupprecht afraid to speak his mind in the highest circles of government, and also at general headquarters, as when, in 1917, he warned, "Return Poland to Russia, or we will lose the war!"

Indeed, even by the autumn of 1916, he was advocating "A peace without victory" and "The renunciation of all conquests, to gain a peace of understanding," thus revealing a bent for statesmanship even after he had achieved his own craft's highest award.

This was his marshal's baton from the hands of the man whom even the Kaiser referred to as "the field marshal," Paul von Hindenburg, on July 23, 1916. Rupprecht's promotion became official the following August 1, 1916, the same date that his royal uncle, Prince Leopold of Bavaria, received his marshal's baton also. More to the cutting point, the German crown prince was never awarded a like staff.

Both Rupprecht and his august uncle hailed from the twelfth-century South German ruling House of Wittelsbach dynasty, whose first monarch had been King Otto I. But for the loss of World War I by Germany, most likely Crown Prince Rupprecht would have succeeded to the very same throne as well, but it was not to be.

The crown prince was a great grandson of King Ludwig I, who had abdicated in 1848 during that year's liberal revolution and had been succeeded by his son, Maximilian II, who died in 1864, when his unstable son, aged eighteen, ascended the Bavarian throne as King Ludwig II.

When the latter drowned under mysterious circumstances at the Starnberg Lake on June 13, 1886, Ludwig I's second son, Luitpold, took over (Ludwig's younger brother, Otto, had long been mentally ill), becoming King Ludwig III on November 5, 1913, reigning until the 1918 Revolution. His son was thus the Crown Prince Rupprecht of our saga.

The latter was born on May 18, 1869, the son of an Austrian princess as well. On August 8, 1886, after being both privately tutored and graduating from grammar school,

Rupprecht was appointed a second lieutenant with the Infantry Lifeguard Regiment, and he would eventually serve in all three branches of the military services of the day, including cavalry and artillery as well.

In 1889—the year of Cpl. A. Hitler's birth in neighboring Austria—Rupprecht began his university studies in both Munich (his familial capital) and the Imperial City of Berlin at rival Prussia and returned to later serious military studies. These included strategy at the general staff level, the leadership of troops in battle, and combat tactics, working his way up in rank until in 1906 he was named general of infantry and 1st Army commander (aged thirty-five).

Besides all thing martial, Rupprecht's hobbies were art and travel, visiting Savoyard Italy, Syria, Palestine, Egypt, Greece, England, Sweden, India, Ceylon, Java, China, and Japan, authoring a trio of published books on his trips in 1906, 1922, and 1923. His military memoirs—also in three volumes—were published in 1929 as *My Wartime Diary*.

He was married twice, first to Princess Marie Gabrielle, also from the House of Wittelsbach, but she died after only eleven years of marriage. The crown prince remarried in 1917 to Princess Antonia, daughter of Grand Duke Wilhelm of Luxembourg, a state occupied by the German Army at the very start of the Great War in August 1914.

By then, Rupprecht was already a colonel general, and he was asked to lead the 6th Army, with his first chief of staff being Maj. Gen. Krafft von Dellmensingen, who was then the Bavarian Army chief of staff also. The two men commanded 200,000 soldiers.

In 1914, each German Army corps comprised two infantry divisions apiece of 17,500 officers and enlisted men, plus 4,000 horses, seventy-two guns, and twenty-four machine guns. Corps troops included heavy artillery and field hospitals, as well as bakeries, bridging trains, and supporting logistical support columns.

The Reserve Corps did not have heavy artillery, while a reserve division possessed but half the number of normal infantry field guns. A cavalry corps comprised two or three horse divisions, each with 5,200 officers and troopers, 5,600 mounts, motor transport, twelve guns, six machine guns, and field radio units.

The overall Imperial German Army in 1914 boasted 2 million soldiers in eight army commands, plus reserve forces, raising the figure to 3.8 million men. On its southern flank—invading both Belgium and Luxembourg—were the 6th and 7th Armies under Crown Prince Rupprecht, tasked with holding the enemy on their line.

Of their commander, Tuchman asserted that he was "Erect and good looking in a sensible way.… He came from a less eccentric branch of his family … and was descended from the Prince Rupert [of the Palatinate] who had fought for King Charles I of England against Cromwell" in the English Civil War.

"In memory of King Charles, white roses decorated the Palace of Bavaria every year on the anniversary of the Regicide," but the Bavarian Army was considered to be thoroughly German.

"They were barbarians!" asserted French Gen. Auguste Dubail (1851–1934) after the first days of 1914 combat, having sacked their billeting houses, ripping up chairs and beds, ransacking closets, tearing down curtains, and smashing already trampled furniture in their wake, looting as well both ornaments and utensils. "These—as yet—were only the habits of troops sullenly retiring—Lorraine was to see worse!"

Rupprecht's initial orders to stay put—protecting the Reich and the German speaking Czech Sudetenland from a possible French invasion—irked the Bavarian crown prince, who was champing at the bit to assault the French. He had little patience with the apparent timidity of general H.Q., which was mainly concerned about the proper execution of the Schlieffen Plan.

Noted Asprey in *The German High Command*: "After several skirmishes, the 6th Army was ordered to withdraw on 15 August 1914 from the impending French attack. The French actually came out of their fortifications, but only slowly followed the withdrawing Germans"—a retreat that Rupprecht felt would demoralize his men if allowed to continue.

"Either let me attack or issue definite orders!" he yelled into a staff telephone. He got his wish, and on August 20–21, 1914, his 6th Army and the 7th then under former German War Minister Gen. Josiah von Heeringen defeated the French with a surprise assault in that very same Lorraine as above.

The battle raged across a front 80 kilometers wide. By evening, the French 2nd Army was overrun, and Moltke agreed to let Rupprecht continue his attack to Nancy, forcing part of the French forces back across their border thereby.

The crown prince had won his point with general H.Q. by telling his superiors: "The French have had huge losses in fruitless attacks on our defensive positions at Sarrebourg and Morhange: an absolute massacre! We must exploit this success! I agree that it is a good thing to pin down the French right wing, but it would be even better to destroy it!"

Still, despite Rupprecht's battle lust, the French under both Gen. Dubail and Gen. Noel de Castelnau (1851–1944) brought the plucky Bavarian's assault to a standstill. Still later, his armies—along with all the other German ground forces—would be stalled again in the overall drive on Paris after First Marne.

As a result, Crown Prince Rupprecht moved his headquarters to St Quentin, during which heavy fighting again took place, this time with the British. The Race to the Sea Battle of Arras occurred during October 1–13, 1914, followed by the Battle of Lille-Ostend, until the enemy flooding of a canal again halted the forces of Rupprecht.

More severe fighting occurred over several months until a stable new German front could be established and held.

During the year 1915, another Battle of Arras took place, as well as the Battle of the Loretto Heights, during which an enemy breakthrough was halted by the German defenders, with heavy losses on both sides.

During the Verdun mauling, the Bavarian heir to the throne stood opposite the BEF. Rupprecht's then chief of staff, Gen. Hermann von Kuhl, was summoned to Berlin to appear before Gen. von Falkenhayn,

Informed of a coming enemy offensive, Kuhl was duly warned of an "impromptu British riposte north of Arras," after which a counterattack of eight German divisions would occur in mid-February 1916. Von Kuhl refuted this assertion as nonsense, noting the alleged complete unpreparedness of the new "Kitchener Armies." Falkenhayn repeated this again to Kuhl on February 11, 1916, adding that he hoped the expected British assaults "Would bring movement into the war once again."

When he heard this, a miffed Crown Prince Rupprecht scoffed: "Gen. Falkenhayn was himself not clear as to what he really wanted, waiting for a stroke of luck that would lead to a favorable solution" on the stagnant, stalemated Western Front.

Rupprecht correctly assessed that the infamous Battle of Verdun would become a bloody maw for both sides, and hardly the decisive victory for them that the embattled Wilhelmine Second Reich and its author sought.

Using his good graces at the imperial court at Berlin with the Kaiser, Crown Prince Rupprecht helped in the general overthrow of the Kaiser's favorite von Falkenhayn. Thus came the eastern duo to the fore, and with Ludendorff postwar, Rupprecht won a later celebrated libel suit in court.

Of his commands, Bongard notes that he "Remained with the 6th Army in Lorraine during the" (September–November 1914) "Race to the Sea" and for most of the two ensuing years of war; was appointed commander of the northern army group comprising the 2nd, 4th, 6th, and 17th Armies in early 1917; and in that position, he exercised overall direction of the German responses to British attacks at Third Ypres/Passchendaele (July 31 to December 7, 1917) and Cambrai (November 20–30, 1917).

Part of Rupprecht's task was to construct the latter famed Hindenburg Line defensive positions. This was an attempt—codenamed Operation Alberich—to shorten the German-held area in front of the later Hindenburg Line so that less troops would be necessary to hold the area. Overall, it was a program of destruction designed by Ludendorff that included houses demolished, wells poisoned, trees cut down, booby traps and mines planted, and also large segments of the Allied populations evacuated. At first, Rupprecht determined that he would resign over what he considered to be a monstrous order, then, on second thought—because he was who he was in wartime—he merely refused to sign the order himself. Thus, responsibility was averted.

In July 1917, the flinty heir to Munich's throne demanded in conference that Ludendorff should stick with his military knowledge and avoid politics. By September 1917, the Bavarian crown prince was also calling privately for the evacuation of Belgium to placate English fears of a later German seaborne invasion of the British Isles, and also perhaps to help save the Hohenzollern dynasty thereby.

In 1917, there occurred the Third Battle of Arras along with the Battle of Flanders, called later by its German survivors "The most difficult of all defensive battles. The point of the Battle of Flanders was to hit the (German Navy) submarine base of Zeebrugge, and that this failed was in part credited to Crown Prince Rupprecht."

In February 1918—observing events unfolding on the Eastern Front from afar—Rupprecht warned against the joining of Litauen, Kurland, and other parts of Russia with Prussia politically. When his advice was ignored, Rupprecht wrote in a letter the following September of "The ostrich-like attitude—a lie in itself!—that was already noticeable in the politics of the prewar years, and is the reason for our military defeat."

"Everyone who speaks up against this is [branded] a pessimist and a weakling," he noted of the doves like himself within the German Empire's ruling strata, attests Blohm.

Militarily, Rupprecht was equally as outspoken as the spring 1918 offensive preparations were being made on the Western Front, arguing that there should be a push toward Hazebrouck-Calais. He asserted that, if it would have been possible to cut off the French, Belgian, and English troops who were standing along that east-west line, pushing them against the sea, as well as to gain the west coast from Ostend to Le Havre, it would have meant the fall of the British and the overall Entente alliance.

At the November 11, 1917 Mons Conference—ironically—there had first been discussed Ludendorff's coming spring 1918 grand assault. Present among others were the first quartermaster general, Rupprecht's chief of staff Gen. von Kuhl, von der Schulenburg for Imperial Crown Prince Wilhelm, and Col. Georg Wetzel to decide both the date and place of the initial attack, to be codenamed overall Michael.

As a reflection of how thoroughly the various chiefs of staff dominated their individual commanding officers, not a single one of them was in conference. It is doubtful that the presence of Rupprecht could have staved off the ultimate defeat. His influence could have meant more limited offensives that might have prolonged the war into either 1919 or 1920, or ended it sooner—say, in March 1918—without the gross casualties on both sides that it produced instead.

Once the overall series of attacks got underway, Rupprecht's Army Group attacked at the Somme River during March 21 to April 4, 1918, launching as well the Lys Offensive of April 9–29, 1918 next.

Recalled Asprey in *The German High Command*, later: "After the withdrawal from the Marne, the first step was taken, and what had begun there four years ago as a victory march was now again become a defeat. Another attack of the troops in Flanders had to be discontinued after 18 July 1918, leading to the 'Black Days of Compiegne.'" On August 15, 1918, Rupprecht expressed his utter amazement regarding their newest enemy on the European battlefields: "The Americans are multiplying in a way we never dreamed of!… At present, there are already 31 American divisions in France!" This led even the normally bellicose Ludendorff to lament to von Kuhl on September 30, 1918, "We cannot fight against the entire world!"

In late October 1918, Rupprecht wrote to the new and last Imperial Chancellor Prince Max of Baden at Berlin:

> Our troops are exhausted.… In general, the infantry of a division can be treated as equivalent to one or two battalions, and in certain cases, as only equal to two or three companies.… In certain armies, 50% of the guns are without horses.
>
> The morale of the troops has suffered seriously, and their power of resistance diminishes daily. They surrender in hordes, whenever the enemy attacks, and plunderers infest the districts around the bases.
>
> We have no more prepared lines, and no more can be dug. There is a shortage of fuel for the trucks, and when the Austrians desert us—and we get no more petrol from Rumania— two months will put a stop to our aviation!

Thus asserted the soldier who in 1914 had taken 12,000 enemy prisoners and fifty guns in his first battle. He was right: within a month, the overall German war effort collapsed, as well as all of the Second Reich's dynasties in their wake on the home front. He ended the war by executing a skilled combat withdrawal through occupied Belgium against sustained and heavy British attacks during August to November 1918.

Crown Prince Rupprecht was now only an illustrious, unemployed former army group leader, a crownless prince without a future throne after the overthrow of his father at Munich.

Two of his former staff officers would find fame in the next world war, however: Col. Gen. Franz Halder as chief of the general staff and Field Marshal Wilhelm Ritter von Leeb, both under the aegis of former 6th Army Group Cpl. A. Hitler.

GFM Duke of Württemberg Albrecht, the Third Royal Heir Bearing a Baton

Albrecht Maria Alexander Philipp Josef von Württemberg (December 23, 1865 to October 31, 1939) lived to see Poland fall twice to German arms, during both world wars. He began his Great War service as the victorious commander of the German 4th Army at the August 1914 Battle of the Ardennes, then took part in the climactic First Battle of the Marne River before its transfer that October to Flanders to wage the First Battle of the Yser River.

He commanded at its second battle as well, overseeing the introduction of poison gas in large-scale combat for the first time ever in warfare. In February 1917, he was honored with the command of Army Group Albrecht on the southern part of the overall Western Front until the war ended.

His father, the king of Württemberg, died in October 1917, making Grand Duke Albrecht heir apparent to the throne, but it was done away with in the German Revolution of November 1918.

When his cousin, the abdicated King Wilhelm II, died on October 21, 1921, the grand duke became titular head of the dynasty. He died at Castle Altshausen, with his son succeeding him as dynastic pretender.

Gen. Max von Gallwitz, a Veteran Commander on Fronts Both East and West

Max Karl Wilhelm von Gallwitz (May 2, 1852 to April 18, 1937) served with great distinction in important combat commands on both of the Great War's major fronts—east and west.

He started 1914 as C.O. of the Guards Reserve Corps in the West, where he took Namur, but he was very soon transferred east to the eastern duo's new 8th Army Command in Prussia, where in 1915, he earned promotion to the command of Army Group Gallwitz, 12th Army. Fighting with Mackensen's 11th Army—and in command of Litzmann—Gen. Gallwitz succeeded the Kaiser's favorite Hussar marshal late in 1915 as he joined the Gallant August to conquer Serbia.

The year 1916 found Gallwitz returned to the west, where he fought the BEF at the Battle of the Somme River as commanding officer of both the 2nd Army and Army Group Gallwitz Somme, which included the 1st German Army.

During 1916–18, Gen. von Gallwitz was C.O. of the western 5th Army, famously fighting the new American Army at the Battle of St Mihiel. After the war, Gallwitz was an elected Reichstag deputy during 1920–24 from the new German National People's Party of the right. He published two postwar volumes of memoirs: the 1929 *My Leadership in the World War 1914–16*, followed in 1932 by *Experiences in the West 1916–18*.

Born a Silesian at Breslau, Gen. von Gallwitz died at the age of eighty-four on April 18, 1937 rather far from home, at Naples in Fascist Italy.

Gen. Max von Hausen, Victim of First Marne

Max Clemens Lothar Baron von Hausen (December 17, 1846 to March 19, 1922) was the initial commander of the German 3rd Army during the 1914 Battles of the Frontiers, Charleroi, and the Marne River, being relieved that September after that catastrophic defeat for German arms.

By title, von Hausen's 3rd Army command was the Royal Saxon Army mobilized under the German forces that summer of 1914, wherein his men reportedly executed 600 residents of Dinant during the Battles of the Frontiers and Charleroi, including women and children. This was followed by the destruction of the French city of Reims that September 1914, but his fortunes changed during the Battle of First Marne wherein all three major German armies were beaten by the French. Finding one of his flanks exposed to the enemy, Gen. von Hausen ordered a retreat.

As with his boss, von Moltke, von Hausen was allegedly retired due to poor health, but never again received another combat command, dying postwar.

Col. Gen. Karl von Einem

Col. Gen. Karl von Einem (January 1, 1853 to April 7, 1934) commanded the German 3rd Army during the Great War after having prepared for the early fighting while Prussian Minister of War beforehand (1903–09), being succeeded by Gen. Josiah von Heeringen. Indeed, Col. Gen. von Einem was one of very few of the Kaiser's general officers to retain the same command during most of the actual fighting, as well as afterwards, from September 12, 1914 to January 30, 1919.

His first combat command in the west ensued when he succeeded Gen. Max von Hausen after First Marne in 1914. He then defeated the French Army's Champagne Marne attack of two separate periods in 1915, following which he led his forces in the entire trio of Battles of the Aisne River. During that fight's second struggle, von Einem held French Gen. Antoine's 4th Army fast as part of the overall Nivelle Offensive of April 16 to May 15, 1917, which led to the French commander's firing.

In the March 1918 Kaiser's Battle, Ludendorff chose von Einem to back his July 15–17, 1918 assault on the German eastern flank in the high casualty Champagne–Marne fighting. This was followed by heavy combat with the recently deployed AEF of U.S. Army Gen. John J. "Black Jack" Pershing in the Battle of the Meuse-Argonne over September 26 to November 11, 1918.

On November 10, 1918—the very day before the Armistice took effect—von Hindenburg relieved Imperial Crown Prince Wilhelm from his long command of Army Group CP, bestowing it instead on von Einem for its demobilization march back into the Second Reich. Col. Gen. von Einem retired from the army the next year, dying on April 7, 1934 at Mulheim, Germany.

Overall, the Allied 100 Days' Offensive lasted from August 8 to November 11, 1918, right up until the day of the Armistice that ended the fighting, and it started with the latest Battle of Amiens, drove the Germans effectively out of occupied Northern France and back behind their crumbling Hindenburg Line.

With the curtailment of the effectiveness of the failed Kaiser's Battle in July 1918, the new Allied Generalissimo French Army Gen. Ferdinand Foch ordered the onset of the long prepared Entente counteroffensive in response, the Second Battle of the Marne River. In consultation with his fellow army commanders, Foch agreed with Haig to strike again at the Somme as in 1916 with the BEF and also to heavily utilize for the first time the AEF of Gen. Pershing.

The open fields of French Picardy were considered good tank terrain, suitable for massive armored thrusts. The attack opened with a French component in the Battle of Montdidier on August 8, 1918, which included ten Entente divisions of BEF, French, Australian, and Canadian forces, boasting 500 tanks. This assault achieved complete surprise, with the Allies rampaging into the German rear areas, punching a hole 15 miles wide in the enemy lines south of the Somme River. This resulted in 330 artillery tubes taken and 17,000 POWs captured, plus an estimated 30,000 Germans killed and wounded.

After three days, the Germans retreated from the gains made during their own earlier attacks to the Hindenburg Line. On the 17th, the French began the Second Battle of Noyon, taking it twelve days later. Three days earlier, the Second Battle of Arras of 1918 also commenced, and the Second Battle of Bapaume saw the fall of that town on the 29th. The Australians crossed the Somme River on the 31st, crashing through the German lines during the Battle of Mont St-Quentin.

A pair of related Entente victories were garnered at the Battles of the Scarpe (August 26, 1918) and the Drocourt–Quéant Line (September 2, 1918), with the French in striking distance of the Hindenburg Line in the Battle of Savy-Dallon on the 10th. The French 10th Army saw it near Laon during the September 14, 1918 Battle of Vauxaillon.

Four days later came the turn of the BEF during the Battle of Épehy on the St-Quentin Canal, with the entire German defensive works about to be brought under direct attack along its full length from Cerny on the Aisne River to Arras.

Prior to Foch's main attack, the line's salients jutting out at both Havrincourt and St Mihiel fell during hard fighting on September 12, 1918, and more fell fifteen days later during the Battles of Épehy and the Canal of the North.

Foch launched what he called his Grand Offensive against the Hindenburg Line on September 26, 1918 in a series of inter-Allied struggles. These included the varied Battles of Somme-Py (September 26), Saint-Thierry (the 30th), Montfaucon (October 14–17), and Chesne (November 1, 1918). The main assault, though, commenced on September 29, during the Battle of St-Quentin Canal by Australians, British, and French in concert, and by October 5, the Aryan defense had been breached across a 19-mile-wide front. By the 8th, two full British armies smashed through the line during the Second Battle of Cambrai, at last forcing the shaken duo to admit even to themselves that the war was lost to Germany and had to be ended. In all, it took until October 17, 1918 for the vaunted but crumbling Hindenburg Line to be pierced at last. Gone were any further thoughts of it not falling until the spring of 1919.

Next, King Albert I of the Belgians launched his Army Group of mixed nationalities in the Fifth Battle of Ypres in Flanders. Now the German armies were retreating back through all the territory they had first taken in the summer and fall of 1914, conceding the loss as well of their Metz-Bruges rail line that was vital to their re-supply.

Meanwhile, on August 21, 1918, Field Marshal Haig had opened his own Battle of Albert, knocking the German 2nd Army rearward 34 miles and taking it the next day.

October was a month of routs for most German forces as well: on October 9, 1918, there began the Pursuit to the Selle, followed by the Battle of Courtrai on the 14th, that of Mont-d'Origny of the 15th, the Selle (17th), Lys and Escaut (20th), the Serre (also the 20th), Valenciennes (November 1), the Battles of the Sambre and Guise Rivers (both on the 4th), and that at Thiérache (the same day), the fighting of the last running up to the very minute of the Armistice occurring. Reportedly, the very last man to die was an American soldier from Baltimore, MD, USA, Henry Gunther.

For his magnificent victory over the Germans, Foch was awarded the baton of a marshal of France in August 1918 by French President Raymond Poincaré.

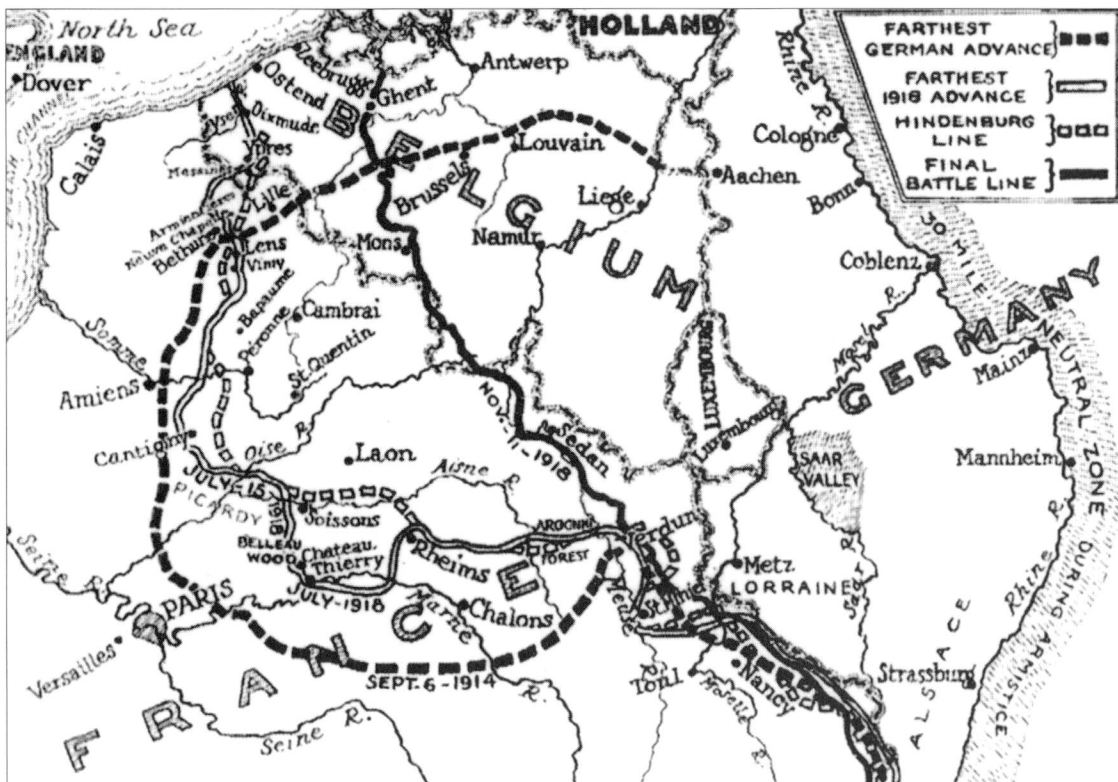

Perhaps the very best map extant of the rather compact German Western Front that included both Northeastern France and all of Belgium. In the final analysis, the Germans got no further until May 1940 under the leadership of the former Great War Corporal Hitler. (*Forward March, 1934, LC*)

This was and remains the very best view extant of German war minister—and later chief of general staff—General Erich von Falkenhayn, seen here in prewar Prussian blue and red collar. He served as chief of the general staff during September 1914 to August 1916. (*ASA*)

Clockwise from top left:

His successor as war minister in 1914 was General Josias von Heeringen. (*ASA*)

Heeringen was succeeded in turn by General Adolf Wild von Hohenborn. (*ASA*)

Hohenborn was succeeded by General Walter Reinhardt, who postwar faced off against a fractious Captain Hermann Goering over whether officers would wear epaulettes or stripes. In time, both got their way. Von Woyrsch took Radom on July 19, 1915 from the Russians. (*LC*)

The 1936 state funeral for the main German loser of the First Battle of the Marne River in September 1914, Colonel General Alexander von Kluck, whose monument marker appears here. (*Heinrich Hoffmann Albums, U.S. National Archives—hereafter HHA*)

"General von Kluck about August 23, 1914, made a desperate effort to 'run around the end' of the Allied line, interposed between it and Paris, and produce another [1870-style victory of Sedan]. He did not quite succeed, and immediately found himself in a very dangerous position during the Battle of the Marne. Thanks to [BEF CO] Sir John French's failure to rise to the occasion, Kluck was able by dint of desperate fighting against the gallant [French] Maunoury to make good his retreat to the Aisne" River, noted one period Great War source.

The general's widow is escorted onto the site, 1936. (*HHA*)

In the first thirty days of the war in 1914, the entire Austro–Hungarian Army proved to be a negligible factor, but on December 2, 1914, it finally captured the Serbian capital of Belgrade. Exulted Ludendorff later: "The storming of Kovno was an intrepid stroke!" and called von Eichhorn "an officer of brilliant intellectual qualities, and had trained his troops in an exemplary manner."

Standing at far left, Mrs von Kluck leads the mourners. (*HHA*)

The defeated German 3rd Army commander at First Marne was Colonel General Max Baron von Hausen, and he was succeeded by General Einem as a result. Initially, General von Hausen served as *aide-de-camp* to the king of Saxony (*ASA*)

Created field marshal by the Kaiser despite his own loss at First Marne was Colonel General Karl von Bülow, brother of Wilhelm's hated and fired 1909 Reich Chancellor Prince Bernhard von Bülow. Note the crossed baton shoulder boards seen here. He has been described by one of his more recent biographers as "a coldly arrogant and self-confident man." (*ASA*)

General Otto von Emmich, wearing Blue Max at the throat with Iron Cross medal and ribbon below, among other decorations. (*LC*)

The commanding officer of the German 10th Corps in the 2nd Army led by General von Bülow, General von Emmich's troops led the assault on Liege and the Meuse River in Belgium in August 1914. He here appears in the military kit of Hanover's 73rd Fusilier/Foot Regiment.

German Imperial Crown Prince Wilhelm seen here cracking a joke with officers and men during an Iron Cross award ceremony for the 1st Company, Bavarian Infantry (Bavarian King's Guard Regiment), during the Verdun campaign, July 7, 1916. (*ASA*)

"At Verdun … he found himself labeled The Butcher.… His armies won a significant victory on the Aisne [River] during the spring offensives of 1918, but he soon realized that defeat was likely to follow. He recommended a policy of retreat to Hindenburg and Ludendorff, but was firmly rebuffed," stated his sole biographer thus far in English, Klaus Jonas.

Right: Chief of staff to the imperial German crown prince, Colonel General Konstantin Schmidt von Knobelsdorf. (*LC*)

Asserted Ludendorff: "The year 1915 was to witness some terrific fighting!"

Below: Lt-General Hermann Josef von Kuhl (November 2, 1856 to November 4, 1958). (*LC*)

In 1914 von Kuhl was deemed to be "one of the most competent commanders in the Imperial German Army, retiring in 1919 to write a number of critically acclaimed essays on the Great War." In addition, General von Kuhl—a chief of staff to Bavarian Crown Prince Rupprecht during November 24, 1915 to November 11, 1918—was, also, "one of only five recipients … with both the military and peace class of the Blue Max." Indeed, von Kuhl was the man whom even the fired Ludendorff suggested to the Kaiser as his own replacement as first quartermaster general on October 26, 1918, but the spiteful Wilhelm II named General Groener instead. Von Kuhl's last command was, rather, as commander of General of Infantry of Army Group "A" during November 12, 1918 (named by Hindenburg) through January 11, 1919.

Of Gens. von der Marwitz and Litzmann, Ludendorff opined in his 1919 memoirs that "both were splendid soldiers and fearless leaders, who cared for their men."

The Hohenzollern motto was "Nothing without God," to which true believer Paul von Hindenburg also subscribed to the end of his life. Indeed, upon swearing in Hitler's first coalition cabinet on January 30, 1933, the Reich president intoned: "And now, gentlemen, forward with God!"

A large staff car is seen as a backdrop here as the crown prince (center, in left profile standing) shakes hands with a trio of staff officers at left, saluted by a sentry at present arms with rifle at far right and watched over by Hindenburg, third from right. (*DH*)

When Romania entered the war against the Central Powers in 1916, its army had 250,000 men to join the Allies' 10 million *versus* the Germans' 6 million, asserted Ludendorff.

The crown prince makes a roadside stop to shake hands with wounded soldiers of his army group on the Western Front at St Quentin, 1918. Note also the imperial crown on his car's rear license plate. (*LC*)

In 1918, the unthinkable happened, with a Socialist prime minister ordering Hindenburg to fire the crown prince as a German army group commander—and then having his order carried out!

Glückliches Neujahr!

Right: Incredibly to all who fought it, the Great War entered its third year in 1916, as the child hands a symbol of the hoped-for peace to a German (*left*) and an Austrian (*right*) soldier. It was not to be for two more years. "Happy New Year!" this period postcard proclaims.

Below: Saluting troops at a wintry 1916 roadside at Verdun, France, is the Kaiser (center, hand to helmet), accompanied by his son and heir, Imperial Crown Prince Wilhelm (second from right, wearing Death's Head-emblazoned fur busby cap. Note also that the greatcoats of both the Kaiser and his heir feature fur collars, while all the others do not. (*LC*)

Left: A *Punch* cartoon by Leonard Raven Hill, published April 12, 1916.

Flawed from its very inception in February 1916, the Battle of Verdun was never the martial success that von Falkenhayn, Wilhelm II, and Crown Prince Wilhelm all hoped it would be. It was suspended in stalemate that summer.

Below: The new German High Command, 1916. *From left to right:* Hindenburg, the Kaiser, Imperial Chancellor Theobald von Bethmann-Hollweg, King Ludwig III of Bavaria, and Ludendorff. By war's end, only Hindenburg would still remain in office of this stellar group. The two reigning monarchs wear black mourning bands, most likely for the late Kaiser Franz Josef I of Austria-Hungary. (*LC*)

King Leopold III (January 7, 1845 to October 18, 1921) "was the last King of Bavaria, reigning from 1913–18," when he was overthrown. His son and heir, Crown Prince Rupprecht, has been touted by his most recent biographer as "the most capable of the commanders of Royal blood."

Wartime front visit. *From left to right*: Wilhelm II, von Plessen, Hindenburg, and others. (*DH*)

Ludendorff called the Turkish C-in-C Enver Pasha in September 1916, "A true friend of Germany," with "sound military judgment." He also characterized Field Marshal Duke Albrecht of Württemberg (1865-1939) as "a real personality," and more military than the two crown princes as well.

Kaiser Wilhelm II inspects troops in captured Riga. In the background is the Museum of Art, 1917. (*LC*)

Above left: The Kaiser's last major ally to enter the war among the Central Powers was Tsar Ferdinand of Bulgaria, "festooned like a Christmas tree!" asserted Wilhelm II. (*LC*)

The German monarch in 1909 caused an international incident prewar by slapping "Foxy" Ferdinand on his behind, never apologizing for it, either. Called "Foxy" Ferdinand by his detractors—as well as by his major biographer—his sons referred to him rather as *le monarch*. On July 15, 1910, he and they became the first major royals in Europe to fly in a biplane, all by the same pilot on the same day, the French aviator *Monsieur* Delaminne, whom Ferdinand decorated with Bulgaria's Order of St Alexander.

Above right: The German emperor in the uniform of his latest and last wartime ally—that of a field marshal in the Royal Bulgarian Army, complete with crossed baton shoulder boards. (*LC*)

"Ferdinand I of Bulgaria [was] Europe's most disliked sovereign," it was alleged, by his foes. Meeting *Foxy* at Imperial HQ Castle Pless, Ludendorff found him to be, "Clever—but no soldier."

Each kitted out as field marshals in the other's armies, Wilhelm II (*left*) and Ferdinand meet at the latter's capital of Sofia in 1916, with "Foxy" seen clutching his ornate German baton on his lap. (*LC*)

Ferdinand reigned as Bulgarian tsar from October 5, 1908 to October 3, 1918, but also reigned prior to that as prince of Bulgaria from July 7, 1887 to October 5, 1908. Tsar Ferdinand (February 26, 1861 to September 10, 1948) outlived not only his ally the Kaiser, but also both of his sons. Tsar Ferdinand abdicated in favor of his eldest son, who became Tsar Boris III on October 3, 1918. Aside from ruling, Ferdinand was a world-recognized "author, botanist, traveler, entomologist, and philatelist." (*LC*)

Above, the Kaiser (left center) and Mackensen (right center) meet troops wearing the new 1916-35 'coal scuttle' helmets." (*ASA*)

In 1918, both rulers would abdicate their thrones, Ferdinand to live out exile on his German properties and Wilhelm in Holland, an ironic ending and twist to their long relationship. In addition to his titles regnal, Tsar Ferdinand held the political office of governor-general of Eastern Rumelia from July 7, 1887 to October 5, 1908. (*LC*)

His Majesty the German Emperor (*left*) orating to a subdued Bulgarian Prime Minister Vasil Radoslavov (1854–1929) at right. Note Wilhelm II's handy cold weather hood behind his overcoat's collar, as well as the crossed marshal's batons on his shoulder boards. (*ASA*)

German General Kurt von Morgen (*center*) renders a hand salute to Bulgarian Army officers at right in a snowstorm at Foscani. (*LC*)

The two allies fought well together for the final two years of the Great War. Ludendorff termed the "Vampire War" against Romania as "big attacks on all fronts of the battle front…. The battles then fought were among the most fiercely contested of the whole war … far exceeding all previous offensives in numbers of men and material."

Mud was the bane of all foot soldiers everywhere.

Ludendorff had high praise for many generals during the Great War, among them Bronsart, Kuhl, Below, Gallwitz, and Loßberg.

REALISATION

("When I went to Bulgaria I resolved that if there were to be any assassinations I would be on the side of the assassins."
STATEMENT BY FERDINAND.)

A cartoon from *Mr. Punch's history of the Great War*, Graves, 1919. How the Allies saw the top three Central Powers' rulers, as murderers all. (*LC*)

Regarding the successful campaign in Romania, Ludendorff asserted that "in the movement battles … German leadership … manifested its superiority.… A victory the laurels of which world history will award to the German soldier," but who afterward needed a rest and was utterly worn out.

Central Powers' martial cooperation on campaign, 1916. *From left to right*: Mackensen, unknown three men, Tappen, Seeckt, Crown Prince Boris of Bulgaria (King Boris during 1918–43), and Falkenhayn. (*LC*)

Together, they defeated the Romanian Army and stalemated those of Greece and the combined Western Allies in the Balkans until the very end of the war. Previously, von Falkenhayn had himself been chief of the German general staff during September 1914 to August 1916.

One persistent rumor that followed Mackensen to the end was that he was the bastard son of either Kaiser Wilhelm I or Emperor Friedrich III, and especially during World War I, the Black Hussar was embarrassed at having continually to deny this charge by his enemies.

Observing military operations underway in Romania are von Falkenhayn (*center*) and von Mackensen, the latter wielding his informal stick baton in right hand, 1916. (*LC*)

Mackensen is credited with achieving the great breakthrough of the Russian Front between Gorlice–Tarnów as well. After having awarded him all of Imperial Germany's top military decorations, a grateful Wilhelm II named a battle cruiser after him as well, but it was ordered scrapped after the war in 1922 under the Social Democratic Weimar Republic, nor did its successor the Nazi Third Reich reinstate it. As boys, Mackensen's three sons played with the Kaiser's six, and Hans-Georg von Mackensen allegedly became the lover of Prince August Wilhelm "Auwi" of Prussia, their affair causing the breakup of the latter's heterosexual marriage.

In command on his segment of the 1916 Romanian Front is Falkenhayn (fourth from right)—where he commanded the German 9th Army—with a coterie of both German and Austro-Hungarian officers as well. As in Serbia the year before, they won. (*LC*)

Von Mackensen's deadly lancers cross over. Truly, Napoleon of a century earlier would have felt at home in this operation. (*LC*)

With his piercing blue eyes and colorful, frogged uniform with bushy shako cavalryman's cap, von Mackensen figured prominently in the weekly cinema newsreels back home, but he made his share of martial errors also, such as attacking impetuously on occasion without artillery support, his men thus suffering bloody battlefield repulses, according to Goodspeed.

A wartime picture postcard of both German and Austrian Army troops (*left*) fighting together against the common foe (*right*) in the invaded Bukovina, 1916. (*LC*)

Notes one 1960s writer: "Von Mackensen conquered Serbia. A master strategist on offense, he was selected to direct the attack against Serbia in October 1915. Before Allied help could arrive, the Serbs were defeated, and were forced to withdraw" by sea to the Greek Island of Corfu.

Astride his white mount, von Mackensen made a dramatic triumphal entry into the fallen Romanian capital of Bucharest on December 6, 1916, an Austrian officer mounted at right. Von Falkenhayn was also responsible for this singular victory over this defeated Allied power. The marshal's informal stick baton rests across the pommel of his saddle. (*LC*)

Noted an earlier German-language biography: "Mackensen never talked negatively in public about Wilhelm II, but praised him as a talented and conscientious ruler with a political eye, thus sailing aboard the Imperial yacht *Hohenzollern* with His Majesty and Princess of Prussia Viktoria Luise."

Mackensen as the celebrated darling of the German home front press as the "Conqueror of Dobrudja" in September 1916. (*LC*)

Mackensen came very nearly to overshadowing the duo during that same year of their own joint glory of 1916. His rivals felt that the acclaim given von Mackensen was "excessive," especially his former subordinate in the Death's Head Hussars prewar, Imperial Crown Prince Wilhelm. Significantly, the duo never brought Mackensen to their Western Front. Prewar, the Kaiser named Mackensen as commander of the elite Death's Head Hussars Brigade at Danzig, of which both the imperial crown prince and princess were also members.

Über top of the Mackensen eagle family crest with plumed helmet is this inscription in old Germanic script type that reads: "We must and can take care that our youth are in the history of Prussia, and learn of the great things done by their fathers and brothers in arms in the World War. Again and again we have to tell them: 'Do not forget the loyal deeds,' and again and again remind them how much was robbed from us." The passage below the helmet reads, "From the exhibit, *The Writing of Germans*, Writing Museum Rudolf Blankertz, Berlin; this exhibit traveled all over Germany." (*LC*)

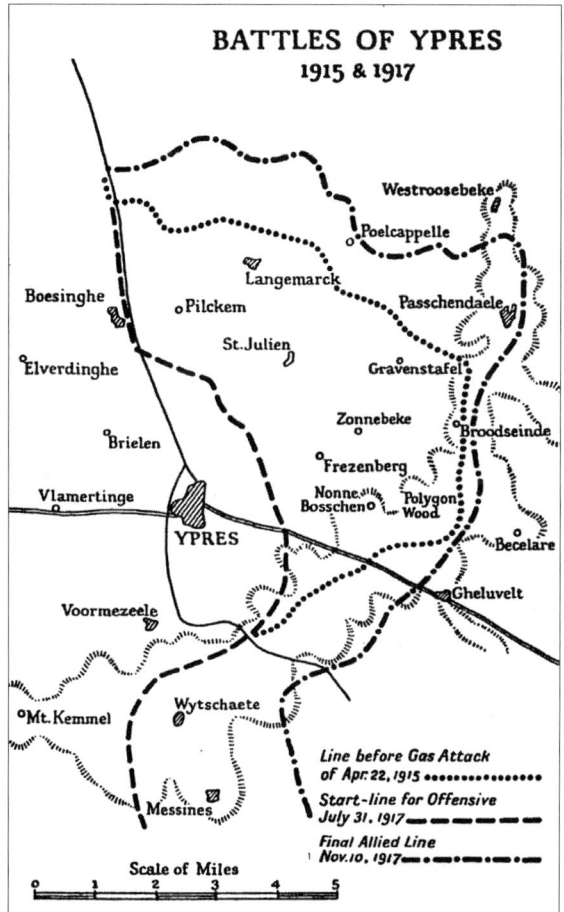

BATTLES OF YPRES
1915 & 1917

The Battles of Ypres took place on the embattled Western Front in both 1915 and 1917, as depicted here. (*LC*)

As correctly noted by Ludendorff, "The enemy's aim was our destruction," *versus* German "internal politics and thoughts of self" that undermined the domestic war effort within the Second Reich: "This meant the ruin of our country." (*LC*)

The Kaiser's aged Austrian fellow monarch and ally, Kaiser Franz Josef I, who also ruled during the earlier reigns of Wilhelm II's father and grandfather. (*LC*)

Most of the German officer corps saw their partners at Vienna as being chained to a corpse. During 1916–17, the duo believed that "Unless we got a peace that safeguarded the existence of our country, the war would be lost," as it was in the end.

Franz Josef's successor was Kaiser Karl I (August 17, 1887 to April 1, 1922) left, seen here with Army Commander Baron Kovess at right, 1917. (*LC*)

Beatified by Pope John Paul II in 2004—long after Karl I's death in 1922—he was declared blessed by the Catholic Church for his attempts to conclude peace during the latter two years of the Great War, 1916–18. The great nephew of the late Franz Josef, it was under the reign of Kaiser Karl I that the rule of the House of Habsburg ended after 642 years. Karl had a pair of titles used simultaneously: Karl I of Austria and Karl IV of Hungary; as such, he was both the last Austrian emperor as well as the final Hungarian king. Ruling during 1916–18, he left his thrones, but never formally abdicated *à la* his wartime ally the Kaiser. In April 1919 he was formally dethroned by the Austrian Parliament and exiled to Switzerland. Karl spent the remaining years of his life attempting to restore the monarchy. He made two attempts to reclaim the Hungarian throne in 1921; both failed due to a lack of support from Hungary's regent Miklós Horthy. Karl was exiled for a second time to the Portuguese island of Madeira, where he soon fell ill and died of respiratory failure in 1922.

The future Austrian Kaiser—the last in the ruling line of the Habsburg dynasty—at his wedding to Princess Zita of Parma of October 21, 1911, the final Austrian empress. She carried on secret peace negotiations with France via her brother, an officer in the rival, and enemy, French Army. The result was the collapse of her ruling house. Kaiser Franz Josef I third from right. (*LC*)

Archduke Karl—not yet Kaiser, but an Austrian commander (center left)—chats with von Falkenhayn (center right), with German Army Colonel Hans Hesse standing at far right, hands on sword pommel. Note also the sentry to the left of Colonel Hesse, rifle borne at shoulder arms. (*LC*)

Prior to becoming Kaiser, Karl was promoted a field marshal by Franz Josef I as commander of the Austrian 20th Army Corps, then led an army on the Eastern Front against both the Russian and Romanian Armies in 1916.

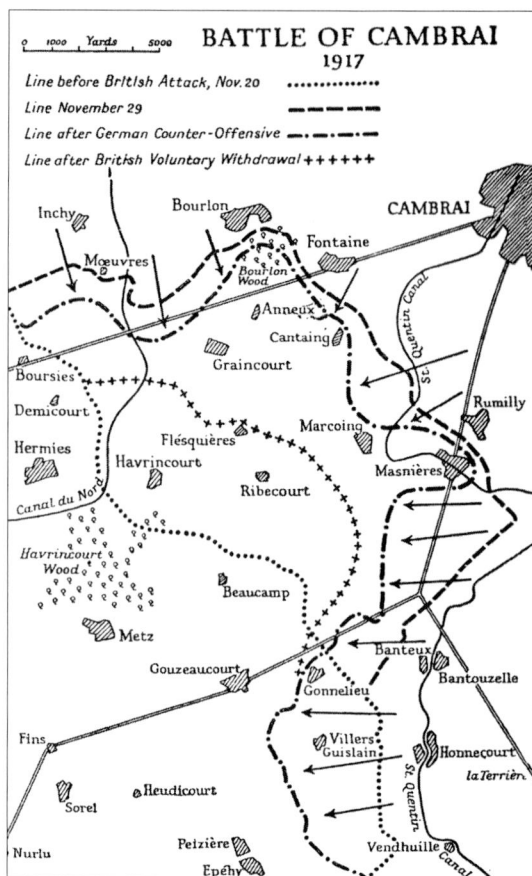

BATTLE OF CAMBRAI
1917

Line before British Attack, Nov. 20 ••••••••••
Line November 29 ━ ━ ━ ━
Line after German Counter-Offensive ▬•▬•▬•▬
Line after British Voluntary Withdrawal + + + + +

Above left: Bavarian Army General Konrad Kraft von Dellmensingen, wearing distinctive Royal Bavarian collar insignia, entirely different from those of both the Prussian and German Imperial Armies. (*LC*)

On November 11, 1918, Kaiser Karl released his officials from their oaths of allegiance to him, departing as well from the imperial castle Schönbrunn at Vienna for castle Eckartsau east of the capital the same day as the Western Front Armistice that ended the war overall. Two days later, the king of Hungary released his officials at Budapest from their loyalty to him as well.

Above right: The 1917 Western Front Battle of Cambrai gave the Germans a nasty surprise when masses of Allied armored vehicles attacked the unready Ludendorff. (*LC*)

Ludendrof lamented of the politicians at home: "They made our people yearn for peace—without making the enemy ready for it!"

Ludendorff's armor and artillery expert—Colonel Max Hermann Bauer (January 31, 1869 to May 6, 1929) introduced the first tank in the German Army in May 1917, but it "was too large and unwieldy; thus few were produced. So they had to use captured enemy tanks."

"Krupp and Daimler designed a light tank, but production was not authorized until French light tanks showed their value, consequently they could not be available until April 1919," when the Great War was already over for six months. In their final attacks of the war in the autumn of 1918, the French and Americans led their assaults with massed armored formations. Right from the very start, therefore, Churchill had beaten the duo in the technically critical aspect of tank warfare, a lead that was never overtaken by Imperial Germany.

German infantry swarm to the assault of an Allied tank in motion on the Western Front. The original Allied propaganda caption of 1919 read, "German attack on a British tank, drawn by F. Martania for *The Sphere,* London, *The New York Herald* Co." (*LC*)

Recalled Ludendorff of his relationship with Hindenburg during the war years: "The field marshal permitted me to participate in his glory.… He always agreed with my views," thus slyly tying the silent older soldier to the ultimate defeats of 1918 as well as the victories prior.

Kaiser Wilhelm II with Kaiserin Auguste Viktoria/Dona, his brother Prince Heinrich of Prussia and wife Princess Irene on their way to church on the Kaiser's birthday, January 27, 1917, at Bad Homburg. (*ASA*)

When his wife visited imperial general HQ throughout the war, the Kaiser's subordinates were outraged. Lamented Ludendorff in 1919, the German home front peaceniks, "Sought to drive a wedge between the field marshal and myself. They dared not attack him, so they … struck at me.… He personified the good principle, I the evil one."

Imperial Chancellor von Bethmann-Hollweg, a civilian in uniform. (*LC*)

Ludendorff opined in 1919 that "those who spread such notions should at least have made him jointly responsible for all the alleged mischief.... The reputation of the field marshal stands secure enough in the hearts of the German people."

Recalled Ludendorff of the duo's daily regimen, at least at the start of their tenure in late 1916, "At noon, we made our report to His Majesty the Emperor," and thus the Kaiser was in overall control of the far-flung wartime battlefronts to that extent.

THE SCRAPPER SCRAPPED.

A cartoon from *Punch* by Leonard Raven Hill, published July 25, 1917.

The imperial chancellor's many political and military enemies combined to have the Kaiser fire him, as cartooned here. The "scrap" refers to his notorious 1914 assertion that the signed 1839 treaty between Germany and England over Belgium was nothing more than "a scrap of paper," without merit; the Second Reich invaded neutral Belgium anyway, bringing the British Empire into the war against the Central Powers.

The fired chancellor's immediate predecessor of 1909 had been former War of 1870–71 cavalry hussar Prince Bernhard von Bülow. For once, the duo failed to have its way with the usually pliant Kaiser, who refused ever to name "Dear Bernhard" as imperial chancellor again.

On his seventieth birthday, on October 2, 1917, Hindenburg (*center*) visited the wounded at a field hospital in the west. (*LC*)

Whined Ludendorff in 1919: "Mine was a life of work … I lived only for the war for four years and was in the office at 6–7 AM to late at night," as he passionately wanted to be!

A cartoon from *Punch* by F. H. Townsend.

Regarding the wartime canard that thousands of Russians were driven into the Tannenberg marshes to die was debunked postwar by Ludendorff himself thus: "That they there perished is a myth! No marsh was to be found anywhere near it!"

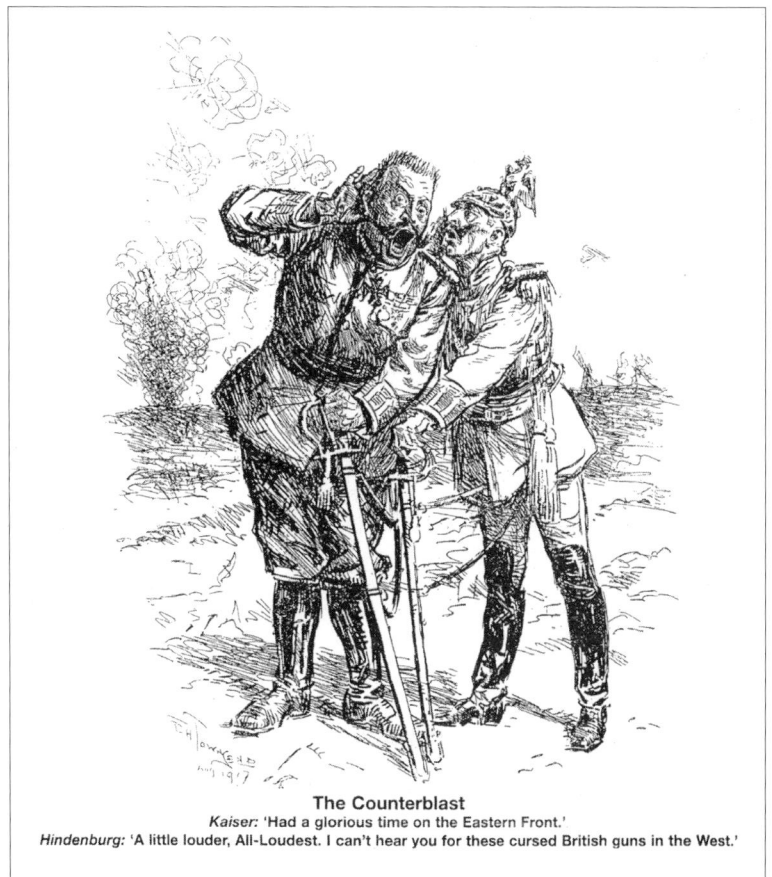

The Counterblast
Kaiser: 'Had a glorious time on the Eastern Front.'
Hindenburg: 'A little louder, All-Loudest. I can't hear you for these cursed British guns in the West.'

A Punch cartoon by Bernard Partridge, published June 13, 1917.

British and other Allied cartoonists delighted in skewering the top two members of the German Imperial House of Hohenzollern, as here. The "contemptible" remark made by Wilhelm II referred to the small professional British Army of 1914 before its vast expansion under Lord Kitchener. The same occurred during 1917–18 with that of the United States of America.

Aside from "Little Willy," the crown prince's other nickname was "The Greyhound," due to his slender figure that women found attractive all his life.

A WORD OF ILL OMEN.

Crown Prince (to Kaiser, drafting his next speech). "FOR GOTT'S SAKE, FATHER, BE CAREFUL THIS TIME, AND DON'T CALL THE AMERICAN ARMY 'CONTEMPTIBLE.'"

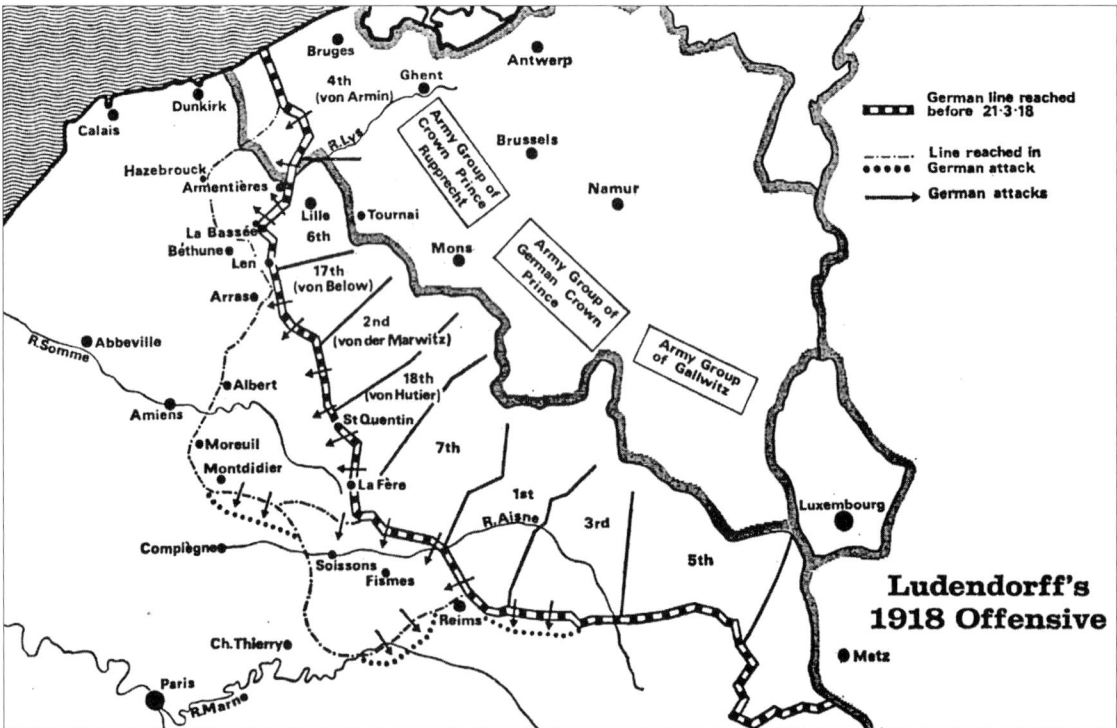

Above and top left of next page: Campaign maps of the 1918 Western Front German Operation Michael/Kaiser's Battle series of five attacks designed by Ludendorff to crush the Allies before enough American help could arrive in France to turn the tide for good against the Second Reich. They failed. (*LC*)

Notes William Gillespie of *International Historic Films' Operation Michael* DVD film presentation: "Dubbed the Kaiser's Battle, the spring 1918 offensives were to consist of four major assaults code-named Michael, Georgette, Gneisenau, and Blücher–Yorck. The first and largest of these offensives—Operation Michael—was intended to strike the BEF along the Somme River, with the goal of cutting it off from the French to the south."

GERMAN OFFENSIVES
1918

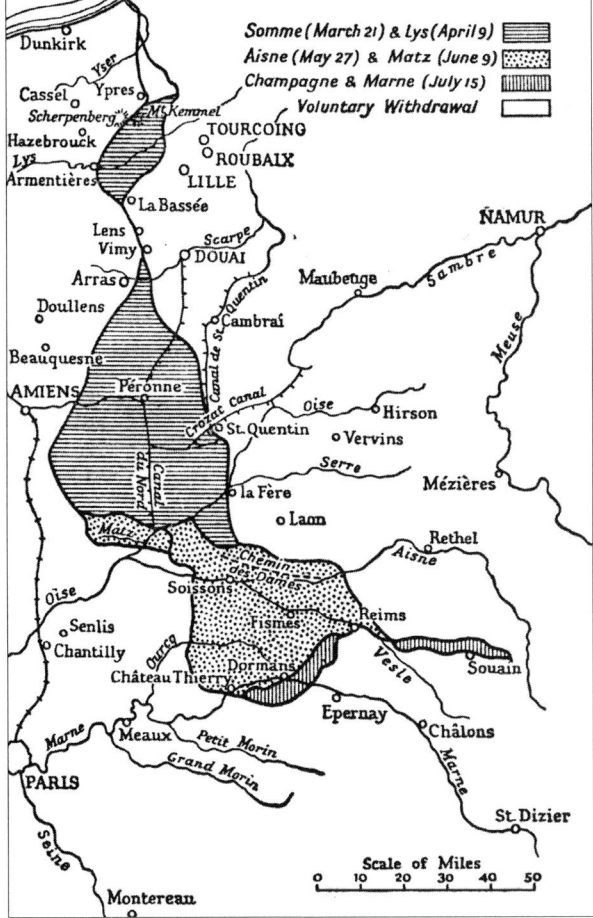

Somme (March 21) & Lys (April 9)
Aisne (May 27) & Matz (June 9)
Champagne & Marne (July 15)
Voluntary Withdrawal

Dunkirk
Yser
Cassel • Ypres
Scherpenberg • M.S.Kemmel
Hazebrouck
Lys
Armentières
La Bassée
Lens
Vimy
Scarpe
DOUAI
Arras
Doullens
Beauquesne
AMIENS • Péronne
Canal de St.Quentin
Cambrai
Crozat Canal
St.Quentin
Oise • Hirson
Vervins
Serre
Mézières
la Fère
Laon
Rethel
Aisne
Chemin des Dames
Soissons
Tismes
Reims
Oise
Senlis
Chantilly
Ourcq
Dormans
Château Thierry
Vesle
Souain
Epernay
Châlons
Marne
Meaux • Petit Morin
Grand Morin
Marne
PARIS
St.Dizier
Seine
Scale of Miles
0 10 20 30 40 50
Montereau

TOURCOING
ROUBAIX
LILLE
ÑAMUR
Maubeuge
Sambre
Meuse

Top right: The German Army's newest tactical gambit, Storm Troopers, to spearhead the 1918 attacks, specially trained soldiers armed with bags of hand grenades. (*LC*)

Later, Hitler named his Nazi political street fighters after these earlier warriors. Noted one account: "Designed by Dr Friedrich Schwerd, the German steel helmet was trialed in 1915, and made a general issue … in 1916. It was not bulletproof unless fitted with a heavy brow plate that fixed over the distinctive side lugs, but was capable of stopping the small splinters and fragments that were the cause of many head wounds. Initially regarded with some misgiving, it was soon a popular—even iconic—piece of equipment."

Right: Besides grenades and standard, bolt-action rifles, the new men also sported sub-machine guns and pistols for trench combat. The new *stahlhelm* (steel helmet), nicknamed the "coal scuttle," replaced the former spiked version during 1916–35. For his Great War service, Hitler wore both. (*LC*)

One recent account described General Hutier's new storm combat tactics thus: "Surprise was the keynote. After a short—but very powerful—artillery barrage of gas and high explosive shells, small groups of *Sturmtruppen* armed with automatic rifles, light machine guns, flame throwers, and trench mortars would move out under cover of a barrage that crept forward as they advanced."

Horse-drawn, wheeled artillery also rumbled up to the front for the coming battles, again, over tough terrain and mud, March 1918. (*LC*)

"The German advance reached—and then briefly crossed—the Marne River, before it was stopped with the help of US Marines and [Army] soldiers." By Armistice Day of November 11, 1918, the AEF—according to one period source in 1919—suffered "274,860" casualties. "These include killed in action, wounded, missing in action, and prisoners." According to Stormtroopers in *Empire & Revolution*: "The German Army in the west was reinforced by troops from the east, and readied for the first big German offensive on that front since Verdun in 1916," and thus also the duo's own initial such action since arriving in the west in September 1916.

The main backbone of any assault force—the infantry—as always moved up on foot, as depicted in this painting by wartime artist Schnurpel, *Again on Assault.* (*U.S. Army Combat Art Collection*)

"The German failure was due to a number of factors. The Germans did not have sufficient mechanical transport to supply their advancing troops, and their artillery was unable to keep up with the advancing infantry. Many of the best German assault troops were killed, and the remainder began to lose their aggressive spirit as a consequence of heavy casualties. Finally—in the face of the abundance of supplies found in the captured Allied dumps—discipline among German troops broke down, and widespread looting developed."

Next page, above left: Period woodcut art entitled *Grenade Thrower* by wartime artist Georg Sluyterman. Its fuse ran along the hollow inside of the stick handle, pulled by the soldier before throwing, as here. Around his waist is a black leather ammunition belt, and resting on his chest a gas mask, a bayonet at his left side. This was the man upon whom the German High Command depended to win the Great War in the final assaults of 1918. (*U.S. Army Combat Art Collection*)

Above right: As with the imperial German crown prince, so, too, was Corporal A. Hitler also a combat artist, as seen here. (*Billy F. Price Collection, Texas, USA*)

"The Germans had made impressive territorial gains and inflicted heavy casualties on the Allies, but they had failed to achieve the decisive breakthrough and split the Allies. The *Kaiserheer* [Imperial Army] had suffered 500,000 casualties, and was exhausted; Ludendorff had run out of strategic options" as well. The Kaiser referred caustically to the abrupt Ludendorff as *The Sergeant Major.*

Gas attack—but from which side and against which side? All too often, it did not matter, as shifts in wind controlled the way the gas drifted. Stated the Great War period caption: "Asphyxiating gases in use. Gases—the soldier's most dreaded peril—advancing to the attack before a favoring wind." (*LC*)

"The German chemist Fritz Haber won a Nobel Prize in 1918 for his synthesis of ammonia from its elements. In World War I, he directed the first chlorine gas attack at Ypres, and was in charge of German chemical warfare," according to Jarvis' *Did You Know?* A Jew, he left Germany after the Nazis took office.

According to *TIME*'s 2017 special issue magazine *World War I: The War That Shaped Our World, 100 Years Later* of this very same photograph, "Deadly gas was first deployed as a weapon on the Western Front at the Second Battle of Ypres in April 1915; used by all sides in the war, gas killed some 90,000 soldiers. Above, a gas attack on the Eastern Front…. Such weapons were banned by the Geneva Protocol in 1925," only to be ignored by Mussolini a decade later and used again in Ethiopia.

One German soldier who ended the Great War in a military hospital at Pasewalk, East Prussia, recuperating from a gas attack was artist Cpl. Hitler, whose work again appears here, of a protective gas mask being worn. He recovered his eyesight. Entitled *Gas Alarm Near Soissons, 1918*, it a watercolor on paper mounted on cardboard. Below it, Hitler added in his own handwriting, "French counterattack on 23 July 1918 near Soissons." It was reportedly, "Originally owned by Piller, a corporal in the [16th Bavarian] List Regiment, according to more modern owner Billy F. Price." (*Billy F. Price Collection*)

THE LAST THROW.

A cartoon from *Punch* by Bernard Partridge, published February 21, 1917.

By naming Operation Michael also the Kaiser's Battle, Ludendorff cunningly shifted the political blame for its military loss from the duo and to the Kaiser, a ploy not lost on a chagrined Wilhelm II.

"Although the Germans were able to stabilize the front … on August 8, 1918 … a major British offensive on the Somme [River] using large numbers of tanks penetrated seven miles into the German lines along a 15-mile front. Six German divisions collapsed, many prisoners were taken, and discipline in the *Kaiserheer* [Imperial Army] broke down."

Top: "1918: On the *Winterberg* [Chemin des Dames] … His Majesty [right, in cap and cape] personally interrogates a captured British officer wearing a gas mask bag and standing at attention before Wilhelm II." Above (fourth from left) is von Plessen, while above the Kaiser (third from right) is Hindenburg, with Ludendorff looking on at far right also. (*DH*)

German "Reinforcements marching to the front were jeered and accused of being strike breakers by troops relieved … Ludendorff was in a state of nervous collapse" and yet, "Still had wild notions that [an Armistice] could give Germany a breathing space, and that a policy of massive territorial annexation" in the west as had already occurred in the east "Was still possible." It was not, as—one by one— the Second Reich's Central Powers' partners dropped out of the war.

   Later, British POWs who met and talked with the Kaiser found him totally unlike his portrayal by wartime British propaganda, but saw him rather as a kindly figure concerned for their welfare, assuring them that he would win the war and that thus they would all be home for Christmas 1918.

Bottom: The Boche/Cabbage Head Looter by artist Captain Harvey Dunn, AEF. This soldier was the very man whom Ludendorff badly needed to continue the forward advance instead: the average hungry German soldier, amazed at what he found in captured Allied warehouses: food and drink of all kinds, long denied him. (*U.S. Official Photo, LC*)

"After a sudden artillery barrage—and under cover of gas attacks and smoke bombs— these [storm trooper] groups would then make a deep penetration of the enemy front, seeking to outflank and get behind enemy units and disrupt communications. Then the non-elite remainder of the infantry would follow up the storm troopers, seek to consolidate their advances, and deal with pockets of resistance."

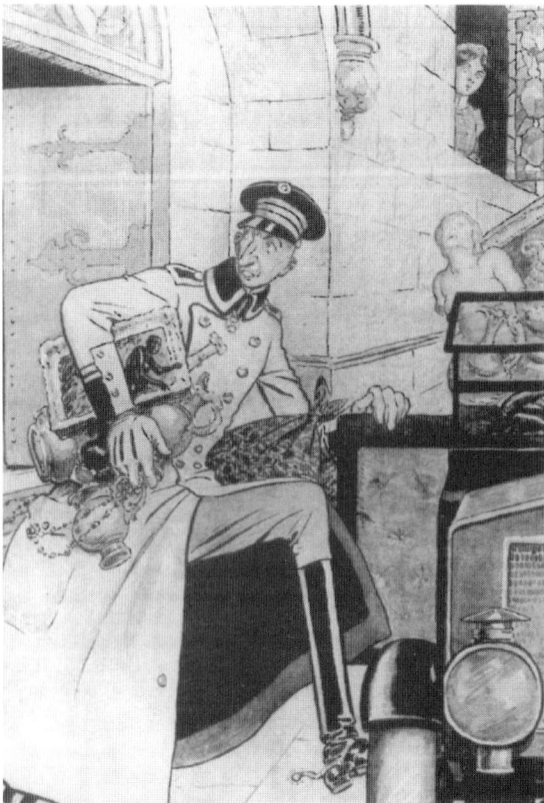

"*Being Unable to Take Paris* by Cartoonist Edwin Morrow, *The Bystander,* October 14, 1914," reviled already as "Little Willy," Crown Prince Wilhelm also discredited his dynasty via his widely known extramarital affairs throughout his life—before, during, and after the Great War, was depicted by Allied cartoonists as "Cowardly, wily, and corrupt.... The British preferred to portray him as a sneak and a thief," as here, "based on a claim by the Baroness de Boye, who reported that the Crown Prince had helped himself to a number of valuables and art treasures from her chateau." (*LC*)

Grenade! by artist Captain Harvey Dunn, AEF. This time (center left), it was one thrown by an Allied soldier, as these Germans rightly recoil in fear from the coming explosion. (*LC*)

"These tactics had been made possible by changes in defensive warfare during the course of the war. In order to reduce casualties to artillery bombardment, both sides had switched to a defense-in-depth system with the forward areas being lightly defended with snipers and machine gun nests, rather than continuous lines of troops, and with reserves held further back, often in artillery-resistant dug-outs."

Even as his armies blazed ahead in the Great War's final attacks on the Western Front, the Kaiser as circus ringmaster had trouble from dissuading his fractious partners from seeking a separate peace on their own as a way out of Ludendorff's no-win strategy for defeat. (*Cartoon by Punch, London*)

A *Punch* cartoon by Leonard Raven Hill, published September 11, 1918.

It was no good, however, as the war in the west would be lost in 1919–20 if not already in 1918.

In his 1919 memoirs, Ludendorff claimed that he—and therefore not Hindenburg—gave the Battle of Tannenberg its historic name: "One of the most brilliant battles in the history of the world had been fought!" he crowed therein.

THE NEW ORIENTATION.

Kaiser. "OUR FUTURE, MY DEAR BOY, LIES IN THE EAST!"
Crown Prince. "WELL, FATHER, FROM WHAT I'VE SEEN OF THE WEST I THINK YOU MAY BE RIGHT."

A cartoon from *Punch* by Bernard Partridge, published May 29, 1918.

Martial prospects in the Middle East also looked grim for the Second Reich, as lampooned here.
    During the subsequent victorious German campaign in East Prussia in the summer of 1914, the winning duo stayed at the very former Russian Army headquarters previously occupied by Gens. Rennenkampf and Grand Duke Nicholas—Nordenburg, Insterburg, and the Dessauer Hotel among them.

Kamerad! by artist Captain Harvey Dunn, AEF. This was seen and heard all along the Western Front, as masses of German soldiers simply surrendered in-place. Note the gas mask on the soldier's chest and the abandoned machine gun at lower left. (*LC*)

"The shock tactics of the storm troopers could prove extremely effective, but the problem for Ludendorff was that he decided to launch them not against Italians or demoralized Russians—nor even against the French—but, rather, against the best troops on the Western Front, namely the British and Commonwealth troops. While German tactics on the ground were to infiltrate the front line and seek out its weakest points, their general strategy contradicted this by seeking out the strongest element of the opposing armies, the British."
    Following the winding down of the defeated German attacks came the inevitable and overwhelming Allied counterattacks that won the Great War at last after four long years. "The other problem with Ludendorff's storm trooper tactics was that they exacted the heaviest toll on the best troops.… Instead of survival of the fittest, they led to culling of the fittest, and the survival of the un-fittest. This was even more true in a situation where resistance was greater than expected The spearhead took almost all the shock, the shaft hardly any at all."

Above left: The overall architect of Allied victory was Army Marshal of France Generalissimo Ferdinand Foch, seen here on August 23, 1918 with his baton, just presented to him in a field ceremony by President Raymond Poincare of France. (*LC*)

A previous biographer of the German duo quotes the aggressive Frenchman as asserting in March 1918, "You are not fighting? I would fight without a break! I would fight in front of Amiens, behind Amiens—I would fight all the time!" He was as good as his boast. Noted a period Great War history: "This is the man whose tremendous thrust routed the Prussian Guard at the [Second] Battle of the Marne [River]. Launched at exactly the right moment, it went through the Guard, 'as a knife goes through cheese,'" routing the whole army of Hausen, and earned for Foch [Marshal] Joffre's verbal decoration as, 'The first strategist in Europe.' A few weeks later—through his generalship and the help of the flower of the British Army—Foch's troops won the terrible struggle that we call Ypres. There is a legend that this time he won commendation from Lord Roberts who—after studying his plans—is said to have remarked to officers of his staff, 'You have a great general.' His appointment as Allied Generalissimo marked the beginning of their final drive to victory."

Above right: Commanding the BEF during 1915–19 was Field Marshal Sir Douglas Haig (*left*), seen here greeting a Scottish unit in the field. Haig had been promoted field marshal by Britain's revered King George V on January 1, 1917. According to John Hussey, the British Tommy thought of him as Douggie, who "Knows what he is doing. He was not only our leader and commander-in-chief, but our friend." At his death, 100,000 mourners passed by his funeral bier. During his time in France—as here—he preferred horses to command cars. With over 80 German divisions directly pitted against 26 British divisions under … Haig, the Germans were guaranteed some kind of advance." (*LC*)

Above: Given a wide political latitude by President Woodrow Wilson (*fur coat, second from right*) was AEF Commander General John J. "Black Jack" Pershing (*far right*), the nickname deriving from his previous command of all-black U.S. units in the American Far West and in Cuba during the 1898 Spanish-American War that made the U.S. a global power at last. Here, the two top men in the American High Command review their AEF in France in 1919. (*LC*)

Of Hindenburg, General Max Hoffmann commented snidely, "Since I have heard that Hindenburg won the Battle of Tannenberg, I have ceased to believe in Hannibal and Caesar!" Regarding Michael, "The Germans also launched mortar attacks, gas, and smoke canisters from their forward positions. Over 3.5 M shells were fired in five hours in the biggest barrage of the war. Next, the storm troopers moved forward … taking advantage of a heavy mist that greatly limited visibility, and isolating the battle area from communications with HQ."

Left: Hindenburg (*left*) and a staff officer at center photographed with a young sentry (*right*) with rifle at shoulder arms at KHQ Spa, Belgium. Soldiers such as he would make all the difference between Red Revolution and stability in the coming weeks ahead for the new, revamped German High Command that the venerated marshal would command in place of the overthrown Kaiser. (*LC*)

"The British put up a dogged resistance, and started making a fighting retreat to gain time for reinforcements to come up.… On the first day, the Germans had heavier casualties. The offensive continued for the next two weeks, but finally ground to a halt."

In the east, the duo made political-military alliances with such breakaway former Russian zarist commanders as the Cossack leader and 1918 ally Pavel Skoropadsky at center, flanked here by the duo of Hindenburg (*left*) and Ludendorff (*right*) and their combined staffs. (*LC*)

"The final result of the [Michael] battle was that the Germans advanced 40 miles at the deepest point, and gained 1,200 square miles of territory ... but it was a Pyrrhic victory of the worst kind. Much of the land gained was already ravaged by former battles—most notably the Somme [River]—and thus difficult to defend. It would soon be recaptured by the Allies."

That past June 15, 1918, the Kaiser (*left*) celebrated the thirtieth anniversary of his reign in the glassed-in solarium of Spa's ornate Hotel Britannique, shown here, with Hindenburg and Crown Prince Wilhelm at right. The man to whom Emperor William is talking at center may be either Captain Mewes or Colonel von Rauch. (*LC*)

Previous duo biographer Asprey asserted: "While hundreds of thousands of German soldiers were being wounded [on the Western Front]—while civilians were dying by the thousands from malnutrition—the 30th anniversary of Kaiser Wilhelm's reign was celebrated at German Supreme Headquarters."

Left: Hindenburg (*center*) makes a point to his imperial superior, Crown Prince Wilhelm. (*LC*)

In later years, Crown Prince Wilhelm would accuse the marshal of having betrayed both his father and the dynasty in November 1918 in advising Wilhelm II to flee to safety in neutral Holland.

"Both sides seemed to have suffered equally. The British lost 178,000 men killed, wounded, and captured, and the French 77,000 for a total of 255,000 [Allies lost]. The Germans lost around 240,000. The difference, however, was that the German losses were overwhelmingly their elite troops, while the Allied losses were standard troops."

Below left: A *Punch* cartoon by Leonard Raven Hill, published November 8, 1916. Did Hindenburg come to dominate his Supreme Warlord? This cartoon seems to imply that.

"In short, Operation Michael effectively represented the culling of the cream of the German Army, for a large patch of churned up mud. It was this—along with other negative trends—that set the scene for Germany's defeat and surrender later that year."

ANOTHER GAS ATTACK.

Kaiser (*to All-Highest-But-One*). "AND HOW GOES IT?"
Hindenburg. "SIRE, I HAVE DEALT THE ENEMY A SMASHING BLOW."
Kaiser. "SO? AND WHERE WAS THAT?"
Hindenburg. "IN THE VIENNA PRESS, SIRE."

Above right: King Ludwig III of Bavaria in a formal portrait with his queen. He bears his baton as field marshal in his right hand. (*LC*)

The surprise Russian thrust that took Memel and Tauganrog in Lithuania on March 17, 1916 was reported to the startled duo via a "telephone girl" at her switchboard as the enemy soldiers entered her location. Later, Miss Erika Rostel was duly awarded a gold watch—but not an Iron Cross.

Above left: His Bavarian Majesty with interim stab informal swagger stick baton. Note also the distinctive collar logo, entirely different from that of the larger German Army seen here earlier. (*LC*)

Where the Austro-Hungarian troops were deployed, the lament was that "the heaviest fighting always fell to the German troops, as at the Battle of Lemberg, that was retaken from the Russians in summer 1916."

It was to Field Marshal Prince Leopold of Bavaria that Warsaw finally fell in August 1915.

Noted a period Great War work, "The triumphant entry of Prince Leopold of Bavaria [occasioned] the looting that often follows a German success," as asserted in Allied wartime propaganda. Notes one of the prince's recent biographers of this "C-in-C of the united forces on the Eastern Front, his very able chief of staff—Major General Max Hoffmann—wrote that the 69-year-old Prince was likable, relatively harmless, but rather unintelligent."

Above right: Two German field marshals: the Bavarian Prince Leopold at left and the Prussian Wilhelm II at right, at Duna on the Dvina River in 1917. (*DH*)

Prince Leopold von Wittelsbach (1846–1930) was born at Munich on February 9, 1846 as a Bavarian prince and later was a son-in-law of Austria's Kaiser Franz Josef I. After having fought against the former foe of Prussia during the Six Weeks' War in 1866, he served as Prussia's ally in 1870 at the climactic Battle of Sedan that defeated the French Army. In 1905, he was named a German Imperial Army field marshal by Kaiser Wilhelm II and took retirement in 1912, two years before the outbreak of the Great War. Recalled to active duty on April 16, 1915 at the age of sixty-nine, Field Marshal Prince Leopold's first command was of the 9th Army on the Eastern Front, then fighting against the Russians at both Warsaw and Lodz that fall. He received the important joint command of both the German and Austrian forces as C.O. on August 5, 1915 of the newly formed Army Group Prince Leopold of Bavaria, and on the 8th was awarded by His Majesty the Blue Max. On August 29, 1916, the field marshal became C-in-C of the entire Eastern Front when the duo succeeded Falkenhayn as chief of the German general staff overall.

During 1917–18, his own chief of staff Hoffmann negotiated with the Bolsheviks the Treaty of Brest-Litovsk that successfully won for the Central Powers the war in the east. Both the prince and his chief maintained their posts until the armistice in the west ended the war overall. Retiring, Field Marshal Prince Leopold—the Conqueror of Warsaw—died at Munich with his military reputation intact on September 28, 1930. Hitler served in one of Crown Prince Rupprecht's regiments during the Great War.

Rupprecht received both the First and Second Class Iron Cross awards for his repulse of the French from Sarrebourg and Morhange.

"Bombs and grenades from Rupprecht's Bavarians. Englishmen in the area will not feel their toothaches much longer... Hail from the artillery," asserted one wartime barb.

The Kaiser (*center*) with cane, von Plessen (*fifth from left*), and the Kaiser's three-man personal flag detail arrive to inspect troops of the Army group of Crown Prince Rupprecht of Bavaria, June 1918. (*LC*)

During autumn 1914 to August 28, 1916, he commanded Army Group Crown Prince Rupprecht of Bavaria, "Conducting mainly defensive operations of the 6th Army from headquarters at Lille and later Douai. On August 22, 1915, he was awarded the Blue Max."

The Bavarian crown prince (*third from left*) is now on-site for the Kaiser's front visit, as Wilhelm II (*right*) troops the line of the men at right, followed by his NCO flag bearer in dark jacket at center, June 1918, a member of the German emperor's "ever-present" lifeguard unit. (*LC*)

"Promoted field marshal on August 1, 1916, Rupprecht passed command of the 6th Army to Colonel General Baron von Falkenhausen towards the end of September, and assumed control of his newly formed army group with HQ at Cambrai, with his Army Group including the 1st, 6th, and 7th armies." The latter was replaced in March 1917 with the 4th Army instead, making Rupprecht "responsible for the entire northern front facing the BEF from the Belgian Coast to the Oise River," added one source.

Rupprecht (*left*) and Wilhelm II (*right*) with staffers inspect their men, June 1918. (*LC*)

On July 24, 1942, Hitler asked his nighttime adherents, "Who cares a rap—for instance—for Rupprecht of Bavaria? Kingship possesses but little wisdom, and the boundary between the throne and the madhouse is a slender one!" In March 1918, Rupprecht fought "a number of desperate defensive battles" when "his command resumed offensive operations on a large scale, advancing as far as the Arras-Albert Line."

A *Punch* cartoon by Leonard Raven Hill, published December 11, 1918. The caption reads, "WANTED. William the Gallant (*to Holland*). "COURAGE! I WILL NEVER DESERT YOU."

Reportedly, in 1945, Rupprecht declined an American Army offer to make him king of Bavaria. His people considered him "the uncrowned king" after the death of his father in 1921 anyway, until his death in 1955. It was also suggested that—had it been offered—Rupprecht was prepared to accept becoming Germany's first Catholic Kaiser. Indeed, Ludendorff—who had moved his official residence to Bavaria postwar—did so partially as a way of becoming a main backer of Rupprecht's claim, until he had his own falling out with the Bavarian field marshal.

WANTED.

WILLIAM THE GALLANT (*to Holland*). "COURAGE! I WILL NEVER DESERT YOU."

Field Marshal Albrecht, Duke of Württemberg, minus baton, commander of the German 4th Army. (*LC*)

Ludendorff rejoiced when the sudden Russian Brusilov Offensive of June 1916 was halted: "Quiet reigned along the front as far as the Carpathian" mountains that it was always feared the Russian would surge over, as indeed they did, but in 1945. "The summer campaign against Russia was at an end," he sighed with relief in 1918.

Duke Albrecht's marshal's baton, as seen today in the Army Museum at Munich. (*LC*)

Ludendorff termed German artillery as "the keystone of the battle and the mainstay of the front." In trench fighting, "The use of the rifle was forgotten, and hand grenades became the chief weapon."

Moaned Ludendorff postwar, "When it came to hand-to-hand fighting, the superiority of the enemy in men was much too great.… Our existing machine guns were too heavy; we needed lighter ones."

On Ludendorff's later lamented Black Day of the German Army, August 8, 1918, Allied armored cars rolled up to a divisional headquarters to take its entire staff prisoner, 600 light and heavy tanks advanced across German lines, and six to seven full German divisions were simply overrun, reportedly, causing a full retreat in Belgium: "The war was lost," he concluded.

Above left: Colonel General Max von Gallwitz. (*LC*)

Stated Towson, MD, USA, translator Hildburg Sherry Baker: "Max Karl Wilhelm von Gallwitz was born May 2, 1852 at Breslau, and died at Naples on April 18, 1937, the same year as Ludendorff. As a volunteer like Mackensen in 1870 in the Franco-Prussian War, Gallwitz was later transferred as well to the General Staff at Berlin. In 1903, he was named Director of the Army's Administration Department in the War Ministry, plus as representative deputy in the Imperial Bundesrat [Federal Council]. In 1911, Gallwitz was promoted General of Artillery and Inspector of Field Artillery simultaneously." he began the Great War in August 1914 at Namur in Belgium, being transferred eastward to the Narew River Front in the east in 1915 with the 11th Army, continuing with it across the Donau River to Belgrade. At the end of 1916, General von Gallwitz commanded the 5th Army at Verdun when it was named an army group. In an important conference in January 1917, Hindenburg was willing to see General Gallwitz replace Bethmann-Hollweg as imperial chancellor rather than take on that post himself. Indeed, there was already a precedent of a soldier replacing a civilian in that very post, when in March 1890, the Kaiser put in Bismarck's position General Leo von Caprivi, a soldier then heading the German Navy.

Above right: Colonel-General Karl von Einem *gennant* (named) von Rothmaler prior to being promoted to field marshal by the Kaiser. A cavalryman by training, Einem replaced the defeated General Max Baron von Hausen after his loss at First Marne in 1914 as C.O. of the German 3rd Army.

In June 1933 in Bavaria, Field Marshal von Einem established the pro-monarchist movement League of the Upright, which claimed 100,000-plus members. In January 1934, von Einem's plans to celebrate the Kaiser's seventy-fifth birthday with a monarchist demonstration at Berlin were crushed by General Goering, who had SA men break it up; Hindenburg let the Nazi infraction stand. (*LC*)

Next page, above: A wide-angle view of the much-touted Hindenburg Line on the German Western Front. Stated the original 1919 caption: "The Hindenburg Line near Le Catelet. At this point—where the Scheldt Canal goes underground—American troops broke through on September 28, 1918, but suffered terrible losses when the Germans came out of the tunnel and attacked their rear." (*U.S. Official Photo, LC*)

Next page, middle: The original 1919 Allied propaganda caption read: "The 'Impregnable' Hindenburg Line. These fortifications—in the invincibility of which the Germans had placed their confidence—yielded to the first onrush of the French at the Somme" River, seen here, photographed by the French Pictorial Service.

On December 12, 1918, the first German troops returning from the then lost Western Front reached Berlin. (*LC*)

Left: The rearmost and older segments of the vaunted line tended to be far more substantial than those newer parts, often built of reinforced concrete above-ground bomb shelters, as shown here. Noted the original 1919 U.S. propaganda caption: "Bombproof cement headquarters in the Argonne Forest of Prince Max, the German commander, who learned right here that bomb proofs could *not* withstand American valor." (*LC*)

7

Armistice and Revolution, 1918–20

Bavarian King Leopold III Overthrown, 1918

Following the Palm Sunday 1919 Socialist assault on Bavarian King Ludwig III's Wittelsbach Palace, one outraged attacker asked another, "Have you seen the King's bathroom? I tell you, it is a scandal! I found a little boat there, and the lackey told me that instead of governing, King Ludwig used to sit in a hot tub for hours on end playing with his little boat!"

Like his Kaiser, the king had been deposed in November 1918 by the first Soci revolt at Munich, fleeing by car with his family into exile, first to Austria and then on into Hungary, where he died in 1921.

This deposition of Bavaria's monarchy included dashing the hopes of his successor-designate, son and heir, Crown Prince Rupprecht. In 1917, the latter had correctly predicted that Bavaria's Catholic middle class would become even more anti-monarchical for the loss of the war than the Social Democratic Party because it blamed the government for its woes already. Their beloved, revered, and much respected wartime army group commander, the Crown Prince, was not among those they castigated for the lost war, however, and many sought his ascension to the throne to the very end of his life more than thirty-five years later.

Dona and the Duo: Kaiserin Auguste Viktoria's Role in the Great War, 1914–18

In 1952, Dorpalen chronicled the until-then largely unknown role played by Wilhelm II's long suffering wife, "Dona" (Kaiserin Auguste Viktoria), over the course of the Great War. It was revealing, indeed.

First, she realized how attuned her husband was to, and fearful of, the duo from the Eastern Front, Hindenburg and Ludendorff. Noted Van der Kiste in *The Last German Empress*:

> Unsure of himself, he was especially sensitive to the brusque, self-assured ways of Ludendorff, who in turn made no secret of his intense dislike of the Kaiser's wavering attitude.
>
> Without saying so, the Emperor seemed to be toying with the idea of abdicating, in order to escape the crushing burden of his immense responsibility.

Like her first-born son, Imperial Crown Prince Wilhelm, the empress was also both pro-duo and anti-Imperial Chancellor von Bethmann-Hollweg. Like him as well, she wanted the first two hired and the second fired, the latter to be replaced by the former chancellor, Prince Bernhard von Bülow, fired by the Kaiser in 1909.

In time, Wilhelm agreed to their first and second demands, but adamantly refused to ever have "dear Bernhard" back as his chief minister again, whom he felt, rightly, had betrayed him in '09. Noted Van der Kiste in *The Last German Empress*:

> Just at this time—when the Emperor needed her encouragement the most—the Empress suffered a stroke. Early in September 1918, William himself collapsed completely.
>
> Again, fears were voiced that the monarch might decide to abdicate. Hardly recovered herself, the Empress rushed to his bedside. She succeeded in giving him new strength and confidence…
>
> Bülow—she was convinced—was the one man with sufficient prestige in Europe who might be able to liquidate the war on tolerable terms.

But it never transpired. When the change in the chancellorship occurred (early in October 1918), Auguste Viktoria was not a party to it, and thus Prince Max of Baden ascended into his fateful, final role.

"It was combined with far-reaching political reforms that transformed the German Empire from a Constitutional into a Parliamentary monarchy," just as the Kaiser's late parents—the "Freds," as I have dubbed them—had always wanted since before his own birth in 1859, thus achieving at last the goals of the aborted 1848 Revolution of fifty years prior.

For the first time, moreover, a number of Socialists were taken into the still Imperial "government," in the end a fatal recipe that spelled doom for first Ludendorff and then the Hohenzollern dynasty, but not, alas, for the Wooden Titan, von Hindenburg.

The Kaiser's surprise decision to leave Potsdam—and thus not meet with his last chancellor as urgently requested—for KHQ Spa was also laid in 1952 to Dona's influence over her husband. In *The Last German Empress*, Van der Kiste wrote:

> She agreed … that the Emperor would be safest with the Supreme Command. Her faith in Hindenburg was unshaken; she was certain that the old marshal would protect his monarch against all pernicious influences, and reject any idea of abdication. She … urged Wilhelm to leave.…
>
> Hindenburg's wish that the Emperor show himself to his troops provided the official reason for his trip. It was this decision that sealed the fate of the German monarchy.

In the final analysis, Dona was wrong in not foreseeing that trusty Hindenburg would save himself at the expense of "His Imperial Master." Thus, "The role she played during the closing days of the monarchy was fateful indeed." Nor was her assessment of Ludendorff without misjudgment, either, as recorded by the man she succeeding in having fired in July 1917, Bethmann.

Adml. von Müller on Bethmann's Assessment of Ludendorff, and the Latter's Fall

Indeed, on October 13, 1918, the chief of the Kaiser's naval cabinet, Adml. Georg von Müller, recalled a remark made by the former chancellor in August 1916 upon the arrival of the duo to head the supreme command in place of Falkenhayn: "You do not know Ludendorff, who is only great at times of success! If things go badly, he loses his nerve. I have seen this happen in the eastern campaign," as occurred again in late summer 1918 as Operation Michael collapsed.

On October 26, 1918—after the Kaiser fired Ludendorff—the admiral added tartly in his exceptional diary, "His Majesty was in excellent form…. The Kaiser had been constantly plagued by Ludendorff throughout the war. The general had committed mistake after mistake. Since Tannenberg, he had suffered from megalomania!"

My Own View

My personal view of this is that the Kaiser should have fired Hindenburg as well, replacing him with Groener, who succeeded him in 1919 anyway upon his boss' second, but not final, retirement. In addition, the most talented man to have become the final imperial chancellor was a Jew whom the Kaiser would never have named in any case: AEG Electrical tycoon and then serving able Imperial Minister Walter Rathenau, assassinated by right-wing extremists in 1922.

This team of Chancellor Rathenau and CGS chief Gen. Groener would have had—in my opinion—the courage and skill to both end the war sooner and save the dynasty, possibly even keeping Wilhelm II on his then "Soci throne."

Stab in the Back!

The war was over and done with. Germany had lost it. Hindenburg had lost it. He, Ludendorff, and the other German marshals and generals allegedly found a convenient excuse for having lost it, though, in the now famous—or infamous, take your pick—"Stab in the Back" legend.

In 1936, Wheeler-Bennett provided what he felt was the origin of this "legend" in *Wooden Titan*:

> Ludendorff was dining with Maj. Gen. Malcolm, head of the British Military Mission in Berlin, and with his usual turgid eloquence was expiating that the High Command had always suffered lack of support from the civilian government, and how the Revolution had betrayed the Army.
>
> In an effort to crystallize the meaning of Ludendorff's verbosity into a single sentence, Gen. Malcolm asked him, "Do you mean, general, that you were stabbed in the back?" Ludendorff's eyes lit up, and he leaped upon the phrase like a dog on a bone.
>
> "Stabbed in the back?" Yes, that is it, exactly! We were stabbed in the back!

Thus, according to this line of reasoning, the German warlords were able to console themselves thereafter that they had not lost the war at all.

They had been grossly betrayed by the people at home, that Wheeler-Bennet and some others have since considered to be a gross historical lie. In like manner, Hindenburg in later years was to blame Groener for the removal of Wilhelm II, whereas it was Hindenburg's responsibility, no matter who voiced the actual words.

The Marshal's Future Pondered

What was von Hindenburg to do now? All that he stood for, or once professed to, at any rate, was gone. Germany was in the hands of the hated Republicans. What path of service was he to follow now?

The Kaiser was gone and later, from his Dutch exile, released all his former officers and civil servants from their oaths via his signed Act of Abdication. Instead of going into exile with his imperial sovereign—or of committing suicide allegedly like the Jewish ship-owner Albert Ballin—Hindenburg decided to remain at the head of the beaten army, to once again "save Germany."

In effect, he replaced the Kaiser as *de facto* supreme warlord, officially taking the title of commander-in-chief of the Army, placing himself and his troops at the disposal of the new acting Republic president, the one-time saddle maker Soci Reichstag Deputy Friedrich Ebert.

Leaving the suppression of the Red revolts within the besieged Second Reich at home to others, Hindenburg busied himself instead with the demobilization of the major part of the army still on enemy soil. He and Gens. Groener and Loßberg brought it all home within the two-week timeframe set down by the Allies in the Armistice—one agreed to by the German signatories.

But how was it—one might well ask—that the man who had lost the Great War for Germany and her defeated partners was even allowed to remain as a prominent figure in postwar affairs for the next six months?

Unser Hindenburg Must Stay!

An extraordinary event occurred, with the German people in the main telling themselves, even silently, "The Kaiser ran away, and Ludendorff lost the war, but our Hindenburg, *he* must remain, to guide and lead us!" At the war's end, therefore, he was more popular than ever. Following the signing of the Treaty of Versailles on June 28, 1919, the aged field marshal retired the very next day from the army for the second time.

Returning home to Hanover once more, this time it was to a guard of honor at the railway station and to a tremendous ovation by his fellow townspeople, in complete contrast to how he had left it that early morning of August 1914 on a deserted station platform in the dark of night. Noted Wheeler-Bennett in *Wooden Titan*:

> The enthusiasm of the welcome did not pass in a day. A perpetual crowd stood before the house … and whenever the giant figure of the marshal appeared in the streets, all traffic ceased, and the crowd gave itself up to joyful demonstration.

His celebrity became a burden to him. [Or so it has been repeated ever since, but I think not so much.] Hating ostentation—and devoid of personal ambition [again, I doubt both]—he chafed at the restrictions that his popularity placed upon him.

"My wife has just gone into Hanover to do some shopping. I used to like doing it myself, but I cannot any longer! If I cross the Georgestrasse, there is such a crowd that the traffic has to stop!" he complained to a visitor.

Memoirs, 1919

In September 1919, Hindenburg rushed his ghostwritten memoirs into print under the title of *Aus Meinem Leben* (*Out of My Life*) that even the usually highly critical Dr Josef Goebbels liked, for their author's supposed moderation. It immediately became a bestseller.

The Treaty of Versailles having been duly, if controversially, signed, many post Great War historians saw it as the real cause of World War II twenty years later, but in the main, it aped what the Germans had enforced upon the defeated French in 1871 in terms of lost land and mandated war reparations payments.

Indeed, that of Brest-Litovsk (March 3, 1918), which victorious Germany had pushed upon defeated Russia, had been far worse than that designed at Paris. The Treaty of Versailles did, however, contain clauses calling for the extradition of the Kaiser and several other top accused militarist war criminals to stand trial, including Hindenburg himself.

Der Alte Herr (The Old Gentleman)

The Hanoverian city fathers pleaded with the old marshal not to give himself up. The "Old Gentleman"—as he was now called—bitterly said: "If they want to shoot an old man like myself—who has only done his duty, and nothing more!—let them come and take me."

To prevent the Allies from taking his Kaiser, however, he even wrote to French Marshal Foch, soldier to soldier, thus (noted in Foch's *Memoirs*):

> In the name of the old German Army … as the supreme head of an army that through centuries has upheld the tradition of true soldier's honor and knightly sentiment as its highest ideal, you will be able to appreciate our feelings!
>
> I am ready to make any sacrifice to keep this shameful humiliation from our people and our name! Therefore, I put my person entirely at the disposal of the Allied Powers, in *place* of my Royal Master! I am convinced that every other officer of the Old Army would be prepared to do the same!

Noted a period biographer, "To this appeal, the French marshal made no reply," possibly viewing it as nothing more than playacting to the Teutonic marshal's future political gallery at home.

Another who volunteered to take his father's place in an Entente dock was the Imperial German Crown Prince Wilhelm, left instead to rot on his own Dutch exile Isle of Wieringen during 1918–23.

In the British Parliamentary Khaki Election, Prime Minister David Lloyd George even ran on the electoral slogan of "Hang the Kaiser!" This was quietly forgotten, however, once he won the election.

The Dutch refused to extradite His Majesty Wilhelm II, even under threat of both economic sanctions and possible Allied military action. Soon thereafter, the Allies dropped their calls for extradition of all accused German war criminals, renewing them in 1945 after the second lost German War, however.

Reichstag War Hearings, 1919

Almost as soon as he had retired for the second time from the German military, Hindenburg sent to President Ebert a statement that he was responsible for everything that had happened since August 1916.

In the latter part of 1919, therefore, he was duly given the chance to uphold his actions in public. In 1935, recalled his German biographer Ludwig Cohn:

> So in the latter days of November, Hindenburg came as a conquering hero to Berlin. A special salon car brought him … from Hanover … and a guard of honor was awaiting him.
>
> Two Regular Army officers were attached as honorary ADCs, and two steel-helmeted sentries were posted in front of Helfferich's villa while the marshal was his guest. Here for the first time since 26 October of the previous year, he saw Ludendorff again.
>
> Their meeting was not hostile, but cool. Huge crowds cheered Hindenburg at his every appearance…Hindenburg and Ludendorff appeared before the Committee of Inquiry on 18 November 1919.
>
> In plain clothes, they drove to the Reichstag Building through streets lined with troops and mounted police who kept back the cheering—and jeering—crowds.

The cross-examination was a tumultuous affair, with Hindenburg doing most of the talking, and after several interruptions by the presiding officer of the marshal's prepared statement, he and Ludendorff nevertheless won the day.

The Kapp–Lüttwitz Putsch, March 13–18, 1920

The major move by the right to overthrow the revolutionary government of the Soci left and replace it with a military dictatorship came during March 13–18, 1920 at Berlin. This was what has come down in German history as the Kapp Putsch, although his purely civilian part in it was not its most important factor. That belonged to a Regular German Army officer instead.

Gen. Walther von Lüttwitz

Gen. Walther Baron von Lüttwitz (February 2, 1859 to September 20, 1942) was born at Bodland near Kreuzberg in Upper Silesia, son of a head forest warden and levee overseer.

Commissioned an officer following his military training of 1878–87, von Lüttwitz graduated from the War Academy in 1890, serving at various postings during the next twenty-two years up to 1912, when he was appointed to the general staff at Berlin. His later commander, Imperial Crown Prince Wilhelm, described von Lüttwitz as "more a leader of men than army chief—more Blücher than Gneisenau." Nevertheless, von Lüttwitz served as Little Willy's own chief of staff in 1916 at Verdun, after having been the C.O. of 10th Army Corps during the Second Battle of Champagne in France.

In November 1916, he was returned to Army corps command of the 3rd, and during the Michael Offensive, he was awarded the Oak Leaves to his already given Blue Max, awarded for his leadership in the Battle of St Quentin/La Fère.

Postwar, on December 28, 1918, von Lüttwitz was named commandant of all military forces at Berlin, as well of the newly formed *Freikorps* units overall. During 1918–19, he earned the title "Father of the *Freikorps*" when he deployed them in place of the less reliable and politically Red-tainted Regular Army troops under his joint command.

With these forces, it was von Lüttwitz who defeated the Red Spartacist Revolt of January 1919 at Berlin, and the following May, the Soci government duly promoted him to command all Reich forces in case of more such risings or renewed war with the Allies. That July, however, he became a plotter to overthrow the very government that had just named him to defend it. When ordered to disband a pair of the most anti-government Marine FKs, Gen. von Lüttwitz instead commanded the Marinebrigade Ehrhardt *Freikorps* to occupy the capital and overthrow the Soci government itself on March 13, 1920.

As the troops carried out their orders, Gen. von Lüttwitz brought into his leadership circle, among others, Ludendorff and Reichstag Deputy Wolfgang Kapp. Their joint goal was to set up an authoritarian regime that would restore the old Bismarckian Reich's 1871 federal establishment, although not necessarily that of any monarchs *per se*.

The leaders met at the Brandenburg Gate on the 13th to launch the coup, and they quickly occupied the downtown central government ministries quarter. Deputy Kapp declared himself the new Reich chancellor, and under him von Lüttwitz as his Minister of Defense.

Kapp located his new government in the Old German Reich Chancellery after the ousted Socis fled Berlin altogether, first to Dresden and then to Stuttgart, in disarray.

Gen. von Seeckt infamously refused to defend the ousted government by firing on the plotters, waiting to see which side would prevail.

This turned out to be the government's own civil servants who refused to work with the plotters, and also Berlin's workers, who called and enforced a general strike of all transportation that simply shut down Reich Capital Berlin. The revolt collapsed.

Gen. von Lüttwitz resigned his commands on March 18, 1920 on the revolt's sixth day, seeking political asylum in Hungary, returning via an amnesty to Germany in 1924. He died at the age of eighty-three at Breslau on September 20, 1942, when it seemed most likely that then Nazi Germany would win both the Battle of Stalingrad and also World War II.

Kapp fled to Sweden, returning from exile two years later in April 1922 to stand trial at Leipzig, but he died of cancer while in police custody before he could be tried.

Mrs. Ludendorff as Insider Eyewitness to the Kapp–Lüttwitz Putsch (My Married Life)

After Ludendorff's return from Sweden, [where he had written his memoirs during his brief 1918–19 exile] we lived in the Hotel Adlon in Berlin ... *Herr* Adlon ... had the tact to give us a room with a separate exit on to the Wilhelmstrasse.

By this means, we avoided contact with the officers of the Entente, [whose Berlin headquarters it also was] and in all the months I was there, we never encountered them. [Later, they moved to a flat] with a view of the Tiergarten....

There were conferences in all the rooms, and all those who later took part in the Kapp revolt were in and out of our house: Gen. von Lüttwitz, Gen. von Oven, Col. Bauer, Capt. Pabst, and many others.... Kapp himself came often, so that I got to know him.

He was a man with an insinuating personality—highly gifted as an orator—so that people listened eagerly to his clever speeches, and yet how pitifully he failed!... What was planned and contemplated was a dangerous game....

Later—when I realized the true state of things—I never understood how it was that Ludendorff was the only person to be snared by the alluring eloquence of these men.... It is inconceivable that a man like him—with his scientific outlook and solidity—should have taken part in an affair that was deficient in any and every detail of organization.

When the Kapp conspirators had fled to the four winds, they left behind them an office that was conducted with almost criminal carelessness and entirely devoid of system.... Ludendorff never possessed any knowledge of human nature, otherwise he could never have been at the mercy of those influences that brought about his downfall. Even quite dubious elements did not hesitate to approach him....

Even before Ludendorff left Berlin, we were already in grave difficulties, and our lives were threatened. Capt. Ehrhardt placed at our disposal a bodyguard of 24 men—splendid fellows!—devoted body and soul to their leader.

They protected us faithfully—and it was imperatively necessary—since the excitement of the populace knew no bounds, and all their rage and all their hate was concentrated on Ludendorff.

His friends saw to it he escaped from this danger, and provided him with a refuge in a Bavarian castle.

Remarkably, he was not brought to account by the restored Soci government afterwards.

The Kaiser *versus* the Field Marshal, 1921

Hindenburg's showy offer to take Wilhelm II's place in the dock of the criminally accused was derided by the Kaiser as nothing more than "A theatrical gesture to win more popularity, to him reeking of the basest hypocrisy. The Kaiser's anger at Hindenburg had turned to a deep hatred, and he now privately accused the field marshal deliberately of having betrayed his Imperial master in order to transfer the affections of the German people to himself."

Indeed, during 1914–21, "It could not be denied that Hindenburg had replaced the Kaiser as the father figure of Germany.... He still remained the greatest man in Germany. His massive frame seemed to breathe an air of confidence and strength, but it was misleading: at heart, he had no courage," as this scribe charged.

"His failure to speak up for the Kaiser" over the past three years "sprang from moral cowardice, not disloyalty. He was a fervent monarchist.... The field marshal was shocked, however, by the reaction of the German people to the news of the Kaiser's flight. He was abashed by the fury and contempt of the monarchists, and suddenly saw the action in a different light."

"In the storm of universal condemnation, he feared that he might be accused of treason for the part he played," and, perhaps, for good reason. Noted Wheeler-Bennett in *Wooden Titan*:

> It was not a creditable performance, and Wilhelm II was not alone in condemning the reticence of the field marshal....
>
> The Kaiser was determined to force Hindenburg into the open and ... in spring 1921, wrote to the field marshal that his exclusion from Germany was the cause of 'Burning anquish in my soul! As you know, I forced myself to the difficult and terrible decision to leave the country only upon the declaration of yourself!

Hindenburg failed to respond to this missive for many more months. In July 1922, he finally wrote to the Kaiser: "Most Serene Highness—Great and Mighty Kaiser!—Most Gracious Kaiser, King, and Lord! I take the responsibility for Your Majesty's resolve to go into exile, a step taken on that unhappy 9th of November as a result of the united demand of all your advisors!"

After his own delay of two months, the Kaiser replied thus: "...I thank you for having now taken this step, that is necessary not only in the interest of historical truth, but equally for my personal reputation!"

Noted the Kaiser's 1962 biographer Virginia Cowles in *The Kaiser*: "Wilhelm II was disappointed to find that Hindenburg's statement aroused little interest. 1918 seemed a long way back; furthermore, most people felt that whatever advice the Kaiser had received, the final responsibility for his flight must remain his, and his alone." There the matter has rested ever since.

Death of Mrs. von Hindenburg, 1922

Noted Ludwig Cohn in *Hindenburg*:

> In 1922, Hindenburg suffered the most cruel blow he had ever experienced. His wife died after their marriage had lasted 40 years. The photographers—who, since the days of Tannenberg—had been more assiduous in their attentions than had pleased him [again, allegedly] have preserved an image of him as chief mourner on this occasion....
>
> A human document, all the more impressive because the field marshal is in full panoply,

much bestarred, surrounded by uniforms and banners, as prescribed by his rank and the custom of his fathers.

Among the thousand photographs showing Hindenburg during and after the war—and also in the days of the final disaster—there is not one to be compared with this picture: heartfelt sorrow!

There is nothing to mitigate it, nor to make his aspect symbolical. An old, old man has lost his only friend. The giant looks broken, [but he went on].

Princes Seek Pensions, Rupprecht & Oskar Ask German War Department for Assistance, *New York Times*, August 22, 1922

Berlin—Three members of German Royal families—asserting that they were unable to support themselves in civilian life—petitioned the Republic's War Office for pensions today [August 19, 1922].

Ex-Crown Prince Rupprecht of Bavaria—who fought against the American Army in the Argonne, and is now unemployed—claims a general's pension.

Prince Oskar of Prussia—the ex-Kaiser's fifth son, aged 34—asserts that the salary of a bank employee is insufficient to enable him to buy a ham sandwich at the Adlon Hotel bar at Berlin, but is advised to postpone his request for a colonel's pension in the hope that a settlement of the Hohenzollern estate will improve his finances.

Duke George of Meiningen demanded a pension as a former Inspector General in the Army, but was refused. A general's pension is $ 10 a month, but is too big a drain on the government exchequer, that is already embarrassed in paying crippled soldiers' pensions—averaging 200 marks—or 20 cents weekly.

The German people are not sympathetic to the Princes' demands, and advise them to go to work, and follow the policy of the Crown Prince of Saxe-Meinengen, aged 30, who—when dethroned—studied law, and today has been appointed to a minor judgeship in Thuringia, getting 1,000 Marks a week.

Ludendorff's Role in the Beer Hall Putsch: An Insider's Account of November 8–9, 1923
"I now come to the Hitler Revolt," recounted Margarethe Ludendorff in *My Married Life*:

For some months, our house [in Bavaria] had become the rallying point … of the National Socialists/Nazis.… Every hour there were conferences.

To avoid all suspicion, Ludendorff … made a point of busying himself in the garden.… He pruned the roses, watered the flowers, and sprayed the lawns.… Hitler … was the focus of universal interest.… I took no part, anymore than I had done in the Kapp revolt.…

Until the afternoon, everything was normal. Towards evening, I saw our servant—Kurt Neubauer—hurrying out of the house in uniform.… 'A meeting in the *Burgerbrau*.… Detailed to guard the hall'.… My son Heinz Pernet was bounding downstairs.…

A motor dashed up at tearing speed and stopped in front of the house. The horn sounded. Ludendorff left the house … and the next moment it had gone."

The next morning, her maid brought her the newspaper: "Adolf Hitler proclaimed national dictator. Gen. Ludendorff nominated commander of the National Army," read the headlines: "An official of the Post Office appeared.… Wireless messages had been picked up. 'Oath of allegiance and participation in the Hitler revolt extorted by force of arms. Hitler and Ludendorff to be arrested wherever discovered.'"

At first, Mrs. Ludendorff believed that her husband had been killed in the police gunfire that ended the coup in Munich. In *My Married Life*, Mrs. Ludendorff recalled:

An hour later, I got news from Ludendorff.… Hitler and he were alive, and only our poor Kurt had been left on the battlefield.…

He [the general] did not appear until evening … due to his examination at the Central Police Station and before the Court, that he had been detained so long. His indignation knew no bounds. In a few hours, the Hitler revolt had been definitely suppressed.…

All those … implicated in the Hitler revolt … were arrested. Ludendorff was the only exception.… A formal statement had been taken from him, he was released.… They felt compelled to arrest … my son Heinz.… My son in prison!…

Ludendorff felt … bitter against Gen. von Seeckt for failing—on the first news of the rising in Munich—to mobilize the whole Reichswehr and advance with fire and sword against the traitors [whom the general at Berlin conversely saw as Hitler, Ludendorff, and their followers!] In this, one must recognize how mistaken Ludendorff was in his judgment of his fellows!…

The result of the Hitler trial is well known. All the prisoners were found guilty with the exception of Ludendorff, who was acquitted [mainly because he had not been present at the beer hall when Hitler and Goering had arrested the members of the legal Bavarian government and military].

My son—after being in prison for five months awaiting trial—was sentenced to a year's detention in a fortress … the sentence was suspended.… In addition, he had to pay a fine of 1,000 marks and the costs of the trial. It was an expensive pastime!

He was found guilty of being an accessory to an act of High Treason by having driven the general's car. In a moment, Ludendorff again became the popular hero, to whom the people's favor veered once more.

He was overwhelmed with flowers and presents, and telegrams and letters of congratulations arrived from all parts of Germany, even from its remotest corners. Shortly afterward when he celebrated his 60th birthday, this day was treated as a national festival of the first order.

Boy scouts, companies of cadets, deputations, clubs and societies, all brought their congratulations. In the evening, a torchlight procession—with thousands of participants—came to greet him.

At its head marched in full dress the leaders of all the Munich Corps, and they were followed by the patriotic societies, with bands playing. It was an imposing spectacle!

Ludendorff Breaks with Crown Prince Rupprecht
Recollected the first Mrs. Ludendorff in *My Married Life*:

> After the Hitler revolt, differences broke out between Crown Prince Rupprecht…and Ludendorff that developed into a public quarrel. The general asserted that the Crown Prince had received Dr von Kahr in the night of 9 November 1923, and that a conference with Munich's Cardinal Faulhaber had also taken place.
>
> It was after this and because of this that Kahr had wavered in his support of the revolt and its failure could be attributed to that cause. Crown Prince Rupprecht denied these assertions … and gave the correct version, namely that … he was not in the city at all, but at one of his castles outside Munich.…
>
> The Crown Prince demanded that Ludendorff … should beg his pardon. This Ludendorff refused to do.… Things ended in the unedifying trial that terminated … in a victory for the Crown Prince.
>
> The consequences were appalling. The well-known public manifesto appeared—signed by 37 generals—that excluded Ludendorff from their society.… The German Officers' League … were thereupon violently attacked by the general.

Ludendorff even self-published a pamphlet entitled *King Rupprecht Against Ludendorff* that contained "facts" that even its author knew to be untrue, his ex-wife later asserted.

Her conclusion: "From all that happened in the following years, I have only one explanation … that his ill success and the blows that fate had struck him had turned his brain. I found his conduct and actions impossible to explain." People also blamed the influence of his second wife.

Hindenburg's First Run for Reich President, 1925
The monarchists used the whispered taunts of *The Spector of Spa* against Hindenburg to force him to several acts allegedly against his will, the first of which was, reportedly, the acceptance of the nationalists' nomination of him as a Reich presidential candidate, after the sudden death of Ebert in 1925. Initially, he opposed the nomination vigorously—sincere or not—because he did not want to become "a political agitator," as Ludendorff had done in both 1920 and again in 1923, each time with disastrous results.

Regarding his oath to the Kaiser, he was persuaded, reportedly, by Grand Adml. Tirpitz, not to let that stand in his way of running, so he accepted. Ludendorff had already run for the post as well in the preliminary election as the Nazi candidate, put up to it by Hitler. He had been disastrously beaten, thus clearing the way in future for a Hitlerian run, just as, reportedly, the Führer had both foreseen and even planned.

Hindenburg had feared that the same might happen to him—no idle fear that.

Lochner Covers Presidential Candidate Hindenburg, 1925
In the evening, a mass meeting took place. The field marshal had now become a civilian—an impressive figure in his solemn Prince Albert attire. He spoke in a fatherly tone,

evidently concerned to assure the world that he was not lusting after more war. Noted in *What About Germany?* Lochner said in part:

> As President of Germany, I would consider my sole duty to be that of doing my best for our fatherland on the basis of the Constitution and the present day position of Germany in the world.
>
> I desire an honorable peace. I am not a militarist! I know war with its attendant misery. I never wish to experience it again! I hope I have convinced you that I will not travel to Berlin on top of a cannon, or in an invalid's chair!

On April 26, 1925, the election was held, and the results were:

Hindenburg/Nationalist 14,655,766

Wilhelm Marx/Socialist 13,751,615

Ernst Thälmann/Red 1,931,151

Asserted one observer, "It had been a very close thing," and Hindenburg's fears had thus been justified in the event. His lookalike son, Oskar, woke him up with the joyous news at 7 a.m.: "Father, you are President of the German Reich!" To which the winning candidate himself replied testily, "Is that so? Well, why did you want to wake me up an hour earlier to tell me? It would still have been true at eight! I think I will turn over and get some more sleep!"

When he officially arose, the new president-elect made a more historic pronouncement on his good political fortune thus: "May God bless the choice of the German people, and make it a prosperous one!" He was duly inaugurated at Berlin on May 12, 1925 with great pomp and ceremony, once again becoming the savior of Germany. At Doorn House in Holland, the former German Kaiser gnashed his teeth anew.

Unknown to Wilhelm II, however, was that—keeping it mainly to himself—the marshal's major reason for becoming Reich president was to prepare the way for the return home of the emperor himself, his version of St John the Baptist and Jesus Christ, but it was never to be, again because of him, the old soldier.

Von Epp!

Gen. Franz Xaver von Epp (1868–1947) was the renowned "Mother of God General" who served Bavarian king, German Kaiser, and Nazi Führer in two world wars, but for our immediate purposes here, he was the main suppressor of the Red Revolution at Munich in 1919.

Soldier, politician, near German presidential candidate in 1932, Franz Xaver Ritter von Epp—after an already stellar military career both before and during the Great War—became notorious and acclaimed as the conservative liberator of Munich, Dortmund, Hamburg, and Essen from German communists.

A colorful, larger-than-life figure like his Nazi ally Capt. Goering, von Epp—oddly—is still rather unknown today, despite having published his 1939 autobiography as, *Ein Leben fur Deutschland* (*A Life for Germany*) at Munich.

Billed as a nationalist who despised Red disorder, Epp became a Nazi to restore law and order to the Reich, and he did so as a fervent Catholic as well. In fact, he was so fervent that—in NS circles—he was called "The Mother of God General."

Active in the Bavarian People's Party until it refused him a leading position, von Epp joined the Nazis, and in the Reichstag election of 1928, he was elected as an NS deputy candidate (along with Goering) representing Upper Bavaria-Swabia, a seat he held until the fall of the Third Reich in 1945.

Like Goering before him, von Epp's main contribution to the party was his famous name, and before that, he was a career soldier of the type that Hermann had hoped to have become until the loss of the Great War ended his martial career plans—for a time.

As a dedicated military man, Epp was in his element as a commander working with a diligent, trusted, handpicked staff that submitted problems and options to him in writing for his final decision. He was, in effect, an ultimate chief executive officer, as was Goering.

The most prominent and able of the "Epp men" was Col. Hans Georg Hoffmann, who, like his boss, was a soldier and a Nazi "Old Fighter" from the party's street fighting days who joined the SA Brownshirts in 1931. Both he and von Epp believed in law and restraint. Of the two men, Col. Hoffmann was far and away the harder worker, though.

In 1943, the colonel fell to the floor of Epp's office, dying with a sheaf of papers in his hands. After having his stricken aide carried to a sofa, Epp picked up the papers with the lament, "Now I will have to do all this damned dirty work myself!"

According to German naval Corvette Capt. Sander-Nagashima of the Military History Records Office at Potsdam, Franz Epp was born at Munich on October 16, 1868, the son of painter Rudolf Epp and his wife, Katherina Streibel. After attending both a lower school at Augsburg and the Munich Military Academy, Cadet von Epp formally entered the German Army on August 16, 1887.

On October 30, 1889, he was promoted to lieutenant of the 9th Bavarian Infantry Regiment, and he served during 1900–01 as a volunteer with the 4th East Asia Infantry with the German Expeditionary Corps led by the Kaiser's celebrated "World Marshal" Alfred von Waldersee sent to China to help quell the Boxer Rebellion. Returning home to the Wilhelmine Reich afterwards, von Epp transferred to the 19th Bavarian Infantry Regiment.

Noted German translator Hildburg Sherry Baker of Towson, MD, USA, on February 2, 1904, von Epp transferred yet again to German West Africa (today's Namibia) as a company commander of the 1st Field Regiment, where "He took part in the bloody 1904 Herero and Namaqua Genocides," being condemned in such books as *The Kaiser's Holocaust.*

Promoted to first lieutenant on October 13, 1896, Epp was raised again to captain on July 11, 1907, following his second and final return from Colonial Africa on November 30, 1906.

Back in the pre-Great War Reich, Epp's military commands included the following postings: December 14, 1906, Chief of the Bavarian Lifeguard Infantry Regiment of King Ludwig III; October 16, 1908 as adjutant of the 3rd Bavarian Infantry Division; and June

22, 1912, commander of the 2nd Battalion of the Bavarian Lifeguard Infantry Regiment.

On August 29, 1914—with the world war having erupted in Europe—his monarch commanded Epp to lead the Lifeguard Regiment into battle, and the following December 26, 1914, he was named its commander on the Western Front. He saw combat action as well, reportedly, against the Serbian, Romanian, and Italian Armies, the latter on their Isonzo River Front facing the Austrians.

While serving in the 5th Army of Imperial German Crown Prince Wilhelm, Epp was awarded the title of Ritter, being knighted with his von on February 25, 1918. On June 23, 1916, Epp had already been given the Max Josef Award by the King of Bavaria personally for heroism in front of the enemy. On May 29, 1918, now von Epp received the Blue Max decoration from his Kaiser. It remained for Chancellor Adolf Hitler to finally award von Epp an Iron Cross in 1943.

According to his personnel file at Potsdam, von Epp was named commander of the Bavarian Mounted Rifle Brigade, and during the final month of the war—from October 15 to November 18, 1918—was also C.O. of the Infantry Lifeguard Regiment again.

Then came the effects of the collapse of the German Army on the Western Front, the overthrow of all the various German ruling Princely Houses—including the Wittelsbach family of Bavaria—and the declaration of the German Republic at Berlin.

This was soon followed by a full-scale Red Revolution to establish Russian Soviet-style communist regimes at both Munich—the Bavarian capital—and also at Reich Capital Berlin. As the Bavarian Soviet was "a dictatorship of the proletariat" or working class, the new regime incited class warfare, putting up posters in those poorer Munich districts exhorting its residents to "Come Out of Your Slums! Flats are Available! Help Yourselves!" as food shortages increased dramatically also.

Centrist local politician Johannes Hoffmann called for the ouster of the Communists and their regime thus:

> Bavarians! Countrymen! In Munich, there rages a Russian terror, directed by alien elements. This insult to Bavaria cannot be allowed to last another day!… You men of the Bavarian mountains, plains, and forests, rise up as one, gather in your villages with weapons and equipment! Select your leaders. Munich calls for your aid! Step forward, now! The Munich disgrace must be wiped out! This is the honorable duty of all Bavarians!

One who responded avidly to this call to arms was then Maj. von Epp, who formed the Free Korps von Epp, composed of army veterans of the Great War, and it soon became the most important of several such organizations established by others to fight the Reds. He hated the Red Republic, and as a devoted monarchist, he dreamed of restoring the fallen dynasties to power.

The major's second-in-command was Army Capt. Ernst Rohm, and the FKE had ties to the Munich anti-Jewish Thule Society as well, the latter sending money to the forces assembling in the farmlands, providing the mass of staunch Nazi voters *versus* the Red workers of most German cities.

The resulting "liberation of Munich" has also been called "The White Terror," and it was achieved with great bloodshed. Notes the Potsdam Military Records Office: "Epp's *Freikorps* was anything but timid! They were responsible for the murder of the revolutionary Gustav Landauer and also for the massacre of the Kolping apprentices in Giesing, a working class quarter of Munich."

As one of Epp's officers told Commandant Graff of the French Military Mission, "You see, most of these fellows are young men who—during the five years of the war—had no paternal discipline, and, as it is too late to train them, the best thing is to wipe them out!"

On April 5, 1920, one of the men in the FKE wrote home to his family: "We shoot even the wounded! The enthusiasm is great, almost unbelievable!" As their overall commanding officer, von Epp was therefore "responsible for various massacres," for which he was never brought to trial.

As Gustav Noske overthrew the Red regime at Berlin, von Epp and von Oven at Munich led a force consisting of two Regular Army Guards divisions, augmented by other *Free Korps* units from Prussia, Bavaria, and Württemberg, with the communists at Munich surrendering on their own holiday of May 1, 1919. Hoffmann's government was reestablished under the joint protection of the new German Army—the Republican Reichswehr—and the civilian FKs.

Both sides had taken and executed hostages during the Bavarian Civil War. In addition to the hatred focused on the now dead local Reds, most Bavarians felt revulsion toward the national capital at Berlin, and also all things Prussian. The hero of the hour—the man who represented this deep-rooted wellspring of popular feeling—was the city's liberator, Franz Ritter von Epp.

He was briefly the veritable military dictator of the entire South German province of Bavaria, an area that became a center of opposition and Nazi activity against the federal government at Berlin and the surviving Communists there, too.

In 1919, Epp and his command entered the new Republican Army, but only as the FKE. Later prominent Nazis who were FKE men included NS Motor *Korpsführer* "Papa Angry" Adolf Hühnlein, NS Party Deputy Führer Rudolf Hess, and Hitler's personal SA adjutant, Lt Wilhelm Brückner.

On October 1, 1919, von Epp was named commander of Reichswehr Brigade 21 in the Regular Army, and exactly a year later, he was also posted as Infantry Leader 7 of the Army's resident 7th Infantry Division, responsible for maintaining all public order in Bavaria.

The anti-Red campaign continued into 1920, when Dortmund was "liberated" by Epp's men on April 6, and industrial Essen fell on the 7th, with the entire Ruhr area "pacified" by the 8th. In the latter, hundreds of Red prisoners were shot "attempting to escape" by FKE men and—once more also, as at Munich and in the Baltic—dozens more received death sentences handed down by freebooter courts martial.

Promoted major general on February 10, 1921 according to his official personnel service records, von Epp was again raised in October 1923 to the rank of lieutenant general.

Once the FKE became part of the official national Reichswehr army, von Epp and Rohm used its funds to hire spies like L/Cpl. A. Hitler. They later established the future Führer's official NS Party newspaper, *The People's Observer*—its first—for 60,000 Reichsmarks.

Despite his initial support for Hitler's Nazis, von Epp soon discovered that he had a tiger by the tail during a meeting held on June 14, 1922 at which now civilian Hitler discussed a future rightist strategy with him, Gen. Ludendorff, Gustav von Kahr, and others opposed to the national government at Berlin.

The others wanted to compromise with Berlin, but the more radical Hitler proposed a cynical deal instead with the Communists—now called the KPD. The group expelled Hitler instead. He stormed out, shouting, "You will live to regret the treachery that you are committing against the German race today! You will recognize too late what power I have behind me!" A decade later, Epp and Hitler would find themselves almost at greater odds again.

On October 31, 1923, von Epp retired from the army after thirty-six years of active service on three continents, having been threatened with replacement in command due to his increasingly right-wing politics. The following November 8–9, 1923, Hitler and Goering launched their ill-fated Beer Hall Putsch to march on Berlin, but it ended instead in a hail of Bavarian State Police bullets.

Von Epp—like Bavarian Crown Prince Rupprecht—played no part in this affair. Hitler moved from fear that monarchists like them would strike first to bring about either a return of the Bavarian monarchy or else a complete break with the still Prussian-led Reich in favor of a new union with fellow Catholic state Austria.

After Hitler left prison, reorganized his party, and promised publicly to seek office through none but legal means via the elective process, now Lt Gen. von Epp duly joined the Nazis. He was elected to the Reichstag on the NS ballot in May 1928, proving to be one of the movement's most successful candidates at the polls to boot.

Despite his election, Epp ridiculed the supposed "qualities" of the statesman thus: "I do not have those qualities! I will never have them, for nothing depends on those qualities!" As a Reichstag member seated next to fellow NS Deputy Goering, von Epp noted in his diary that it was "an attempt by the slime to govern—church slime, middle class slime, military slime," and in the latter category, he included Gen. Wilhelm Groener as well.

In 1932, Gen. von Epp was posted as leader of the Party Defense League. After the appointments to national Reich offices of Hitler and Goering on January 30, 1933, Epp was named by the new Nazi chancellor the following March 8, 1933 as his Reich commissioner and secretary of state for Bavaria, and during April 10, 1933 to April 30, 1945, he was governor of Bavaria as well.

The real power in Munich, however, was Nazi *Gauleiter* (Regional Leader) Adolf Wagner. In 1941, von Epp challenged Wagner over the latter's notorious Crucifix Order that mandated all such crosses be removed from State Catholic School classroom and other walls, being replaced with pictures of Hitler.

When von Epp protested the order to his Führer directly, the latter ordered the mandate rescinded immediately, privately informing his equally anti-Catholic aide Martin Bormann that "the problem of the churches must wait for solution until after the war!"

When he felt that Rohm's open lawlessness in Bavaria had gone too far, Epp also threatened to call out the army to restore order, and few doubted that the celebrated 1919 liberator of Munich would do so if pushed too far; he was not, but he did complain privately to Hitler thus:

> Government cannot exist this way! Such a system is impossible! Every existing authority will be destroyed.... An irrational policy on all sides and at all levels.... Unworthy happenings (in the concentration camps).... Terrorist acts against Jews are known in Berlin. Since there are no orders to intervene, one must do good things secretly.

Added Peterson in 1969: "Epp candidly wrote that the non-Party member was helpless and terrorized; the people no longer dared to speak, and no one knew what they really thought. Thus spoke Epp, the man supposedly in charge, with 11 more years in which to regret."

Epp was named head of the Colonial Bureau of the Party on May 5, 1934, devoted to the eventual return of Imperial Germany's former overseas colonies seized by Japan, France, and Great Britain during and after the Great War. He held that post until it was dissolved on February 17, 1943, in the wake of the Stalingrad defeat of the German 6th Army in Russia that ended all such overseas fantasies.

On July 7, 1935, Hitler promoted von Epp to the military rank of general of infantry, as well as chief of Infantry Regiment 61 on October 16, 1938. He also served under Goering as Reich Master of the Hunt for Bavaria.

Von Epp often found himself on the opposite side of Nazi pet causes: he opposed the SS camp at Dachau outside Munich, blocked Nazi race-baiter Julius Streicher from becoming mayor of Nuremberg, told Hitler that Nazi Germany could not win another war against the Allies, and also asserted that a cruel fate would await the Third Reich over the Jews.

Finally, like his slain aide, Capt. Rohm, von Epp wanted the SA to supplant the Regular Army. To that end, Epp headed the Army Political Office until the Blood Purge ended its relevance for good. In all these political battles, the Mother of God General would be bested, but not slain.

One that he almost won, however, was that of the succession to the dying Reich President Paul von Hindenburg in 1934. The army—upon whose whim at that time Hitler's future entirely depended—was openly considering three choices for the new president of Germany: von Epp, former Imperial Crown Prince Wilhelm, and Hitler himself. When it was learned that Hitler secretly promised to purge Rohm and the SA leadership corps before Hindenburg's death, the army decided to back the Nazi Führer as his successor.

During World War II, von Epp held no military commands, as Hitler may well have considered such an authoritative and outspoken man as he far too dangerous to entrust armed troops. For his part, Epp held himself aloof from the many plots to either remove and/or kill the Führer to whom he owed all his appointive offices.

As the war went on, von Epp received letters at his office in Munich from people decrying being, "Delivered to a pack of hangmen!"

In the spring of 1945, he may or may not have had a hand in the surrender of Munich to the U.S. Army. One source states that "Epp was one of Hitler's internal critics who was involved in the revolt of the Freedom Action of Bavaria against the NS in 1945."

Another asserts that "he was arrested on [then *Gauleiter*] Paul Giesler's orders in 1945," being associated with the above named anti-Nazi organization, "lead by Rupprecht Gerngross.… Epp, however, did not want to be directly involved with the group, as he considered their goal—surrender to the Allies—a form of backstabbing of the German Army."

Virtually unrecognized for who he was other than as only a member of the Goering surrender entourage on May 8, 1945 to the Americans, von Epp was never tried after the war for anything, but died instead of natural causes, two dates being given for his demise: December 31, 1946 and January 31, 1947.

The entire Hindenburg line fell nonetheless to the hard-charging Allies, resulting in thousands upon thousands of captured German Army POWs. Their Great War was at last over. (*LC*)

When the Treaty of Versailles's terms were signed by the Germans on June 28, 1919, it meant virtually the complete disarmament of the Second Reich: only a 100,000-man army, no military draft, the general staff dissolved, and Germany forbidden to have any aircraft, tanks, or artillery. The reduced army would have twelve years of service for enlisted men and twenty-five for officers, with no reserves. Hindenburg resigned from the army the same day, according to Walter Gorlitz.

Allied soldiers stack discarded German steel pots. Noted the period Great War original Allied caption: "Boche helmets—mementos of Cambrai. Steel helmets were all taken from Boche prisoners captured during the memorable advance on Cambrai." (*LC*)

After the Treaty of Versailles was signed, the Germans established *Grenschutz Ost* (Frontier Force East) of 30,000 men under arms with armored cars to ward off marauding Poles. It reminded Hindenburg of the 1813 iron wedding rings instead of gold during the Wars of Liberation in German history.

A postwar allegorical picture postcard of a dead German soldier of 1914 being posthumously awarded an Iron Cross by an eagle, as—in the far distant future of 1933—Hitler's Nazis restore lost Prussian martial glory via a march-past with banners near Berlin's Brandenburg Gate, still there today. (*LC*)

When Hindenburg turned seventy years old on October 2, 1917, the Kaiser himself came calling to wish him a happy birthday, while at KHQ Kreuznach, the marshal ordered a full salute for a boy he called, affectionately, "My little soldier!"

On September 10, 1918—two months to the day before his flight to Holland—the Kaiser visited and spoke with workers at the Krupp Arms Plant at Essen in the German Ruhr heavy industrial area. Note that he wears a sidearm and carries a hatchet style walking stick. He told them: "Each of us has his duty to perform and his burden to carry: you at your lathe, and I on my throne!" (*LC*)

Above, left and right: Wilhelm II's last appointed imperial chancellor, Prince Max von Baden, wearing a black mourning band on left uniform sleeve. He died in 1929. (*LC*)

On April 9, 1917—Ludendorff's own fifty-second birthday—Lord Haig's BEF rolled over three successive lines of the overall Hindenburg Line, while the man it was named for took his normal, daily, calming hour-long walk through a nearby wood at headquarters. His being eighteen years older than the more excitable Ludendorff helped.

The Kaiser's Chief of Naval Cabinet Admiral Georg von Müller believed that Ludendorff was a megalomaniac, while the news of the latter's notorious mental breakdown on September 11, 1918 spread like wildfire through the various command staffs on the embattled Western Front. He had other things to worry about, however, such as the unchecked spread of the deadly Spanish Flu disease among the already weakened troops.

Left: His first wife, Margarethe Pernet Ludendorff, wearing black in mourning for two of her sons slain in the war.

Angry soldiers in Crown Prince Rupprecht's command asserted that "The Prussians will fight until the last Bavarian!" With revolution staring all of them in the face in the autumn of 1918, Hindenburg roared: "I'll not allow my epaulettes or my sword to be taken from me!" In the event, no one tried.

A *Punch* cartoon by Leonard Raven Hill, published September 26, 1917, that preceded the Kaiser's flight to Holland on November 10, 1918.

In his 1935 biography of Hindenburg, author Ludwig Cohn noted that no one had ever even imagined a scenario in which the Kaiser might have had to flee, but maybe he himself did. First, he recalled when his grandfather, as "The Cartridge Prince," had to flee Berlin for asylum in the UK during the 1848 uprising of fifty years before. Second, he never ordered his army to invade neutral Holland, perhaps foreseeing it as a possible place of personal refuge someday, as now dawned upon him.

THE INSEPARABLE.

THE KAISER (*to his People*). "DO NOT LISTEN TO THOSE WHO WOULD SOW DISSENSION BETWEEN US. *I WILL NEVER DESERT YOU.*"

The man who told the Kaiser he had to go on November 9, 1918: Lt General Wilhelm Groener (November 22, 1867 to March 5, 1939), born at Ludwigsburg, Württemberg. A longtime personal rival of—and successor to—Ludendorff, of his later boss, General Groener asserted that, "As a man, Hindenburg is certainly to be respected, but he is not a strategist, and as a statesman, he does not have the least talent!"

Groener was one of the very few men whom Hitler actually feared. General Groener died in 1939. (*LC*)

Above: Defense Minister Groener (*third from left*) on German Army maneuvers in Fall 1930. At far left stands another man whom Hitler feared, General Kurt von Schleicher—the Reich Chancellor just previous to the Nazi Fuhrer—whom Goering had murdered during the Nazi Blood Purge of June–July 1934.

In 1930, Nazi Dr Josef Goebbels asked rhetorically in the pages of his newspaper *The Attack*, "Is Hindenburg still alive?" as his camarilla seemed to be omnipresent instead, and the rabidly pro-NS General Litzmann subtly threatened the marshal with assassination if Hitler was not named to office, just like Erzberger and Rathenau before him. (*ASA*)

Previous page, below: Castle Wilhelmshöhe, a post-Spa headquarters of the new duo of Hindenburg and Groener. In 1870, the captured Emperor Napoleon III of the French had been interned there following his surrender after the Battle of Sedan, an event that Hindenburg as a younger officer had witnessed from afar.

When the Reich president accepted the 1930 Young Plan to pay the Allies their demanded wartime reparations, Ludendorff charged publicly that "Field Marshal von Hindenburg has forfeited the right to wear the field gray uniform of the German Army, and to be buried in it!" He was largely discounted by the public, however.

Having succeeded the Kaiser as commander-in-chief of the German Armed Forces on November 10, 1918, Hindenburg (*right*) here salutes their soldiers returning home from the Western Front to defeated Germany. Notice that he salutes with his right hand only, his informal stick baton held at his side, perhaps in submission, a first. (*DH*)

Hitler had crossed the Rhine River by train, heading west into France in 1914; four years later, the defeated soldiers walked back eastward. They knew that they had lost the war, but not the people at home in the main.

"Hindenburg on an elk hunt in Kurland, 1915," with a Reich hunting ranger at left. (*LC*)

There is no mention that he and later Reich Master of the Hunt Hermann Goering ever hunted together, surprisingly. Kurland is referred to in the 1935 Ludwig Cohn Hindenburg biography as "a coastal district of Latvia, just south of the Gulf of Riga," much coveted by both Imperial and Nazi Germany in the two world wars.

According to his 1935 biographer Ludwig Cohn: "He soon became known as an excellent shot. His record from 1904–24 shows that—in addition to minor game—he shot 104 wild boars, 76 roebuck, 27 red deer, 24 does, six black cock, six chamois, and, further, during the war, one bison and one elk. His game book and trophies on the walls of his house meant as much to him as sleeping and eating; they were the only true delights of a man full of life and vigor, whose professional duties had drawn to a close."

Left: Corporal A. Hitler in wartime, his first one. (*HHA*)

The former Kaiser Wilhelm II handlebar moustache gave way to a new one that is still recognized worldwide as that belonging to Adolf Hitler. Initially, even Kaiser Wilhelm was a fan of the future Nazi Führer, calling him, "One of my brave soldiers," telling Prince Schaumburg-Lippe that "No bourgeois/middle class government has called me back! This Cpl. Hitler will run them all out, and not forget his Supreme Warlord!" In the event, the Kaiser was right about everything but his final assertion, alas.

Below left: Artist Hitler depicts in this graphic what Hindenburg and Ludendorff verbalized and wrote postwar, namely that the men on the fighting fronts had been betrayed by the "stab in the back" at home, here shown at right by a rebellious Red soldier. (*Billy F. Price Collection, Texas, USA*)

Previous page, below right: Seen postwar are Germany's most famous field marshals of the just lost Great War: Hindenburg at left and Mackensen at right, both bearing the formal versions of their staffs of office, awarded to each by their former imperial master, Kaiser Wilhelm II. Standing between and behind the two marshals at rear in cut-out cavalry helmet is Colonel Oskar von Hindenburg.

Here—clasping his bejeweled baton—the storied von Mackensen appears in his favorite dress uniform of the Death's Head Hussars. The skull-and-crossbones motif on the façade of his fur Perlmutze busby shako cap was adapted by the Nazi SS as well. The Black Marshal's career martial spanned all three German emperors as well as the Nazi Führer. He was promoted to lieutenant general and division commander in 1903, and the following year outraged his fellow officers by kissing the Kaiser's gloved hand in public at the Danzig train station. (*LC*)

Right: The defeated Kaiser. The victorious Allies wanted to try him as a war criminal, but the Dutch refused to extradite him. The Socialist German republic likewise balked at either extraditing all the other alleged war criminals on the Allied lists as well as conducting domestic trails. All died free of any such proceedings.

The Kaiser's signed abdication was dated Nov. 28, 1918, at Amerongen, Holland. (*ASA*)

By 1926, Hindenburg had fully supplanted the former German emperor as the public's father figure and ruling authority. In this church ceremony, his spiked helmet and formal marshal's baton tests on the stool at left, behind which stand the Baron Konstantin von Neurath couple in the first pew. In the second pew can be seen Dr Otto Meissner just past Hindenburg's head, and next to him at right, Colonel Oskar von Hindenburg. In that same pew at far left can be seen the head of German Navy commander Admiral Dr Erich Raeder. (*LC*)

Hindenburg in mourning at the grave of his late wife, 1922, his military *aide-de-camp* standing at right rear. (*LC*)

One postwar British biographer of the ex-Kaiser called him "The Fabulous Monster," and—many felt—justly so, too: "A wildcat whose mustaches want uncurling, a man-eating tiger!" ran the hyperbole. In 1911, one English lord termed Wilhelm II, "A howling cad!"

Crown Prince Rupprecht of Bavaria (*second from left, seated*) with his deposed royal father, the former King Ludwig III of Bavaria, two beaten field marshals postwar. (*LC*)

Ludwig Cohn in 1935 speculated that if Rupprecht had been sent to East Prussia in August 1914 instead of Hindenburg, he would have been the acclaimed victor at Tannenberg. Had he become dictator of Germany during 1916–18 instead, his more moderate advice—such as not demanding the return of the overseas German colonies as a peace condition—might very well have ended the Great War earlier in a negotiated peace acceptable to all.

Bavarian Army Colonel Franz Ritter von Epp, 1917. (*Courtesy Michael D. Miller*)

Reportedly, the former Kaiser had kept diaries during the entirety of his long Dutch exile, and, upon his death in 1941, Crown Prince Wilhelm took them home to Berlin, where the Red Army reportedly seized them in 1945. It would be great to see them published some day!

Top right: Lt-Colonel von Epp (*right*), C.O. of the Royal Bavarian Lifeguard Infantry Regiment. (*Courtesy Michael D. Miller*)

Had the Kaiser returned to his lost throne, he meant to establish a real dictatorship during his renewed reign. It was never to be, however. In 1920, he had written to Mackensen from Doorn that until he himself came back, his Black Marshal must serve as his stand-in, "with Ludendorff in charge of military matters and Karl Helfferich … of domestic affairs … or von der Goltz … or Lettow-Vorbeck," according to his most prolific biographer, Rohl.

Von Epp and General Karl von Wenninger (*center*) were with the staff of 28th Reserve Corps in Romania on September 7, 1917, with the latter being killed in action at Muncelul the very next day, according to noted author Michael D. Miller.

Still, it was Ludendorff whom the former emperor blamed the most for the debacle of 1918: "It was he who lost his nerve in Spa … that in an audience with me, he urgently demanded that we offer an armistice, as well as … a changed form of government with a new chancellor—and that immediately! With that, he set the stone of revolution rolling, and cost me my throne!"

The Kaiser wrote to Ludendorff thus: "I still hope one day to have you at my side as my Chief of General Staff when— together!—we will rebuild our glorious Army!" Perhaps that is why Ludendorff later rejected Hitler's offer to name him a field marshal under the new Nazi Third Reich.

Above right: Lt-Colonel von Epp wearing Blue Max as regimental commander in 1915 on the Somme River Front, with the Royal Bavarian Lifeguard Infantry Regiment. (*Courtesy Michael D. Miller*)

Thirsting for revenge from Holland, the Kaiser wrote to his favorite wartime field marshal, August von Mackensen, "Then order will be restored to the country, and then I shall come back to sweep the country clean with an iron broom, starting at the top! I have noted down the names … and once we have restored order at home … we shall gallop full tilt at the enemy!"

In May 1921, Wilhelm II again warmed to his favorite postwar topic—his Restoration—thus: "There must be a levy *en masse* of volunteers, even if they are armed only with scythes and hunting rifles! Then we will first throw out the Poles, and then move against the Entente!"

The Gorlitz Free Corps enters liberated Munich on May 1, 1919 as part of von Epp's anti-Spartacist/Communist force. (*HHA*)

Von Epp would go on to free Essen, Dortmund, and the rest of the Red-held industrial Ruhr in April 1920. For these deeds, the Nazis on November 8, 1935 created Ritter von Epp Plaza from the renamed Promenadeplatz.

Epp (dark horse, right) salutes his victorious Free Corps cavalry and infantry as they parade past at Munich on May 1, 1919. (*HHA*)

Unlike Goering—who ran away to Scandinavia—and Hitler (not yet a force), the combat general of the Great War von Epp actually did something against the hated Reds during this volatile period. Added the Kaiser in May 1921: "In the old days under a King, it would have been a different matter. He would simply have issued the mobilization order, called the Army together, and ordered it to attack," as he had done, indeed, just so in August 1914.

There was a mass grave outside Munich for the German Communists slaughtered during the freebooter takeover of Bolshevik Munich in May 1919 and its liberation afterwards. For these crimes, Epp was never brought to stand trial.

On Hitler in May 1932, the Kaiser wrote: "We see that Hitler thinks of only himself.… Megalomania, and like Ludendorff, mentally over-excited."

Epp (second from right) and others kneeling after the liberation of Munich, May 1, 1919. (*HHA*)

In January 1933, the Kaiser saw himself as the only foil to Hitler's Nazis in power: "Call me, and I will come!" but then exulted along with his second wife, Hermo, when Hindenburg named the Führer as Reich chancellor on January 30 that year. She called it "The best birthday present!" that had occurred three days before, on the 27th.

Epp (*center left*) in May 1919 as the liberator of Red Munich. Note the boy standing at far right, an onlooker to history-in-the-making, and thus even a part of it himself. (*Eva Braun Hitler Albums, U.S. National Archives, College Park, MD, USA*)

On the Nazi Day of Potsdam of March 21, 1933, the Kaiser viewed himself as "The Steel Helmet Kaiser," returned to his throne anew, just as his portrait was hung that day at its place of honor in the Berlin City Hall.

A stern-looking formal portrait of von Epp as a German general wearing the pre–1935 "coal scuttle" style steel helmet and Blue Max at the throat. This is also, perhaps, the best photographic extant of that cover's bolted lugs at both right and left. (*HHA*)

Even though Epp persuaded Rohm—his personal ADC during 1921–23 as 7th Military District C.O.—to surrender the Nazi rebel-occupied Military Academy; General von Seeckt fired him, in December 1923. On May 8, 1945, Epp surrendered to the U.S. Army as part of the overall entourage of Reich Marshal Goering, dying at the age of seventy-nine as a POW on New Year's Day 1947.

At the September 1929 Nazi Party Congress at Nuremberg. *From left to right*: unknown SA man, Epp in steel helmet, unknown SA officer, Hitler carrying SA coffee can-style kepi cap, and Captain Hermann Goering following behind. Both Hitler and Goering wear boots, while General von Epp sports instead low-quarter shoes. (*HHA*)

Above left: Martial leader of the Kapp–Lüttwitz Putsch at Berlin in March 1920 was General Walther Baron von Lüttwitz, holder of the Blue Max. (*LC*)

In 1917, the Kaiser's many admirers touted him as "Wilhelm the Truly Great," while instead the very next year he became "Wilhelm the Last." (*LC*)

Above right: General von Lüttwitz (*center*) with German Socialist Defense Minister Gustav Noske (*right*), the man mainly responsible for the suppression of the German revolution of 1918–19. (*LC*)

Angered when the upstart duo forced the firing of Bethmann-Hollweg as imperial chancellor on July 13, 1917, the Kaiser stormed aloud, "I might as well abdicate straightaway!" as Hindenburg and Ludendorff had, in effect, abrogated his right to name the imperial chancellor and Prussian prime minister, but he stayed in power another eighteen months instead. (*LC*)

Right: Another major figure in the March 1920 Berlin takeover was Captain Hermann Ehrhardt (*left*) of the Naval Brigade bearing his name. General von Lüttwitz ordered him to start the revolt by occupying Reich Capital Berlin, and he complied. Just a week later—his self-confidence restored—Wilhelm II blurted out, "Democracy ends there, where my Guards are in command!" but on November 9, 1918, not even they supported him, it was alleged. (*LC*)

Marauding troops and armed civilians at Berlin. Only a socialist general strike defeated the revolt within a week. (*LC*)

In 1918, the Social Democrats felt that for years they had been ruled by a madman, none other than the last German Kaiser: "The best thing would have been to send him to an asylum!"

The civilian instigator of the March 1920 revolt was former Reich government official Dr Wolfgang Kapp. (*LC*)

In 1918, the Kaiser's loyal courtiers felt that "He would delude himself to the last that his soldiers would fight to keep him on the throne!" They did not.

As the March 1918 Michael Offensive pushed the Allies back, reportedly the Kaiser yelled from his passing royal train to a sentry standing on the platform that, "The battle is won! The English have been totally beaten, and must kneel before the Imperial Standard!" His boast was premature, however.

Mrs Ludendorff was an eyewitness to the March 1920 revolt who recorded astute recollections in her memoirs.

As the truth from the battlefields became known in the summer of 1918, Wilhelm II showed a different side to his stalwarts: "I see that we must take stock. We are at the limits of our capabilities. The war must be brought to an end." He was right, and gave the order to the beaten duo to proceed accordingly.

Top left: The duo's "unknown" August 21, 1922 Munich visit that is barely mentioned in the past literature on the period, and even then only as a mere stopover by the field marshal on his way elsewhere to hunt chamois! As shown here, it was rather more than that, indeed! (*DH*)

Noted Anna von der Goltz in 2009, however: "In the summer of 1922, Hindenburg … chose to ignore well-informed republican warnings … with his controversial visit.… *En route* to his annual summer hunt in the Bavarian town of Dietramszell, Hindenburg visited the nationalist politician Gustav von Kahr in Munich, an advocate of Bavarian separatism." What follows is the previously unpublished, in-depth photographic coverage from the exiled Kaiser's own albums in Holland that reveal the depth of the postwar collaboration among the still-talking duo themselves, as well as with both Crown Prince Rupprecht and the later ill-fated Gustav von Kahr. It is presented here in detail for the very first time. Before the march past of the Reichswehr/National Army reads the period caption showing Hindenburg with baton at left and Ludendorff looking down at right, listening to the welcoming address of His Excellency General von Mohl at the Academy of Art.

Top right: Hindenburg at center with baton chats with General von Danner at Munich's Academy of Art. (*DH*)

Von der Goltz asserted, "At this time, the Bavarian capital was an El Dorado for extreme right organizations and leading personalities of right wing radicalism. The divisive side-effects of Hindenburg's public appearances were visible once more."

Above: From left to right: hands behind back, Ludendorff stands in right profile; Dr Stumpf in dark spiked helmet; two unknown officers; Hindenburg also in right profile; His Excellency *Graf* Bothmer (white beard); Gustav von Kahr (dark coat and top hat, back to camera); and General Petz, also back to camera and wearing dark spiked helmet, all at the Munich *Hofgartentor*. (*DH*)

Left: Standing outside the Academy of Art at Munich are Ludendorff (*fifth from right*) and General von Mohl, the latter wearing the cutout cavalry steel helmet. (*DH*)

States von der Goltz: "The government envoy reported back to Berlin: 'The streets were so packed that one could hardly get through! There were blue and white [the Bavarian colors] and Red flags everywhere. Social Democrats and Jews were insulted, and sometimes even beaten up.'"

Above left: General von Mohl (*center*) raises his saber at center to commence the day's events, as Marshal von Hindenburg in turn raises his baton in salute at left, the officers at right rendering hand to helmet salutes instead, at the Art Academy. The 1922 caption reads: *Das Hoch auf den Feldherrn/Cheers for the General* .(*DH*)

Above right: General von Danner stands between the honor guard commanding officer at left with saber and the marshal at center as the latter gestures with his baton to the men standing at Attention at right, as he prepares to inspect them.

Von der Goltz—quoting the official government report on the duo's visit—"The field marshal himself behaved rather quietly, but he was steered by Kahr … and Ludendorff, who both used the occasion to further their own popularity by bathing in Hindenburg's glory." Note that there is absolutely no mention at all of Hitler and his Nazis. (*DH*)

Right: Beginning his inspection of the National Association of German Officers assembled in his honor, the marshal at far right is followed by Dr Stumpf carrying a bouquet of flowers at center left and Colonial Service Maj. Fehn at center right in front of the Bavarian capital's Army Museum in the *Hofgartentor.* (*DH*)

Hindenburg (*center*) troops the line of the assembled Bavarian National Border Police as the men he inspects stand with rifles at present arms. Note the guard commander at left center with drawn saber, Maj. Fehn, followed by Dr Stumpf. (*DH*)

On September 2, 1918, the Kaiser soberly reflected aloud, "We have lost the campaign."

The marshal striding by at center with Dr Stumpf at left center, with flowers in left hand. Note also the man between them at rear raising his top hat in a civilian salute. (*DH*)

Following the failure of the Michael Offensive, the Kaiser left Reich Capital Berlin for the last time, by rail, on October 29, 1918, never to see it again, to take refuge at KHQ Spa, Belgium, among the most loyal of his paladins, the German general staff—or so he thought.

Hindenburg (*fifth from left*) makes a point to stop at the saluting figure of Infantry Leader General von Epp to personally congratulate him for ending the Munich Red Revolt of 1918–19, as the others render hand salutes in this photograph by Spiess. (*DH*)

In 1920, British Prime Minister David Lloyd George speculated on a Napoleonic-like island exile for the ex-Kaiser, perhaps in Dutch Batavia or Java, or maybe the still British Falkland Islands off Argentina.

Left: The duo at center chat outside the Art Academy. Note that only they in this group wear the 1914–16-style spiked helmets, while both also sport sashes across their chests. (*DH*)

When the former emperor remarried in exile, it was termed by his courtiers, "The elderly monarch's sexual Indian Summer," he being considered, "no longer normal." The Kaiser, however, viewed Hermo as the new Kaiserin of his second reign instead; so did she.

Previous page, middle: From left to right, in their car: Hindenburg (about to take his seat), Ludendorff at center, and Dr Stumpf at right holding the marshal's baton in his left hand, the driver awaiting the command to go, outside the Art Academy. (*DH*)

One wonders if Hitler was but a face in the crowd during all this—most likely, yes. The Kaiser remarried on November 15, 1922, he wearing the uniform of a general of the 1st Guard Regiment, even designing her wedding gown himself.

Previous page, below: The car at the Army Museum in the *Hofgartentor*, with—seated, from left to right—driver, Dr Stumpf, Hindenburg, and von Kahr, the latter murdered by the Nazis during the Blood Purge of the summer of 1934. (*DH*)

At the Kaiser's second wedding, his brother, Prince Heinrich, toasted the bride as "Her Majesty the Empress and Queen," while her passport identified her instead as "Princess Hermine Reuss, wife of Kaiser Wilhelm II." By August 1923, the new couple was to be seen bickering, he "Having very little liking for her own five children" from her widowed previous marriage.

Members of the Bavarian royal house, including the former King Ludwig III of Bavaria, who stands at center in white beard in right profile, grasping baton in his right hand, just visible, outside the Army Museum. This time, almost everyone sports the former spiked helmets of a bygone era. (*DH*)

Hindenburg looks into the camera's lens at left center. (*DH*)

The Kaiser had been named a field marshal in a trio of armies: his own and those of both Great Britain and Austria. In 1928, he called the hated Woodrow Wilson "a paralytic madman."

Top left: Standing on the steps at center, Rupprecht raises his baton in a right-handed salute to the man at left raising his top hat, while Hindenburg follows behind at far right, looking down and carrying his own baton of office as well. Dr Stumpf stands at center between them, at the Army Museum. (*DH*)

Middle left: Hindenburg stands in majestic repose on the carpeted staircase baton in hand, as Ludendorff is at left, behind whom stands an officer at attention, others rendering hand salutes at right, at the municipal Cultural Museum. (*DH*)

The Kaiser admired Benito Mussolini for having stormed to power in Italy in October 1922, having been appointed premier by the man he called "The Dwarf," Savoyard King Victor Emmanuel III.

Below left: Standing on the landing below a lineup of colorfully-garbed university students are, from left to right, Ludendorff, Hindenburg, Dr von Kahr, and Dr Stumpf. Standing on the step above and between the marshal at left and von Kahr at right is, perhaps, Dr Stumpf's son, later Luftwaffe Colonel General Hans-Jürgen Stumpff, who on May 8, 1945 surrendered the beaten German Air Force to the Soviets at Berlin's Karlshorst Army Engineering School. (*DH*)

Hitler's Nazi SA Storm Troopers parade past two of the trio of wartime Bavarian field marshals, Prince Leopold (*left*) and Crown Prince Rupprecht (*right*), both standing in the far left bottom of this frame. The Nazi Führer does not seem to be present, however. (*LC*)

Notes one account: "Rupprecht had no sympathy for the Nazis, and during 1939–45 lived in exile in Italy. However, his second wife and their children were captured in Hungary by the Nazis during World War II and ended the war at Dachau concentration camp in Bavaria."

Crown Prince Rupprecht reviews the 19th Bavarian Regiment of the new German Army in December 1924, its men presenting arms.

Hitler stated on July 5, 1942, that the Bavarian crown prince had offered him a dukedom if he would give up the post of Reich chancellor in 1934. During the entire interwar period, Rupprecht hoped to see a constitutional monarchy established in his homeland, one that has yet to happen. As for Rupprecht himself, he never ascended the throne of his fathers, dying in 1955 at Castle Leutstetten, being given a state funeral with full honors and buried in Munich's Theater Church with other members of his family, the Wittelsbach dynasty.

When the botched Nazi Beer Hall Putsch/Revolt failed in November 1923, the Kaiser wrote von Mackensen that "Only he was in a position to restore order. You cannot set up a new Reich from a beer hall!" Regarding Hitler, he asked, "How does he imagine his future?"

Above left: Ludendorff at far left, Goering at far right, with unknown officer talking with the latter. (*HHA*)

In 1932, when his son and heir Crown Prince Wilhelm wanted to run against Hindenburg for Reich president, the angry Kaiser wrote him: "If you do that … I shall disinherit you, and throw you out of my House!" The crown prince stood down.

Above right: As with both the war and the Berlin revolt of March 1920, once again, Margarethe Ludendorff was a recording eyewitness to the events surrounding her husband's involvement in the Beer Hall Putsch of November 8–9, 1923.

Wilhelm II fulminated that "It was impossible for the Hohenzollerns to return" via the Red republican seat of the dead Ebert!

Berliner Tageblatt (*Berlin Daily News*) reported the Hitler–Ludendorff trial in Munich, with the far lesser known Hitler getting top billing: "The Reich Against the Traitors." In 1932, Hitler privately mocked the crown prince for his "Jewish girlfriends swimming at Cecilienhof," but the Kaiser endorsed the Nazi Führer for Reich president over Hindenburg anyway. (*LC*)

The New York Times.

THE WEATHER

VOL. LXXIII No. 24,930 ... NEW YORK, FRIDAY, NOVEMBER 9, 1923 TWO CENTS

BAVARIA IN REVOLT, PROCLAIMS LUDENDORFF DICTATOR;
ITS MONARCHIST FORCES REPORTED MARCHING ON BERLIN;
CAPITAL CRIES TREASON AND MASSES TROOPS FOR DEFENSE

The American newspaper *The New York Times* reported the failed BHP, by giving it a royalist cast instead—and no mention of one A. Hitler in the main headline, although he was noted in the subhead. (*LC*)

For his part in 1932, Wilhelm II called Hitler "A dreadful howler!"

Revolutionary Nazi artist Hitler's self-portrait of him and Ludendorff at the volley of Green Police gunfire on Munich's Odeonsplatz on November 9, 1923: the general standing at center and the former corporal gone to ground at right, just as his enlisted man's training had taught him to do, from *Adolf Hitler: The Unknown Artist*. (*Billy F. Price Collection, Texas, USA*)

From Holland, the ex-Kaiser snorted: "The new Reich will not come from a beer joint!" in December 1923—he was right.

As General Ludendorff (center) looked during the 1924 Beer Hall Putsch Trial at Munich.

The major defendants posed for a group photo after the BHP trial, February 26, 1924, in front of the red brick Infantry School Building at Munich. Ludendorff was acquitted of all charges, having thus escaped the legal penalties for having taken part in not one but two separate uprisings against his governments. His adopted stepson, Lt Heinz Pernet (far left) later gave Hitler's niece (and alleged lover), Geli Raubal, voice lessons—reportedly. (*HHA*)

Above left: The Ludendorff family servant, Kurt Neubauer, was among those Nazis killed by Green Police gunfire on the Odeonsplatz, as here memorialized after Hitler took office in 1933. (*HHA*)

Hitler, sniffed the ex-Kaiser, "was no statesman." After his Reichstag speech celebrating his first year in office as Chancellor on January 30, 1934, Hitler had Goering dissolve all monarchist associations, prompting the irked Kaiser to call him, "The enemy on the right!" three days after his own seventy-fifth birthday.

Above right: Ludendorff with the son of his first wife behind leaves the courtroom after one of the trial proceedings, 1924. Unlike the general, his stepson, Lt Pernet (September 5, 1896 to June 30, 1973), spent jail time incarcerated as his stepfather's driver in the BHP. Convicted along with Hitler in 1924, after his release from prison, Lt Pernet became a brigade leader in the Nazi SA.

As Hitler was in prison, Ludendorff took over as protector of the banned SA. In the elections for Reich President in 1925, Hitler put up the general as his candidate against Field Marshal von Hindenburg. Ludendorff's political career ended when Hitler dropped him after Hindenburg's victory, and his friendship for the Nazi leader turned to icy rejection," asserts his most recent biographers. (*HHA*)

8

Weimar Republic, 1921–31

When Future Nazi Führer Feared Bavarian Crown Prince, 1923

Above all else, Hitler before, during, and long after his failed Beer Hall Putsch of November 8–9, 1923 feared that Crown Prince Rupprecht would seize the vacant Bavarian throne. He worried that a King Rupprecht would lead his kingdom out of Bismarck's former Reich, either as an independent state of its own, or into union with Catholic Austria, in either case separate from the Protestant Prussia that Hitler needed to run his even then projected World War II against the Allies of the Great War.

It was also not impossible that a crowned Rupprecht might ascend the steps of the former Hohenzollern imperial throne as Germany's Kaiser at Berlin. The Allies themselves might have accepted such in order to prevent either a Red Reich, a completely reactionary new Germany, or even a Munich-Vienna-based monarchy that would steal away the Führer's own future plans to unite his former homeland to his current one. Thus, Hitler felt compelled to send a messenger to "His Majesty" at the latter's Berchtesgaden castle for an endorsement of the NS rising. The outraged crown prince was having none of it, however, and instead sent his own note to the responsible local police and military authorities: "Crush this movement at any cost! Use troops if necessary." They did. He was more opposed to his old nemesis—the anti-Catholic, pagan, haughty Ludendorff's participation—than he was to the largely unknown former Cpl. Hitler, however.

Hitler felt disdain for Rupprecht, as noted by Gordon thus: "He was deeply scornful of a Bavarian Crown Prince who would only take back his throne by acclamation. Hitler expected to have to take anything he wanted by force, and was quite prepared to do so."

This was but one of many basic differences between him—a "front soldier" of the trenches as he saw himself—and the high-born, aristocratic elite represented by Army Group commander Field Marshal Crown Prince Rupprecht.

Nevertheless, practical politician Hitler was forced to retain at least a healthy, if feigned, outward respect for and fear of his former commanding officer, and he was right to do so.

Adolf as Ludendorff's Drummer, 1924

Asserts Showalter in *Hindenburg*:

For a time, Hitler even considered himself the *drummer* of Ludendorff or someone like him, but the strain of years of war service combined with the influence of his second wife lead Ludendorff down the path of alleged crackpot religious and political activity.

As Hitler moved closer to power, Ludendorff withdrew even further into a shadow world, alienated from Hindenburg and from most of his wartime colleagues...

The Tannenberg Memorial Debuts, 1924

Authority Peter K. Gessner, of the University of Buffalo, State University of New York, on January 19, 2017 in *Tannenberg*: "The concept of erecting a monument ... was first advanced in 1919 by the Association of Veterans of East Prussia ... a contest was staged for a design ... [that] resulted in over 400 projects, and was won by brothers" and Berlin architects Walter and Johann Kruger, who built the first of many versions during 1925–27.

This was dedicated by Marshal von Hindenburg on the tenth battle anniversary in 1924 at a bare hillside site near Hohenstein in East Prussia, now at Olsztynek, Republic of Poland.   This was to commemorate what had come to be called the Second Battle of Tannenberg in the decade since it had been won. Watching him dedicate the site's foundation stone were 60,000 people, mostly veterans like him of the Great War themselves. Reportedly based in part on the U.K.'s famous Stonehenge and Holy Roman Emperor Frederick II's Castle of the Mountain, its octagonal design featured eight towers 67 feet tall each.

States Tannenberg battle chronicler Showalter in *Hindenburg*:

> The Krugers ... blended myth and acoustics. Eight large towers—placed in a circle large enough to contain 100,000 people [visually speaking, this figure I doubt] were linked by heavy walls.
>
> Each tower had a specific function. One was a youth hostel, one housed battle flags, a third was a chapel, and so on. Together they defined what George L. Mosse calls a "sacred place," with the participants at the center of the festival rather than looking upward and forward at a ritual performer....
>
> There were simpler, homelier memorials as well. Stones and plaques marked individual sites of the battle. Nor were the graves of the fallen collected—as in the west—into huge plots suggesting anonymous mass sacrifice.
>
> Even after the Memorial's erection, these remained places of pilgrimage. School children from all over the Reich came by train on reduced fare excursions, backpacking from Allenstein or Neidenburg to the graves, completing the trip by standing open-mouthed within the Memorial to East Prussia's German identity.

In addition, the Tannenberg Memorial—dedicated to the slain soldiers killed in the battle—encompassed the earlier Anglo-French-American Unknown Soldier concept of honoring all German Great War dead.

Notes Brownell in *First Nazi*: "The memorial was built in a prominent place in a shape reminiscent of the castles of the Teutonic Knights. Its location on a hilltop was accentuated by massive earthworks and landscaping designed to look as if nature alone had shaped the site."

In contrast, Gresser attests in *Tannenberg*:

> Standing on a manmade rise in the ground, the monument—a structure of imposing proportions—took the shape of a regular octagon 325 feet across. In the middle of each of the eight sides rose a 75-foot-high tower 30 × 30 feet at its base.
>
> Linking the individual towers were 30-foot-high walls—solid on the outside—but the inside forming an arcade facing the monument's central plaza. The overall appearance … was strongly suggestive of a Teutonic castle, an indication that the Germans viewed the 1914 victory as in some way a reprisal for the defeat suffered 500 years earlier in an encounter with Slav armies.
>
> In the middle of the plaza was located a tomb of 20 unknown German soldiers who had died during the 1914 battle. Above the tomb rose a wooden cross 40 feet high sheathed in brass.
>
> The unveiling of the monument took place on 18 September 1927 [just prior to Hindenburg's eightieth birthday, on October 2, 1927].

Hindenburg's Seven Reich Chancellors, 1925–34

During his tenures of presidential office, Hindenburg had seven appointed Reich chancellors: Hans Luther, 1925–26; Wilhelm Marx—the man he had defeated in 1925 for the presidency—May 16, 1926; Hermann Müller, June 28, 1928; Heinrich Brüning, March 29, 1930; Franz von Papen, June 1, 1932; Gen. Kurt von Schleicher, December 2, 1932; and Adolf Hitler, January 30, 1933 to April 30, 1945.

Hindenburg's *Camarilla*, 1925–34

The word *camarilla* is defined by *Webster's Seventh New Collegiate Dictionary* (1967) as "a group of unofficial—often secret—and scheming advisors," and thus it has been wrongly used in connection with both the Kaiser and now, here, with Hindenburg, as all of them were officials, appointed by them.

Oskar von Hindenburg

Lt Gen. Oskar von Beneckendorff und von Hindenburg (January 31, 1883 to February 12, 1960) served his father both as a wartime military *aide-de-camp* when field marshal, and during his nine-year Reich presidency as his top personal advisor as well.

Neither Oskar's early military superiors nor Hitler found the only son and heir to be very bright, but he was smart enough to outlast them all and prosper. One of his early postings was to his father's old regiment, the 3rd Guards, and it was here also that he met the man whom he would help make Reich Defense Minister and Chancellor of Germany, Gen. Kurt von Schleicher.

After his father was promoted field marshal, Oskar was advanced to major, serving on his father's headquarters staff throughout the war and beyond. When the marshal was elected Reich president in 1925, Oskar stayed on as the new chief executive's aide, a post wherein he controlled most personal access to his father the president.

He was instrumental in having Hitler named Reich chancellor on January 30, 1933—the day before his own fiftieth birthday—and also helped him gain electoral acceptance at the polls in August 1934 as his late father's successor as Reich president.

Reich Presidential State Secretary Dr Otto Meissner

During the entire nine-year period of the von Hindenburg presidency, the dominating influence was that of Dr Otto Meissner, a monarchist civil servant. It was he who—along with von Papen and Oskar—persuaded the "Old Gentleman" to usher in Hitler to appointive office, in the Nazi National Revolution of 1933. This the Reich president actually supported, rather than being merely a disinterested bystander and onlooker, as some historians have asserted.

Otto Lebrecht Eduard Daniel Meissner (March 13, 1880 to May 27, 1953) headed the office of the president of Germany during its initial triad of incumbents: Soci Friedrich Ebert, Field Marshal Paul von Hindenburg, and Cpl./Reich Chancellor Adolf Hitler, no mean political feat.

In 1937, Hitler created Dr Meissner a federal/Reich minister, entitled "Chief of the Presidential Chancellery of the Führer and Chancellor." Dr Meissner also managed to survive his postwar trial as a convicted war criminal at Nuremberg without being hanged.

It was lawyer Dr Meissner who guided the aging marshal throughout all of his long presidential tenure, from Weimar Republic into Third Reich, covered in his 1950 post-war memoirs *State Secretary Under Ebert, Hindenburg, and Hitler*. This was allegedly ghostwritten by his son, Dr Hans-Otto Meissner (1909–92), who was also a biographer of Magda Quandt Goebbels.

Along with fellow *camarilla* members Franz von Papen and Oskar von Hindenburg, the elder Dr Meissner helped hoist Hitler into the saddle of governmental office in 1933 against great political odds.

Tannenberg Memorial Opening and Dedication, September 18, 1927

On September 18, 1927, now incumbent Reich President Marshal von Hindenburg headed a cast of thousands at the joint opening and dedication of the brand-new Tannenberg Memorial. His speech pleased Germans and angered non-Germans in rejecting 100 percent German war guilt for 1914, with an extract of it engraved by the Nazis in August 1933 on to a bronze plaque in a place of honor inside one of the eight octagonal red brick towers.

The ceremony aped the later mammoth proportions of Nazi rallies thus: "Ten kilometers of veterans—resplendent in Imperial uniforms—paid homage to Hindenburg and the 20 Unknown Soldiers from 1914" who were buried at the memorial site as well." The star of the show himself boasted his Masurian regimental colonel-in-chief uniform awarded to him by the Kaiser of long ago.

The Return of Neudeck, October 2, 1927

On the occasion of the Reich president's eightieth birthday on October 2, 1927—as organized and then supervised by Oskar von Hindenburg—the marshal and his family had restored to them the formerly lost estate of Neudeck. This was paid for, upgraded, and even lavishly furnished to their "station" in life by both German governmental and private financial contributions.

The property had fallen into grave disrepair and poor financial straits the year before under the management of Hindenburg's cousin, Lina, but now all was set right on the spur of Elard von Oldenburg-Januschau to provide clear title to the property. The rebuilt manor house was both deeded and titled to Oskar and not Paul, thus avoiding German inheritance taxes due at the time of the Reich president's eventual demise.

Hitler extended this windfall as head of government in 1933 to make their male descendants as well officially tax-exempt, as sweet a financial deal as could be legally enacted. Indeed, the new Maj. Gen. Oskar von Hindenburg, his wife, and their family resided on the estate throughout the entirety of the end of the Weimar Republic and all of the Nazi Third Reich as well.

It took the storming Communist Red Army in January 1945 to chase Clan Hindenburg off the vast Neudeck premises into Medingin in Lower Saxony during the hasty evacuation of their beloved East Prussia, it never to be seen again.

Invading the house, Soviet soldiers both looted and set it afire. At the Potsdam Conference of August 1945, the property became part of the hated Republic of Poland, with the German populace expelled from their lands, replaced by vengeful Poles anew.

In 1950, the manor house remnants were finally and completely demolished. Located today in the Warmian administrative district—formerly German Masuria—in modern northern Poland, it has had a long and checkered historic past like the rest of the former Prussia. The region had been settled by Pomeranian tribes subjugated starting in 1234 by the brutal Teutonic Knights, with Neudeck Village being established in 1320 by them as well, the area being thrice devastated by wars during 1414–66. It became part of the Duchy of Prussia beginning in 1525. In 1755, the marshal's ancestor Prussian Army Col. Otto Friedrich von Hindenburg bought the estate as his clan's new country residence.

It was inherited post-death by nephew Otto Gottfried von Beneckendorff (1747–1827), who united the two family names as one in 1789 under special permission granted from King of Prussia Frederick Wilhelm I, father of the later marshal's first Kaiser-commander, Wilhelm I.

During 1773–1922, Neudeck was incorporated within the Royal Province of West Prussia, but its remnants were granted to the newly reborn State of Poland on June 28, 1919 under the Treaty of Versailles. What little remained of West Prussia became part of East Prussia simultaneously.

Tannenberg Monument, *Time* magazine, October 3, 1927

Erect and martial, President Generalfeldmarschall Paul Ludwig Hans von Beneckendorff und von Hindenburg arrived at Tannenberg, East Prussia, there to unveil a war memorial to the soldiers who fell in the historic Battle of Tannenberg.

More than 100,000 people gathered to witness the ceremony. Six miles of veterans lined up to do honor to their old military chief. Some of them were dressed in field gray; others were resplendent in plumed helmets and gold-braided tunics of Imperial days.

Gathered there, too, were many of the highest Reich authorities, from Chancellor Wilhelm Marx and several of his cabinet to Marshal von Mackensen, Gens. von François and [Ludendorff].

Clad in his marshal's uniform, with the baton of his rank in his left hand, the aged Hindenburg—almost 80—passed through the cheering throng, stopping now and then to say a few words to a former comrade-in-arms.

He is grim, cool, calm, yet genial enough on occasion. Germans recall a story about their President that exemplifies his peculiar wit: one of his old friends is alleged to have asked him:

"What do you do when you get excited?" "I whistle," replied the President. "But I have never heard you whistle!" "I never have!" the Old Gentleman answered, slyly.

And with memories of his famed battle "thick as autumnal leaves that strew the brooks of Vallombrisa," Germany's greatest warrior showed no sign of emotion as he approached the massive octagon memorial, surmounted by huge, lofty towers.

Noted in Brownell's *First Nazi*, Hindenburg said to the dense mass of people around him:

The Tannenberg National Monument serves primarily as a memorial in commemoration of those who fell in freeing their fatherland from enemy invasion.

Not only in their memory—but also in honor of my living comrades—I feel it is my duty here on this occasion to say the following: "The charges that Germany is guilty of the greatest of all wars, we—the German people!—repudiate in all its phases."

Not envy, hate nor eagerness for conquest caused us to resort to weapons. War was a last resort for us, and the requiring of the greatest sacrifices of the entire people was the last means of maintaining our prestige against a host of enemies.

With pure hearts we marched out to defend the fatherland, and with pure hands the German Army wielded the sword! Germany is ever ready to prove it before impartial judges!

Far away in Doorn, the ex-Kaiser, too, bethought him of the Battle of Tannenberg, and recalled that if Hindenburg and Ludendorff were its heroes, it was only because he had sent them there.

With magnificent effrontery, he wired the President of the German Republic: "At today's dedication of the memorial of the Battle of Tannenberg, I am in deep and unforgettable gratitude with all those who participated in this gigantic Cannae [where Hannibal scored his famed victory over the Romans in 216 BC].

"Instructed by me to free East Prussia from the enemy, your and Gen. Ludendorff's superior leadership, supported by the devoted cooperation of your subordinates—who were most of them trained in the school of my old Chief of the General Staff Count Schlieffen—succeeded in gaining a splendid victory with our incomparable and brave troops!

"Tannenberg showed the world again what German power was capable of under strong and definite leadership! May the heroic spirit of Tannenberg penetrate and unite our divided nation!

"Then it will achieve wonders, and the brave men to whom this memorial is dedicated will not have fallen in vain. Then—with God's help—Germany will rise again! Wilhelm, Imperator, Rex [Emperor, King]."

All over Germany there were great rejoicings and preposterous prognostications; many saw in the President's words the beginning of a real move to clear Germany of the charge of being solely guilty for starting the war.

A Polish Site of a German Victory Avenging a Defeat by Lithuanians in 1410

The site of the 1924–27 observations was located in what is today the Polish *voivodship* of Marmia and Mazury (Masuria in German). "In part the battle took place," continued Gessner in *Tannenberg*:

> … in the vicinity of the village of Tannenberg, the location where some 500 years earlier the combined Polish-Lithuainian forces had dealt a crushing defeat to the Teutonic Knights, a German military order.…
>
> On this latter [1914] occasion, the German victory had been total: of the 150,000-strong Russian 2nd Army, 92,000 had been taken prisoner, and another 30,000 were killed or wounded.
>
> Only around 10,000 of [Gen.] Samsonov's men had escaped. In the face of the defeat, Samsonov walked off into the woods and committed suicide.

Hindenburgian Branding, Marketing, & Merchandising, 1925–34

In 1929, there was released the "silent, non-fictional film," *The Iron Hindenburg in War & Peace*, four years after his first inauguration as president of Germany on May 12, 1925, produced by Allgemeine/General Film-Union Haussler & Company.

It reenacted not only his Great War battles, but also the 1918–19 Berlin street fighting under the subhead of "The Red Terror," both of which had been central to the launching of the twin Hindenburgian Reich presidencies. All were at the core of the overall Hindenburg legend and now myth.

Stated writer Anna Menge von der Goltz in 2008's *Hindenburg*: "*Two* recent public controversies—about a possible retraction of Hindenburg's honorary citizenship of Berlin and about the plan of a hotel owner to re-erect a Hindenburg statue on Mt. Kyffhauser in Thuringia (Germany)—point toward the public's renewed interest in Weimar's second President."

Indeed, the late Irish actor Peter O'Toole played the marshal-president in an American television dramatization of the rise of Hitler that was panned by TV comedian and talk show host Jay Leno.

Continues Ms. von der Goltz in *Hindenburg*:

> There was a massive readership of Hindenburg books and special Hindenburg issues of the illustrated press, and also a receptive audience for Hindenburg films, and the President's frequent speeches on the radio....
>
> The files of the Reich President's Bureau ... contain a wide range of rich sources, including negotiations with publishers of popular novels, and with companies wishing to deploy Hindenburg's image in commercial advertising....
>
> His much-trumpeted personal modesty and lack of ambition were central elements of the mythical narrative ... Hindenburg in fact frequently put pressure on writers, filmmakers, radio producers, and advertisers ... to uphold a particular account, or to suppress variations of the mythical narrative that he considered damaging.

Film

"Hindenburg was deeply involved in promoting his own myth," with Presidential State Secretary Dr Meissner being his main agent. The 1929 film *The Iron Hindenburg* was part of this film genre effort, in which the marshal was featured as "The hero of wartime Germany.... The film premiere took place at the *Primus-Palast,* one of Berlin's newest and largest 'cinema palaces,' with over 1,000 seats.... By 1930, 5,000 cinemas with a total number of two million seats had been built in Germany."

Three of German filmdom's biggest fans were Hitler, his later wife, Eva, and Dr Goebbels, and they were not alone. "In spite of the crippling effects of the economic crisis, 4.5 million Germans still went to the cinema every week in 1932," the very year that Hitler ran against Hindenburg twice for president of the Reich. In *Hindenburg*, Goltz stated:

> *The Iron Hindenburg*'s key messages—that Hindenburg's leadership was Germany's destiny and that he had "saved" the country from the Russians, from postwar domestic strife, and from prolonged international humiliation—clearly perpetuated the central theme of the Hindenburg Myth....
>
> The President and his staff observed the documentary's production with an eagle eye ... Germany's first President Friedrich Ebert—in contrast—had hardly ever appeared in films...

They asked for and got the deletion of a line uttered by the actor portraying "The Wooden Titan" of the Great War because it alluded to his alleged "physical frailty" thus: "I am dead tired, but as long as this old body is still good for something, I will stand up until I collapse!'"

His 1932 presidential re-election effort was the theme of the film *One for All!*, which showed the Russian hordes invading East Prussia in 1914 until "a giant shadow in the shape of Hindenburg's iconic square head was then shown approaching from the west ... [and] bold letters herald *Tannenberg!*" rolling back the beaten enemy into Russia.

That same presidential year of 1932, there was also released *Tannenberg*, directed by Heinz Paul, in response to the anti-war film *All Quiet on the Western Front*, whose screenings were both boycotted and disrupted by Dr Goebbels' SA men that September, after the elections. The film cost 500,000 RMs, cast 8,000 actors, and was produced by the Zurich firm of Preasenfilm GmbH as "a documentary on the historic battle." It featured "a human tragedy affecting the lives of ordinary East Prussians. Small children crying for their mothers and asking with innocent eyes whether the 'Cossacks really eat dogs?' were as much a part of the film as Hindenburg and Ludendorff studying military maps."

Indeed, in his postwar memoirs, Hindenburg had mentioned the plight of fleeing refugees streaming past him as he planned the battle to save them. His head was used in the official film poster against flaming houses and bold lettering stating *Tannenberg*.

Both the Reich president and Dr Meissner complained that the actor portraying the victorious general—Karl Koerner—did not do so heroically enough. As a result, many of the actor's scenes were simply cut from the finished film by the official German government censor board that reported to these same two top officials of the regime.

Radio

"At 8 PM on 24 April 1925, Hindenburg made German broadcasting history…the first program broadcast simultaneously throughout Germany by hooking up various stations," an outright campaign speech to elect him president.

"It is estimated that 10–11 million people regularly listened to the wireless in the Republic's last year," of 1933–34, "The German government … regulated the airwaves from the very beginning," and thus under Hindenburg, eight years before the Nazis took office.

"It featured prominently in the Presidential contests of 1925 and 1932 … [Red] Presidential candidate Ernst Thälmann had been excluded from using the new medium," as were the Nazis until the Reichstag election of March 1933, when they were then part of the official Hindenburg final regime.

While none of the president's opponents were allowed to broadcast, the incumbent candidate "was given extensive airtime on 10 March 1932.… Reich Chancellor Brüning and other Cabinet Ministers spoke in favor of Hindenburg in the wireless the same week, too."

The communists had attacked this governmental monopoly in their own unique fashion during the Reich president's December 31, 1931 nationally broadcast radio address when an unknown voice broke in shouting Red propaganda slogans. This was achieved by simply attaching "their own microphone to the single cable broadcasting Hindenburg's speech," as discovered by the later Berlin police inquiry.

The successful stunt received both widespread and global news coverage, creating a sensation. Still, Hindenburg remained the main German political speaker on radio until Hitler claimed that position during 1933–45.

Books and Articles

"A bibliography of 1938—not even counting unfavorable works—listed … 3,000 Hindenburg articles and books…. In addition to the front novels, Hindenburg's media presence was further enhanced by numerous large-size, illustrated, coffee-table books," one such in several editions during 1922–35 sold over 145,000 copies.

Again, the marshal-president avidly protected his image during his lifetime: "Hindenburg was keen not to appear as the chief instigator of the Kaiser's 'flight' into exile," that, in fact, he actually had been.

Magazines

There was a "near insatiable demand for all things Hindenburg-related…. The Reich President was the undisputed star of the genre after 1925; no other politician was pictured as frequently in the major illustrated weeklies," especially regarding the coverage of his eightieth birthday in 1927, outdoing that of his seventieth during the Great War in 1917.

Again, this all changed as Hitler overtook the dead warrior during 1934–45.

Advertising, Marketing, and Merchandising of the Hindenburg "Brand"

"Hindenburg became one of Germany's first true advertising icons—selling anything from cars [especially Opel] to liver sausage," with the Nazis aping their rival's head with that of Hitler on their 1932 election posters that appeared on news kiosks all over Berlin and Germany.

The iconic image of Hindenburg appeared on vases, teapots, mouth organs, matchboxes, cigarettes and other tobacco products, ashtrays, and also wine and champagne.

Since Hindenburg failed to register his own name in 1917, everyone was free to use it and his image, and they did, until he relented eleven years later, regarding Hindenburg eyeglasses and oil lubricant products.

The newly elected President Paul von Hindenburg arrives at Reich Capital Berlin via car motorcade with cavalry escort for his first inaugural in 1926 with the Brandenburg Gate at left. (*LC*)

Hermo took longer to be disillusioned with the Nazi Führer, telling Mackensen in December 1935, "God preserve this man!" After Hitler took back the German Rhineland on March 7, 1936, she declared herself "enchanted" by his policies.

Two days after Hitler invaded Poland, Doorn Village was occupied by 3,000 Dutch Army troops on September 3, 1939, the day that Great Britain declared war on Germany for the second time. Chortled Wilhelm II: "The Polish campaign was marvelous!" accomplished by the army officers of "My school!"

Artist Hugo Vogel's 1927 formal portrait of newly inaugurated Reich President von Hindenburg, for the second time the hero of his nation. This was the last painting done by Vogel of *Der alte Herr* (the Old Gentleman), and as chronicled in his 1927 book *When I Painted Hindenburg*. Vogel (February 15, 1855 to September 26, 1934) survived his famous subject by seven weeks, and during 1915–17 had stayed with the duo at GHQ as official painter to "the field marshal," as Ludendorff always referred to his boss. Buried at Wannsee Cemetery, Vogel today has streets named after him in both Berlin and Magdeburg. (*LC*)

Above left: Reich President von Hindenburg wearing the exact same clothing and medals, but in this photograph also displaying the kindly visage so well remembered by all his subordinates over the decades of both his martial and political service. (*LC*)

As World War II progressed, Hermo noted that the Kaiser was "Delighted by all the blows raining down on England!"

Above right: A formal picture postcard of the new Reich president in uniform with informal marshal's baton: an elected republican official bearing a staff surmounted by a monarchist crown, surely a contradiction in terms. (*LC*)

The German Army finally invaded Holland on May 10, 1940, and on the 14th, the Kaiser was startled to see sentries in German field gray uniforms guarding him again for the first time since November 9, 1918 at his very own gate.

A kindly-looking, be-medalled President von Hindenburg (*right*) in formal tuxedo at a diplomatic dinner at the Reich President's Palace, Berlin during the late Weimar Republic period. Dr. Meissner at center. (*ASA*)

A foreign political cartoon of 1925 noting the duality of Hindenburg's position as Reich president: soldier, civilian, or both? He won his first of what was to be two seven-year terms of office "By a plurality of 986,749 votes" on a Sunday, beating—among others—the Catholic Central Party's candidate, former Chancellor Wilhelm Marx. In general, he wore civilian garb throughout most of his first term in office, thus reflecting his new, chameleon-like image. (*LC*)

At one time during the Great War, Hindenburg considered General von Gallwitz as a serious candidate for the post of imperial chancellor, just as the Kaiser had named a general to succeed the great Prince Bismarck in 1890. For his part, Hindenburg disdained the same office for himself, however.

Lamented the Kaiser at KHQ Kreuznach on May 28, 1917, "What is there for me to do at Kreuznach? I am only Hindenburg's adjutant, and I have nothing to say!" Actually, he was rather more than that right to the very moment he left by rail for Holland on November 10, 1918.

Top right and above: Troop review of the Berlin Garrison Honor Guard outside the Reichstag Building in the company of black-clad civilian Defense Minister Otto Gessler (obscured) and Army Commander Colonel General Hans von Seeckt (wearing saber at his left side). Gessler almost ran against Hindenburg in 1932, but a sex scandal kept him out of the race ultimately, while General von Seeckt "did much to pave the way for the revived German air service," long before Hermann Goering took office as the first Reich Air Minister in 1933. (*LC*)

Above left: A welcoming drink to Bavaria. (*LC*)

During an Eastern Front Visit on July 25–26, 1917, the Kaiser at the Tarnapol battlefield reviewed "wild looking" Turkish Army troops, who were "capable of cutting the throats of Russian POWs!" the Kaiser averred. From a hilltop, Wilhelm II watched gleefully the retreat of the Russian Army.

Above right: A nocturnal martial band serenade in the park of the Reich president's Berlin Palace. (*LC*)

At another front visit in wartime occupied Poland, an onlooker noted: "A very banal speech by the Kaiser that did not touch the men's hearts." After the overthrow of Chancellor Bethmann-Hollweg in July 1917, Wilhelm II toyed with the idea of naming Hindenburg as his successor. Hindenburg's mantra was "First weigh the cost, and then dare!"

It must have galled the exiled monarch Wilhelm II even more when his successor as head of state took to aping a formal practice of his late grandfather, Kaiser Wilhelm I, who made celebrated appearances before crowds in a famous window setting. Here, Hindenburg stands in the far right "historical corner" window of the Reich president's palace to bask in the acclaim. (*HHA*)

In 1939, his successor as Reich president, Hitler, gave this very same room and window to girlfriend Eva Braun of Bavaria when she stayed at Berlin during World War II. Indeed, it was from this very site that she filmed in color with her home movie camera the famous scene of his return by car into the RP Park on July 6, 1940 from the victorious French campaign, as shown often on T.V. on The History Channel, from the viewpoint of her motion camera lens. To put an even finer point on it, Cpl Hitler won the very campaign that the venerable Field Marshal von Hindenburg had lost, no less. Note the latter's grandchildren in the other two windows. As for Eva, her first of a trio of suicide attempts came on August 12, 1932, the very day before Hitler's first official meeting with the Reich president who had just defeated him for that office earlier that same year.

The battle flags of Prussia are dipped in salute to Hindenburg at Berlin on the occasion of his eightieth birthday, October 2, 1927. (*LC*)

At KHQ Pless on January 30, 1917, Admiral Henning Holtzendorff told Admiral Georg von Müller that "Ludendorff overreached himself with ambition, though he was highly talented and worthy."

Above left: To celebrate the same national event, every German picture magazine devoted its cover to the birthday boy of October 2, 1927. (*LC*)

On February 8, 1917, Ludendorff informed the Kaiser that the duo would no longer make the daily trip from Berlin to Potsdam's New Palace to brief the Kaiser—that task to be delegated instead to a staff officer, with the Kaiser allegedly being "content to being left out in the cold."

Above right: Special obverse and reverse of a medal struck on the occasion of President von Hindenburg's 80th birthday on October 2, 1927. (*ASA*)

The gift of the German nation was the return of the former Hindenburg family estate of Neudeck in West Prussia, seen here after his death in 1934, its flag flown at half-staff in mourning. (*HHA*)

Noted Ludwig Cohn in 1935, Neudeck was "The ancestral family estate of the Beneckendorff-Hindenburgs, near the town of Greystadt in East Prussia, 30 miles south–southeast of Marienburg, 60 miles south–southeast of Danzig."

Hermann Goering's Nazi Luftwaffe flew overhead to honor the master's passing, August 1934. On October 10, 1917, the Kaiser took "a superb [train] trip through Serbia," and was received in a ceremonial entry at Sofia, where he visited his latest ally, "Foxy" Ferdinand. On the 12th, Tsar Ferdinand admitted that he feared assassination, but in the event lived another thirty-one years, into 1948.

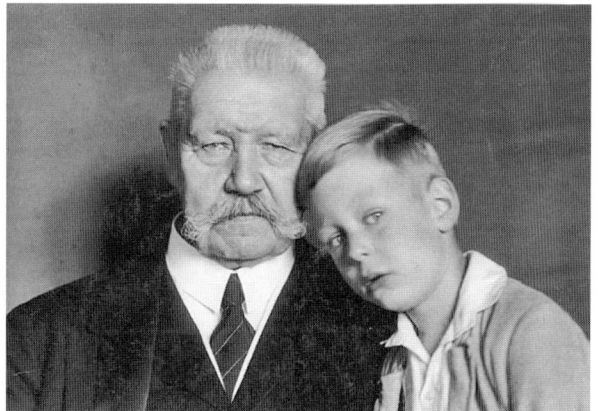

Left: Hindenburg's grandchildren assemble on the front steps of Neudeck on his eightieth birthday, October 2, 1927. Note the one "breaking ranks" at bottom—there is one in every crowd! (*LC*)

The Kaiser was pleased to visit the ancient Roman battlefield at Philippi in Macedonia, where those who had assassinated Julius Caesar were defeated by the forces of Marc Antony—death to regicides! For his part, "Foxy" wanted the site as part of his future projected Bulgar Reich.

Above: Grandfather von Hindenburg with his grandson, the son of his own son, Oskar von Hindenburg. (*ASA*)

In charge of the financial renovations of Neudeck, Colonel Oskar von Hindenburg spared no expense. This is the hall, complete with fireplace, wall-mounted hunting trophy antlers, and oil portrait of the master of the house over the mantelpiece. (*LC*)

"The new house was built by the architects Berlberg and Moser, close to the old family residence that had endured for centuries…. Over the huge mantelpiece, a verse is written that characterizes Hindenburg's way of looking at life, 'Loyalty is the Marrow of Honor,' according to Helene Nostitz von Hindenburg. In the fall of 1918, Ludendorff's "mad rage" and "nervous breakdown" was common knowledge among the higher staffs of the German Army on the Western Front. Indeed at the latter's firing by the Kaiser on October 26, 1918, Admiral von Müller noted that "His Majesty was in excellent form" at Castle Bellevue. That very same day, though, the Austro-Hungarian war effort collapsed.

"Hindenburg's niece—Helene Lina Olga Vera von Nostitz-Wallwitz von Beneckendorff und Hindenburg (1878-1944)—wrote a book, seemingly under the pseudonym O. C.Hiss, *Hindenburg: Eine Kleine Streitschrift,* Potsdam: San Souci/Without Care Press, 1931. The literal translation is *Hindenburg: A Little Polemic,* and this is probably the same book that was published in the same year in English under the title of *Hindenburg at Home: An Intimate Biography,* according to author-publisher Alan Sutton.

This is the Neudeck library, the formal marshal's baton seen resting on the table at right amidships. (*LC*)

"In his writing room [office] hangs a portrait of the great Count Moltke [the Elder] by Lenbach," who also was later one of Chancellor Hitler's own favorite portraitists. "Not far off is the portrait of King Frederick the Great…. A large bust of William II stands in a corner of the room, and a smaller statue on the writing table [desk]. On another wall hangs a portrait of Hindenburg's wife…. From above the bookshelves in the library, the ancestors of the Beneckendorff family look down at us, and their gaze seems to rest on the profusion of documents that lie on the tables. Some of these proclaim Hindenburg honorary citizen of various states and cities…. On the floor are carpets presented by Oriental and African potentates, resplendent in gorgeous colors. The library is well stocked with works on history, especially Roman history."

The rear façade of the Neudeck mansion, with father and son von Hindenburgs on its spacious, sunlit veranda, umbrella at right. (*ASA*)

Reich Chancellor Franz von Papen's Presidential Cabinet in 1932 that often met there included Defense Minister General Kurt von Schleicher, Foreign Minister Baron Konstantin von Neurath, and others. History has referred to it as "The Cabinet of Barons."

Original Tannenberg Memorial architects Johannes and Walter Kruger with an assistant look at a scale-model mock-up rendering, "Of their winning design entitled, *Gode/Good Wind*," for the site near Hohenstein, East Prussia. (*LC*)

Continues Ms. Hindenburg in her 1931 presentation of Neudeck: "In the dining room is a porcelain service given to him by the Berlin porcelain factory … a copy of a set made for Frederick the Great…. The old linden tree under which he played as a child and listened to the injunctions of his parents still stands near the house."

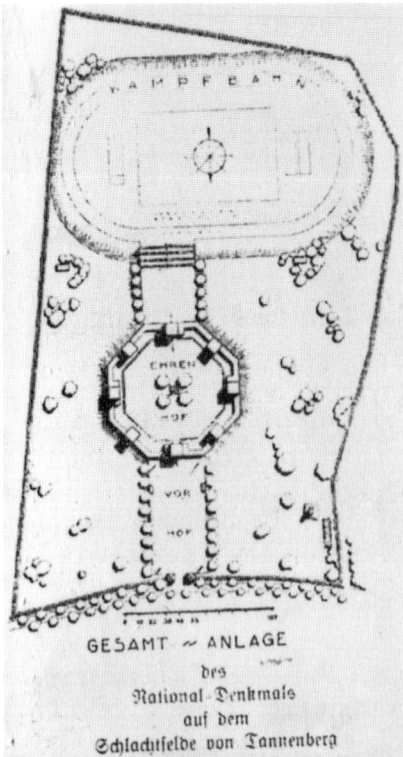

GESAMT ~ ANLAGE
des
National - Denkmals
auf dem
Schlachtfelde von Tannenberg

A full plan for the overall original concept of the Tannenberg Memorial that was both later altered and never completely finished. What appears in most of the illustrations herein is the central octagonal portion that was finished, however. (*LC*)

"The old family residence is gone, but the new home carries on the traditions.… The little family burial ground stands nearby, close to the forest and under the shade of the great trees. There sleep the ancestors of the Beneckendorff-Hindenburg family, my own father among them," wrote Ms. von Hindenburg in 1931.

Prussian banners held aloft at the Tannenberg Memorial dedication on August 27, 1933. (*HHA*)

In June 1945, many of these very same standards were heaped in front of the Lenin Mausoleum on Moscow's Red Square at the feet of Marshal and Generalissimo Josef Stalin during the massive Soviet victory parade over Nazi Germany. "He has one passion that he indulges in, and which has lasted from his early days: It is the sport of deer stalking. He loves to shoot chamois in Bavaria, and his only ailing is a little rheumatism 'that I caught in the snow when a chamois once kept me a long time waiting,' he told me," asserted Ms. von Hindenburg.

Inside the interior of the 1927 dedication of the Memorial's tomb containing the remains of twenty unknown German Army Great War veterans—also designed by the architect Kruger—with giant granite block at right, emblazoned with Iron Crosses on its sides. (*LC*)

"When he goes on these hunting excursions to Bavaria, he lives with his friends in a small shooting box. He gets up early in the morning. Before the door stand some peasants waiting to join in the day's sport. He shakes hands with them all. And then starts off on the shooting adventure."

Hindenburg stands bareheaded with baton at left on the official opening of the Tannenberg Memorial on September 18, 1927, with Ludendorff standing apart in light overcoat—head also bared—at right. (*LC*)

"Then it became clear to all how matters stood between them. Ludendorff publicly refused to stand side by side with Hindenburg … and made his own appearance dependent on this condition." Snorted Ludendorff, "I will go my own way!" "Where that led him he neither saw nor dreamed," his divorced former wife concluded. As his superior officer still, the field marshal could have ordered Ludendorff to stand by him, but did not.

Above left: Another view of the same scene, with Ludendorff having donned a rain cape. The final break between the former duo came in 1925 after Hindenburg's first election as Reich president, when he cancelled his former annual visit to the Ludendorffs at Ludwigshöhe, this on the advice of Reich Chancellor Dr Hans Luther, most likely because the former had already twice been an outlaw rebel against the Weimar Republic—reason enough. (*LC*)

"We are all familiar with a picture of the President walking between his son and his host, clad in rough sporting clothes and using a big stick as he tramps through the snow."

Above right: The field marshal dedicates the Unknown Soldiers' core monument at the memorial. (*LC*)

Recalled Mrs. Ludendorff later, "Ludendorff foamed with rage. He felt himself deeply wounded" over the final breakup of the duo after so many years. Now that ideal, too, was shattered, but remained unknown to the public at large. "There is a shooting lodge also near Berlin, in the Schorfheide, that officially belongs to the President of the German Republic," later taken over by Goering. "Here Hindenburg goes for weekends to shoot deer," Ms. Von Hindenburg wrote of her august uncle.

The September 19, 1927 Tannenberg Memorial lineup. *From left to right*: Hindenburg, Mackensen in fur busby, and Ludendorff at center, left hand on sword hilt pommel. (*LC*)

Previous page, below: After losing the 1925 presidential election that Hitler had put him up to, noted Mrs. Ludendorff: "The general felt himself impelled—without any visible reason—to publish in the press … that all relations between Adolf Hitler and himself had been sundered." Later, he told his wife also that he regretted being fired by the Kaiser: "I ought never to have let myself be dismissed! It would have been better while the war was still in progress if I had snatched the dictatorship for myself!" Wilhelm II, it seems, knew his man well enough! In the BBC dramatization of these events, *Fall of Eagles*, Ludendorff does protest his firing, whereupon the Kaiser tells a sentry nearby, "Arrest that man!" Choking, Ludendorff then backs down, accepting his fate. Mackensen's first wife, Dorothea, died in 1905 after a long illness. In 1907, the Black Hussar met his future second wife, Leonie, then aged twenty-nine, and "exactly half his age, shocking many people." Despite the daily love notes he sent her, the happy couple never had children. They married in 1908, when groom von Mackensen was already ten years older than his new mother-in-law.

Aerial views of the second inner core at the memorial. The square granite block has been replaced by a Christian cross. (*LC*)

"He does not smoke except when he is at some social function where the others are smoking cigars. He does not play cards, and he drinks only a little wine at his meals," on Hindenburg.

Horse-head sculpture-surmounted water trough on the grounds for cavalry, with the memorial seen in the distance. Asserted its original caption: "[Architects] Walter and Johannes Kruger with Erna Becker-Kahns realized a fountain in the form of a horse pond as a monument to the horses fallen in the historic battle in 1914." (*LC*)

Cattle grazed peacefully at the site as well.

"On the occasion of the President's 80th birthday, there was a great round of official celebrations in Berlin, but the most touching moment of all was reached at the children's reception in the Stadion. Thousands of them were gathered there to receive him.… The young girls sat in a circle on the huge lawn … All arms waved handkerchiefs … They jumped over the ropes and barriers and surrounded the motor [car] in which Hindenburg sat, smiling and beaming kindly on the youngest of his nation."

A ground-level view of the entire red brick structure mock-up of 1935 reflecting Hitler's own later architectural changes to the Krugers' original design, its closed gates rendering a fortress-like visage. It was abandoned to the Red Army in January 1945 without a fight, however. (*LC*)

"Paul Hindenburg was the eldest of four children, there being two other brothers and one sister [Ida]. His second brother, Otto, became a cavalry officer with the rank of major, and received the Iron Cross for bravery on the field in the war of 1870; he died in 1908."

A ground-level view of the new Christian cross central concrete courtyard feature. (*HHA*)

"The youngest brother—Bernhard—still lives [in 1931]. He has written several novels and some dramas. He also wrote a monograph on the field marshal in 1915 ...

"The only sister was a very remarkable woman, and in her own way became quite famous [Ida]. She was an acknowledged expert in graphology, on which subject she published a book, but she was best known for her religious activities ... and undertook important works of charity, always giving to the poor whatever money or means came her way."

Successor to von Papen and predecessor to Hitler as Reich chancellor was army General Kurt von Schleicher, seen here wearing the cap and icons of the German Republican Army of the interwar years, changed by the Nazis with Hindenburg's approval in 1933. Von Schleicher saw himself—and not Hitler—as the strongman that Weimar Germany needed. (*LC*)

A Nazi monument to the interwar *Freikorps* created by von Schleicher was dedicated in 1942. The inscription below read "*Gedenktafel zum Gedächtnis der gefallen Freikorpskämpfer*" ("Commemorative plaque to remember fallen Free Corps"), according to former Sudeten German translator Mrs. Erika Burke of Pearland, TX, USA.

"In the garden in which Hindenburg played, there was an old gardener who had served as a drummer under Frederick the Great. The stories of military prowess that he related to the young boy must have had an influence in shaping the character of the future field marshal."

An intercepted bouquet of flowers intended for the Reich president, who wants it! *From left to right*: saluting officers, intercepting Army officer and policeman, restrained damsel, motorman, an amused General von Schleicher, saluting officer, the Reich president reaching out with gloved right hand, Colonel Oskar von Hindenburg reacting, obscured presidential military ADC, saluting policeman, and officer. Note also the high-ceilinged car, designed to accommodate the Reich president's spiked helmet. (*LC*)

The men who ushered the Nazis into office in 1933—Hindenburg's inner circle or *camarilla*—often met at a table outside Neudeck in casual attire, as shown on August 31, 1932 in the *Munich Illustrated Press*—for them, anyway. The magic circle included Chancellor Franz von Papen, Colonel von Hindenburg, Defense Minister von Schleicher, and State Secretary Dr Meissner. They appeared in jaunty caps, knickerbocker trousers, and sporty Argyle socks.

A previous photographic book author called these men, "the gravediggers of the republic."

Taking their places at the Tannenberg Memorial on September 19, 1927; *from left to right*: Hindenburg the elder, Hindenburg the younger, Mackensen, and others. (*LC*)

Like Hitler later, Mackensen hated the press, and kept them away from his wartime military headquarters, reportedly. He was criticized during the war for having his soldiers bring in the harvest on his mother's estate at Gelgenfelde, and also for forcing his relatives to serve in his army.

Trooping the line of standard bearers at the same event, Hindenburg at center leads the pack, followed by at center left Mackensen, then Defense Minister Otto Gessler in dark suit, Colonel Oskar von Hindenburg, and the president's martial aide. At far left is General Alexander von Linsingen, most likely. The men reviewed wear the cavalry cut-out helmets seen here before. (*LC*)

Mackensen had seen the Great War coming, and—like the imperial crown prince as well—"Said that a real war would not be totally unwelcome."

In the latter part of his presidential terms, Hindenburg felt safe enough to revert to type, abandoning his early civilian attire for his more natural uniforms of yesteryear and century, as here. *From left to right at this troop review in 1932*: Army commander General Kurt Hammerstein-Equord looking forward, Schleicher looking down, the guard commanding officer with drawn saber, and Hindenburg. (*LC*)

Hindenburg approaches the color guards, the band now behind him, opposite the front gate of Reich presidential palace, Berlin, its tops flanked by a brace of stone lions. (*LC*)

"Paul von Hindenburg—this strong character!—had an innate antipathy to pigs and mice: he could scarcely stand the sight of them. This idiosyncrasy became a favorite subject for teasing on the part of his brothers and cousins."

He also attended the annual fall military maneuvers at Mecklenburg as in imperial times past, here seen with map in the rear of his official car, military ADC at right, and Colonel Oskar in right profile behind and outside. Note also the uniformed chauffeur at the wheel. (*LC*)

"In his character, the boy von Hindenburg was very unselfish. When he happened to get a little money, he never thought of himself, but always bought some small presents for his grandmother, his mother, his sister, and his brothers."

The marshal wears wind goggles on the visor of his cap at right on maneuvers. (*LC*)

"One day he had a few pennies that he spent for a glass of wine as a present to his mother, who never allowed herself such luxuries. On bringing it across the street, not a little of it was spilled." Reportedly, he made a will at the age of eleven, leaving all his toys to his sister and brothers, on March 12, 1859. A later will would become infamous under Adolf Hitler.

The Reich president (left, with informal stick baton—note the length) is greeted at center by his smiling Army Commander General von Seeckt during the autumn 1928 Reichswehr (National Army) maneuvers, plus visiting woman and child at center. Note also the foreign military observer at far left in raincoat and garrison cap. (*LC*)

In 1889, as a major at the Prussian war office—the year Hitler was born in Austria—Hindenburg demonstrated his mutual attachment to his soldiers with his motto of "Every individual must be treated differently."

Mounted lancers with pennants pass by the Marshal-President in review. (*LC*)

Of his Polish soldiers serving in German uniforms, he averred, "They were untidy, I suppose because of their poor education, but when one treated them well, they were faithful and affectionate. I must say that I have been pained by the news of their cruelty towards the Germans since the last war. I would not have believed this of my former soldiers."

Seeckt (*left center*) and Hindenburg (*right center*) each bow to the other as they shake hands on maneuvers, as Defense Minister Gessler rubs his face at right and Seeckt's staff render hand salutes at far left, 1925. (*LC*)

Well before the advent to office of Hitler and Goering, Seeckt and Hindenburg were building Germany's sparse armed forces for the next war.

Seeckt's grave was at Berlin's Invalidenhof Cemetery in 1936, featuring the honorary title of "Chief of Infantry Regiment No. 67," surmounted by his ornate familial crest above and centered.

"Last year [1930] the French ambassador in Berlin made an official call on the President. As the ambassador was about to take his leave, Hindenburg asked him to tarry a moment. He left the room, and reappeared shortly afterwards carrying in his hand a richly ornamented sword … one of honor that had been taken during the Battle of Sedan in 1870 from a high French officer, and had lately been presented to Hindenburg. As the President did not consider it right to keep the sword, he gave it to the ambassador with a kindly gesture, asking him to return it to the heirs of the owner, or to the French State. Monsieur de Margerie, as I heard, was much touched by this act of courtesy."

On the annual 1932 fall maneuvers, Reich President von Hindenburg (*right*) is rejoined by his former colleague of the Great War era and immediately afterwards, General Wilhelm Groener (*left*), this time as the Weimar Republic's civilian defense and interior minister. The marshal holds his informal swagger stick baton in his left hand. (*LC*)

Ludendorff denigrated Groener publicly as "The Spa Villain" for having told the Kaiser that he must go to Holland, blasting Reich President von Hindenburg for accepting Groener's appointment as defense minister, asserting that the field marshal, "Had forfeited the right to wear the gray uniform of the German Army," thereby. This had some traction to it, as "Hohenzollern princes left the room when Hindenburg entered." Thus, the field marshal never entirely escaped the ghost of his own role on November 9, 1918 in the so-called "Specter of Spa."

An interwar reunion of naval and military holders of the former imperial decoration, the Blue Max. (*HHA*)

As a young cadet, Hindenburg had trouble with arithmetic, gave away his food to others, and once refused a warm cloak: "He felt that the comfort of extra warm clothing would be against his sense of loyalty towards the military severity of his school," or so the legend has it.

9

Nazis, 1932–34

Imperial Crown Prince Wilhelm and Cpl. A. Hitler

"Where a Hitler can lead, a Hohenzollern can follow!" asserted the imperial crown prince's younger brother, Prince August Wilhelm—nicknamed Auwi—prior to the Nazi Party's being appointed to national and provincial office by President von Hindenburg on January 30, 1933. Both royals had affiliations with the party, the older with the Nazi Motor Corps (reflecting his love of cars) and the latter as a member of the brown shirted SA Stormtroopers.

Both also had hopes that Nazi Party Führer Hitler and former air ace under the imperial crown prince's command in World War I, Capt. Goering, would restore the Hohenzollerns to power once their NS "national revolution" occurred.

Indeed, to that end, the rising Bavarian politician Hitler approached the former army group commander at his home Cecilienhof at Potsdam outside Berlin for an interview in 1926.

According to the crown prince's sister Princess Viktoria Luise's memoirs, Wilhelm told Hitler, "I agree that I would once have been Kaiser, but now I am a private citizen, and have duties only towards my family. As you can see, I am wearing a tweed jacket and knickerbockers," leading Hitler to sneer to his wartime intimates at Führer H.Q. in East Prussia on January 31, 1942, that the Nazis should thank the Social Democrats of 1918 for having gotten rid of the House of Hohenzollern for them.

Still, the family had its value for promoting Hitler within right-wing monarchist circles as long as that was needed. The imperial crown prince alleged later that Hitler never fooled him, though, calling the Führer "a demagogue and a little Philistine!"

Chancellor Brüning's Failed Gambit: The Hohenzollern Restoration of 1932

As the 1932 German presidential election approached, Hindenburg's incumbent Reich Chancellor Dr Heinrich Brüning concocted a secret plan for what, allegedly, his boss most wanted—namely, the restoration of the Hohenzollern dynasty to their lost throne.

What he proposed to the marshal was that a regency be established under one of the sons of the disgraced Imperial Crown Prince Wilhelm, his older son, Prince Wilhelm, or the younger, Prince Louis Ferdinand.

To Dr Brüning's astonishment, Hindenburg rejected all three contenders, holding out instead for the return of Wilhelm II only. Realistically, both men knew that this was impossible, and that it always would be, too.

Neither the Socialists nor the trade unions—both of which had helped overthrow the monarchy in 1918—would countenance either the abdicated father or son, while they might have accepted a regency under one of the two grandsons of Kaiser Billy.

Meanwhile, both the Nazis' private armies—the SA and SS—were believed to be threatening a takeover by force, with the conservative army facing a possible divisive civil war with both sides, Black right and Red left. Its older officers of Great War vintage sided with their commander-in-chief, the venerable marshal, but the younger ones were leaning heavily instead to the former frontline enlisted man, veteran Cpl. A. Hitler of that same conflict.

This generation gap split along lines of both age and especially class distinctions. The men in the enlisted ranks supported Hitler—the Führer—while the workers and unions were either Soci or Commie.

The 1932 Presidential Election

In spring 1932, however, the matter seemed to come to a head for the first time when the initial term of the aging President von Hindenburg was set to expire. The marshal would either have to retire—as he allegedly wanted to do—or run again for re-election to a second seven-year term of office that, reportedly, he had no wish to do.

Mentioned as both nationalist candidates in his place were Bavarian Gen. Franz Ritter von Epp and the former Imperial German Crown Prince Wilhelm. Unexpectedly, however, the marshal was persuaded to stand again to prevent either a Communist takeover or one by Hitler and his Nazis. Had the crown prince run and won as president, he might later have become emperor as well, as Napoleon III had done in 1852.

After much hesitation—and negotiations with his father in Holland—the crown prince dropped his candidacy and threw his support not to Hindenburg but to Hitler, who then ran against the marshal instead. Here is how it evolved, in one of the strangest delayed election results in modern political history.

The winner of two hard-fought national contests back-to-back appointed his twice-defeated rival to his own top governmental operational office in the land a mere eight months later. The incumbent president—the aging Marshal von Hindenburg—was not expected to live out his second term if elected to 1940, when he would be ninety-three years old. He ran anyway, to keep Hitler out.

In his august personage, the marshal-incumbent stood for the stability of traditional law and order, as well as racial tolerance. His challenger from the right was a Great War veteran like himself, but a fringe candidate who was not then even a citizen of the land whose top post he was seeking for the very first time. Hitler stood for racial intolerance, radical change, and ultimate personal dictatorship for himself and his party.

The communist candidate, Ernst Thälmann, from the very far left likewise represented even more radical change, with the rest of the nationalistic, conservative bloc vote being split yet a third way by a fourth candidate. This was the Jewish Theodor Duesterberg, deputy leader of the German Great War veterans' organization, the *Stahlhelm/Steel Helmet*, of which the incumbent Reich president himself was the honorary head.

It was all thus a very confusing Reich presidential sweepstakes. The seeming impasse was broken when Hindenburg reluctantly announced on February 15, 1932 that he would run for re-election. One week later—at a giant Nazi rally in the Berlin Sports Palace—Dr Josef Goebbels announced that his own chief Hitler would challenge the president.

There was a danger in this, however. If the brash Nazis were beaten, their aura of winning several elections in a row since 1930 would be broken, their more radical elements might attempt a coup, and the army could crush the party outright. There was a hidden threat as well: incredibly, potential candidate Hitler, an Austrian—even though he had lived in Germany since 1913 and fought in the German Army in World War I and won both classes of the coveted Iron Cross—had never bothered to formally become a German citizen and could even be, thus, deported back to Austria.

Hitler Becomes a German Citizen, February 25, 1932

On February 25, 1932, however, this pressing political problem was solved when Hitler was appointed *attaché* of the German legation of Brunswick by fellow Nazi Dr Wilhelm Frick in a Berlin announcement. With his acceptance of that minor posting, Hitler automatically became both a citizen of Brunswick and Germany, and thus legally eligible to run for president and serve if elected. He was on his way at last to office.

The First Election, March 13, 1932

When the polls closed on Sunday, March 13, 1932, the incumbent Hindenburg had garnered 18,651,497 votes, or 49.6 percent of the total of those cast, while the main challenger—Hitler—fell far shorter, with but 11,339,446 and thus 30.1 percent.

The Red candidate got 4,983,341 at 13.2 percent and the third nationalist—also the fourth man overall—received 2,557,729 for a mere 6.8 percent.

The Second Election Run-Off, April 10, 1932

All four candidates were thus disappointed, because none had won the required absolute majority needed for election under the constitution, exactly as had occurred to Hindenburg in 1925. Thus, a run-off second national election was mandated by federal law, in which the candidate receiving the most votes would win. Undeterred, losing main challenger Hitler asserted: "The first election campaign is over! The second has begun today! I shall lead it."

He then introduced national German campaigning by aircraft for the first time, chartering his very own airplane for an aerial barnstorming campaign from one end of the country to the other, visiting four major rallies daily in different towns and cities. Meanwhile, the losing fourth candidate withdrew from the race, throwing his support to the main losing challenger: a Jew backing Hitler. All three nationalist candidates were united against the Reds.

Thus, on April 10, 1932, the polling results were 19,359,983 or 53 percent for the incumbent, the main challenger Hitler receiving 13,418,547 or 36 percent, and the Red standard bearer getting 3,706,759 at 10.2 percent. With two national elections held within just thirty-three days of each other, the incumbent had been re-elected for a second term. Asked for his reaction, the twice-defeated main challenger pouted to the media thus: "He is 84. I am 43. I can wait!"

He did, and over the course of the next eight months, the re-elected president's appointed chief executive officer and his cabinet were unable to effectively govern the country. Violent revolution threatened from both opposite poles, the Red left and the Brown right.

"Meanwhile, the armed forces demanded that something be done to forestall these twin brewing revolts, with martial law looming on the horizon. Even so, the President was secretly informed that—if the Left and Right somehow joined forces against them at the Center, it would not hold, and the country's core would be swept away by the two extremes."

Winner Confronts Loser, August 1932

According to *Time Capsule 1933*, the re-elected Reich president initially saw Hitler as "a political opportunist" when their first in-person meeting took place in August 1932 at the Presidential Palace in Berlin. "With what power, Mr. Hitler, do you seek to be made Chancellor?"

"Precisely the same power that Mussolini exercised after his March on Rome!" "So! Let me tell you, Mr. Hitler, if you do not behave, I will rap your fingers!"

Afterwards, the miffed Nazi politician complained to the assembled reporters: "It is impossible to head a ship on the right course in a moment! It takes time. All I ask is four years!" He got it, 1933–37, and then extended it as long as he could, until April 30, 1945.

The really improbable happened: the man who had twice defeated him in outright electoral contests was persuaded by his son and aides to name Hitler as Reich chancellor to head his own government.

After their first encounter of August 1932, the haughty Reich president had chortled that the only post he would ever name Hitler to was as Minister of Posts, "So that then he could lick the backs of stamps bearing his own image." In other words, Hitler could kiss Hindenburg's ass.

The Rupprecht Spector Rises Again, 1933

In January 1933—just as he was being named Reich chancellor by von Hindenburg at Berlin—Hitler was again threatened by a royalist plot hatched in Bavaria to make Crown Prince Rupprecht king at Munich, this time with the latter's own tacit support. The Nazi Führer forestalled this there, though, via Gen. von Epp.

Goering's Secret Meeting, January 28, 1933

Domarus presents this recollection in *Speeches and Proclamations*:

It is incomprehensible how Hindenburg's State Secretary—Dr Meissner—was able to conclude from the discussion with Goering on 28 January 1933 that the National Socialists upheld a positive reinstitution of the monarchy.

Goering had declared that it was possible only if two thirds of the German population were to deem it their will in a free election, a remark that appears to indicate the opposite.

Who was to constitute the two-thirds majority if the NS, the Socis, and the Communists comprised three quarters of the German voting public?

The question was left unanswered.

Ludendorff's Curse on Hindenburg: January 30, 1933

As the incumbent Reich president appointed his former rival as his own Reich chancellor, he received an angry telegram from Ludendorff: "This man will one day ruin the entire country! Coming generations will curse your name for having named this accursed man—one of the greatest demagogues of all time!—Chancellor." The Reich president never heard from or saw crusty Ludendorff again, and the latter died at the age of seventy-two, three years after the field marshal, in 1937.

This was long enough to see the former lance corporal tear up the hated Treaty of Versailles, rearm Germany, reintroduce the military draft, recover the Saar, and take the Rhineland by force. Ironically, Hitler—the man despised by both men—attended both of their funerals. At last, the duo had been sundered apart.

The Nazi Berlin Night Parade of January 30, 1933

It was the night of January 30, 1933, and the Nazis were celebrating Hitler's appointment. Recalled eyewitness Ludwig Cohn in *Hindenburg*:

> A gigantic torchlight progression passed endlessly along the Wilhelmstrasse, and from the open window of the Chancellery, Hitler leaned far out to receive the acclimations of his followers.
>
> Further down the street, in the Presidential Palace—behind closed windows to protect him from the damp night air—Hindenburg, too, watched the throng. Thousands of cheering Germans marched beneath him, but they were acclaiming another....
>
> The events of the day had undoubtedly excited him.... The Hindenburg Legend had suddenly blazed up again in the white-heat of enthusiasm, and his old mind went back to past glories as he watched the marching thousands.
>
> The Brown Shirts passed at a shambling pace, to be followed by the field gray ranks of the *Stahlhelm*, moving with a precision born of discipline. The old marshal watched them from his window as in a dream, and those behind him saw him beckon over his shoulder.
>
> "Ludendorff," the old voice said ... "how well your men are marching, and what a lot of prisoners they have taken!"

Shades of Tannenberg!

Hitler Morphs into Hindenburg

Hitler sought, successfully, to pass himself off as the natural continuance of German history. The Nazis sold a picture postcard with the heads of Frederick the Great, Bismarck, Hindenburg, and Hitler on it, but with no visage of the disgraced Wilhelm II there.

Under the image was the caption: "What the King [Frederick] conquered, the prince [Bismarck] moulded, and gave form; the field marshal defended, and the soldier [Hitler] saved and unified." To an extent, that was all true.

A second postcard showed the field marshal and corporal alone, with the words, "The Marshal and the Corporal fight with us for peace and equality!" Once again, the Kaiser—as well as his imperial father and grandfather—was left out in the cold, and once more Hindenburg silently acquiesced in their absence.

Within sixty days, democracy was totally dead, one-man rule virtually completed, all other parties outlawed for the next dozen years—their leaders in jail—and the winning presidential stalwart of 1932 himself largely marginalized.

Hindenburg had been co-opted by the man he had twice beaten. Allegedly, Hindenburg once asked, "How will posterity judge me? I lost the greatest war in history!" But that has been rather overlooked in recent decades in place of his having held the stirrup so that Hitler could hoist himself into the saddle of office. As one period scribe asserted, "Hindenburg's record is a bad one." Such is his legacy.

Hindenburg and the Nazi Heroes' Memorial Days, March 1933 and 1934

Explains Domarus: "Hindenburg issues a decree permitting the swastika flag to be flown next to the black-white-red Reich flag [1933] and provides for the introduction of the sovereign symbol of the Party to the *Reichswehr* [1934]."

The Day of Potsdam, March 21, 1933

This was celebrated, oddly, on the very day that the former duo launched their last Great War offensive against the Allies in the west—that of Operation Michael on March 21, 1918, fifteen years earlier. Now it was 1933, and the Nazis were launching their new Third Reich to replace the defeated second one of Prussia's former glory of 1871. Hitler's great tribute to Hindenburg was his ceremony in the Potsdam *Garnisonkirche* (Garrison Church) that same day also marking the opening of the new Nazi elected Reichstag.

Recalled French Ambassador André François-Poncet in *The Fateful Years*:

> [The Garrison Church]—The great shrine of Prussianism aroused in so many Germans memories of Imperial glories and grandeur—for here lay buried the bones of Frederick the Great....
>
> As the old field marshals, generals, and admirals from Imperial times gathered in their resplendent uniforms ... led by the former Imperial Crown Prince and Field Marshal von Mackensen in the imposing dress and headgear of the Death's Head Hussars, the shades of Frederick the Great and the Iron Chancellor hovered over the assembly.
>
> Hindenburg was visibly moved, and at one point in the ceremony, Goebbels—who was staging the performance—observed that the old field marshal had tears in his eyes.

Flanked by Hitler … the President—attired in the field gray uniform with the Grand Cordon of the Black Eagle, and carrying a spiked helmet in one hand and his marshal's baton in the other—had marched slowly down the aisle, paused to salute the empty seat of Kaiser Wilhelm II in the Imperial gallery, and then in front of the altar read a brief speech giving his blessings to the new Hitler government.

The Nazi Führer shrewdly played on the old man's known sympathies in his own remarks, that were broadcast by radio live all over the country: "By a unique upheaval in the last few weeks, our national honor has been restored, and—thanks to your understanding, *Herr Generalfeldmarschall!*—the union between the symbols of the old greatness and the new strength has been celebrated. We pay you homage!"

Hitler then shook the "Old Gentleman's" hand, and the historical deed was done. Hitler had played his cards right: Hindenburg was deeply impressed. Indeed, he trusted Hitler explicitly after that, and because of this trust, he retired—more or less—to Neudeck. This let Hitler do the actual ruling of the new Third Reich under his august aegis and *imprimatur*, with all this but a mere two months after having been appointed to office himself.

Eyewitness François-Poncet added these aspects to the first great Nazi show of the new regime in *The Fateful Years*:

> The citizenry had decked the houses with flags and bunting. Huge swastika-crested banners hung from the rooftops side by side with the black-white-red flags of the former Empire.
>
> The bells rang out in full peal as the official automobiles sped down the road between two lines of Brown Shirt militiamen. At the Garrison Church, the public was admitted to the gallery only.
>
> The central gallery was reserved for the Imperial Family: in the foreground stood the chair of Kaiser Wilhelm II, empty, and immediately behind it the Imperial Crown Prince in the uniform of a colonel of the Death's Head Hussars. Beside him, I noticed his wife—the Imperial Crown Princess Cecilie—his brothers, and his sons.…
>
> Suddenly, the door opened, and the audience rose to their feet as one man as Marshal Hindenburg entered.… Although grown stouter and obviously laced tightly into a tunic that no longer fitted him, he still possessed all the dignity of a veteran leader.
>
> The audience admired his high stature, calm, poise, and grandeur that stamped his melancholy face. He advanced slowly, leaning heavily on his cane. As he reached the front of the Imperial gallery, he turned to face it squarely and raised his marshal's baton to salute his master's empty seat and the Princes of the blood gathered about it.
>
> Hitler—advancing by his side—looked like a timid newcomer being introduced by an important protector into a company to which he does not belong. Who could have believed that this wan man with such vulgar features—dressed in an ill-fitting coat and in appearance so respectful and so modest—was the more powerful of the two personages?
>
> A multitude of uniforms streamed behind the marshal and his chancellor. Goering and Goebbels in their turn saluted the Imperial Highnesses, but in a breezier way, with the

back of the hands [rendering what was, in fact, the Nazi casual salute so often wrongly described by authors as a wave].

Hindenburg and Hitler sat down facing each other in a vacant space in the center of the choir. The marshal put on his heavy tortoise-shell spectacles and read a speech.… Hitler's hand and the marshal's met in a firm grip as the Deputies rose to their feet. The image of Kaiser Wilhelm II dominated the scene.

It was as though the Third Reich—bent upon continuing the labors of the Second— intended, before burying the Weimar Republic, to bring back the Imperial exile of Doorn so soon as circumstances permitted.

At the end of the ceremony, a military parade took place before the doors of the Garrison Church. The Imperial Crown Prince—standing in the first row of spectators—looked for all the world as though the review were being given in his honor, and he inspecting his own troops.

But it was all a mirage, just as Hitler and Dr Goebbels had intended it to be.

Passing the Nazi Enabling Act, March 23, 1933

In *The Fateful Years*, eyewitness François-Poncet recalled of how Hitler was voted his dictatorial powers:

Within five minutes, the proceedings were over.… Parenthetically, he dashed all monarchist hopes to the ground when—alluding to possible reforms of Reich and Constitution—Hitler stated that the return of the monarchy was for the moment impossible.

How speedily the Potsdam ceremony was relegated to the background!… Hitler had won … valid for four years and based upon a semblance of legality, Hitler had become absolute master of the Reich.…

There was no longer need for either the Reichstag's sanction or Hindenburg's signature to legalize his decrees. The marshal had been ousted with—for only recourse—the faculty of expressing lack of confidence in the Cabinet.

This he could not do without risking the horrors of civil warfare. Hindenburg's Chancellor was stronger than Hindenburg himself.… And so—in sum—the solemn act in the Garrison Church proved to be no more than a solemn swindle.

His Majesty's Reaction to the *Tag von Potsdam* (Day of Potsdam), March 1933

Noted Wilhelm II's grandson, Prince Louis Ferdinand of Prussia, in his 1952 memoirs *The Rebel Prince*:

I witnessed his reading an enthusiastic telegram from one of his sons [possibly *Auwi*] who had been present … [at Potsdam]

Hitler … had tricked old President von Hindenburg into enabling him virtually to become the sole ruler of Germany. In amazement and disgust, my grandfather exclaimed, as he stamped angrily with his foot, "These idiots believe they can jump from the Rococo Age into that of the motor car and airplanes!"

A somewhat elliptical comment, it seems to me. It is interesting to note that had the 1918 overthrow of the Hohenzollerns not occurred, Wilhelm II would have continued to reign until his death in 1941, a run of fifty-three years (1888–1941), followed by the reign of Kaiser Wilhelm III (the crown prince) of ten years (1941–51), and then that of Kaiser Louis Ferdinand of forty-three years (1951–94), but, alas, none of that was to transpire in the actual event.

Von Epp's Nazi Coup in Bavaria, March 1933
In *The Fateful Years*, Eyewitness François-Poncet recalled this event after the Second World War:

> Commissioners charged with executive police functions were sent into the *Lander.* When Bavaria gibed, Gen. von Epp was at once detailed to take office as Reich Commissioner for Bavaria.
>
> He proceeded to depose the lawful government of Bavaria, to seize its ministries, and to set up Nazi leaders like Rohm and Wagner in them. Held—the Bavarian prime minister—and his colleagues gave way without a struggle.
>
> One—the Minister of the Interior—was seized in his bed and was marched barefoot to the Brown House, the SA [and Nazi Party] headquarters. All this was simply a foretaste of what was to come [as the Nazis took control all over the country swiftly].

Anti-Hindenburg Jokes, 1933–34 (Wheeler-Bennett's *Wooden Titan*)
A bitter Berlin story ran:

> "Have you heard?" a man would ask his friend—glancing over his shoulder to make sure he was not being overheard—"Hindenburg was at the Oranienburg Concentration Camp yesterday?" "Oh, why?" "He wanted to visit some of his voters!"
>
> "That is nothing! They say that the Old Man signs anything now! The other day Meissner left his sandwich bag on the table, and when he came back, the President had signed it!"

Hindenburg was outliving his renown and popularity rapidly. The former "Wooden Titan" was falling. Actually, according to some observers, Hindenburg knew very little of what was going on, but was merely "kept informed" by Dr Meissner, who had already sold out to Hitler and Goering, both of whom were clearly the coming masters.

In time, the Hindenburg legend was gradually put to rest. Many Germans hated the way in which Hindenburg had betrayed them to Hitler and his Nazis by his signature of the Enabling Act passed by the new Reichstag that gave Hitler full executive power to govern as he liked and did.

The Big Three at the Tannenberg Memorial, 27 August 1933
In August 1933, Hitler and Capt. Goering accompanied their Reich president to Tannenberg for the first summer celebration of 1914 since their own appointment to

national office. Although it was an embarrassment, all three men accepted the offer of the Poles to allow 1,500 cars transit via the Polish Corridor that separated the two German Prussias, east and west, so as to even hold the gala celebration. Among the passengers were Vice Chancellor Franz von Papen and Nazi *Gauleiter* Erich Koch.

German period journalist, chronicler, and eyewitness Max Domarus noted in *Speeches and Proclamations*:

> Hitler had scheduled a large rally at the Tannenberg Monument in East Prussia in memory of the battle … not only to commemorate the two battles of Tannenberg in 1410 and 1914, but also to pay a personal tribute of gratitude to Hindenburg.
>
> He directed Goering to give the Old Gentleman the gift of the Prussian domain of Langenau and the Preussenwald Forest, and to install a tax-free manor, Hindenburg-Neudeck.
>
> At this Act of State on 27 August 1933, Hitler [spoke], after Goering had read the deed of gift, [from a framed plaque seen in the famous photographs of the event, and here identified as such at last].
>
> *Herr* General Field Marshal!… Salvation came with the name Tannenberg!… The fate of Germany took a decisive turn! East Prussia was liberated, and Germany was rescued. This day marked the beginning of that tremendous series of battles in the east that overwhelmed Russia as a warring nation, showered the German armies with immortal glory, and obliged the German nation to forever owe loyal gratitude, *Herr* General Field Marshal, to your name.

The old man could not have recalled his own legend any better. Hindenburg recalled in *The Great War*:

> At that time, fate allowed me … to join and fight in the ranks of my brothers and comrades for the freedom of our people as a simple musketeer.…
>
> Today … I speak … in deepest reverence the gratitude of all.… The German Reich government … has resolved and made law that the plot of land in this province that is today connected with your name … shall remain free from the public duties of the Reich and the *Lander* as long as it remains bound to the name of Hindenburg by a male heir.

This male heir was none other than Maj. Gen. Oskar von Hindenburg, in whose name and legal title the property was and remained until the unexpected undoing of the above transaction by the Hindenburgs' foes of 1914 a mere thirty-one years later—another Russian Army.

Domarus added a pregnant clause that was to have fateful consequences for the entire German Armed Forces ever afterward: "Hindenburg showed his appreciation by appointing Goering General of Infantry on 30 August 1933," just three days after the Tannenberg deed bestowal. As noted in *Speeches and Proclamations*:

> To prevent the appointment from attracting too much attention—and perhaps prompting opposition in the ranks of the Reichswehr—[Werner von] Blomberg was simultaneously appointed colonel general.

The following official notice was published on 31 August 1933: "With effect as per yesterday's date, the Reich President has promoted the Reich Minister of Defense—Infantry General von Blomberg—to the rank of colonel general. Within the framework of other promotions, he also conferred upon the Prussian Minister-President—former Capt. Goering, Knight of the *Pour le Mérite*—the rank of general of infantry in recognition of his extraordinary merits both in war and peace, by virtue of which he is entitled to wear the uniform of the Reich Army."

This was the last time in which he had appeared at Doorn House in Holland during his final visit to their former emperor, Kaiser Wilhelm II, in 1932.

Pointed out the always astute observer Domarus in *Speeches and Proclamations*:

Goering's promotion from captain to general of infantry—bypassing five military ranks!—was in all probability a unique incident in the annals of German military history.

With the exception of the later SS generals, Goering was the only Wehrmacht general who achieved his rank as a result of a revolutionary step. The astounding thing was that it was not Hitler—but the Imperial Field Marshal von Hindenburg—who made this highly unusual appointment.

It was far more than that, however, for the two Nazis had discovered a very important secret lever of power for their future dealings with all top German military officers: they could be bribed with titles, batons, lands, housing, and tax-free financial gifts.

In effect, on August 27, 1933, they had just succeeded in bribing the most important of all such officers, and if they could bribe one, they both could and would bribe them all—and did.

Von Papen on the "Eastern Help" Scandal

As a major player in the dramas of 1932–34, von Papen's 1953 postwar memoirs are a very revealing and important work, in which he commented on the alleged effect of the East Prussian *Junker Osthilfe* financial scandal on the Hindenburg males at the time. As noted Wheeler-Bennett in *Wooden Titan*:

It is the old fable of the *Osthilfe Scandals* of the Junkers, of Reich President Hindenburg and his son, who—fearing disclosures—forced the Head of State, against his own will, to consent to Hitler's appointment as Reich Chancellor. This thesis has long been refuted by documentary evidence.…

One finds [in historian Alan Bullock's 1952 biography of Hitler] the never authenticated assertion that Hitler had planned to indict openly the President and his son for involvement … and for tax evasion.

It is an insult to the memory of the Reich President even to consider that he might have abandoned the path of dutiful decisions under the influence of such machinations!… Hitler did become Chancellor as the only way to avoid a breach of the Constitution and civil war.

On 2 December 1932, Hindenburg expressed the fervent hope that [an appointed Reich Chancellor von Schleicher] would relieve him of the unpleasant necessity of choosing between civil war and parliamentary government with Hitler.

Successors to Hindenburg: Epp and Imperial Crown Prince Wilhelm, 1934?

As Hindenburg neared death in the summer of 1934, the question arose as to who would succeed him as Reich president, and once more the names of both von Epp and Imperial Crown Prince Wilhelm were floated anew, but this time with covert German Army support.

Behind the scenes, Hitler made a deal with the army generals that if they guaranteed him the presidency after the "Old Gentleman's" demise, he would purge the top leadership corps of the rebellious SA leaders of Capt. Rohm that the army perceived—rightly or wrongly—as a threat. The deal was struck, hatched, and kept.

On May 10, 1934, Hindenburg had already made out his Will and Political Testament, in which he recommended to Hitler the restoration of the Hohenzollern monarchy. Then, commander of the army, Col. Gen. Baron Werner von Fritsch, called all the senior generals to Bad Nauheim for a discussion of the succession question.

At its start, it appeared that Imperial Crown Prince Wilhelm might be the winner, as most of the men present were fervent monarchists, but this changed entirely when Fritsch's boss, German Defense Minister Col. Gen. Werner von Blomberg, declared that Hitler becoming president would, indeed, sacrifice his own SA, hated rival of the army.

The generals then agreed to accept Hitler as their future supreme leader over the imperial crown prince. Thus, when Hindenburg died on August 2, 1934, Hitler within the hour had it announced that both offices—of Reich chancellor and of Reich president—would be combined in a single person alone: his.

That very day, the entire German Armed Forces took a personal oath of allegiance to Hitler alone, and not to either the ignored Weimar Constitution or even to the nation state of Germany. This remained the state of affairs until Hitler's own death in 1945, before which he ordered the two offices split in two once again. Thus, Hitler unified the two posts into one entity, becoming dictator of his new Nazi Germany in one of the most bizarre twists of political history ever recorded.

The Reich President's Post-Blood Purge Telegrams, July 1934

The Reich president's last official act was a sorry one, many historians assert. After the Nazi Blood Purge of June 30 to July 3, 1934—in which Hitler and Goering exterminated several of their enemies not only in their own ranks but also prominent soldiers and civil servants—Hindenburg sent them both congratulatory telegrams read all over the Third Reich.

That to Hitler read: "From the reports placed before me, I learn that you—by your determined action and your brave personal intervention—have nipped treason in the bud. You have saved the German nation from serious danger! For this, I express to you my most profound thanks and sincere appreciation. Hindenburg."

The world was shocked: what had Hindenburg come to? What, indeed! Privately, Hitler called him "the old coach horse." The outside world was astonished that the knightly, Christian von Hindenburg would publicly endorse blatant mass murder by shootings without trial in such a way. Not to be outdone, though, seven years later, the exiled Kaiser would also send the Führer one of his former infamous telegrams, congratulating Hitler on the fall of Paris in 1940.

It has been posited that the real author of the Hindenburg–Hitler–Goering telegrams of 1934 was Dr Meissner, who had already sold out to them as the coming powers until the very end in 1945.

Acquitted of war crimes at Nuremberg after World War II, in 1950, Dr Meissner published his memoirs, *State Secretary Under Ebert, Hindenburg, and Hitler,* and died at the age of seventy-four in Munich in 1953, eight years after the Führer, and nineteen years after the field marshal, viewed by some as the Talleyrand of Germany.

Hitler's Succession as President Illegal?

Domarus asserted that it was illegal: "In 1934, he had appropriated the position of Commander-in-Chief of the Reichswehr—in violation of the Constitution—the day before Hindenburg's death," or on August 1, 1934.

The Death of President von Hindenburg: Sir John W. Wheeler-Bennett, 1936 (*Wooden Titan*)

> Now he was quite quietly dying. On the afternoon of 1 August 1934 [at Neudeck in East Prussia], he called the great Dr Sauerbruch to his bedside: "You have always told me the whole truth, and you will do so now…. Is Friend Hein [Matthias Claudius's euphemism for Death] in the castle and waiting?"
>
> "No, *Herr* Field Marshal, but he is walking around the house." … "Thank you, Sauerbruch, I wanted to know, and now I will confer with the Lord a little!… I have known by heart for a long time what I want to read," from his Bible.…
>
> He read for a while; then laying down the book, he called to the doctor again. "It is all right, Sauerbruch, now tell Friend Hein he can come in."

It is interesting to note that the eminent surgeon operated on both the Kaiser before the Great War and on Hitler in 1936, on both occasions for throat cancer that each patient survived.

The Death of President von Hindenburg: John Toland, 1976

In 1976, the late American biographer and historian John Toland published his massive biography *Adolf Hitler*—based mainly on his own, personal interviews with survivors of the era—introduced at the U.S. National Archives at Washington, D.C. I attended that event and spoke with the author.

He said that Hitler arrived at the ill president's home Neudeck on August 1, 1934, as he was already sinking fast:

Oskar von Hindenburg led the Führer into the President's bedroom.

"Father," he said, "the Reich Chancellor is here." Without opening his eyes, the marshal said, "Why did you not come earlier?"

"What does the President mean?" Hitler whispered to the son. "The Reich Chancellor could not get here until now," Oskar told his father, who only muttered, "Oh, I see." After a silence, Oskar said, "Father, Reich Chancellor Hitler has one or two matters to discuss."

This time, the Old Gentleman opened his eyes with a start, stared at Hitler, then shut them again, and clamped his mouth shut. Perhaps the President had expected to see his Reich Chancellor, his *Franzschen*—Papen.

Hitler emerged, "tight-lipped," and would not discuss the scene.

Actually, later he did, asserting that the delirious octogenarian kept calling him "Your Majesty!" mistaking him for the absent "Exile of Doorn." Hitler left, never to see the marshal alive again: "The Old Gentlemen died with the words: 'My Kaiser … My fatherland' on his lips. He was laid out on the iron cot with a Bible in his hands."

Nazi Requiem for a Prussian Field Marshal, August 6–7, 1934

The Berlin Kroll Opera House at noon on August 6, 1934 was the setting of the initial phase of the late president's state funeral events: "Where his coffin was carried past the ranks of Army field gray and brown and black of the SA and SS. These diverse groups were at last united by similar oaths of loyalty to the Führer."

Recalled Toland forty-two years later: "It was symbolic that the music for the occasion was the funeral march from [composer Richard Wagner's] *Götterdämmerung*."

Birth of the Hindenburg Legend, August 30, 1914—as Revealed by Hitler

More importantly for our saga here, Domarus revealed the exact nature of how, when, in what way, and by whom the Hindenburg legend of 1914–34 was born, as stated in Hitler's own memorial address of August 6, 1934.

The German Reich chancellor as head of government had done his homework—via Dr Meissner—in researching the official imperial archives of two decades before. As noted in *Speeches and Proclamations*:

On 22 August 1914, Hindenburg was assigned the task of assuming supreme command of an army in East Prussia. Eight days later [i.e., on August 30, 1914] the German people and the world are first told of this appointment, and thus become acquainted with the name of the new colonel general!

Wolff's Telegraph Bureau makes the following official report: "Our troops in Prussia under the leadership of Col. Gen. von Hindenburg [and thus not Beneckendorff] have defeated the Russian Army advancing from the Narew River in a force of five army corps and three cavalry divisions in a three-day battle in the district of Gilgenburg and Ortelsburg, and are now pursuing them over the border." Quartermaster Gen. von Stein.

Hitler called it right: "Tannenberg was won! Front now on, the greatest battle in world history was bound up with this name!"

Eyewitness Domarus described what happened next, after the conclusion of Hitler's *Krolloper* memorial address: "When the mournful strains of Wagner's *Götterdämmerung* died out, the funeral party went outdoors … the Reichswehr gave its first official salute to the new commander-in-chief."

From Neudeck to Hohenstein: Hindenburg's Final Journey to Tannenberg, 1934
Notes Goltz in the most recent account, *Hindenburg*:

> It began with the transportation of the deceased President in the dark of night on a gun carriage, from Hindenburg's East Prussian home Neudeck.
> Following a torchlit route—and escorted by infantry and cavalry—the cortege made its way to Hohenstein [during the night of August 6–7, 1934].

How Christian Hindenburg Entered the Nazi Pagan Valhalla, August 7, 1934
"Burial took place the next noon [August 7, 1934] not where Hindenburg had wished—at Neudeck—but, on Hitler's insistence, at the scene of the marshal's greatest triumph, Tannenberg," asserted Toland in *Adolf Hitler*:

> The body was placed on a catafalque in the center of the monument to the battle, an impressive structure with eight square towers some 60 feet high with fires flaming at the top of each.
> It reminded [French] Ambassador François-Poncet of a castle built by the Teutonic Knights. Hitler strode forward to face the coffin. At the podium he discovered that an adjutant [SA Gen. Wilhelm Brückner?] had laid out the wrong speech, and there was an embarrassing pause that must have puzzled radio listeners all over Europe.

One of these was my later and today still living former history professor Dr Armin E. Mruck, then of East Prussia and post-World War II a resident of Maryland, a retired professor at now Towson University, Maryland:

> But he quickly collected himself, and began extemporizing one of the shortest speeches Lochner, for one, had ever heard him deliver. Hitler ended with fulsome praise of Hindenburg's military and political achievements in words befitting a Wagnerian hero, not an orthodox fundamental Lutheran, "And now, enter thou upon Valhalla!" the ritualistic abode of ancient Germanic pagan worthies!

In far-off Holland, fellow Christian Wilhelm II might have stifled a smile, if not an outright derisive laugh.

Toland concluded: "At the end of the services, Hitler kissed the hands of Hindenburg's daughters," as Mackensen once did those of their imperial majesty so long ago, in better times:

Moved by the solemnity of the moment—if not by opportunism—Gen. von Blomberg impulsively suggested that the Armed Forces should henceforth address him not with the customary Mr Hitler, but as Mein Führer.

Hitler accepted the proposal, and returned to Berlin.

Goltz's *Hindenburg* expanded on the above version thus: "Originally, it was planned for the late marshal-president to be interred in the yard's central axis," but the Hitler–Speer duo changed this: "A special crypt was built in the former exit lower, a huge monolith with Hindenburg's name being placed over the entrance. The cross was also replaced by a paved field for military parades, the central point for official anniversary meetings." For the immediate present, however, the Nazi state funeral had the deceased's coffin placed on a raised bier for Hitler's funeral oration, followed by deposition inside the crypt to ringing bells and staccato artillery fire.

Several accounts mention Hitler's overly "pagan" oration: "In this place among the infantry soldiers from victorious regiments who are sleeping here, our field marshal will find his place of rest. Our late marshal—enter you your Valhalla now!"

The Domarus Account (*Speeches and Proclamations*)

On the morning of 7 August 1934, funeral ceremonies for the Reich President commenced in the courtyard of the huge Tannenberg Monument.

Hitler had once again conceived of something new: he greeted the bereaved and kissed Frau von Hindenburg's hand [that of Oskar's wife], thus reinstituting a ceremony that had no longer been practiced in official German society since 1918…

"After an address by the Chief of Chaplains Dr Dohrmann, Hitler stood before Hindenburg's sarcophagus and delivered the following speech," as published officially the next day, August 8, 1934; but did the Nazi Führer actually give it, considering what Toland wrote above?

In any event, there were published some pertinent facts, such as the actual date of the late soldier's first retirement from the army, March 18, 1911, and blamed the Kaiser for appointing the victor of Tannenberg "too late" to head all of the Reich's ground forces in summer 1916.

Hitler also took a veiled oratorical shot at that third great actor in the Hindenburg saga by according the "Old Gentleman" pride of place militarily thus: "In 1925, the best representative national Germany could find was the soldier and field marshal," duly elected Reich president, and not, therefore, his allegedly more brilliant and accomplished understudy, Ludendorff. As noted Wheeler-Bennett in *Wooden Titan*:

It is here—in the midst of the slumbering grenadiers of his victorious regiments—that the tired commander shall find his peace. The towers of the castle shall be defiant guards of this, his last great headquarters in the east. Standards and flags shall salute him!

And the German people will come to its dead hero to gather new strength for life in times of need, for even when the last trace of this body shall have been obliterated, his name will ever more be immortal.…

A magic power lay in the very name of the field marshal who—with his armies—ultimately forced the greatest military power in the world to its knees in the Russia of that time!

Dead commander, enter into Valhalla now!

François-Poncet's Version (*The Fateful Years*)

The marshal's obsequies were magnificent, and fraught with that romanticism that intoxicated the Nazis, criminals or not. The body—set on an artillery gun carriage drawn by six black horses—was transported by night to [*sic.,* from?] Neudeck—passing mile after mile between two rows of torches.

Next day it was placed on a catafalque in the center of the Tannenberg Monument—whose eight square, massive towers, and battlemented wall connecting them—were reminiscent of a castle built by the Teutonic Knights.

Great lights burned at the top of each tower, soldiers formed a chain under the walls, oriflammes fluttered from the enceinte, but not a single swastika banner among them. To this extent at least, the feelings of the deceased had been respected.

Following an embarrassed and banal pastor, Hitler made an address, he was more nervous than ever, excited, spasmodic, flushed, and in no sense in keeping with the rapt gravity of the spectators…

Reporter Louis P. Lochner's 1942 Version (*What About Germany?*)

Two State funeral ceremonies were staged by the Nazi regime—the first in the Reichstag in Berlin—the second at the Tannenberg Monument of East Prussia, in one of whose towers Hindenburg's remains were laid to rest.

Hitler decided to deliver the eulogies at both obsequies.

Everything went according to schedule in the Reichstag. Hitler read from a prepared manuscript, lauding Hindenburg's career and personality.

At the Tannenberg Monument, Hitler again had a manuscript before him. He read a sentence or two—both of which had a familiar ring to me—then faltered. The next moment, he was improvising.

Speaking haltingly, then briefly—and visibly ill at ease—he ended amazingly abruptly for a marathon talker, saying, "And now, enter thou upon Valhalla!"

That was about the most inappropriate final salute anyone could make in the case of a personality as devoutly Christian as the old field marshal had been—what had happened?

Hitler's adjutant had mistakenly brought the Reichstag address of the previous day to Tannenberg, instead of the script intended for the second oratorical effort, and had placed it upon the lectern.

Hitler soon became aware of his mistake. He "ad libbed" and—instead of giving his words a Christian turn, or at least omitting any digression into heathenism—fell back upon his craze for Wagnerian mythology, and consigned the field marshal to the reception hall for warriors of the ancient Teuton god Wotan!

There is also another, political possibility: politician Hitler might very well have been throwing a bone to his own pagan wing of the Nazi Party: Alfred Rosenberg, Heinrich Himmler, and, not to be overlooked, Hindenburg's own acolyte (and Hitler's former mentor as well) Ludendorff. Political utterances serve many purposes.

Eyewitness Papen on the Tannenberg State Funeral, 1953 (*Memoirs*)

The day after he died, I arrived at Neudeck at the invitation of his family. I was overcome at the memory of the many private and official conversations I had had there with Hindenburg, who had become almost as much a father to me as a friend.

It was a solemn and unforgettable moment when Oskar von Hindenburg left me alone to take my farewell of the President.

He was laid out on an iron camp bed in his spartan little bedroom, with a Bible clasped in his hands, and on his face the expression of wisdom, kindliness, and determination that I had known so well.

I had honored him, and given him the best years of my life, and now I had to say goodbye. He represented a whole era of German history. He had fought at Sadowa, and had attended the coronation of the German Kaiser at Versailles.

In his declining years, his sense of duty had led him to take over the leadership of his country. Now—when the whole weight of his authority was most needed to guide future developments—he had been taken from us....

Hindenburg had left instructions that he was to be buried next to his wife, near his own home at Neudeck [and, thus, not at Hanover at all]. Hitler had other ideas—of a grand State Funeral.

The family was subjected to a storm of requests that the burial should take place inside the great Tannenberg Memorial, and the President's body be laid to rest in one of its towers.

In the end, they gave way. It was—I must confess—highly impressive to see the old field marshal surrounded for the last time by the flags and standards of his regiments, spoiled only by the appalling tactlessness of Hitler in wishing such a devout Christian "entry into Valhalla."

Hindenburg belonged to an era that had in fact ended with the First World War—and the penalties of peace. He was the last imposing representative of a world that had disappeared, and he could no longer halt the avalanche that descended on us.

Only 11 years later, his East Prussian home had become part of Asia, the Tannenberg Memorial had been razed to the ground, and the fate of Europe was in the balance.

François-Poncet Reflects on Hindenburg (*The Fateful Years*)

After the ceremony—on my way back to Berlin by train—I thought of the old man whom we used to see in the course of our diplomatic duties four or five times a year. His tall stature was striking; he was almost a colossus.

His face was divided into two parts by a heavy moustache that rose on either side like tusks over the corner of his lips. His hair was cut short—stubble, like the hairs of a brush—was gray and close-set.

His features were full and regular, suggestive of martial power and robust equilibrium, were it not for their sadness and weariness, accentuated by a waxen complexion and lusterless eyes overcast by leaden eye lids.

Yet there was a kindness in his glance and in his great, gruff voice that spoke in monosyllables and in military tones. He impressed one as an aged and weary leader of men, a kindly grandfather who was annoyed at having to leave his armchair.

He remembered having been detailed as page to Marshal MacMahon in 1861 when Napoleon III had sent MacMahon to represent him at the coronation of Wilhelm I as King of Prussia.

Whenever Hindenburg met me, he would repeat the same anecdote. A huge African tent set up in the garden of the French Embassy had struck the young page's attention, and the old marshal never failed to allude to it.

I would attempt to steer the conversation to MacMahon, whose destiny and Hindenburg's had much in common [as the French marshal was elected president of France after the second and final fall of the deposed Bonaparte dynasty]. But Hindenburg did not know—or had forgotten—the story of MacMahon.

He was a typical representative of the generation that grew up under Wilhelm I. He read the Bible every evening before going to sleep. He did not relish luxury, he lived stingily, and was a miser.

He wished to recoup the family fortunes—that had once been prosperous—and the Neudeck estate in East Prussia—a gift from the nation—turned him into a *Junker* [landowner].

"Was Hindenburg Senile During 1932–34? A Medical Viewpoint," *Stroke*, Vol. 3, July–August 1972, by Walter J. Friedlander, MD

It was this senile old man who found it impossible to resist Hitler, even though it is reasonable to theorize that a less demented man occupying Hindenburg's position of President … might well have defeated the Fuhrer's ultimate seizure of power.…

An inquiry concerning Hindenburg reveals a progressive exaggeration of personality traits as his brain disease increased, until he presented a caricature of what he had been.

Biographers do not record any distinct cerebral ischemic episodes, but all agree that advancing age took its explicable toll, and this seems most likely to have been due to cerebral arteriosclerosis, [or in its generic, lay person definition, hardening of the arteries].…

[By 1932, Hindenburg] Was so far gone mentally that his Secretary of State, Meissner—now an intriguer for the extreme right—had to write down for him word for word the questions the President put to his callers, and the vague statements he was to make after they had their say.

Hindenburg was described as no longer capable of prolonged concentration, and often dozed off during lengthy conferences. His conversation … would often wander off to the happier days of the Prussian-Austrian War of 1866.

"He could recall the names of noncoms who served under him then, although even the memory of his famous victory on the Eastern Front at Tannenberg in 1914 was hazy.… The decline of his physical state served to reinforce his natural lethargy," noted Andreas Dorpalen.

> In June 1934, Hindenburg left Berlin for his home *Neudeck*. He declined rapidly and died quietly.… Senility—probably secondary to cerebral arteriosclerosis—had run its natural course in an old man—not just another old man, but an old man, who—at least in the last years of his life—may have held the chance and then lost it to prevent history running its tragic course…

Lochner Contrasts the Hindenburg of 1925 and 1933–34 in 1942

Associated Press reporter Lochner first met the future Reich president in 1925 via the famous marshal's sister, Ida von Hindenburg. Lochner recalled in *What About Germany?*:

> I visited her … in an old ladies home for noblewomen in Potsdam.…
>
> The white-haired sister … looked surprisingly like her distinguished brother, except that her head seemed somewhat rounder than the field marshal's more rectangular cranium.… She usually referred to her brother as the field marshal, but from time to time her affection found expression in the good, good brother!…
>
> The Hindenburg of 1925 was very different from the senile President of 1933.… On 19 April 1925, he seemed healthy and vigorous despite his age. The demonstration fell on an unusually hot day.…
>
> I managed to wedge myself into an observation point directly opposite Hindenburg's front door [of his Hanoverian homestead]. As the church clocks tolled the hour of noon, the marchpast began.
>
> The field marshal—then 77 years old—took his stand before the door, clad in the full dress uniform of his rank, with many rows of decorations. With his left hand resting on the hilt of his sword and with his right hand frequently saluting, the Presidential candidate stood almost like a statue for 90 minutes.
>
> Gaunt, erect, towering, he scarcely as much as shifted his feet. The heat did not seem to bother him. Members of his entourage soon retired to the cooler inside of the mansion. I nearly fainted.

This is the trick of both professional actors and now politicians, become one and the same well before Hindenburg took the stage, and the gambit is called playing to the gallery.

In that, at least, the marshal and his later "Bohemian Corporal" Hitler had much in common: both were thespian troopers of the very first order.

Papen's Hindenburg Senility View (*Memoirs*)

> We had all been aware of the danger inherent in re-electing so old a President … Brüning … maintains that Hindenburg suffered a breakdown in September 1931 that impaired his faculties for about 10 days.

Meissner … has denied this, as has Herr von der Schulenburg, Hindenburg's military ADC. The Old Gentleman often had attacks of faintness, but his intellect remained unimpaired.

When I became Chancellor in June 1932, the President still had all his wits about him, and his powers of decision did not fail during this critical period.… It was not until the end of 1933 that his physical condition started to deteriorate, but even then, there was no sign of any intellectual decay.

It was clear, however, that he could not last forever, and with so critical a situation in the country, I realized that his death would have serious consequences.… If the President should die, it was highly undesirable that his mantle should fall on Hitler, or one of his Party colleagues.

Chief among the latter category was Goering, whom rumor had it already saw himself as the future Kaiser Hermann I, and the Hohenzollerns be damned. To preclude this—and also to facilitate the return of those very same former Wilhelminians—Papen met with Hitler in March 1934, with the latter asserting that, "He had no objections to the Hohenzollern dynasty, although he felt that a new Kaiser might be handicapped by no longer being King of Prussia," as before, during 1871–1918.

In June 1934—partly at least at von Papen's instigation—Reich Chancellor Hitler made his first state visit outside Germany to a country that he had not first conquered, to the hybrid state of Savoyard-Fascist Italy to meet Italian Premier Benito Mussolini.

He was shocked to see the subservient role that "*Signor*" Mussolini was forced to play as merely the appointed head of the government of His Majesty King Vittorio Immanuel III. Hitler returned, allegedly, a changed man, according to Papen: "He was full of sarcasm about the 'monarchist meddlings' in Italy, and said to me, 'If I have never been anti-monarchist before, I am now!'… He was offended by the snobbish attitude of the Italian court," a feeling that increased dramatically during and after his second state visit to Italy in May 1938.

The First Hindenburg Will Flap, 1934

Reportedly, Hitler simply called von Papen on the telephone to inquire if the "Old Gentleman" had left a will, to which his former vice chancellor replied that he would ask Oskar von Hindenburg.

Asserted the Nazi Führer: "I should be obliged if you would ensure that this document comes into my possession as soon as possible!" When it arrived from Neudeck and was given to the NS dictator, he told Papen coldly: "These recommendations of the late President are given to me personally. Later, I shall decide when—and if—I shall permit their publication." When his foreign press secretary Ernst Putzi Hanfstaengl told Hitler at tea that the foreign journalists were alleging that Hitler planned to suppress the papers altogether, Hitler snorted angrily, "I do not care what that pack of liars thinks!" Indeed, he no longer needed to, and never did again, either.

Recalled François-Poncet in *The Fateful Years* regarding the will:

It had taken 11 days to discover the document!… One half of it—the old part—had been written in Hanover in 1919, and the other, the recent part, was drawn up in Berlin, and signed as of 11 May 1934 [prior to the Nazi Blood Purge, moreover].

In the latter, Hindenburg waxed lyrical in praise of Hitler. Now such feelings in no wise agree with those the old marshal was known to have entertained shortly before his death.…

To recommend Hitler to the German people as his chosen successor could never have entered the marshal's mind, for he was much too sincerely a monarchist and legitimist. In fact, the secret drama of Hindenburg's existence was that Kaiser Wilhelm II … resented the fact that Hindenburg was occupying Wilhelm's position, if not his throne.

Can the clauses of the Will—though couched in full and lucid style—be ascribed to senility? Such was not the version current in Berlin in August 1934!

Talk in the capital was that Hindenburg's Will had been tampered with, that the entire second part was bogus and written by the man who had recently helped Hindenburg edit his memoirs [reportedly Col. Mertz von Quirnheim].

The whole operation suggested the complicity of several persons. It was made possible only with the connivance of Col. [Oskar] von Hindenburg, Meissner … and of Papen.

Well, shortly thereafter, Col. Hindenburg was appointed general; Meissner … remained at Hitler's side [as Secretary of State], and Papen—becoming a taboo personage—enjoyed the attentions … of the regime in his foreign missions.

All of them would seem to have received the just reward of their good offices. I have never heard it said that the Allies after World War II apprehended Col. von Hindenburg in Germany, but Meissner was arrested, and Papen imprisoned in Nuremberg.

Reported Toland in *Adolf Hitler* in 1976:

On 15 August 1934, the testament was released for publication.… There was talk in the capital that the document had been doctored by the editor of Hindenburg's memoirs, and that Oskar von Hindenburg and his father's advisor—Dr Meissner—were co-conspirators in the deception.

A measure of credence was given this rumor when Oskar swore in a radio speech to the nation that his father had always supported Hitler. The cynics notwithstanding, the son was not lying.

Despite Hindenburg's repugnance for some aspects of the Hitler regime, he had seen the Führer as his direct successor.

I believe that this assessment is correct. Whichever way things turned out, Hindenburg's own legend would be burnished anew: if Hitler brought back the Hohenzollerns, the marshal's own historic mission had been achieved; if not, he took another swipe at the ex-Kaiser in death for firing him in 1911.

He counted on Hitler starting the next world war—so much the better—but few, if any, of them reckoned on the full scope of the Nazi murder machine during that war. He was, however, entirely opposed to his chancellor's plans to enlist Fascist Italy as

Nazi Germany's military, diplomatic, and political ally: "I do not care *what* you say, Hitler! You will never make anything out of the Italians but spaghetti benders!" the "Old Gentleman" roared.

The Domarus Will Flap Account (*Speeches and Proclamations*)

Von Hindenburg's Will was opened on 15 August 1934. It bore the inscription: "My Last Will & Testament. This letter is to be given to the Reich Chancellor by my son" ... dated 11 May 1934, and began with the words, "To the German People and its Chancellor" ... and closed with the following section dedicated to Hitler:

"I thank Providence that it has allowed me to experience the hour of resurgence in the twilight of my life!... My Chancellor Adolf Hitler and his Movement have taken a decisive step of historic significance toward the great goal of bringing the German People together in inner unity beyond all differences of rank and class.

"With this firm belief in the future of the fatherland, I can rest in peace. Berlin, 11 May 1934 von Hindenburg."

As an aside, I assert here that the phrase, "I thank Providence" was, most likely, written by Hitler himself, and not von Hindenburg. Hitler used "Providence" instead of God throughout his political career.

The Second Hindenburg Will Flap, 1946–47 (*Speeches and Proclamations*)

Notes Domarus: "After World War II, the de-Nazification Court at Nuremberg"—in von Papen's trial—took up the question of whether a second Will (that Hitler suppressed) did not indeed recommend the reinstitution of the monarchy, and, if so, who had been responsible for the text, in particular for the section devoted to Hitler?

Oskar von Hindenburg vehemently insisted that there had been only *one* text, and that its full wording had been published. Von Papen—who had drafted the document—originally maintained a different view, claiming that he had not been responsible for the section addressed to Hitler.

However, he was ultimately forced to admit that he might have been the author of these remarks as well. This revised view most probably reflects the truth, for von Papen stated on 4 August 1934 in Neudeck after visiting Hindenburg's bier:

"No one acknowledged the historic achievement and human greatness of Hindenburg more highly than Adolf Hitler. We can fulfill Hindenburg's legacy no better than to unite our efforts once more for our immortal Germany and its peaceful European mission" ... from von Papen's de-Nazification trial in February 1947.

According to the testimony of Oskar von Hindenburg at his own respective trial before the Denazification Court at Uelzen in March 1949, the Reich president had merely requested in a personal letter to Hitler that he consider reinstating the monarchy at a later date. Such never occurred.

The 1934–35 Tannenberg Memorial Evolution

The late marshal had always reportedly intended that he would be buried at Hanover in the clan's family plot next to his late wife, Gertrud, lain there since 1921, but now Hitler had other ideas instead. Continues Gessner in 2017's *Tannenburg*:

> Hitler had decided that the monument should become a mausoleum for Hindenburg and his wife. To effectuate the change in purpose, Hitler had the grave of the unknown soldiers removed, and the level of the plaza lowered by eight feet, with stone steps surrounding it on all sides.
>
> A vaulted burial chamber was built in the crypt of one of the towers. The entrance to the crypt was guarded by two 13-foot statues of soldiers.… Special brass sarcophagi were placed in the burial chamber.
>
> Behind the sarcophagi stood two crosses joined at the arms. Inscribed on them were two of the field marshal's favorite sayings: "Love is eternal" and "Be faithful till death." On the wall hung a black Prussian eagle.
>
> In the tower above the crypt, another chamber housed Hindenburg memorabilia, and within it stood a 13-foot-high statue of the Field Marshal in dark green porphyry.

The Nazi State Funeral of August 7, 1934

On August 7, 1934, Hitler had German architect and Nazi rally planner Dr Albert Speer stage the most elaborate state funeral seen in Germany since imperial times to honor the deceased "First Soldier of the Reich."

Conducted to the pealing of church bells and Hitler's own, unique, high-flown oratory of macabre hyperbole, it concluded with his ringing charge, "*Toter Feldherr, geh' ein in Walhall!*"—"Supreme field lord, enter Valhalla!"

Oskar von Hindenburg's Radio Speech, August 18, 1934

> My now immortal father himself saw in Adolf Hitler his immediate successor as head of the German Reich, and I am acting in accordance with my father's wishes when I call upon all German men and women to vote that my father's office be passed on to the Fuhrer and Reich Chancellor.

This was the actual title that Hitler had already bestowed upon himself, with that of Reich president being retired until it reappeared in his own "Last Will and Testament" of April 30, 1945.

"And thus, the marshal's cry sounds from the Tower of Tannenberg still!" Oskar's radio address continued: "Gather together, stand united, and form behind Germany's Führer! Demonstrate inwardly and outwardly that an unbreakable bond firmly encompasses the German people in a single will!" he asserted over the national airwaves. Hitler duly "won" the plebiscite vote of 89.9 percent of those registered to vote on August 19, 1934.

Thus, the Nazi leader was "not only Chancellor for life, but President as well," even if that actual title disappeared for the next decade-plus. Truly, "the Clan Hindenburg had hoisted Hitler into the saddle," as Showalter puts it.

The Nazi Upgrade of the 1927 Tannenberg Memorial

Hitler directed that the architects Kruger again utilize the Stonehenge motif over the entrance to the marshal's crypt. Goltz recalled in *Hindenburg*:

> A giant stone—symbolically from Königsberg—was placed, with the field marshal's name inscribed upon it.
>
> This stone was so large that railway bridges had to be strengthened to aid its transportation. Two giant stone soldiers—as if on guard—were placed outside the tomb. A porphyry statue of the victor—by the East Prussian Friedrich Bagdons—dominated the Hall of Honor above the tomb.
>
> The concourse grass was replaced with stone and, and around the memorial, landscape were placed [historically inaccurate] interpretations of the Aryan German presence in East Prussia since the Stone Age.

It was there that the marshal had been buried, in the plaza or "central yard" of the monument, on August 7, 1934, with Hitler himself officiating. Adds Gessner in *Tannenberg*:

> The Tannenberg monument itself was elevated to the rank of a Monument of German Pride, the only such in all of Germany. It became a symbol, myth, and a place of pilgrimage for thousands of Germans.
>
> School children were required to visit it, and it was the site of the annual reunions of the veterans of WWI.

The Nazi Führer designated the final version to be known as *Reichsehrenmal*, or National Memorial Tannenberg.

Ludendorff Rejects the Hitlerian Marshal's Baton, April 9, 1935

After sending Hindenburg into "Valhalla," the Nazi Führer fully intended to do the same with Ludendorff when the latter died as well. Recalled Domarus in *Speeches and Proclamations*:

> Consequently, he issued an order on April 8, 1935 that read as follows:
>
> "Tomorrow, on 9 April 1935, Gen. Ludendorff is celebrating his 70th birthday. With sentiments of deepest gratitude, the German people recalls … the immortal accomplishments of its greatest commander in the World War. In … this sentiment of a national debt of gratitude, I order that all State buildings exhibit flags on 9 April 1935."…
>
> Ludendorff … celebrated … in his house on the banks of the Starnberg Lake in Tutzing [Bavaria] on 9 April 1935.… Hitler had an honor guard appointed to the celebrant, and dispatched Reich Minister of Defense von Blomberg and Chief of Army Command Werner von Fritsch.
>
> … to relay his congratulations in Tutzing. Blomberg was also instructed to present the marshal's baton to Ludendorff, but the latter—the victorious commander *per se*, rejected

the appointment. Naturally, the German people heard nothing of this affront ... and the absence of any word of thanks.

The Second Nazi Upgrade of the Tannenberg Memorial, October 2, 1935

On the occasion of what would have been Hindenburg's eighty-eighth birthday (October 2, 1935), "The President's bronze coffin was relocated to a new, somber chamber, where he was joined by his late wife Gertrud, who was moved from the family plot in Hanover," their former home.

"The new crypt—that was completed in the fall of 1935—was located directly below the south tower. To create an entrance to the crypt," explained Gessner in *Tannenberg*:

> Hindenburg and the 20 unknown German soldiers ... were temporarily disinterred, and the level of the plaza was lowered by eight feet, with stone steps surrounding it on all sides.
>
> The unknown soldiers were reinterred in the side chapels. Designed by the Kruger brothers and carved by Paul Bronisch, the entrance to Hindenburg's crypt was dominated by two 14-foot sculptures of *The Eternal Watch*, carved out of more than 120 tons of imported Königsberg marble. The mausoleum had a dramatic vaulted ceiling.

Hindenburg's Second Nazi Burial, October 2, 1935

"The sarcophagus was draped in the Reich War Flag for the ceremony, at which Hitler performed the rededication." Again, contemporary eyewitness Domarus provides the best personal account of the 1935 event (*Speeches and Proclamations*):

> On 1 October 1935, Hitler paid a visit to East Prussian troop units. The next day he attended Hindenburg's "final interment" in a newly erected vault in the Tannenberg Monument near Hohenstein.
>
> On the evening of 2 October 1935, he declared the Tannenberg Monument a "Reich Memorial," and dispatched the following official announcement: "I ...bestow upon it the name Tannenberg Reich Memorial.... It shall be consecrated for all eternity.... To sincerely thank them in this hour is both my duty and a matter dear to my heart!"

The Hindenburg/Tannenberg Decade, 1935–45

After 1935, Hitler himself visited the sacred site once more, in August 1941, as his armies were storming across European Russia vanquishing Hindenburg's prior enemies of August 1914: the reborn Russian Army of Josef Stalin, Lenin's 1924 successor.

During 1936–39, there was a traveling exhibition on the Masurian region centered on the battle, that the 1936 *Baedecker Guide* edition described the memorial site as "Where President Hindenburg rests beside his fallen comrades as a place of national pilgrimage."

Projected plans for busts of those figures involved in Hitler's own Polish campaign of 1939, including tablets exhibiting his own quotations and a full-length statue of the Führer to complement that of his former boss, von Hindenburg, were never placed.

In addition, the August 1939 commemoration of the twenty-fifth anniversary of the battle was scrapped due to improved German-Russian relations, with the signature at Moscow of the Nazi-Soviet Non-Aggression Pact of August 25, 1939 that led to the next fall of the Polish state.

Hitler Bribes von Mackensen, October 22, 1935
Reported Domarus in *Speeches and Proclamations*:

> Field Marshal von Mackensen had aided Hitler in defeating the *Stahlhelm* [national German Great War veterans' association] by renouncing his honorary membership ... on 31 July 1935, because "The most important battle aim of the *Stahlhelm*" had been "realized with the reinstitution of general conscription," [i.e., the national military draft for all males of service age].
>
> In return for this support, Hitler assigned to Mackensen the title to the ancestral estate *Prussow* near Stettin—that was State property—on 22 October 1935.
>
> It was a well-known fact that Hitler showed a marked generosity in bestowing material and financial endowments [i.e., bribes] upon persons who were devoted to him.

One of the former Kaiser's six sons—Prince August Wilhelm of Prussia, nicknamed "Auwi"—was a featured speaker for the Nazis as a member of Hitler's SA Storm Troopers during the election campaigns of 1928, '30, '32, and '33. He was in hopes that the Nazis would elevate him as the successor Kaiser to his father Wilhelm II once they took office, but it never happened. He is surrounded here by Nazi SS guards. (*HHA*)

Another royal who flirted politically with the Nazis in the same vain hope was the former Imperial German Crown Prince Wilhelm, seen here being lionized by a crowd in the Steel Helmet Student Ring at Naumburg in 1933. (*DH*)

Prince Wilhelm was allowed to return home to Germany from his Dutch exile of 1918–23 on the very day of the Hitler–Ludendorff Revolt at Munich, thus infuriating his chagrined father in Holland, never permitted the same. Crown Prince Wilhelm wears his Blue Max at the collar, photographed by Heinrich Classens.

On September 3, 1932, the Hohenzollerns turn out in force to attend Berlin's thirteenth annual Reich Front Soldiers' Day, showing (seated in the front row) from left to right, Crown Prince Wilhelm; his younger brother, Prince of Prussia Eitel-Frederick (nicknamed "Eitel-Fritz"); the latter's wife, Princess Ina Marie, who is turned to talk with another brother, Prince Oskar of Prussia; and, finally, one of the latter's sons. Between the Eitel-Fredericks in the second row are, perhaps, the surviving two of the then living five brothers, the sixth, Prince Adalbert, having committed suicide in 1920. (*U.S. Army Signal Corps and also DH*)

Like Auwi, the imperial crown prince also joined an NS political formation, in his case the Motor Corps, as seen here, at center, hands in pockets of what he called "the funny pants." (*HHA*)

Previous page, below: Hitler held Auwi in basic contempt, and the feeling was mutual. Friedrich Karl Holtz—editor of the Berlin Nationalist weekly publication *Fridericus*—published an article on March 20, 1932 that "astounded all of Germany," entitled "Our Reich President Crown Prince Wilhelm." Hitler had met secretly with the crown prince—as he had in 1925 with Ludendorff—urging him to run against the incumbent Hindenburg for the post.

On March 29, 1932, the crown prince held a secret meeting of his own at his Castle Oels in Silesia, where Crown Princess Cecilie, Colonel Eberhard von Selasen-Selasinsky, and the NS propaganda chief for North Westphalia convinced him to run. Had he done so, Hitler's hope was that Hindenburg would himself decline to stand against the Kaiser's own first-born and heir, leaving the Nazi Führer with an easier opponent to beat in the person of the crown prince.

The plan for a Reich President Wilhelm von Hohenzollern would need Hitler's full support as well as *Der alte Herr's* own retirement, with Mackensen being delegated to accomplish the latter. First, however, Crown Prince Wilhelm wanted his father's agreement, but the "Old Man of Doorn" refused and also forbade his son to run; "Little Willy" obeyed, Hitler was foiled, and Hindenburg was duly re-elected.

The Kaiser may have objected to both possibilities: that his son would win or lose, thus damaging in either case his own possibilities of returning to the throne himself. A winning Crown Prince Wilhelm might well have aped President Louis Napoleon of 1848–52 in France who declared himself emperor of the French as his term in office expired, ruling 1852–71 as a result. Wilhelm II was taking no chances. (*HHA*)

Reich Chancellor Heinrich Brüning—a machine-gun company commander veteran of the Great War—is seen here campaigning for Hindenburg's re-election as Reich president in the spring of 1932. His oratory helped ensure the aging marshal's victory at the polls, twice. The poster mounted on the speaker's stand reads "Our Reich President" underneath a woodcut print of his candidate's massive square head. (*LC*)

Top of next page: One of Hindenburg's electoral opponents in 1932 was the deputy head of the German veterans' organization, the *Stahlhelm*, of which—oddly—Hindenburg himself was the honorary president. This was the partially Jewish Theodor Duesterberg, sixth from left, his banners being carried behind. During the heated campaign, the Nazis revealed that Duesterberg had an as yet unknown Jewish grandfather in his family tree. (*LC*)

Candidate Hindenburg had exclusive use of the German state radio during the campaign, and read his major re-election campaign speech over the public airwaves.

Hindenburg tried to spare the lives of his soldiers. His other mottos included "God's will be done" and "Above all, no adventure!" A man of some contrasts, however, the Reich president insisted that his Chancellor Brüning borrow his own fur coat during a journey to wintry East Prussia in 1930–31, but then fired him ungraciously after the latter had helped re-elect him to office against Hitler twice in 1932.

"Hindenburg tells how one day he walked with the Kaiser over a battlefield on the Western Front, and saw the monarch kneel and cover up the faces of his dead enemies, one after the other." He also denied that he had retired in 1911 at the age of sixty-four because he had offended the Kaiser by being too successful opposite him in the annual fall military maneuvers.

Left: Pro-Hindenburg re-election posters appeared during his candidacy for the second, run-off election of April 10, 1932 that he won with Leftist votes. The script read: "On 10 April, think of the future of your children, vote Hindenburg." (*LC*)

Reportedly, Hindenburg once picked flowers for his wife during a battle. "He seemed a piece of nature itself," his niece recalled, "as if he had come out of a big forest … He had not one vain or self-conscious gesture. He always spoke as if he stood alone amid some landscape and in the presence of God." Turning to an Austrian general, he "Patted him on the shoulder, saying, with a charming air of comradeship, 'We will do our job well together, won't we?'"

Denkt
am 10. April
an die Zukunft
Eurer Kinder

wählt Hindenburg

Mackensen reviews from a car the massed banners of the *Stahlhelm* on Tempelhof Field, Berlin, on September 4, 1932. The 1A license plate denotes a Berlin-registered vehicle. He was then still the much-revered Marshal Forward of the Great War, a title awarded him by German propaganda in 1916. (*LC*)

Mackensen told one of his three sons, "Life's highest pleasure comes from struggle, work, and—as by soldiers—in victory. The career of a soldier was both serious and holy," he asserted. The imperial crown prince called the Black Hussar, "the true soldier."

On January 30, 1933, Hindenburg did what he had vowed never to do, namely, appoint a Hitler Cabinet to office. Here it assembles after Hitler's being appointed Reich chancellor, von Hindenburg's last. *From left to right*: Nazi Press Secretary Dr Walter Funk; *Stahlhelm* chief and Labor Minister Franz Seldte (complete with left hand prosthesis, the result of a Great War wounding); Hermann Goering; Hitler; and Vice Chancellor Franz von Papen (seated). *From left to right, standing*: unknown man, Finance Minister Schwerin von Krosigk (the only one still in office the day Germany surrendered on May 8, 1945); Interior Minister Dr Wilhelm Frick; Defense Minister General Werner von Blomberg (in 1936 named Hitler's own first baton holder); and Food Minister Alfred Hugenberg. Note Minister Seldte's prosthetic left hand. (*HHA*)

That night, the Nazis celebrated with a torchlight parade that included the iconic Brandenburg Gate, depicted here in a painting later commissioned by Nazi Reich Propaganda Minister Dr Josef Goebbels. Here, passing SA troops at right received straight-armed Nazi salutes from the crowd at left. (*HHA*)

Hindenburg admired the ancient Romans, of whom General Scipio Africanus was his hero, but not the Italians of his own day: "I don't care what you say Hitler!" he boomed out, "you will never make anything out of them but spaghetti benders!"

The Reich president (*left*) and his final chancellor (*right*) share a carriage ride together at Neudeck, 1933. (*HHA*)

Previous page, below: On February 1, 1933, Ludendorff sent his former military commander Hindenburg this famous message: "By naming Hitler as Reich Chancellor, you have delivered up our holy Fatherland to one of the greatest demagogues of all time! I solemnly prophesy to you that this accursed man will plunge our Reich into the abyss and bring our nation into inconceivable misery. Because of what you have done, coming generations will curse you in your grave." Another source amends the above by asserting, "I predict most solemnly that this man will die in incredible misery."

Actors portraying, from left to right, Hitler, Papen, and Hindenburg in a later dramatic rendering. (*LC*)

On January 4, 1942, Hitler recalled: "When I wished to influence the Old Gentleman, I used to address him as *Herr General Field Marshal*. It was only on official occasions that I used to say to him, Mr. President. It was Hindenburg, by the way, who gave prestige to the Presidential title. These fine shades may seem to be trifles, but they have their importance! They are what give the framework its rigidity."

On May 21, 1942, Hitler added: "Once I had won him over to my side, the Old Gentleman's solicitude towards me was truly touching. Again and again, he said that he had a chancellor who was sacrificing himself for his country" as had Brüning before him.

Above left: March 1933 poster featuring both the old and the new leaders of Germany, its slogan reading: "The Reich will never be destroyed if we are united and loyal." This linking by Nazi Propaganda Minister Dr Josef Goebbels of the old and the new paved the way in the public mind for the Führer to be seen as the marshal's logical successor as German head of state in August 1934. (*HHA*)

Above right: The Imperial Crown Prince Wilhelm (*left*) shakes hands with his former Great War aerial subordinate, Captain Goering (*right*) in 1933. Each sought to use the other. (*HHA*)

In time, Goering personally came to be in charge of all Hohenzollern lands and monies in the new Nazi Third Reich, thus reining in on the royals via the power of the purse. In effect, he paid all their bills during 1934–45, including those of the former German emperor in his enforced Dutch exile.

Crown Prince Wilhelm (*right*) is photographed at a 1933 air show by another of his former Great War air aces, the daring Ernst Udet (far left). (*HHA*)

Like Udet himself, Hitler saw Crown Prince Wilhelm as a woman-chasing, muddle-headed fool, and, in fact, had had to complain to Hindenburg about Wilhelm's trying to pick up the wife of Hitler Youth Leader Baldur von Schirach, Henrietta "Henny" Hoffmann von Schirach, in his famous, elegant red Mercedes-Benz sports car. The embarrassed Reich president promised to "straighten out" the crown prince.

Captain Goering (*left*) in new 1933 Air Ministry kit with Prince "Auwi" (*right*). Both dreamed of being the next Kaiser, Goering as "Hermann I," but neither ever did. (*HHA*)

On January 30, 1933, Goering chortled, "How gloriously the Old Gentleman has been used as an instrument of God!" Indeed.

As I wrote in 2015, "The giant D2500 passenger airliner *Field Marshal von Hindenburg* at Tempelhof Airport, June 1933," Berlin. "The four-engined, 42-seater airliner was the pride of Lufthansa, with Goering personally christening it."

In the second photo—from left to right—are seen Defense Minister General von Blomberg, unknown man, Vice Chancellor von Papen, a smiling, pointing Goering, unknown man in dark coat carrying silk top hat, a trio of German *Orpo* (Regular) Police, and the honoree himself, Reich President von Hindenburg. (*HHA*)

A conservative triad arrives for a martial function from left to right Colonel Oskar and Field Marshal Paul von Hindenburg, with then Reich Chancellor Franz von Papen, the old man's all-time favorite holder of that embattled post. Note also Colonel Oskar's cut-out cavalry helmet worn once again. (*LC*)

Yet another von Hindenburg arrival (*right*), this time accompanied by his military ADC at left in steel pot and a civilian at center.

Loving flowers and beer evenings, Hindenburg today would dispute the oft-asserted claims of historians that he was the tool of his ministers. "He had accepted the present without renouncing the past." (*LC*)

Hindenburg awash at center in spiked helmet in a sea of German soldiers during a Berlin military parade. The steel helmets now feature the new Nazi eagle and swastika decals on their left sides. At far right is seen in right profile Defense Minister General Werner von Blomberg. The shiny black leather helmets seen from the rear are those of Berlin Regular *Orpo* (Police). (*HHA*)

Hindenburg (*left*) raises his informal stick baton in salute as the color guard unit of the Potsdam Garrison approaches him on Heroes Memorial Day, March 1933, Berlin. (*HHA*)

"In the afternoons during the winter months, Hindenburg's daughter-in-law often holds big receptions. During the first years of his Presidency, Hindenburg used to appear towards the end, and it was quite touching to experience the hush of reverence that passed over the hubbub when the tall figure came in, towering over the assembled guests."

Potsdam Day interior views: seen first is Chancellor Hitler's address (left at the lectern) inside the *Garnisonkirche* (Garrison Church) at historic Potsdam, spiritual cradle of Prussian militarism, March 21, 1933, where Imperial Chancellor von Bismarck had opened the first Reichstag of the Second Reich on that same date in 1871 after the Franco-Prussian War. In selecting this same date sixty-two years later, Hitler and Dr Goebbels opted for a display of theatrics celebrating the Nazis' Day of National Renewal.

In the first view, Hindenburg and Goering are seated at right, with Hitler's own empty chair also seen. On the other side of all of them are, standing, from left to right, unknown army officer holding helmet before him, Air Ministry State Secretary Erhard Milch, Goering's deputy; and seated, from left to right, Dr Hans Heinrich Lammers, Franz Seldte, Navy chief Admiral Dr Erich Raeder, Hugenberg, General von Hammerstein-Equord, Schwerin-Krosigk, unknown man turning face (blurred, perhaps, Gerecke), Dr Frick, and, behind him, Dr Goebbels, von Neurath, Transportation Minister Eltz-Rübenach, and von Blomberg in army overcoat and belt. Just behind Dr Lammers in the congregational pews is Nazi Deputy Führer Rudolf Hess in SS black.

In the second, vertical view of the same scene, Hindenburg stands to read his own address at left, and all the others thus stand also. Behind them are Dr Meissner (*left*) and Oskar von Hindenburg (*right*). Note the box above left, with the navy admirals flanked by Prussian standards at both left and right of their box. (*HHA*)

The official governmental lineup in the imperial box of the Berlin Opera House during Heroes' Memorial Day, March 1933. *From left to right*: Colonel Oskar von Hindenburg, Hitler, Reich presidential military aide, the marshal wielding his formal baton from Wilhelm II, unknown, Papen, and unidentified man. (*HHA*)

Dr Goebbels had joined the first Hitler coalition cabinet officially on March 13, 1933 and in the Garrison Church later reported seeing tears in Hindenburg's eyes during the ceremonies in the place where he had been personally present in 1871. Hitler stated—according to Stefan Lorant—"By a unique upheaval … our national honor has been restored, and thanks to your [Hindenburg's] understanding … the union between the symbols of the old greatness and the new strength has been celebrated!"

March 21, 1933, the celebrated Day of Potsdam; *from left to right*: an attentive Hitler, Crown Prince Wilhelm making a point to the new Reich chancellor, the Führer's SS adjutant Julius Schaub, Goering in formal tuxedo morning attire, and Mackensen talking into the former's right ear, his formal baton held at lower right. (*HHA*)

At Potsdam, Hindenburg (*left*) shakes hands with Crown Prince Wilhelm at center, as Mackensen watches at far right. (*HHA*)

Fully twenty-three Beneckendorff ancestors of von Hindenburg had died on battlefields, his niece asserted in 1931. He had "an antipathy to all forms of exaggeration," she added. "On one of the glass windows in Castle Marienburg, one still sees the coat-of-arms of the Beneckendorffs—a Bull's Head."

Faces at Potsdam. *From left to right*: Navy C-in-C Admiral Dr Erich Raeder (wearing his naval blue bi-corn hat in the fore-and-aft position), Mackensen with formal baton, and a smiling Crown Prince Wilhelm, hands in pockets of his long military greatcoat. (*HHA*)

"The principle of balance" was Hindenburg's "dominant characteristic," his niece claimed, "that has ruled every situation in his life."

With the high tower of the famed Potsdam Garrison Church forming a backdrop in the distance, Crown Prince Wilhelm salutes German troops passing in review—his first since late 1918—on March 20, 1933. The men march with their rifles slung at carry arms. (*HHA*)

"Hindenburg's own dog used to accompany him each morning as he took his after breakfast walk in the Presidential park at Berlin", in which both Hitler and the Goebbels family later had their first burials in May 1945. "For some time, people had noticed that the dog was missing, but nothing was said. I asked Hindenburg at last what the matter was and why he would not get another dog. He replied simply, 'My old companion is dead. I do not want to have a new one.'" That may also be why he never remarried, as had both the Kaiser and von Mackensen.

Reich President von Hindenburg (*center*) reviews an army honor guard at Potsdam on March 21, 1933, followed by his son, Colonel Oskar. Also seen, from left to right, are Gens. Werner von Fritsch and Gerd von Rundstedt; Admiral Raeder; and Gens. Hammerstein-Equord and von Blomberg. (*HHA*)

The best known photograph of Chancellor Hitler (*left*) bowing to Hindenburg (*right*) while shaking hands at Potsdam, with Mackensen's busby visible at upper left and an unknown officer at center. (*HHA*)

Reportedly, one of *Der alte Herr*'s favorite sayings was, "How the rabbit continues running."

A panoramic view of the entire handshake moment at Potsdam. *From left to right*: von Blomberg, Papen, a pair of unknown colonels, Dr Meissner, Minister Frick, Chancellor Hitler, two unknowns at rear, the marshal, and his son the colonel wearing cut-out cavalry helmet. (*HHA*)

The same scene afterwards. *From left to right*: Blomberg, the marshal, Hitler, Foreign Minister Konstantin Baron von Neurath, Goering, and Colonel von Hindenburg. (*HHA*)

Asserted the Reich president's niece in 1931: "One might compare Hindenburg to one of those big, firmly-rooted oaks of the Prussian landscape under whose shade so many find protection and rest."

From left to right: Colonel Oskar von Hindenburg, the marshal, unknown officer back to camera, Blomberg rendering a hand salute to his helmet, another officer doing the same, Papen, and Hitler. (*HHA*)

Interestingly, Hindenburg retained the trees that Bismarck so loved in the Chancellery Park, while their successor Hitler had them cut down.

Following the German surrender of 1918, Hindenburg shifted his headquarters to the east to Kolberg on the Baltic Sea, the scene of a fierce and lost battle against the French during the Napoleonic Wars. In 1945, Dr Goebbels released an epic film on that same battle in hopes that it would spur German resistance to defeat the Red Army; it did not.

Preparing for the gala march past at Potsdam. *From left to right*: Blomberg, four unknown army officers, German Student Corps members with banners, Hindenburg with formal baton at the ready, Hammerstein-Equord and von Rundstedt advancing and saluting, followed by another unknown officer. (*HHA*)

Once, a rushed Hindenburg closed a letter to a relative thus: "I have to cross the Narew River, and I have not time for poems—many greetings!"

An offshoot action of the Day of Potsdam was that the former Kaiser's portrait was re-hung in the Berlin City Hall, the closest the real one has come to returning to this very date. Note that he holds his ornate formal marshal's baton therein, as well as the imperial crowns still emblazoned on the chair backs. (*LC*)

Right: Period postcard celebrating the Day of Potsdam entitled *Der Potsdamer Kurs* (Fellows), featuring portraits of (*left to right*) Hitler, Prussian King Frederick II the Great, and Hindenburg, with the famous Potsdam Garrison Church tower seen above. (*HHA*)

Below: Period picture postcard featuring (*from left to right*) Frederick, Bismarck, Hindenburg, and Hitler. The NS inscription read "What the King [Frederick] conquered, the Prince [Bismarck] unified, the Field Marshal [Hindenburg] defended, and the corporal [Hitler] saved," thus eliminating in one bold brush stroke all three German Kaisers: both the Wilhelms and also Frederick III, the middleman. (*HHA*)

After the Great War, Hindenburg "was assailed by a thief in his house at Hanover … 'When I came into the room, I saw a man touching things on my writing table [desk] I asked him, "What are you doing there?" "Leave me alone, or I will shoot!" he answered. I grasped his arm and held it down. He shot, but the bullet went into the carpet. Then I kept a firm hold of him and led him to the door, and rang the bell. A servant came, and he was arrested.' Hindenburg's voice hardly changed its tone while he was relating this incident."

Above left: NSKK Leader Franz Ritter von Epp, leader of the anti-Socialist government coup at Munich of March 1933 that firmly entrenched his Bavarian Nazis in office. (*HHA, Michael D. Miller*)

His obituary as published in the *New York Times* on February 9, 1947 stated that, "In the First World War, he commanded an army corps under Bavarian Crown Prince Rupprecht in France."

Above right: Goering (*left*) and Epp at the former's country estate outside Berlin, Carinhall, named for his late Swedish-born first wife, on June 20, 1934. Von Epp had joined the Nazi Party on April 1, 1928. (*Hermann Goering Albums, LC*)

Hindenburg's chauffeur, Mercedes-Benz car, and presidential flag, all later replaced by Hitler when he assumed the office on August 2, 1934. (*LC*)

His niece marveled at Hindenburg's "Magnetic power that awes an assembly and fascinates a crowd, but in this, Hindenburg is quite modest, for in his public position, he feels himself an instrument in the hands of God. One day when the public cheered him, he exclaimed, 'Thank God, not me!'"

Above: A pair of von Hindenburgs in the rear seat of the over-sized presidential parade car on their way to Potsdam on March 21, 1933. The car's ceiling was raised to accommodate the spike atop the marshal's helmet, reportedly. (*HHA*)

Neither the ex-Kaiser nor his heir, the former crown prince, accepted the public image of Hindenburg's wanting always to retire; rather, they asserted that he was loathe to "give up his throne." I concur: like Hitler and them also, he was an actor, always on.

Below: Now Hitler occupies the seat formerly held by Colonel Oskar von Hindenburg in the previous photo, May 1, 1933, he and the Reich president on their way to the Berlin *Lustgarten* (Pleasure Park) as SS men hold back the throngs. The Mercedes-Benz car is license plate 1A-2545 of Berlin registry. Note also the supercharged compressor valves on the right-hand side of the hood. (*HHA*)

Knecht and Klein of DaimlerChrysler AG stated that, "The car that took part in the Day of Potsdam [on March 21, 1933] is—in our opinion—based on a Mercedes-Benz 400 Pullman chassis. The bodywork was done by Josef Neuss of Berlin, [and] was specially built for … Hindenburg, and differs from a 'normal' … 400 Pullman cabriolet. The roof line was extremely high, in order to shelter the passengers safely when they drove through the crowds." Truly, this was probably the most unique Mercedes of all in the Third Reich era, but there are no photos available of Hitler ever using it alone after he had succeeded Hindenburg as Reich president in August 1934, as he might well have done.

The same occasion, but with an SS escort car behind. (*HHA*)

Alexander Stahlberg in *Bounden Duty: Memoirs of a German Officer 1932–45*: "When they were seated in the church [at Potsdam], the President's two cars arrived, the big, high Mercedes special models well known to all Berliners, built high enough for Hindenburg to get in and out without difficulty wearing the spiked helmet of the Imperial Army."

Both of the limousines have 1A license plates, thus registered as Berlin vehicles. (*HHA*)

Stahlberg: "A genuine living memorial to Imperial might and greatness—his marshal's baton in his right hand—he strode to the entrance of the church.… When the march past was over, the President's huge car arrived first to pick him up, followed by the open black, 7-liter Mercedes of the Chancellor."

Riders with different reactions to the same crowds. (*HHA*)

Eyewitness Stahlberg's account of the Garrison Church occasion on March 21, 1933: "While Hindenburg drove away without bodyguards, there was not an inch to spare, as usual, in Hitler's State limousine when his black-uniformed SS Lifeguard had been packed as tightly as possible onto its running boards. I estimate that there were 10–15 guards."

The Reich president (*left*) must wait while his young chancellor at right is acclaimed by a Hitler Youth boy instead, a new experience for him. The chauffeur salutes at right, as do a pair of policemen across the street, as Colonel Oskar von Hindenburg smiles at center, watching Hitler. (*HHA*)

The Reich president is also honored with a bouquet of flowers by another Hitler Youth on his arrival at the *Lustgarten*, a Nazi SA officer looking on at center. (*HHA*)

"The social regulations that are followed in his household are quite simple, but in very good taste. On the staircase, one is received by stalwart-looking footmen, many of whom have been soldiers under Hindenburg. Flowers are used profusely in decoration, as the master of the house has a particular love for them. In these later years, he gives only a few dinners ... Sometimes, however, he gathers his friends together for a simple beer evening that recalls the older days."

Stated Toland in 1976, "Chancellor Hitler played a secondary role during an address by Hindenburg at a youth convention in the *Lustgarten* in May 1933." The Reich president addressed the crowd from a balustrade adorned with both the older Iron Cross and former Imperial colors and the newer NS swastika pole-mounted mobile standard, a subtle but important addition. Behind him were Hitler and Goebbels chatting during his remarks. In front, SA band members played.

The marshal's last living appearance at the Tannenberg Memorial, August 23, 1933, one of my own favorite views. He renders a hand salute only, with Colonel Oskar von Hindenburg standing behind him, obscured, and thus perhaps holding his baton. *From left to right, behind the elder Hindenburg:* Hitler, NS Press Secretary Dr Walther Funk, Captain Goering, and Nazi *Gauleiter* of East Prussia Erich Koch all entering the vast amphitheater. (*HHA*)

Dying in 1987 as a Polish political prisoner, Koch outlived them all by many decades. Note the photographer kneeling at left.

The very same scene later memorialized in a plaster frieze. (*HHA*)

"There is a charming story told of an incident that happened during the memorable conflict that raged around the question of the colors that had been chosen for the flag of the new German republic. A large section of the nation fought for the maintenance of the old colors: black, white, and red—instead of the new republican colors: black, red, and yellow. When Hindenburg entered the *Stadion* for the celebration of his 80th birthday, a child greeted him with the old flag, under which he had fought in so many battles. It was hoped that he would carry it in his hand. Hindenburg bent down and smiled, but with exquisite tact, he gave the flag back to the child, saying, 'Keep it in memory of me, this flag whose memory lives in my heart.' He was President of the Republic, and as such, he would be faithful to the new colors." Hitler had no such notion, and in 1933 replaced them both with his own swastika banner of the Third Reich, which was also allowed by political chameleon von Hindenburg.

Another favorite view of mine, with the three principals seated, the Reich president's ornate throne slightly higher at center than the other two, as befitting both his rank and station. Captain Goering holds the framed gift plaque regarding Neudeck's male tax inheritance status that would benefit Colonel Oskar von Hindenburg for the next dozen years. In return, Goering will be made a general in the German Army, even after having left it altogether in 1919. (*HHA*)

A line-up of monarchists and Nazis that reflected the reality of the new hybrid state of the NS Third Reich. *From left to right*: Litzmann with cane, Mackensen rendering a hand salute to his busby cap, a pair of helmeted officers, Captain Rohm's right hand traveling upward for a Nazi salute, Goering rendering same full tilt, RFSS Himmler at attention, SA man, unknown officers, standard bearer, Prussian Finance Minister Dr Johannes Popitz, and NS Education Minister Bernhard Rust. The occasion is September 15, 1933, a celebration of the new Nazi Prussian State government under Goering, with a special parade being held on Berlin's *Unter den Linden* (Under the Linden Trees). (*HHA*)

Two marshals confer during an indoor rally of the *Kyffhäuserbund* in the famous Berlin Sports Palace on January 14, 1934: Hindenburg at left and Mackensen at right, neither with their batons visible. An SS officer smiles at rear between the pair. (*LC*)

Notes one account: "Mackensen's early support of the Nazis was more obvious than any other officer from World War I, and lent legitimacy to the regime," at a time when Hitler really valued it. Thereafter, he became known as the "Show-off General" as an important Nazi display piece. Thus, the soldier whom "Wilhelm II most liked and admired accepted an estate and honorary titles" from the Nazi Führer. Mackensen saw war as "Generals Luck and Human Butchery."

Another major round of bowing and scraping before Hindenburg by Hitler for public consumption had occurred on March 16, 1933 for the renamed Nazi ceremony at Berlin of Heroes' Memorial Day for the slain of the Great War, as seen here. The Reich president at center accepts his chancellor's homage, as Colonel Oskar von Hindenburg looks on at right, holding in his left hand his father's interim stab informal swagger stick baton. Behind Hitler stand Dr Meissner (*left*) and the marshal's military aide. Note also the open door of the high-roofed presidential limousine, followed by the second such convertible car. At far left, a section of black-coated SS men render the stiff-armed Hitler salute. The scene is in front of the Berlin Guard House War Memorial Building that still exists there today. (*HHA*)

A better-known detail close-up view from another angle of the same scene. (*HHA*)

A wider angle and thus more complete view of the the March 16, 1934 event, showing, *from left to right*: Blomberg, Fritsch, Frick, unknown, Dr Goebbels in silk top hat, Goering, and the others. To the far right is Colonel Oskar von Hindenburg, wearing a rather streamlined version of the steel pot helmet. (*HHA*)

The handshake ended, the principals listen to the Reich president's response to Hitler's greeting. *From left to right*: Frick, Fritsch, Goebbels, Gen. Goering, Papen, Hitler, tall naval officer, and Admiral Raeder. The columns of the Berlin guardhouse are seen at rear. This was the aging soldier's last major public appearance, March 16, 1934. (*HHA*)

The "Wooden Titan" had not changed since 1915, but the real man had. (*HHA*)

In 1931, his niece described his visage thus: "White and impassive, as if hewn out of a marble block," a splendid bit of adoring, hero-worshipping hagiography. Meanwhile, his son, Oskar, was a chief aide, and also the father of two daughters and a son, the Reich president's grandchildren.

The only picture I have ever seen of President von Hindenburg speaking at any lectern emblazoned with a Nazi Party swastika on its front, the black-white-red nationalist colors on its side, with son Oskar standing at right to help his father if needed, August 1933, the last Tannenberg Memorial event the Reich President lived to attend. Note also the various Prussian battle flags in evidence, as well as the officer carrying the memorial wreath at center. (*ASA*)

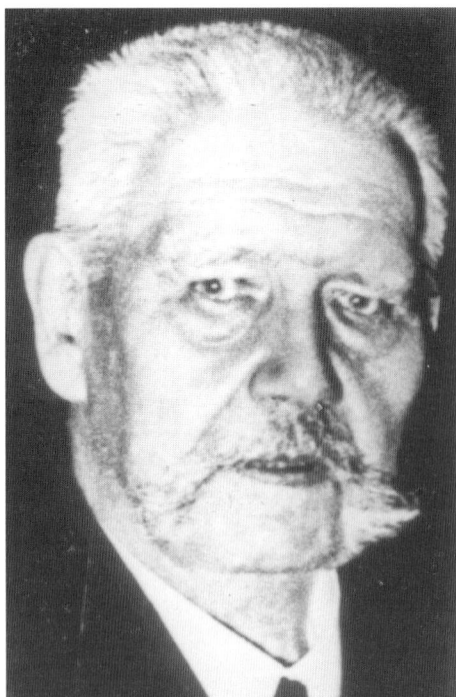

Above left: He was aging and growing frail in health. As the Reich president disliked going about with bodyguards, he chose to remain at home, performing his daily work regimen. So, too, did his last Chancellor Hitler, at least as long as his boss lived. Then he resumed his life as an artist, working only in spurts, very much akin to Hindenburg's former boss, the Kaiser. (*HHA*)

Above right: A cane replaced his sword at his final brief appearances in 1934, seen here with his ever-present military ADC in tow at left. (*HHA*)

Hindenburg's hobbies were drawing and painting, and collecting Madonnas from his retirement days at Hanover after the Great War. Of Napoleon at the Battle of Leipzig in 1813, the famed marshal opined, "He ought to have encircled his enemy!" as he and Ludendorff had done at Tannenberg two decades earlier.

The Führer and his entourage arrive at Neudeck on August 1, 1934—the day before the Old Gentleman's death—to pay a courtesy call on their ailing chief. *From left to right*: SS Schaub, SA Brückner, Dr Meissner, son and heir Oskar, and the Reich chancellor ascend the broad front steps to see the patient, 87. (*HHA*)

Noted another account: "That evening, Hitler had his Cabinet agree to a law combining the offices of Reich President with Reich Chancellor."

The same group departs after their visit. *From left to right*: Hitler, Brückner, Oskar von Hindenburg, and Dr Meissner. Note also the artillery piece flanking the main entrance to the house, with another opposite it to the far left, off-frame. (*HHA*)

"Von Hindenburg died the next day—August 2, 1934—and Hitler assumed the title of Führer and Reich Chancellor" that of Reich chancellor not revived by him until his will of April 1945.

Dr Meissner survived in his post under the Third Reich until its end in May 1945. Here, wearing richly embroidered tuxedo jacket fronted with gold braid (*left*), he shakes hands with then Nazi Field Marshal Goering, the pair watched by Poland's Ambassador to Berlin Josef Lipski. (*HGA*)

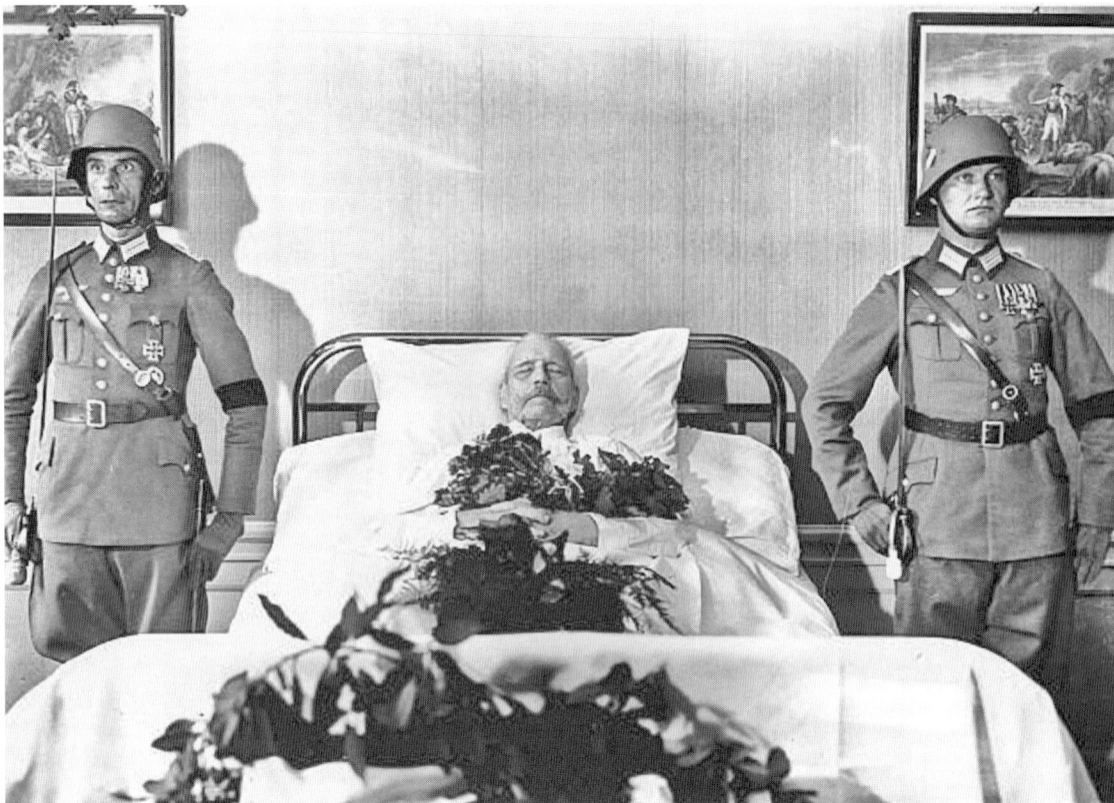

The great man's initial deathbed, guarded by army officers with drawn sabers and wearing black armbands, August 2, 1934, Neudeck. (*HHA*)

The Reich president died at 9 a.m., and at noon, it was announced that at a Cabinet meeting the previous day, the offices of chancellor and president had been combined, with Hitler as both head of state and C-in-C of the German Armed Forces, thus at once succeeding Hindenburg and the former Kaisers all in one fell swoop. Later that same day, all officers and men of the armed forces took a personal oath of allegiance to the Führer himself.

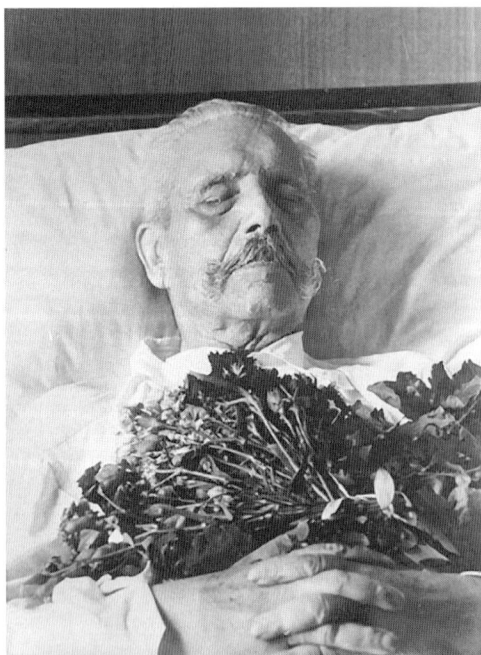

Close-up of the dead man. (*HHA*)

Author Tony Le Tissier, "General Blomberg arranged for every member of the Armed Forces throughout Germany to swear [the oath]. This move clearly involved prior preparation and presumably clearance with Hitler, but the initiative came from Blomberg in the hope of binding Hitler to the Reichswehr. It was to turn out the other way round."

Hindenburg's death mask. (*HHA*)

The German Armed Forces' Personal Oath of Allegiance to Hitler of August 2, 1934 read: "I swear by God this sacred oath, that I will render unconditional obedience to Adolf Hitler—the Führer of the German Reich and people, Supreme Commander of the Armed Forces— and will be ready as a brave soldier to risk my life at any time for this oath," and therefore thus not to either the German people or even state, much less the now defunct Weimar Republic Constitution of 1919.

Hindenburg's office at Neudeck, desk at right, behind which is a white plaster bust of Kaiser Wilhelm II. On the table at left is his souvenir helmet from the War of 1870–71. A portrait of Wilhelm II is seen on the wall at far left, plus a trio of others at right. (*LC*)

The same room, but now with Hindenburg's floral bedecked coffin inserted between the portraits at left and right. Another group of officer honor guards with drawn sabers stands watch, and the flowers are surmounted by a wreath and ribbon from the former German emperor, the monograms for Wilhelm at left and Hohenzollern at right. (*HHA*)

The Kaiser thus had outlived the man he felt had usurped his own rightful place in German society.

The same room but with a different stationing of the guards, and looking rightwards, towards the dead man's desk. Note also that now the corpse is also visible at left center.

In 1915, Hindenburg visited Vienna, where his niece, Helene, was then the wife of the Saxon ambassador to the court of Kaiser Franz Josef I, like the field marshal a universally revered figure both then and later. (*HHA*).

This close-up reveals the white plaster bust of the Kaiser in the right corner. (*HHA*)

Hindenburg's presidential palace on the Wilhelmstrasse at Berlin—later occupied by Hitler as well—was built in 1734 for a certain Count Sacken in a French architectural style. First sold by its private owners to the Prussian crown, the palace later was acquired by the new republic. "In spring and summer, Hindenburg uses the ground floor," wrote his niece, "the windows of which nearly all look out on a park where a number of majestic trees tower above the flower beds."

A close-up view of the late man's desk at Neudeck. The framed picture at far left appears to be that of the former Imperial German Crown Prince Wilhelm, while the standing bronze statue at far right is of Wilhelm II. Note also the oak leaf branches of memory on the portfolio. (*HHA*)

At Berlin's presidential palace, Hindenburg's "desk is on the ground floor. Over the desk hangs a scroll of yellowed paper on which are written the words *Ora et Labora* [pray and work]"—both of which Hitler ignored—"that belonged originally to Hindenburg's father. On a table nearby stands a beautifully carved model of a ship named after the President. I remember how interestingly he went over its constructional points with my youngest son."

The Reich president's office at Berlin, with a portrait of Prussian Army Field Marshal Gebrecht Prince von Blücher on the wall behind the desk. (*LC*)

"Oskar von Hindenburg now lives with his father in the Presidential home with his wife and three children … The whole family share in the enjoyment of the big park. Hindenburg loves walking there with his dog and watching the play of the children." In 1939, Hitler fed squirrels there.

The same scene has altered somewhat by the time of its former owner's death, with a memorial wreath placed on his chair, the portrait shifted to the far wall at right, and a rack of possible government manuals mounted on the wall behind it. (*LC*)

At Berlin, the living Reich president had taken a walk in his palace's park after the morning work session, then lunched, took a nap, and received guests in the afternoon. According to Wheeler-Bennett in 1936 regarding the postwar German Army: "For this remarkable army of 100,000 men, it was found necessary to have a Ministerial staff of 300 officers and 670 staff officers … In addition, there were 55 generals."

Above: A close-up of the Reich presidential standard, replaced by Hitler right away with a more ornate personal version that is still sold worldwide as a collectible. (*LC*)

"One hundred and twenty-three colonels appeared in the Army List, of whom 23 were in the Reichswehr Ministry, and in 1926 the military budget amounted to 776.6 million marks. In proportion to its size, it was the most expensive army in the world."

Above left: In times gone by, the Reich president had spoken before the German Reichstag, as here, reading his speech from a text just below his official standard mounted on the wall behind him at upper right. Note that everyone stands. (*LC*)

"The 18 regiments of cavalry … were commanded by three generals of divisions and nine inspectors with the rank of general, and 42,000 horses were required for them."

Perhaps the scene outside the Reichstag in August 1934 during the Hindenburg memorial service that preceded his state funeral at East Prussia. Assembled here, from left to right, are two unknown officers, von Hammerstein-Equord, Fritsch, Dr Meissner in top hat and overcoat, maybe Mrs. Oskar von Hindenburg, and her husband wearing black mourning band on his left sleeve. (*HHA*)

Above left: Inside at the memorial service held stands a white marble bust of the great man by sculptor Edwin Geharff underneath a draped Nazi swastika banner as a backdrop. (*HHA*)

Le Tissier: "Von Hindenburg had expressed the wish to have a military funeral at the old Garrison Church in Potsdam that held a particular place in his affections," but Hitler decided otherwise. After Hindenburg's first election to the presidency in 1925, "Immediately the Army pledged its loyalty to the marshal—not in his capacity as President—but as its commander-in-chief … Hindenburg had assumed the position as Chief of State that the emperor had once occupied."

Above right: A formation of army standard bearers approach Neudeck at night, August 7, 1934. (*HHA*)

Le Tissier, "On August 7, 1934, Hindenburg was buried at Tannenberg with full military honors in a dramatic ceremony masterminded by Albert Speer. Brought to Tannenberg the evening before, the coffin was placed on a bier in the center of the Court of Honor that was filled with formations bearing the traditional flags of German regiments of World War I."

As the coffin is carried out Neudeck's front door, German Army troops at left present arms with rifles with fixed bayonets for the most famous soldier in Prussian history since Frederick the Great. (*HHA*)

Wheeler-Bennett in 1936, "On October 1, 1927, Oldenburg–Januschau and the aged 'Paint King' Duisburg presented the [Neudeck] title deeds to the marshal—on behalf of German agriculture and industry—but it was not discovered until three years later that, thoughtfully but illegally the deeds had been registered in Oskar's name to avoid death duties [inheritance taxes in the U.S.] and that payment of other taxes had been deferred" as well.

As the flag-bedecked coffin is mounted in the artillery caisson at left, Colonel Oskar von Hindenburg salutes from the front steps at right, his assembled mourning family standing behind him and above on the landing. (*HHA*)

At Tannenberg in 1927, the former wartime duo—Hindenburg and Ludendorff—"Bowed coldly, and did not shake hands," noted Wheeler-Bennett. In 1930, after the marshal had endorsed the American Young Plan to help pay defeated Germany's postwar reparations to the Allies, Ludendorff sniffed publicly: "Mr. Paul von Hindenburg has destroyed the very thing he fought for as field marshal."

Amid blazing torches, the caisson begins its nocturnal journey to the Tannenberg Memorial at Hohenstein, East Prussia, the next morning. (*HHA*)

"A visitor to Berlin [Wheeler-Bennett] well remembers seeing Hindenburg one brilliant morning in October 1931. Some military ceremony was taking place, and a guard of honor awaited the President's arrival. A large closed car drew up, an orderly opened the door, and out jumped two smart staff officers. Then, a pause, and slowly—very slowly—there emerged, backwards and bareheaded—an enormous figure."

Surrounded by torches, helmets, and soldiers, the coffin is covered with an over-sized Iron Cross on the former imperial colors of black, red, and white, atop which can be seen its occupant's martial regalia and spiked helmet. (*HHA*)

"Again a pause—though shorter this time—while one of the young officers extracted from the interior of the car a *Pickelhaube*, that was ceremoniously placed upon the great square head with its hair brushed back."

The sun is up, but the helmet and regalia are unseen in this view. Nazi salutes predominate. This photo, therefore, seems to conflict with the Le Tissier timeline of events. (*HHA*)

"Then the figure turned about, and one had the momentary impression of a gigantic clockwork doll waiting for the spring to be released that galvanized it into movement. His eye caught the motionless line of soldiery. At once, the absent glance changed—the spring had been released—and, one hand grasping his baton and the other resting on his sword hilt, Hindenburg moved stiffly and erect towards the guard of honor."

The funeral cortège arrives at the red brick memorial, August 7, 1934, flanked by a honor guard of cavalry with drawn sabers at left and the same at right, other riders behind those front ranks with rifles at sling arms. Likewise, this photo also seems to conflict with the Le Tissier timeline of events of Hindenburg's body arriving at night. Could this and the previous photo be the re-arrival of the body for the 1935 reburial? Maybe. (*HHA*)

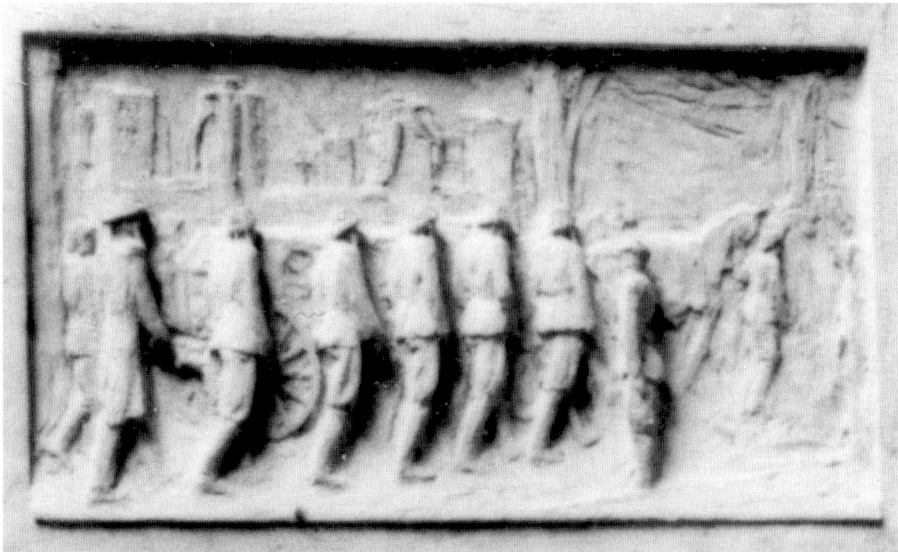

The very same scene later commemorated in bas relief. (*HHA*)

Wheeler-Bennett: "The episode [of the car entry scene] has always seemed to the writer symbolical of the marshal's whole career. The moment of suspension—while the mind was in a plastic state awaiting an impression—and then, once received, the immediate and vigorous action in the direction in which service and duty had pointed."

In charge of Hindenburg's first state funeral, Hitler placed not his propaganda minister, Dr Goebbels, but instead one of his major architects, Dr Albert Speer (seen here at center) who explains his plans to Himmler (left center) and the latter's deputy, Reinhard Heydrich (holding document under left arm, far right). (*HHA*)

German Army standard bearers carry Prussian battle flags onto the grounds of the Tannenberg Memorial, August 1934 for the State Funeral of the German Reich President, Field Marshal von Hindenburg. (*ASA*)

Twin horizontal views of the same scene, Hindenburg's first state funeral at the Tannenberg Memorial, August 7, 1934. In front are soldiers holding medal display cushions, with the flag-draped coffin behind, below Hitler's speaking rostrum. Note also the huge Iron Cross banner draped on the tower behind all in the second photo, and the Christian cross in the center of the plaza. Almost no NS Party swastikas are seen anywhere. (*HHA*)

Above left: A vertical close-up of the very same scene, with a better view of all the main components of this theatrical visage: army officers holding medals cushions, the coffin with the spiked helmet atop at center on the flag, two army and two navy officers flanking the funereal bier, a row of officers behind, Hitler at the lectern, the pastor at left below, soldiers standing at order arms, color guards behind, and, finally more troops, and others. (*HHA*)

Above right: Hitler's bungled funeral oration over, the coffin (lower left) is carried toward the tower at right where it will be placed for viewing. The crowd renders the Nazi salute. (*HHA*)

On the thirteenth anniversary of November 11, 1918, the Reich president and his Reich chancellor Dr Brüning found themselves in a spontaneous debate as to exactly how it transpired that the Kaiser had fled to Holland the day before the Armistice with the Allies was signed. Hindenburg did not want to run for reelection as president, asserting: "In the campaign, they will reproach me all over again with the events of November 1918. It will be worse this time."

Left: Hitler (also lower left) follows the coffin inside the tower, he being followed by his official funeral wreath for display with the coffin inside. The saluting is done. (*HHA*)

Hindenburg: "I meant well by His Majesty! There have been other occasions when monarchs have left their thrones, and been recalled by their peoples when times have changed. I thought it would be like that when His Majesty went to Holland. I still believe his abdication was inevitable, and his flight, too. The front was not holding, the troops were mutinying and—as an old Prussian officer—I had no choice but to protect the person of my King."

The actual pagan "Valhalla" columned building at Regensburg, Germany—built during 1830–42 by architect Leo von Klenze—to which the nominally Catholic Hitler consigned the spirit of the late Protestant marshal. (*HHA*)

Brüning surprisingly contradicted his chief in this "flight debate:" "Brüning had been through those November days as a company machine gun officer. He had experiences gained personally, and not from headquarters' reports, and he felt it his duty to defend the Army—as he knew it—from the general charge of mutiny. Moreover, he had been at Herbesthal from whence came the reports that finally decided the marshal that the Kaiser must fly."

The Hindenburg family cemetery was at Neudeck, to which the marshal's remains were not consigned.

"'With all respect,' he said, 'I hold a different opinion to Your Excellency! At Herbesthal, for instance, everything was Red when we occupied the station, but we had order restored in a very short time. If our messages had been received at GHQ as we had sent them out, the emperor might not have been induced to leave! The mistake was made in the telegraph office at Spa.' He added that he had deposed to this effect before Groener's Court of Honor in 1922, and that his evidence had influenced the verdict" in which Groener had been acquitted of dishonor, "but Hindenburg had no recollection of this."

"'You may be right about Herbesthal,' he said, 'but I am certain of one thing, the 2nd Division of Guards behind you was no longer loyal!' 'They could have been made loyal in 24 hours,' said Brüning earnestly, 'We never believed in their defection.' But Hindenburg would have no more of his established pet theories challenged. The case that he had built up to convince himself was too flimsy to permit of searching cross-examination. He grew petulant."

The Tannenberg memorial before (*bottom*) and after (*top*) Hitler's 1935 architectural revisions, as carried out by the Krugers, Walter and Johannes. The trees were cut down and the grass in the Court of Honor covered over with a concrete plaza instead. (*HHA*)

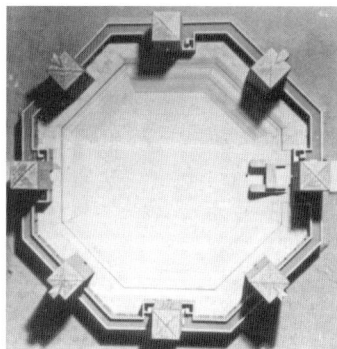

A model of the 1935 Hitlerian architectural revisions to the memorial: the raised stone mound with the Christian cross has been removed, with a new entrance way to Hindenburg's tomb placed before the central tower at rear in this model. (*HHA*)

Detail close-ups of the 1935 model's new entrance way to Hindenburg's tomb at rear before the tower. (*HHA*)

"'No, no, no!' Hindenburg cried out to Brüning, shaking his head energetically. 'I know you are wrong! They were all wrong! I knew already in February 1918 that the war was lost, but I was willing to let Ludendorff have his fling!'" meaning the failed Michael Offensive of March–July that same year in which thousands of German soldiers died or were maimed. It had all been for nothing, as the marshal already knew that he had lost the Great War.

A 1935 publicity still photo of the actual scene as finished: "Tower in which rested Hindenburg's sarcophagus," was the period caption. Note also the tall twin concrete sentries at stand arms. Here they rested until just before the Red Army arrived in January 1945, and they were then blown up by German Army engineers. (*HHA*)

Top left: There were twin aerial flyovers.

Thus it was that Dr Brüning came to be summarily dismissed as chancellor by the Reich president after having been the main force behind his twice defeating Adolf Hitler. Hindenburg wanted him to stay on as German foreign minister, however, along with his cabinet, but Dr Brüning refused: "I, too, have my name and my honor, Mr. Reich President, and I give you the resignation of my cabinet," as well as his own. His contradicting the old man about the events at Spa of 1918 had no doubt continued to rankle the marshal.

Above left: The completed, revised 1935 Hitlerian makeover: the Christian cross has been replaced with a more Germanic Iron Cross in the center of the now flagstone plaza that took the place of the former green grass. (*HHA*)

As the marshal strode by his dismissed Chancellor Dr Brüning to review a naval guard of honor outside, he muttered, " Now I can have a cabinet of my friends," from the German right, and not the left that had just reelected him to keep Hitler out of the Chancellery. "And the man who had been 'the best Chancellor since Bismarck' walked out into the sunlight of the park with the sound of the trumpets in his ears."

When General von Bredow heard that the Reich president had fired his colleague as Reich chancellor and meant to replace him with Hitler, "in a rage he unwittingly started the rumor that came to be known in the history of the marshal as the Potsdam Putsch that never was."

Above right: The marshal's cap and greatcoat, perhaps in the memorial's main tower commemorating his life and career. (*HHA*)

Without restraint, General von Bredow had cursed the House of Hindenburg for its perfidy, and cried in the fury of his rage that Schleicher should—or would—summon the Potsdam garrison and restrain the Old Gentleman (but this was not what Bredow actually called him) by force from committing the monstrous crime of giving the supreme power to Hitler.

Another such hallowed scene, with white plaster bust at left of Hindenburg, one of Wilhelm II in an alcove on the wall at rear, display cases, and battle standards. (*HHA*)

General von Bredow added that Papen, Oskar, and the Führer himself "should be confined in the fortress of Lotzen ... The Potsdam garrison would never have changed their loyalty from Hindenburg to Schleicher ... The news that young Werner von Alvensleben brought to the [presidential] Palace—and that soon spread to the [Nazi HQ at the Hotel] Kaiserhof threw both camps, already in a state of nervous tension, into complete panic."

As we have seen, the handshakes happened, but never with Hitler wearing Nazi uniform as depicted here by the sculptor taking dramatic license: the marshal at left and the corporal at right. (*HHA*)

At the presidential palace, the Hindenburgs made sure that no such arrest orders reached their loyal garrison at Potsdam, while Goering alerted Hitler, who briefly pondered calling out the local SA and SS, then stood down.

Heroes' Memorial Day, March 17, 1935, with horse-drawn artillery caissons and cavalry drawn up at Berlin. (*HHA*)

In the event, there was no uprising against Hitler's being named Hindenburg's last chancellor, and the Potsdam Garrison itself paraded past both the president and NS chancellor together on March 21, 1933.

Army standard bearers at attention with Prussian battle flags, their commanding officer with drawn saber at left, front rank, March 17, 1935. (*HHA*)

In late 1932—when it became clear that Hindenburg was balking at naming Hitler chancellor—he was publicly assailed by the openly Nazi General von Litzmann: "Sixty years ago, I was at the military academy with Mr. von Hindenburg; 30 years ago, we stood side by side as commanders in the 14th Army Corps. In the world war, I was, for years, one of his subordinates. During all this time, however, Mr von Hindenburg never showed any comradeship towards me!" Thus did he break with the illustrious marshal in the way of Ludendorff before him.

Prussian banners dipped in salute. (*HHA*)

In June 1945 at Lenin's tomb in Moscow, Red Army men tossed them at the feet of Soviet dictator and Generalissimo Josef Stalin instead, and they remain on display at Moscow to this day.

At the age of forty-nine, Oskar von Hindenburg asked his friend Chancellor General von Schleicher to be promoted general, but his Guards crony of yesteryear refused: "There were many senior staff officers with higher claims to promotion," claimed Ludwig Cohn, an excuse set aside by Hitler himself less than two years later. At the Day of Potsdam ceremony on March 13, 1933, the Reich president spoke first, and then Hitler, according to Ludwig Cohn as well.

Again dipped at Berlin on March 17, 1935, the banners receive ribbons tied to their staffs. (*HGA*)

At the Potsdam Garrison Church on March 13, 1933, the ceremony inside came first, followed by the military parade outside. The ex-Kaiser's place of residence in exile at Doorn, Holland, is 12 miles southeast of Utrecht, the capital of the Dutch Utrecht Province.

Another Hitlerian entourage follows a memorial wreath at Berlin on Heroes' Memorial Day, March 17, 1935. *From left to right*: Raeder, Fritsch, Air Force General Goering, Mackensen, Hitler taking the salute as the senior man present, and Blomberg. Troops present arms at left. (*HGA*)

Mackensen received many postwar civilian honors, among them being principals of the Universities of Halle, Greifswald, and Budapest, Vienna's agricultural high school, and Danzig's technical high school, as well as being named Canon of the Merseburg Cathedral.

The same group in different positions troops the line of men presenting arms opposite them on the same occasion. (*HGA*)

Postwar, von Mackensen made three trips to see his former Kaiser at Doorn: on his seventieth birthday in 1929, the eightieth in 1939, and for his state funeral on June 9, 1941, weeping at the last. KHQ Spa is 20 miles southeast of Liege, Belgium, the site of Ludendorff's having won his Blue Max in 1914.

Period picture postcard of Chancellor Hitler (*right*) shaking hands with the ghostly visage of a bygone era—Marshal von Mackensen (*left*)—with Blomberg smiling at center, in front of the Berlin Guard House, still there today. (*HHA*)

The Black Marshal retired from active military duty in 1920, living in retirement at Stettin on the Baltic Sea. In 1935, Hitler gave him a country estate at Brüssow, and in 1936 made him chief of Cavalry Regiment No. 5.

With the old Hussar marshal looking on at right, the Führer (*left*) shakes hands with former Imperial Crown Prince Wilhelm (*center*). Note also the sentry presenting arms at right on the steps of the Berlin Guard House that contained inside the *Ehrenmal* (Hall of Honor). The latter two men were members of what was known as the Hussars of the Dead. (*HHA*)

The interior of Goering's Berlin state opera house for the March 1934 ceremony, Hindenburg's last. (*HHA*)

Tannenberg is 80 miles southeast of Danzig, Poland, and 85 miles southwest of Königsberg, in 1935 having a population of 725 people. It was "too small to be marked on ordinary maps," according to Ludwig Cohn.

Next page, above left: The same scene on March 15, 1935, with a giant 1914 Iron Cross—complete with the former Kaiser's first name Wilhelm W. monogram—instead, his lost crown above at center to boot, as yet not returned. (*HHA*)

In his various writings, French Ambassador to Germany André François-Poncet often compared Hindenburg to a former president of France who had been defeated by Germany in the Franco-Prussian War of 1870–71 and—like the German marshal—elected later despite that. This was the Count de MacMahon (1808–93), Marshal of France. Miffed, Hindenburg chose to ignore these repeated comparisons made by the Frenchman.

Above right: Ludendorff in retirement at his home at Tutzing, Bavaria, *circa* 1935 with his dog. (*LC*)

As an old man, the marshal reflected: "For a soldier, war is the normal condition of affairs; and, anyway, I am in God's hand. If I fall, my death will be of the most honorable kind; if merely wounded, I shall have to make the best of it; and if I return uninjured, all the better!"

Right: The second Mrs. Ludendorff was Dr Mathilde Spiess von Kemnitz (1877–1966), a reported nerve specialist whom he called "the wisest of human beings," according to *Life* in January 1938, and also served as his "literary collaborator." The general married her on September 14, 1926. He thought her beautiful, and she believed him to be "The greatest soldier of all time, and said so, with unmistakable sincerity," noted Goodspeed. "*Frau* Kemnitz, a widow, was always properly adoring, and was a Nazi woman of intellect, not merely someone who knew how to dress well, and preside over a drawing room."

Her third husband was General Erich Ludendorff, who married her at Tutzing, Bavaria. Together with her general-spouse, she founded the *Society for the Knowledge of God,* that was reportedly officially banned during 1961–77. The authoress of several books, she opposed both religion and the occult. By 1961, the widow Ludendorff had 12,000 followers.

The bridal pair posed on the front steps of her Tutzing home where they lived together—eagle soaring in flight above on the general's seventieth birthday on April 9, 1935. (*HHA*)

Notes one source: "In 1936, he wrote *Total War* that expounded on his theory that modern war involved the whole nation … Hitler paid final tribute to him by walking behind his … casket." Rumor had it that she had earlier asked Hitler to marry her, but the Nazi Führer refused.

Reportedly, nude photos of her were given to Hitler, who refused to allow their publication. Noted NS era survivor Ernst Hanfstaengl in his 1957 memoirs: "Schaub one day had come across some pictures of the nude Mathilde Ludendorff—taken when that eccentric lady was attending a nature cure of some sort—and these were handed round with appreciative guffaws."

Above left: The general steps out on his seventieth birthday, April 9, 1935, followed by von Blomberg, whose offer of a Hitlerian Nazi marshal's baton was rejected by Ludendorff, the haughty soldier having already conceived for himself the more lofty title of Field Lord of the World War, despite his having lost it. The sentry at right stands at attention at shoulder arms. Fritsch is at the left of Blomberg, behind Ludendorff. (*HHA*)

The general "became increasingly involved in the occult, expressing agitation toward Jews, Catholics, and Freemasons," co-authoring books with his new wife from their home, near where he was buried in December 1937.

Above right: Hitler went in person to wish Mackensen a happy eightieth birthday on December 6, 1934 at the latter's country estate. Over the marshal's right shoulder is seen his younger second wife, Leonie, and behind her Mrs. and German Foreign Minister von Neurath, the latter turning to share a laugh with a rarely smiling von Fritsch behind him. At far left, Blomberg also shares in the general merriment, turning to face the marshal's son, later Colonel General Eberhard von Mackensen, with whom the present author corresponded from Vietnam to Germany in 1967. (*HHA*)

The Führer (*left*) prepares to take his leave, his overcoat being held for him by SS guard Karl Wilhelm Krause, nicknamed "Hitler's Shadow." To the right from rear, Brückner in SA kit renders the marshal a Nazi salute. The Mackensen couple is at center left. (*HHA*)

In 1914 to capture Lemberg, Mackensen's soldiers marched 20 miles a day for eight days. They reached the San River in May 1915 and took Fortress Przemyśl after a famous siege that made military history.

The Hussar marshal meets little NS HJ fans at left, some saluting. (*HHA*)

The Kaiser had named Mackensen to command the Death's Head Hussars on his birthday, January 27, 1894, and in 1901 this was followed by his being promoted to lead the entire brigade of regiments as well, having been raised to major general the previous year. In 1908, this was included in his new command of the 17th Army Corps at Danzig-Langfuhr in East Prussia.

Mackensen with baton (*left*) and Blomberg (*right*) are seen in front of the Berlin Guard House on another occasion. (*HHA*)

Noted one of Mackensen's admirers: "He was the Hussar field marshal, nobody's enemy, beloved by everyone." Recalled Hindenburg of his own career, he opined: "If I were asked what were my feelings before the battle, I should say, 'First of all, a certain sense of pleasure that I was at last going to smell powder, followed by a disquieting nervousness lest so young a soldier might fail in his duty.'"

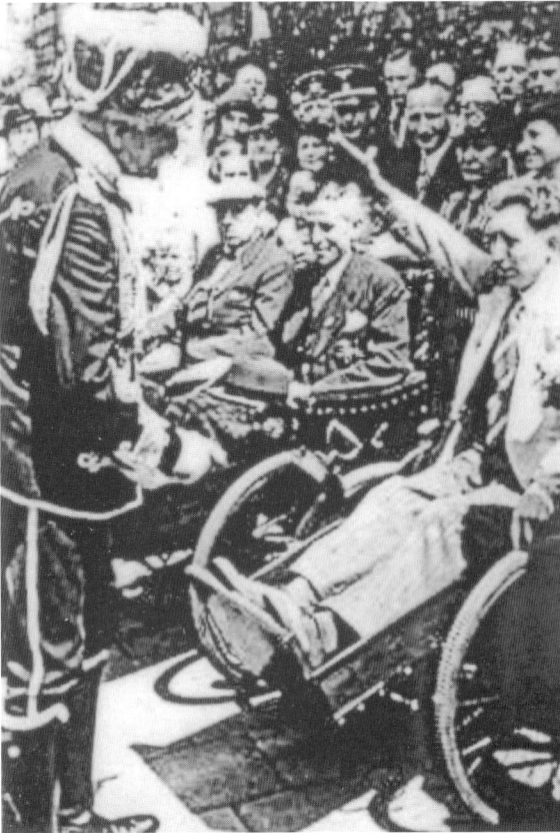

The Black Marshal greets saluting wounded war veterans, perhaps on the same occasion. (*HHA*)

He had impressed the Kaiser in 1892 when he published his own work entitled *The History of the Lifeguard Hussars.* On June 22, 1915, the Kaiser named Mackensen a field marshal, personally presenting him with his baton of office at a banquet in his honor.

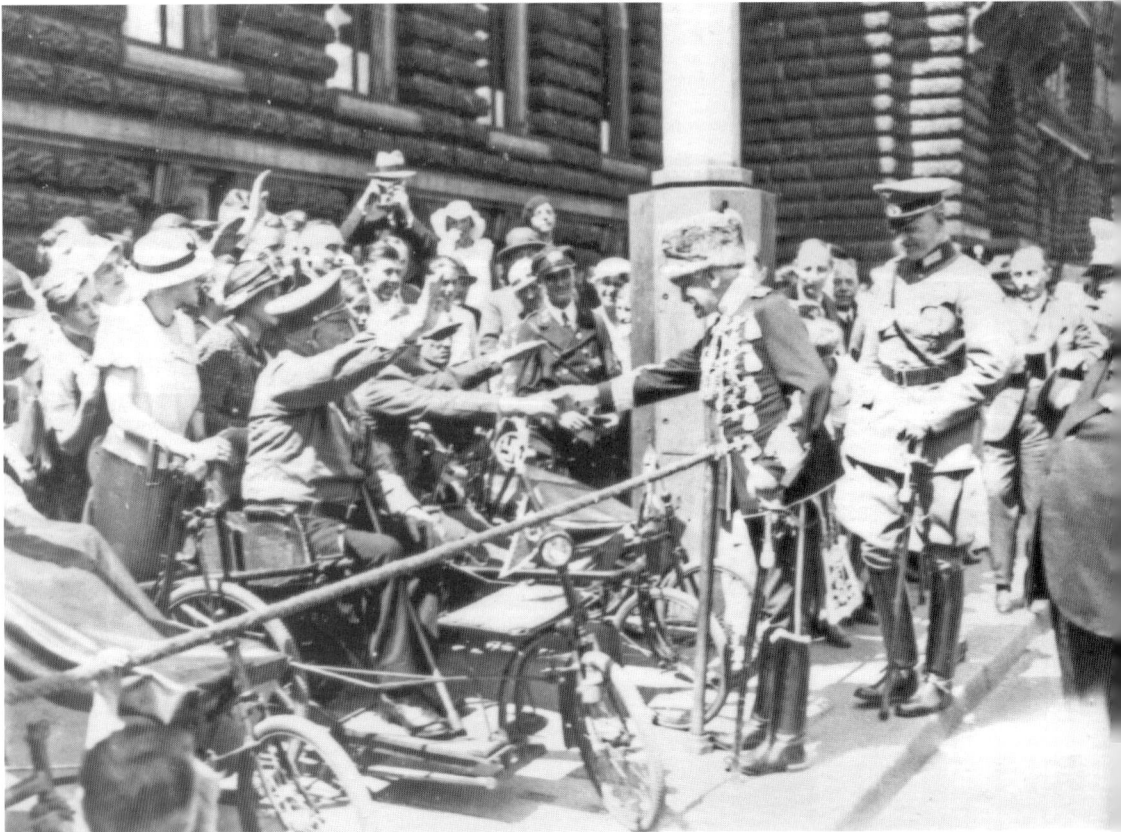

The Führer and his entourage arrive at the Tannenberg Memorial on October 2, 1935 for Hindenburg's second state funeral. *From left to right*: General SS men at attention, Hitler wearing black mourning band over his swastika version, SS man, RFSS Himmler, and unknown others, with Himmler's deputy SS General Karl Wolff third from right as well. (*HHA*)

The pastor (*left*) and the Oskar von Hindenburg family arrive, followed by other mourners. He salutes. (*HHA*)

Hindenburg in his post-combat recollections: "But the sound of the first shots produced a feeling of elation—they were greeted with scattered cheers—and I said a short prayer, gave a few thoughts to the dear ones at home, and to the ancient name I bear, and then, forward march!"

Men in SS black arrive with floral wreaths. (*HHA*)

The number of wounded caused my enthusiasm to wane," remembered Hindenburg decades later, "and to give place to cool-headed-ness or to indifference in face of danger. One is not fully stirred until the fight is over, when one has more time to contemplate the ghastliness of war … My aim on the battlefield has been achieved, I have been given a smell of powder, I have heard the bullets whistle by, bullets of every kind, shells, grapeshot."

The Hindenburg medals and coffin on caisson return for a second time, again flanked by mounted cavalry. (*HHA*)

"I am slightly wounded," Hindenburg recalled, "and am, therefore, an interesting person! I took five cannon, etc., etc.! Above all, I have come to recognize God's grace and loving kindness. Honor to Him forever and ever, amen!"

Stone sentries flank the tomb's entrance. (*HHA*)

Wounded at the Battle of Königgrätz in the Seven Weeks' War with Austria in 1866, Hindenburg wrote later: "A bullet went clean through the eagle on my helmet, grazed my head without causing any serious damage, and passed out behind." It remained in a place of honor in his offices until his death in 1934, sixty-eight years later.

Wearing Great War spiked helmet and uniform, Franz von Papen smiles and is greeted by Hitler, with Hindenburg women in funereal black looking on. (*HHA*)

Noted Ludwig Cohn in 1935: "Before their son had left for the [1866] war, the parents had taken the eagle off the helmet and had secreted a text from the Bible behind it, and the devout father—who was attached to an ambulance throughout the campaign—wrote to his wife, 'O, God, what a rod of discipline is the firebrand of war in Thy hand! Praised be Jesus Christ that our child has been so graciously saved, and has not had to enter that place where the face of horror stares down on one and the tears of woe have flowed so profusely and are destined to continue to flow so long!'"

The official mourner's lineup for the 1935 event. *From left to right*: Perhaps General Wilhelm Ritter von Leeb in steel helmet, Hindenburg family members in black, Hitler, Marshal von Mackensen with formal baton, Blomberg, Fritsch, Goering, Raeder, officers at statue (they and it providing each other with a sense of scale), and standard bearer. (*HHA*)

On November 10, 1918, Hindenburg ordered Mackensen to retreat with his troops from Bucharest to Silesia, while he continued fighting into the 12th, one day after the Armistice had been signed in the west, and on December 1, 1918, his last troops crossed the Hungarian frontier.

The official Tannenberg Memorial lineup at the 1935 and last such event, from left to right: Chancellor Hitler, Field Marshal von Mackensen, General von Blomberg, General von Fritsch, General Goering, Admiral Dr Raeder, and others. Note the over-sized sentry statue at far right. (*ASA*)

The coffin (below) makes its second trip to the tower at left, via its new entrance way commissioned by architect Hitler. Note the Christian cross mounted on the tower's façade, perhaps a sop to the dead Protestant marshal. (*HHA*)

After 1871, Hindenburg recalled: "I have to admit that the French fought bravely … A curious feature of the engagement was that—since we were approaching from the northeast—we had to take care not to trespass on Belgian territory," but there was no such forbearance on Imperial Germany's part in the next war, forty-four years later.

Into the waiting crypt the coffin goes, the concrete on the nameplate on the facade above appearing not quite dry. (*HHA*)

When France surrendered in 1871, the young combat lieutenant wrote home: "Hurrah, Paris has capitulated!" and then rode for the second time in a victory parade, by the age of twenty-three, underneath Berlin's still standing Brandenburger Tor (Brandenburg Gate). There was to be no such third ride, alas. His favorite horse was a light chestnut-colored mount, aptly named Patience.

Inside are two crosses, one for each dead Hindenburg, husband (1934) and late wife (1921). At center can be seen the marshal's spiked helmet and formal baton on pillow cushion atop the flag-draped coffin. A brace of officers stand with drawn sabers at port arms. (*HHA*)

"As a [court] page, he had kissed [Prussian] Queen Elizabeth's hand … When William I died, Hindenburg—then a man of 40—had … begged to be given a block of gray marble, part of the paving in the cathedral upon the coffin of which his beloved master had rested. This piece of stone was always to be found on his desk, a pendant to the perforated helmet" of 1866.

Later, the army officers are replaced by enlisted men sentries with rifles at parade rest, flowers surrounding the bier and the late soldier's medals displayed on the cushions below. (*HHA*)

Before his death in 1898, Bismarck had told Wilhelm II: "So long as the officers' corps remains loyal, Your Majesty can continue to reign in all tranquility." But in 1918 that was not the case, and the Kaiser was in part overthrown because it was his own top officers who left him in the lurch when the crisis of his regime came.

Ludwig Cohn of 1888, when, "the first William's grandson—arrogant and neurotic—came to the throne, Hindenburg and his colleagues were quick to recognize the danger. None were so quick to recognize the danger constituted by the character of young William as was the General Staff," among them both the later duo.

Above: A period artist with a painted rendering of the same scene, a saluting crowd added to the canvas at right for effect. (*HHA*)

"William II whole-heatedly reciprocated Hindenburg's dislike. It was not to be expected that a nerve-ridden, restless, theatrical creature could appreciate a quiet, limpid, and simple nature such as Hindenburg possessed. Just as the field marshal found William's histrionic logorrhea unbearably irksome, so was the latter, a man with a crippled arm, irritated at the sight of the hale and mighty form of Hindenburg."

Right: Inside the crypt, now it is the turn of a Hindenburg (right center) to bow to Hitler (*left*), in this case Maj. General Oskar von Hindenburg, to whom each owed the other almost everything. Looking on at left is Mackensen. (*HHA*)

"According to William, sentries alone had any right to be of an outsize among men—like that Potsdam grenadier of long ago who had served the emperor's ancestors and from whom the field marshal had inherited his magnificent proportions."

Marshal (*left*) and corporal (*right*) leave the crypt, 1935. (*HHA*)

On January 3, 1919, Mackensen and his immediate staff were interned by the Hungarians at Castle Foeth near Budapest, later being taken from it by French Moroccan Spahi cavalry as a POW to Castle Futak in southern Hungary. When the Treaty of Versailles was signed by Germany on June 28, 1919, Marshal Foch ordered his German counterpart removed to Saloniki in Allied Greece, suffering malaria at the age of seventy, and not freed until November 17, 1919, over a year after the war ended.

General von Litzmann in retirement, wearing golden Nazi Party membership badge in his left jacket lapel. After Mackensen, he was the most NS of all the old imperial era soldiers. (*HHA*)

Upon his return home to Germany in 1919, Mackensen was treated as the conquering hero that he was by right, and was welcomed at Passau by Gens. Ludendorff and von Seeckt, his former chief of staff.

The general at home, enjoying his golden years in retirement, but at left, portrait over the mantelpiece, and living man at right, daughter standing, and grandchildren also present. (*HHA*)

When the elder Hindenburg at the age of sixty-four retired the first time in 1911, he wrote to the younger one, a grown man and also an officer in the army: "Have just retired, but am retained attached of the 3rd Regiment of Foot Guards. His Majesty has graciously bestowed on me the distinguished Order of the Black Eagle. May this come your way, too! Warmest Greetings! Father."

Rally lineup. *From left to right*: unknown army general, Mackensen, a Kaiser son in the third row (behind the man in the dark suit), unknown man, Hitler, unknown officer, General von Litzmann with cane, five unidentified officers, General Gerd von Rundstedt, and unknown others. (*HHA*)

After Hitler came to office in 1933, the field marshal issued this official statement: "We German officers are called representatives of the Reaction, when in truth we are representatives of the tradition, and in the meaning of this tradition, Hitler spoke at Potsdam. This was the great German unification!"

Litzmann, third from left, stepping out with cane, with Mackensen second from right. (*HHA*)

On May 10, 1915, von Mackensen had been awarded the *Adler* (Eagle) medal by Kaiser Wilhelm II, his devoted lifelong patron. Mackensen was seen as "the moralistic anchor of the Army." Recalled Ludwig Cohn, "After the Battle of Tannenberg, he had for the first time omitted the Beneckendorff, and signed simply, Hindenburg." Thus are historic legends born!

Mackensen (*left*) and Litzmann (*right*) on a reviewing stand, waiting for the parade to begin. (*HHA*)

In 1933, Mackensen ventured successfully into the business world with his father-in-law, Georg Westerman, as partner, and with brother-in-law, Everhard Westerhard, ran a publishing company with great skill. "The two men who had really won the hearts of the Prussians had been Blücher and Wrangel" (both marshals), noted Ludwig Cohn. "It was to them that Field Marshal von Hindenburg was henceforward compared, and his new rank, conferred in November 1914 [by the neurotic Kaiser] contributed to the growth of the legend" that the holder himself so patently built up over the next two decades.

Mounted former imperial-era cavalry canter past same in review. (*HHA*)

Mackensen's first wife was the sister of a Lt Von Horn who had been a regimental colleague of her future husband's until he was killed in action in France during the Franco-Prussian War of 1870–71. This same account mentions "Mrs. Ludendorff, daughter of a rich Jewish tradesman" raising the question: did General Ludendorff marry a Jewish woman?

Hitler greeted Litzmann on an arrival in 1935. The SS men at left stand at present arms. (*HHA*)

Asserts Ludwig Cohn of when painter met subject: "When … Vogel arrived … and at once began to depict Hindenburg as Blücher, the field marshal felt that at length recognition had come his way.… Of Vogel's first sketch—as compared with earlier essays—he said, 'That is not a picture for home consumption—it is genuinely martial!' … Thenceforward, he would not part from his portrait-painter-in-ordinary, keeping Vogel employed until the end of the war."

Having given the general a Mercedes-Benz limousine for his eighty-fifth birthday, Hitler extends his warmest greetings, watched by Daimler-Benz official Jacob Werlin at right in leather overcoat. Just behind Hitler can be seen a smiling Dr Goebbels. (*HHA*)

"For weeks now, morning after morning, at the eastern headquarters, Hindenburg sat for his 'little professor' … and was above all deeply interested in the buttons, the gold braid, and the decorations displayed in the portraits."

Litzmann's state funeral followed on June 6, 1936 as the coffin here is seen being lowered into the ground at center at Dagow Cemetery. Flag bearers with Prussian battle flags abound, as the official mourners salute at center. *From left to right*: Hitler, Rudolf Hess, Goering (military hand salute to cap brim), Fritsch, Frick, Raeder, and Dr Goebbels. (*HGA*)

10

Scepters, 1935–36

After 1934, the Hohenzollerns—and especially Imperial Crown Prince Wilhelm—were really in a quandary. Their extensive financial holdings, cash emoluments, and landed estates had been basically left alone by the Weimar Republic government after the 1926 referendum vote was passed, returning to them and all royals their funds and estates.

This now continued under the new Nazi Third Reich—as long as the clan stayed out of politics altogether. Thus, the retired crown prince was free to attend horse races, chase pretty girls, and drive on the new Autobahn highways in his elegant red Mercedes-Benz roadsters, his bills being paid for by the Nazi Prime Minister of Prussia Goering.

Gen. Litzmann's State Funeral, June 3, 1936

Recorded eyewitness Domarus in *Speeches and Proclamations*:

> … on 1 June 1936, Hitler ordered a State Funeral for Gen. Karl Litzmann who died 28 May 1936 at age 86. For many years, Litzmann had supported Hitler and helped him through difficult times.
>
> The ceremony took place 3 June 1936 in Neu-Globsow, District of Mark Brandenburg, where the deceased had resided. All high-ranking generals were present.
>
> The new Field Marshal von Blomberg delivered the commemorative address, and Hitler placed a huge wreath on Litzmann's grave, reading, "To Party Comrade Litzmann, the old soldier and loyal fighter for Germany's greatness and resurrection."

11

Swastikas, 1937–45

The Death of Ludendorff, December 20, 1937
Hitler sent a telegram of best wishes to von Mackensen on the Black Marshal's eighty-eighth birthday on December 6, 1937, and the very next day, he visited his former ally and foe, the mortally ill Gen. Ludendorff, at Munich's Catholic Josephinum Hospital. He died there on December 20, 1937 of "circulatory debility at age 73," according to Domarus.

In an official statement, the Reich chancellor noted that "his love and prayers belonged to our people; his hatred to his foes!" and sent a condolence telegram to his widow, Dr Matilde Ludendorff: "I and the entire National Socialist Movement are forever indebted to him since it was he who—in a time of great need, at the risk of life and limb—stood with those fighting for a better future for Germany!"

The widow Dr Ludendorff foiled Hitler's plans for a second "Valhalla" sendoff *à la* the late Hindenburg by having her warrior husband buried at Tutzing, however, "the family's last place of residence."

Hitler got the last laugh in his own way, though. Domarus recalled in *Speeches and Proclamations*:

> Despite her opposition, Hitler would not desist from staging a magnificent State ceremony in front of the Munich Field Lord's Hall on 22 December 1937.
>
> All dignitaries of State, Party, and Armed Forces were instructed to attend the service. Field Marshal von Blomberg delivered the commemorative address. Hitler stepped up to the coffin that had been placed on a bier.
>
> He stood at attention, and called out in a stentorian voice, "Gen. Ludendorff! In the name of the unified German people, I place this wreath before you in deep gratitude." A 19-gun salute was fired after the wreath had been laid. The funeral procession then passed through the city, [with Hitler leading it, at any rate, as photographs show].

"Germany Buries the Greatest General of the War," *Life* magazine, January 17, 1938
> The ablest general developed by the World War was—according to today's military experts—Erich Ludendorff, a Prussian commoner whose father was a minor railway official.

Forty-nine in 1914, Ludendorff was with the 2nd German Army approaching Liege when he personally led a small column ahead of the main body and rapped open the gate of Liege's main fort.

For this, he was made Hindenburg's chief of staff on the Eastern Front. Ludendorff was Hindenburg's strategic brain. He believed in the military theory of annihilation, and annihilated Russian armies at Tannenberg and the Masurian Lakes, Rumanian Armies in 1916 [*sic*.], more Russian armies in 1917, and an Italian Army at Caporetto [*sic*.].

In August 1916, Hindenburg and Ludendorff took complete command of the German armies, and became so indispensable to German victory that even the Kaiser took orders from them.

Though his face and manner were the perfection of Prussian Junkerism, Ludendorff was actually an hysterical man who fell apart in defeat. In 1918, he fled to Sweden wearing a false beard and dark glasses, returned quietly the next year, and promptly married the wife of his host.

He bent an ear to every conspiracy including Hitler's Beer Hall Putsch in 1923 against the Republic, and marched beside Hitler. He decided that he had lost the war because the Jews, Jesuits, and Freemasons had softened Germany.

His wife divorced him for "egomania," and he married a mental healer who converted him to paganism. When, at 72, the military peer of Robert E. Lee died at a Catholic hospital in Munich 20 December 1937, Germany gave him a funeral worthy of his place in history.

The Kaiser Turns Eighty, January 27, 1939

For this gala event—in addition to the major luminaries—all of the Clan Hohenzollern traveled to Doorn, as did both Crown Prince Rupprecht and Field Marshal von Mackensen, the pair of still living baton holders of the Great War, three days before Hitler commemorated his own sixth year in office as Reich chancellor at Berlin. Nine months later came the advent of World War II.

Death of Prince Wilhelm of Prussia in France 1940

The death in action of Imperial Crown Prince Wilhelm's oldest son and former heir, Prince Wilhelm, in France in 1940 lead to a demonstration of 50,000 monarchists at his Berlin funeral, infuriating Hitler.

This led the Führer to remove all Hohenzollerns from the armed forces, including the crown prince's second son and new heir, Prince Louis Ferdinand, the latter sparing not a single word of regret for his slain elder brother in his 1951 memoirs *The Rebel Prince*.

It was this rather mismatched Prince Louis Ferdinand, therefore, who led the House of Hohenzollern even longer than his august father had, all during 1951–94—to his own demise.

Until the crown prince's death, the second son never tried to seize the former's primacy of place in favor of his own, to his credit. Both were present at the deathbed of the former Kaiser in 1941.

Death of the Kaiser, June 4, 1941

Kaiser Wilhelm II (1859–1941)—a self-created German Army field marshal and formerly one also in the British Army until 1914—died at the age of eighty-two at Doorn House, Holland, of a pulmonary embolism.

German Army soldiers guarded his estate since the Nazi invasion of the Netherlands on May 10, 1940. His remains still reside today in a mausoleum on the property, along with five of his pet dachshunds also buried on the grounds of the park. These include his favorite, Senta (1907–27), who spent years of peace, war, and exile with her imperial master.

In 1945, the Dutch government appropriated the estate, replanting the many trees felled by the "Woodchopper of Doorn," and in 1956, the house reopened as a museum, "just as Wilhelm II left it." It was declared a national monument in 1997 and had 25,000 visitors a year as of 2012, despite occasional Dutch political party attempts to close it.

Built in the ninth century, the house was rebuilt in the fourteenth and bought by the former Kaiser in 1920, where he resided until his death twenty-one years later. Its nineteenth-century park was laid out along English country manor lines, permitting the half-British former German emperor to live the life of the U.K. squire that he always imagined himself to be.

Its formal address is Langbroekerweg 10, Doorn, Netherlands, and long before his death, its main resident learned how to speak Dutch so that he could converse daily with the local friendly villagers, tipping his hat to them as he took his walks. Both his late wives, meanwhile, are buried near each other in Potsdam's Antike Temple.

In 1938, his grandson and successor as head of the House of Hohenzollern, Prince Louis Ferdinand of Prussia, was married at Doorn House to Grand Duchess Kira Romanova of Russia, of the House of Romanov.

Imperial Crown Prince Wilhelm Touted as Reich Regent Post-Stalingrad, 1943

Imperial Crown Prince Wilhelm's cause of succession to the then still-vacant throne was floated yet again after the surrender of the German 6th Army at Stalingrad in February 1943, after Hitler had turned him down in 1939 for a renewed army group command, *à la* 1914.

Hitler Blames Imperial Crown Prince Wilhelm for the July 20, 1944 Bomb Attack on Him

On July 20, 1944, during the army's failed bomb blast attempt on Hitler's life, Imperial Crown Prince Wilhelm's ever-hopeful adherents touted him yet again—and for the last time—as a "National Regent" based at Berlin, while Rupprecht of Bavaria had long since removed himself to safety at Florence in Savoyard-Fascist Italy in 1939 under the protection of its king, Victor Emmanuel III, safe from the Führer's vengeance.

This was followed by the protection of the American Army in 1945, and it was they who returned Rupprecht to Bavaria later that same year. Asserted Domarus in *Speeches and Proclamations*:

Hitler was especially angry with the House of Hohenzollern, and with its Imperial Crown Prince Wilhelm, whom he mistakenly believed to be behind the assassination attempt.

However, Hitler greatly overestimated the importance of the former ruling house in Germany and its influence on the public.... He said to his entourage on 20 July 1944, "You can believe me! Soon we will find out that all along the *Kronprinz* was behind it all!"

While kept informed, he was not. One who was more deeply informed was his second son, Prince Louis Ferdinand, who was even questioned by the Gestapo/Secret State Police on it, signed a statement, and was left uncharged as a result.

Goering Speaks at Tannenberg, July 31, 1944
Domarus well described the last ever official function at Hohenstein in *Speeches and Proclamations* thus:

On 31 July 1944, a State ceremony at the Tannenberg Memorial took place in honor of the chief of the Luftwaffe General Staff, Günther Korten.

He had been seriously injured in the assassination attempt [against Hitler] of 20 July 1944, and had died on 23 July. Hitler promoted him to the rank of colonel general, and had Goering place a wreath.

Thus ended the last public usage of the Tannenberg Memorial in the life of the Third Reich.

Shadows Over the Tannenberg Memorial (*Tannenberg*)
Recalls Gessner in 2017: "On 20 January 1945—as the Soviet armies advanced [anew!] in East Prussia—the German military, fearing profanation by the Russians, evacuated the remains of the field marshal and his wife." Indeed, they were right to have been so afraid, as Red Army soldiers looted the coffin of Karin Goering, and used the skull of Prussian Napoleonic Wars Field Marshal von Blücher as a football—literally.

Showalter states that the Hindenburg coffins—husband and wife—went by road to the port city of Königsberg on the Baltic Sea, where they were taken aboard the German Navy cruiser *Emden* for shipment to the German mainland.

Dr Goebbels meantime promised the German people that the blown up Hindenburg Memorial would be rebuilt after the Nazis won the war. This never happened, and many East Prussian sites found themselves with new Polish names instead: Osterode became Ostróda, Allenstein as Olsztyn, and Neidenburg morphed into Nidzica.

In 1960, the Communist People's Republic of Poland again celebrated its victory of Tannenberg—that of 1410, however.

Regarding the removed Hindenburg remains, though, Gessner explains: "After a perilous journey, these found a lasting resting place ... in Marburg Cathedral. A day later, at night, the Germans blew up the entrance tower and the one that had housed the Hindenburg Tomb."

The Tannenberg Memorial Blown Up, January 21, 1945

German Army engineers emplaced demolition charges "inside the entrance tower and that previously housing the Hindenburg coffins, causing both towers to collapse. On January 22, 1945, 30 more tons of explosives were detonated by military engineers."

Adds *A Monument Dispersed*:

> On Hitler's orders, German soldiers blew up the entrance and the Hindenburg Towers at night during 21–22 January 1945, managing to salvage at the last moment the coffins of both the marshal and his wife.
>
> Being short of explosives, the retreating German Army failed to destroy the damaged memorial completely. Soon afterward, Red Army troops entered Polish Olsztyn, burning about 40 % of it, including many cultural monuments.

"The Russians did not complete, though, the destruction of what remained of the memorial, but instead shot a documentary film on the devastated site," just as they would later do of Hitler's captured New German Reich Chancellery Berlin and also of the Reichstag building.

The Hindenburgs Leave Tannenberg, January 1945

There was a lot more to the travelogue saga of the Hindenburgs than that, however. Over the previous decade of 1935–45, the remains of the dead Hindenburgs—husband and wife—had rested in lead coffins, surrounded by Prussian Army regimental banners in their tomb as well. The German Army on Hitler's orders removed them all initially to a Berlin bunker, and then to the salt mine outside Bernterode Village, Thuringia, in north central Germany.

Marked with red crayons identifying the occupants, the two coffins and others were reburied behind a 6-foot-thick wall deep in a 14-mile mining complex, an estimated 1,800 feet below ground.

On April 27, 1945, U.S. Army Ordnance forces found the entire historic mother-lode, transferring it to Marburg Castle an der Lahn River, Germany. Reburial followed yet again twenty months later in August 1946 by the Americans within St Elizabeth's (Protestant) Church at Marburg in Hesse, where they have remained for the last seventy years, according to Polish translator Marzena Beata Guzowska.

The 1949 Polish Destruction of Tannenberg

Postwar looters stole both bronze and metal from the blown-up site, with stones and bricks being used to rebuild nearby Olsztynek, Poland, much as, earlier, the Soviet War Memorial at Treptow-Berlin had used pirated red marble from Hitler's destroyed 1939 New German Reich Chancellery.

In addition, "Much of the fabric of the stone-and-granite memorial was used to build the Soviet War Memorial in Olsztyn, the Monument to the Ghetto Heroes in Warsaw, and for the new Communist Party headquarters in Warsaw," a city taken four times during the world wars by the Germans.

Adds Ms. Guzowska in Gessner's *Tannenberg*:

> Granite pavement of the courtyards were torn away, some of them being used as material for the construction of the Palace of Science & Culture in Warsaw, as well as steps of the stairway between the level of the street and the ground floor of the edifice of the Central Committee of the Polish United Workers/Communist Party (KCPZPR); the plinth of the Monument to a Guerilla—also called The Monument to the Fighters for People's Poland or The Monument to the Guerilla of Folks' Army—a bronze sculpture designed by Wacław Kowalik.

The latter stands on a granite pedestal carved by Polish sculptor Stanisław Żaryn, the monument's surroundings designed by Zygmunt Stępiński and Kazimierz Marczewski. In addition, another segment of pavement was used in the construction of the Monument of Gratitude to the Red Army still there, but since renamed as the Monument of the Liberation of Varmie & Masuria Lands in Olsztyn.

This latter was designed by former Auschwitz-Birkenau death camp prisoner sculptor Xawery Dunikowski, aided by fellow Krakow sculptors Tadeusz Sieklucki and Edward Koniuszy, with Warsaw masonry workers also taking part.

At the moment, the site where the monument stands functions as a car park. The tiles from Hindenburg's mausoleum are left in the strip along the axis of composition, and in a low wall separating the square from Piłsudskiego Street, itself named for yet another famous marshal—that of Poland's Józef Piłsudski:

> Another object into which a part of the mausoleum was incorporated is also in Olsztyn, *Stefan Jaracz's Bust,* made from 350 kg of bronze from molten plaques and letters of Hindenburg's mausoleum.
>
> The bust is placed on a marble plinth, also part of that, and erected in 1946, still standing in front of an Olsztyn theater.

In the spring of 1949, the Polish Communist regime at Warsaw mandated the complete dismantling of all that remained of the Tannenberg Memorial, and yet still enough stayed behind for local pirates to use as well.

Thus, the destruction continued for another three decades, into the 1980s. "Today, only a protruding island in an isolated field remains to mark the extensive 120 acre site" of long ago.

The Memorial's Court of Honor—that measured somewhat larger than an American-sized football field—has been reduced to little more than an overgrown pit of scattered debris and rubble: "Several significant remnants of the structure can still be seen elsewhere. Among these is the perfectly preserved sculpted stone lion that once topped a six-meter pillar at the entrance to the monument, and is now displayed in the nearby Olsztynek town square."

Ironically—for the August 2014 centennial of the battle itself—nothing of any note beyond that remained. Concluded Gessner: "Nothing remains of the monument today other than its buried foundations. The area is now an Olsztynek [Poland] park." The majority of the Polish razing was accomplished during the immediate postwar decade of the Red 1950s.

The Tannenberg *Denkmal* (Memorial) 2017

In 1919, there was established for the battle's fifth anniversary of the Commission of the Tannenberg Association managed by Johannes Kahns, chairman of the Prussian Association of Veterans, and also a member of the German Union of Officers.

On August 31, 1924, the cornerstone was laid by Field Marshal von Hindenburg personally, "At a hill between the towns of Sudwa and Olsztynek, selected as the monument's future site." The competition announced in 1919 drew "389 projects prepared by 352 artists and architects sent to the Commission." Robert Traba states in Gessner's *Tannenberg*:

> The winners were the Berlin architects, brothers Johannes Kruger (1890–1975) and Walter Kruger (1888–1971), who proposed an architectural composition [alluding to a traditional seafarers' calling] *Good Wind.*
>
> Their monumental design embraced a complex spatial development—250 by 450 meters—in the central element of which would be an octagonal building made of East Prussian traditional material.
>
> This was red brick crowned at its corners by massive, 23 meter-high towers of a base of 9 × 9 meters. Each of the towers had a different proposed use, and, consequently, different furniture.
>
> Tower #2 was devoted to German victories during the war. The third—called the *East Prussian*—was supposed to accommodate exhibits documenting the East Prussian stage of the war.
>
> In the fourth—the *Flag Tower*—there were banners, and other insignia of all the regiments. The sixth—*The Soldier Tower*—contained motifs linked to the fates of simple conscripts [draftees], with an archive in the attic.
>
> The seventh was a lay variation of a chapel to the glorious memory of the war victims. The eighth—called *The Generals*—accommodated the busts and biographies of 15 of the chief commanders of the battle.
>
> The whole of the architectural layout culminated in an octagonal construction, the beginning of which was formed by a stadium—its building in 1939 proved unfeasible—linked to the monument by an avenue of trees.
>
> The inner area of the courtyard—measuring about 80 meters corner wise—was devoted to patriotic rallies. Initially, a huge effigy of a lion to the glory of the 147th Regiment of Grenadiers, was planned to be moved from the outside of the area to the center, within the walls of the courtyard.
>
> It was planned that the lion would be placed within a ring of oaks; however—during the building work—the concept was changed. Instead of a lion, a huge bronze cross—about 20 meters high—became the central point of the courtyard.

The designers' intention was not to allude to either a Teutonic cross or "the cross of orn," but simply the cross of a tomb, typically placed on Christian graves, of which the marshal's was one.

Four cobblestone avenues led from Towers 1, 3, 5, and 7 to the cross finished by steps, facilitating the mounting of the platform upon which the cross was located, bearing the inscription on the socie [thus]:

> Here lie 20 German soldiers who fell in the Battle of Tannenberg 28 August 1914. It is here where the Germans worship the memory of their people who died in the World War 1914–18—184,000 of them falling either on foreign soil or to the sea bed; 206,000 finding their place of final rest in their Homeland.

According to Jürgen Tietz, a German historian: "The towers were 20 meters high." Continues Traba in *Tannenberg*:

If the cross constituted the central point of memory within the monumental octagon, the 55 just projecting along the inner side of the wall served as votive places—monuments to the particular Army units taking part in the battle.

As historians of architecture claim, Tannenberg National Memorial as a whole was one of the most interesting architectural concepts of its time, alluding to ideas of medieval style, but based on the classical principles of modernist buildings.

The very fact that the edifice was placed in a free, unlimited space was a case study for modernism that, additionally, did not shy away from the current trends of its time like art deco and expressionism.

"Prussian Relics Found," Wiesbaden, Germany, Newspaper Report, June 17, 1945 (*Tannenberg*)

The remains of Frederick the Great, Frederick Wilhelm I, and President Hindenburg have been found in a salt mine at Bernterode near Nordhausen. The Prussian regalia—formerly kept at Potsdam—225 battle flags dating from the early Prussian wars—and 271 paintings were also found.

The discovery was made by six American soldiers on 27 April 1945, and had been kept secret until now. Workers said that the relics were deposited about 16 March 1945, with great secrecy, and the entrances sealed on 2 April 1945—British United Press.

"Hidden Shrine Yields Two Kaisers' Bodies," Wiesbaden, Germany, *New York Times* June 17, 1945

The bodies of Field Marshal Paul von Hindenburg, former President of Germany; Frederick the Great and Frederick Wilhelm I—as well as that of *Frau* von Hindenburg—have been removed from a secret underground shrine at Bernterode near Mühlhausen, where they were found last 27 April 1945 by a six-man detail of the United States 350th Ordnance Depot.

The removal was so secret that the American troops handling the caskets got the impression that they were handling Adolf Hitler's body. With the bodies was a vast treasure hoard of Imperial jewels, crowns, historic Prussian battle flags, State Seals, and other paraphernalia of departed German glory.

The cache was discovered by Americans while they were searching for an underground ammunition storage vault. They saw fresh mortar signs on the wall, and investigation led to the hidden flag-banked shrine where all four caskets lay surrounded by jewels and other treasures.

An officer representing the fine arts branch of the military government said that the names of the occupants had been labeled on each casket with red crayon. The Germans had lavishly decorated the casket of Frederick Wilhelm I—The Soldier King—with red silk ribbons, swastikas, and other symbols in the name of Hitler.

The bodies of both Kaisers [*sic.*], they were royal kings, but neither was of imperial status] had been removed from the Garrison Church in Potsdam. When the Russians moved into Prussia, the Germans announced that Hindenburg's remains had been withdrawn.

Among the collection was a short sword presented by Pope Pius II to *Kurfürst* Albrecht Achilles in 1406, and an *Adam & Eve* painting believed to have come from the Uffizzi Palace in Florence, [Italy].

But that was far from being the end of what turned out to be a fascinating saga of both history and detective work, as revealed by Will Lang in 1950 in *Life* magazine, some excerpts following:

The coffins were found 1,800 feet below ground. It was 27 April 1945 … and US [Army] Ordnance troops were scouring the Thuringian countryside for hidden ammunition depots.…

In the Bernterode salt mine's 14 miles of dark corridors, they had already discovered 400,000 tons of ammunition, when they came upon a freshly mortared wall blocking one passage.

Tunneling six feet through masonry and rubble, they broke into the secret room … crammed with tapestries, hundreds of brilliant regimental Prussian banners, paintings by [Lucas] Cranach and Watteau, swastikas—and four coffins.

Across the coffins, someone had hastily scrawled a few words in red crayon … identifying the contents of the coffins as casually as if they were shipping crates. So began one of the war's strangest stories—until now, a closely kept secret of the US Army.

For the coffins contained the remains of three of three of Germany's most glorified militarists: King Frederick [II] the Great, most famed of all Prussian conquerors; King Frederick Wilhelm I, his father and the real founder of the Prussian Army; and Field Marshal Paul von Hindenburg.

The fourth coffin contained the remains of *Frau* von Hindenburg, [Gertrud].

But the removal of Hindenburg from Berlin and the Fredericks from nearby Potsdam … had an … inspiration: the corpses were to be concealed until some future moment when their reappearance could be timed by resurgent Nazis to fire another German generation to rise and conquer again.…

After transferring the coffins from the salt mine to the cellar of a heavily guarded castle in Marburg, the Army passed the dilemma on to Washington, and sat tight.… It was not until a year later—in April 1946—that the then US Deputy Military Governor for Germany LTG Lucius D. Clay got his instructions.…

The two kings to be buried in the US Zone [of Occupation] and the two Hindenburgs in the British Zone near Hanover, their former home.

A trio of Americans in the U.S. Army Monuments, Fine Arts, and Archives were tasked with carrying out what became known as Operation Bodysnatch: Theodore Heinrich; Everett P. Lesley, Jr.; and Francis W. Bilodeau, "but to entrust the actual burials to the German government of Greater Hesse … the whole operation was to be considered top secret."

Two possible, early burial sites considered were both castles: Reinhartshausen on the Rhine River near Wiesbaden, and Burg Hohenzollern—"Imperial Crown Prince Wilhelm … owned the [latter] castle, though he lived in a villa nearby" in the French Zone.

"The French answer was unequivocal: they wanted no Hohenzollerns—not even kings—buried in their Zone!" Another castle then considered was Kronberg in the Taunus Mountains near Frankfurt, another such site owned by Hesse.

Yet another possible location was Castle Wilhelmshöhe, the late marshal's next-to-last military headquarters in 1918 as the Great War had wound down. This site at Kassel, Germany, failed muster, however, because it had no suitable burial crypt:

> With delight, they discovered one church answering all their qualifications … in Marburg itself, only a few hundred yards from the spot where the bodies had rested during all the months of search.
>
> St Elizabeth's Church seemed ideal. Begun in 1235 to contain the body of the German saint who had died four years before, it was the first pure Gothic church built in what later became modern Germany … used for centuries as a burial place for princes.…
>
> … suffered no serious war damage and … so conspicuously located in a large city that it could hardly be used for secret nationalist rallies … a large church 700 years old.… They finally selected two separate sites. The two kings would be buried below the floor in the north transept near a medieval shrine marking the supposed resting place of St Elizabeth, a Hohenzollern ancestor.
>
> *Todesraum* for the two Hindenburgs was found at the base of the north church tower… The French authorities refused to let Imperial Crown Prince Wilhelm leave their Zone for any purpose … [so the officers traveled to him for his assent].
>
> The Imperial Crown Prince … brought out a bottle of champagne. He also gave full family approval to the plans for burying the two kings.

Trouble Finding Oskar! (Gessner, *Tannenberg*)

There remained the Hindenburg family. A discreet telegram sent to Hindenburg's son—living in the Province of Hanover—was answered promptly. Prussian Maj. Gen. Oskar von Hindenburg replied that he would be in Wiesbaden the next day to discuss whatever private business was referred to in the telegram.

He never appeared. Quite by chance he was found in the custody of the local American security police, howling to be released. On arriving at a Wiesbaden hotel, he had broken the law by signing the register with his full military title.

Sprung from his cell, the Prussian was a meeker man the next day when he was taken to Marburg to view the site for his parents' graves, and was pleased with the tombs. He was also pleased that the State of Hesse would bear most of the costs for reburying his parents.

"My family," he lamented, "is now as poor as church mice!" [*Sic transit Gloria!*—Glory is fleeting!]

It would have been out of character for the Hindenburgs to go down without incident.… "We have struck water while digging under the north tower. What do we do now?"… Not water, but bedrock only 24 inches down.

This meant that the large Hindenburg caskets could not rest beneath the floor as planned. They considered blasting the graves out of the bedrock, but someone pointed out that the same dynamiting might also bring down the 236-foot, 14th Century tower.

A local architect was brought in and instructed to raise the church floor in the tower by several steps so that the large caskets could be accommodated … Bilodeau noticed that the burial slabs had not arrived.…

Immense, two-ton sandstone blocks with which the graves could be sealed, and thus discourage any fanatic Germans who might want to steal the bodies on a dark night.

This specter was not entirely fanciful, either, as both the remains of Mussolini and Marshal Pétain were, indeed, stolen by grave robbers postwar, as noted by me in articles. Gessner states in *Tannenberg*:

The slabs had already been shipped by rail from the quarry, 150 miles away from Marburg, but they were five days overdue.

A frantic check of German railroad stations was launched, and finally the errant flatcar with the grave lids was found … just about to wander mistakenly into the Russian Zone. It was quickly routed back toward Marburg.

The actual burial of the kings and the Hindenburgs—accomplished before the formal funerals—was noteworthy … that for once nothing whatsoever went wrong. All arrangements moved on schedule.

The coffins were secretly transferred at night … to St Elizabeth's Church, and the next morning—with the edifice locked to outsiders—a five-man crew of German workers lowered the coffins by means of a small derrick.

The graves were sealed with a sheet of steel and a layer of cement as an added anti-burglar precaution, and the sandstone slabs were laboriously pushed over the openings. Through the night, a stonecutter worked with hammer and chisel, cutting inscriptions on the unmarked burial slabs.

The inscriptions were simple, giving only names, birth and death dates, and no titles. It was purposely intended that only Germans should even recognize the simple new tombs. All was ready for the ceremony the next day.

The 64-year-old Imperial Crown Prince Wilhelm declined an invitation to attend the consecration of the kings' tombs. His explanation was candid: "I have reached an age when funerals depress me," but Imperial Crown Princess Cecilie and three other Hohenzollerns were there, [as he should have been, as titular Head of the Family and Kaiser-in-Pretense].

But as the cars entered the churchyard … the Americans were appalled by what they saw. More than 500 Germans had already gathered there. They hung out of nearby windows, over the courtyard wall, and gaped at the official cars debouching more Hohenzollerns than Marburg had seen in years.

Only the Hohenzollern funeral could be held on this day, however, because the Hindenburgs failed to show up! Two days later they did, and their ceremony was a model of Prussian simplicity.

Oskar von Hindenburg, his wife, two daughters, and his sister were dressed in mourning as if their parents had died only that week. Oskar politely refused the original cars offered, and announced that—out of respect for the dead—his family would walk to church instead.

Walk they did, in long and solemn single file through crowded streets across all of the City of Marburg to St Elizabeth's Church. It was exactly 15 months and four weeks [*sic.*] since the GIs had come across the four coffins in their salt mine.

12

Imperial and Royal Exits, 1951–55

Death of Imperial Crown Prince Wilhelm, 1951

The ex-imperial crown prince followed his father to the grave a decade later on July 21, 1951 at the age of sixty-nine following a severe heart attack from nicotine addiction at 1:30 a.m. on German soil. Ironically, in death, he was compared to his grandfather, Kaiser Frederick III, "With whom he shared the well-known 'fate of a Crown Prince' … having to stay on the sidelines of inactivity and renunciation during the best years of their lives."

He was buried at Castle Hohenzollern at Hechingen, Swabia, in what is today a reunified Germany once more, if even still a republic. Recalled his still sole biographer Klaus Jonas, "The hall of the ancestral Burg Hohenzollern was chosen for the funeral services on 26 July 1951," as Allied troops battled those of Communism yet again, in Korea.

The State Funeral of Crown Prince Wilhelm

Hundreds of funeral wreaths—many of them with Royal crowns—decorated the forecourt and the chapel.… The coffin was covered with the Hohenzollern flag … and in front of it lay a wreath of 400 yellow roses from the Imperial Crown Princess Cecilie, [the much cheated on wife].

> Four princes of the two Houses of Hohenzollern held the guard of honor at both sides of the coffin.… There were delegations from all the regiments in which the Imperial Crown Prince had served, as well as from the *Stahlhelm* and the student Corps Borussia, in which his father the late Kaiser had also been a member…

"In the uniform of the Death's Head Hussars, the Imperial Crown Prince was laid to rest," preceded by "the cushion for medals," as was traditional in German military funerals. A group of trumpeters sounded a last farewell over the grave. "The mortal remains of the last Imperial German Crown Prince rest under St Michael's Chapel in the oldest part of the ancestral Burg."

In glaring contrast, Hitler's ashes were burned in a Berlin ditch, while those of Goering were dumped into the Isar River at Munich in the autumn of 1946. The last German Kaiser and King of Prussia still lays today in his flag-draped tomb at Doorn, Holland.

Requiem for Kaiserin Cecilie, 1954

On May 6, 1954, the *New York Times* ran an obituary entitled "Princess Cecilie of Prussia Dead. Widow of Heir to the German Throne Before World War I Succumbs at Age of 67:"

> Bonn, Germany—Cecilie Auguste Marie of Prussia, widow of Imperial Crown Prince Wilhelm, died in Bad Kissingen today of a stroke. She had been ill with circulatory ailment for some time....
>
> She was married to Imperial Crown Prince Wilhelm in 1905. They had four sons and two daughters.

When her husband died in 1951, Cecilie became dowager princess or even possibly dowager empress, since there then was no surviving German Kaiserin, former or otherwise. She was buried next to her husband at Castle Hohenzollern.

During 1933–45—separated but not divorced from her husband—she lived at her Potsdam home, Cecilienhof Castle, but had to flee in early 1945 from the advancing Red Army. Moving to Bavaria in the American Army Zone of Occupation, she resided at Bad Kissingen, and during 1952–54 at Stuttgart before her demise.

There is a final tale to be told here. In 1945, the last Allied Big Three meeting of World War II was held at her home, Cecilienhof, officially known to history today as the Potsdam Conference.

Two decades before—after Hitler had departed the premises—Imperial Crown Princess Cecilie ordered all the ground floor windows thrown open to let in fresh air, as the Nazi Führer had a well-known propensity for farting.

Death of His Majesty "King" Rupprecht, 1955

After the second lost German war, many Bavarians regarded their former crown prince as their uncrowned king without a throne. When he died in 1955 at the age of eighty-six, his state funeral was attended by tens of thousands of mourners.

Noted one recent German historian, "He represented an older, nobler Bavaria ... as a figure known everywhere."

The last meeting between Ludendorff (*left*) and Hitler. (*HHA*)

Jack Sweetman in 1973 stated that,Ludendorff asserted: "I will not have a lance corporal make me a field marshal! I am a general, and I will enter history as such!"

On the evening of May 3, 1942 at FHQ, Hitler told his inner circle that "he did not favor any interference in last wills and testaments unless they infringed on the rights of State and People in the most flagrant fashion…. He had had to deal with this problem when Ludendorff died. Ludendorff had expressly stated in his will that he wished to be buried not in the soldiers' cemetery in Berlin and not at the Tannenberg Memorial, but in Tutzing. Even though this testamentary request had been a great annoyance to him [Hitler], he had nevertheless respected it so as not to create a precedent," that of Hindenburg notwithstanding.

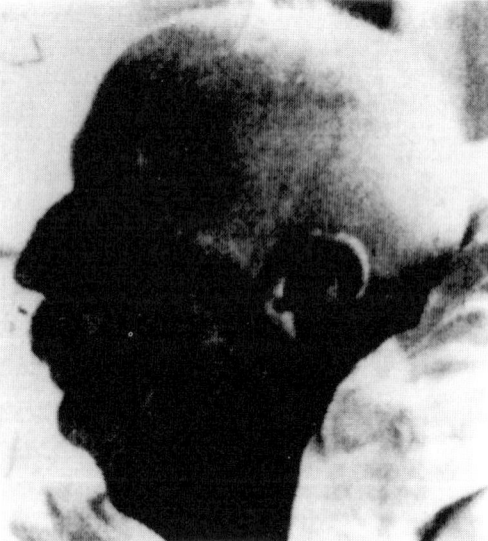

Above left: Dead Ludendorff as he appeared in *Life* magazine, 1938: "Ludendorff's corpse lies in state, December 20, 1937, Munich…. He died of heart failure following an operation for the same bladder complaint that killed Hindenburg," ironically. (*LC*)

To artist Vogel, his subject Hindenburg wrote during the war, "You have never served! A cloak without a button is like a flower without scent!" Their wartime collaboration began on February 15, 1915 and continued until Hindenburg's first official portrait as Reich president a decade later.

Above right: A somewhat clearer print I found in the Hoffmann albums in 1992: Ludendorff on his deathbed, aged seventy-two, on December 20, 1937, having refused Hitler's offer to make him a field marshal. (*HHA*)

At one point in their painter-subject relationship, Hindenburg actually grabbed Vogel's brush, sat down in front of the picture in the artist's studio, and, "with his own hand, painted in a pair of spurs!"

Above: The Ludendorff funeral cortege at Munich as *Life* showed it, 1938 (it occurred on December 22, 1937). Here, the medal cushions with eighty decorations precede the standard horse-drawn artillery caisson with coffin aboard. (*LC*)

On another occasion, Hindenburg wrote his court artist the following instructional letter: "According to Army regulations, it is essential to have an officer's sash for the attachment of the field marshal's baton and the binoculars! In the uniform of the 147th Regiment, there is neither a yellow tab nor a white band on the collar, so that—as everyone knows!—is gray, right up to the red border." At least, therefore, he and the Kaiser had this much in common: attention to detail regarding martial *minutiae*.

After a visit by Crown Prince Wilhelm, Ludendorff asserted that he had been "the only Hohenzollern who has always met me with the same lasting respect."

Noted *Life*: "The war helmet of Ludendorff … The band played 'The Good Comrade' … only family and close friends were present" at the Tutzing burial later. On March 16, 1918—within but days to the start of Ludendorff's last major offensive juggernaut of the Great War on the Western Front—Hindenburg wrote thus to his court painter Prof. Vogel regarding the latter's epochal painting on the 1914 Battle of Tannenberg: "My trousers are not dark enough! There is no reason why black trousers should not be most impressive. Then you must not forget to paint in the [red] stripes of a General Staff officer! Jack boots, black, with the box spurs—not brown gaiters!" This fetish for uniform accuracy Hindenburg shared as well with his prissy, detail-oriented first quartermaster general, Erich Ludendorff.

As it appears in the Hoffmann albums, the coffin being either put aboard or taken off by its handlers at rear, flanked by saber-wielding naval (*left*) and army officers (*right*). Note also the pylon with burning flame atop at right, a fixture at all such NS events, December 22, 1937. (*HHA*)

To get all the details right, Prof. Vogel was duly dispatched to the actual 1914 site of the Tannenberg struggle, and the corrections to the topographical locale took two more years to complete.

The scene at the Odeonsplatz at Munich's famed Field Marshal's Hall, where—fourteen years before—the dead hero and Hitler faced Green Police bullets that ended their brief attempt to seize power. The same scene still stands to this day. (*HHA*)

"Hindenburg was even more interested in a picture painted in accordance with his recollections … the day of his arrival at Marienburg" in August 1914, before the defeat of the Russians. "A huge figure in a cloak, he was standing on the river bank near the castle, lighted up by the red glow of the sunset, while he watched the women refuges from beneath his bushy eyebrows," according to Ludwig Cohn.

Above: Hitler spoke briefly: "Now you can go to Valhalla, great commander!" thus aping his remarks at Hindenburg's state funeral on August 7, 1934, and again also re-linking the two famous soldiers together anew. Lined up for the events was his personal staff. *From left to right:* unknown army officer, naval liaison officer, Luftwaffe adjutant Colonel Nicolaus von Below, SA General Wilhelm Brückner, SS General Julius Schaub, SS Führer Escort Physician Dr Karl Brandt, NSKK aide Albert Bormann (younger brother of Martin), and two unidentified army officers, December 22, 1937. A trio of unknown air force officers stand at far left in the second row. (*HHA*)

Left: Today, Ludendorff has the best memorial of them all: a simple concrete plinth with—from top to bottom—bust, last name, unsheathed sword. They say it all. Nothing more is really necessary. (*LC*)

"For once—standing before his [Marienburg] picture as Blücher, Hindenburg said to Vogel, 'Here I look as if I were saying, 'I shall not rest until I have drowned all the Russians—not one of them shall escape me!''" Once—wanting to see the massive canvas at night—the field marshal ordered, "See that the studio is well lighted within a quarter of an hour!"

Next page, above: Behind and to the right rear of his unused New German Reich Chancellery at Berlin desk at which he never sat was a bust of Hitler's predecessor as Reich president, Paul von Hindenburg on a raised plinth, as seen here in 1939. (*Hugo Jaeger*)

Regarding historic paintings done after a fact, it seems, Hindenburg joined the ranks of both his predecessor and successor, Kaiser and Nazi Führer.

The Kaiser's final place of exile in Holland, Doorn House, where he died at the age of eighty-two in June 1941, a few weeks before his successor as German head of state—Hitler—invaded the USSR. The white tower at far left was where the Kaiser had his last office, and from the bridge at far lower right, Wilhelm II famously fed his ducks every morning. (*DH*)

On August 20, 1942, Hitler opined that "but even Bismarck's criticism is not as damning as are the speeches of the Kaiser himself! Bismarck shows how the eyes of the whole people were fixed on the Kaiser, and what great things could have been accomplished had there been a monarch endowed with more tact, more human charity, and a greater readiness to accept the responsibilities of his exalted position. Instead, the last of the Kaisers did everything possible—by speeches that were as tactless as they were stupid!—to alienate the German princes, with a complete disregard for the consequences. It was the quintessence of stupidity on his part—as a youthful monarch—to treat all the other princes as mere vassals. I might as well adopt the same attitude towards [Hungarian Regent Admiral Miklos] Horthy and Tiso [puppet ruler of Slovakia]." In fact, the frosty admiral believed that Hitler did just that regarding him by 1944.

Just as with his subordinates Imperial Crown Prince Wilhelm and Marshal von Mackensen, the last Kaiser loved his silver-and-black Death's Head Hussars' dress uniform, as seen here, in a formal portrait with his second and final empress, Kaiserin Princess Hermine of Reuss. (*DH*)

On August 20, 1942, Hitler continued: "The irresponsibility of that young man is past comprehension … and—into the bargain—as the vainest and most stupid peacock!"

THE CRYSTAL-GAZER

British interwar cartoon by Bernard Partridge, published September 6, 1939. *The Crystal-Gazer.* "Watched by the shade of Germany's past, Hitler peers into his crystal ball and does not flinch at what he sees," regarding the emperor's overthrow of November 1918. (*ASA*)

On September 21, 1941, Hitler asserted that "a dynasty's domination ceases to be justified when its' ambitions are no longer adjusted to the nation's permanent interests.… I am grateful to Social Democracy for having swept away all these royalties! Even supposing it had been indispensable, I do not know that any of *us* would have so definitely set himself against the House of Hohenzollern!"

A cartoon from the *Evening Standard* by David Low published August 1, 1934. The caption to this British political cartoon by David Low reads, "Hitler: 'The world refuses to realize that violence, when used by Germans, is justified and righteous. What can I do? What would you do?' Ex-Kaiser: 'Do? I did!'" In both cases, the ultimate outcome was the same: defeat for Germany in two world wars. (*LC*)

On May 31, 1942, Hitler argued that "the example of Wilhelm II shows how one bad monarch can destroy a dynasty!" and on August 20 that same year, he added, "Had Wilhelm II been a monarch of character and vision … he would have won the affection of his people, and Social Democracy could never have become the power it did become in Germany!"

My view is maybe, maybe not. The social issues separating rulers and ruled were too great, I believe.

Stated Low of his work in *20 Years After*: "This cartoon appeared on 1 August 1934, the 20th anniversary of the German invasion of Belgium during the First World War, but—even in a symbolic sense—a conversation between the Kaiser and Hitler is largely fantasy. One of the Kaiser's grandsons did join the Nazi Party … Hitler not only abused the Hohenzollerns in his speeches; his plans for conquest as outlined in *Mein Kampf* followed a different pattern than the Kaiser chose. Hitler berated the Kaiser for having gone to war with England, but unlike the Kaiser, he assumed that he would have to fight Russia. The Kaiser and his descendants never gave up hope of a Hohenzollern restoration. Hitler believed that the Third Reich he established would last a thousand years," but World War II and its aftermath proved them all wrong.

Following the death in action in the 1940 French campaign of Imperial Crown Prince Wilhelm's eldest son and heir presumptive, Prince Wilhelm, his younger brother, Prince Louis Ferdinand (1908–94)—nicknamed "Lulu" within the family—succeeded as the Hohenzollern's future chief. Thus he ruled during 1951–1994 after the death of his father, a period of forty-eight years in all. Today, his son holds sway in case the dynasty is ever restored in the now Fourth Reich. Here Lulu is seen with his Russian-born Romanov dynasty wife, Princess Kira. (*DH*)

Noted his *Baltimore Sun* obituary of September 27, 1994, he was eighty-six years old at his death at Bremen, Germany: "The prince worked in a [Ford] Detroit auto plant in the 1930s and … was head of the House of Hohenzollern that ruled Brandenburg from 1415 and Prussia from 1701–1918 … In 1938, he married Countess Kira Kirilovna, a member of Russia's Zarist Romanov family. She died in 1967. He is survived by five of their seven children."

Above left: The official engagement photograph of His Majesty Kaiser Wilhelm II and his bride-to-be, Princess Hermine of Reuss (1887–1947). (*ASA*)

Above right: His Majesty in festive mood and garb at the gala 1938 Doorn wedding of his grandson Prince Louis Ferdinand of Prussia to Russian Grand Duchess Kira Kirillovna. (*ASA*)

Previous page, above: In May 1940, as the German Army overran neutral Holland as he did not do during the previous Great War. The Kaiser found himself guarded once more by armed men in field gray, for the first time since November 9, 1918, a generation before. Here, they assemble in front of the grand staircase at Doorn House, Utrecht Province, as he stands at the doorway behind them, also in German uniform. (*DH*)

On September 27, 1941—a few months after the Kaiser's demise—Hitler told his intimates: "The injustice committed by the Kaiser at Bismarck's expense finally recoiled upon him [in November 1918]. How could the Kaiser demand loyalty from his subjects when he had treated the founder of the Reich with such ingratitude?"—by firing him in March 1890.

Previous page, below: From the very same doorway a little over a year later, on June 9, 1941, the Kaiser's coffin is aboard his Mercedes-Benz car as hearse below for his funeral services outside. Standing just above it at right center is the then technically Kaiser Wilhelm III, the former imperial crown prince, hatless. Above him and to the left is the latter's younger brother, Prince Eitel-Frederick of Prussia. Between the two in funereal black are the late monarch's widow Kaiserin Hermine (*left*) and daughter, Princess of Prussia Viktoria Luise, Grand Duchess of Brunswick by marriage (*right*). Down below, in front of the car, is a pastor standing between two officers in spiked helmets holding the Kaiser's medal pillows, waiting for the marching soldiers in the foreground to pass. (*DH*)

Hitler said on August 20, 1942 of Bismarck's memoirs, "I know of no more trenchant criticism of the Kaiser than that given us in the third volume of Bismarck's own memoirs! When I read it, I was appalled! Had Wilhelm II … possessed the virtues of his grandfather [Wilhelm I], he would have kept Bismarck close to his side … The dismissal of Bismarck undoubtedly shattered the nation—and not only the fact itself—but the manner in which it was accomplished! For Bismarck after all was the symbol of national unity.… On the day he dismissed Bismarck, he gave a ball!"

The royal contingent of the official mourning party. *From left to right*: unknown hat-less naval officer; Kaiser Wilhelm III with his father's widow on his right arm, hat-less; Prince Eitel-Fritz and wife, Princess Viktoria Luise of Prussia; unknown naval officer; unknown female in black; Princess August Wilhelm of Prussia and her former husband, Prince Auwi; and in between them at rear in Luftwaffe steel helmet, uniform, and mourning arm band is Prince Louis Ferdinand of Prussia, crown prince and heir presumptive of the House of Prussia, 1941–94. (*DH*)

Hitler's historical summation of the late Kaiser was as "A mighty wielder of the bombastic word, but a coward in deed; a saber-rattler who never drew sword, though God knows he had opportunities enough!"

Princess Viktoria Luise was the third living member of the Death's Head Hussars present that day, the other two being her brother and Mackensen.

Exiting from the house is the political contingent of official state mourners. *From left to right*: German Naval Head of Military Intelligence/*Abwehr* Admiral Wilhelm Canaris; unknown officer; Dr Artur Seyss-Inquart, German Protector of the Netherlands as Hitler's main representative, hanged by the Allies as a convicted war criminal on October 16, 1946 at Nuremberg Prison; two unidentified officers; Mackensen carrying formal baton and wearing full Death's Head Hussar dress uniform and busby hat; and further unknown army officers. (*DH*)

On September 1, 1942—the third anniversary of his invasion of Poland—Hitler asserted that "the most insignificant letter of Bismarck is of more value than the whole life work of this Kaiser!"

The aged marshal (*left*), ninety-two years old, shakes hands with his fourth German Kaiser, Wilhelm III (*right*), formerly his subordinate at Danzig, Poland, before the Great War that saw them both command army groups against the Allies, as helmeted officers of Hitler's new victorious army watch from right. Here, both the older men wear the undress uniform of the Death's Head Hussars. (*DH*)

On May 31, 1942, Hitler added of Wilhelm II: "His bad taste and familiarity with other monarchs—backslapping and the like!—robbed Germany of much sympathy. A monarch must learn that self-restraint and dignity must be observed in everyday life."

The two groups of mourners merge during the funeral. *From left to right*: unknown officer; the peering face of Admiral Canaris; possibly now heir presumptive, Prince Louis Ferdinand of Prussia in Luftwaffe kit; Princess Viktoria Luise (*left*) and Kaiserin Hermine, both in black; the new Kaiser-designate, Wilhelm III; court official, Dr von Seyss-Inquart of Austria; perhaps Maj. Sigurd von Ilsemann, the late Kaiser's most loyal retainer in exile; and Marshal von Mackensen, bearing baton in right hand and busby in left. (*DH*)

On August 20, 1942, Hitler mentioned Wilhelm II's "Jewish ancestry … the heritage of [which] comes out … in his whole attitude … the completely cynical lack of self-control that was characteristic of him."

Mourners *in extremis. From left to right*: Princess of Prussia Viktoria Luise's nephew, Prince Wilhelm Karl, as an army colonel; Kaiser Wilhelm III; and Marshal von Mackensen. (*DH*)

On September 1, 1942, the Nazi Führer noted: "The era of Wilhelm II and the bad taste that was its hallmark! … The upstart! … The Old Wilhelm was a *grand signeur*, but Wilhelm II was a strutting puppet of no character! … He who was then the Kaiser [Wilhelm II] was a man lacking the strength to resist his enemies!"

Above: Where Kaiser Wilhelm II has lain since June 9, 1941 to now, the tomb on the grounds of Doorn House, Holland. As the senior man present, Field Marshal von Mackensen was the final person allowed to pay his respects at the coffin's side in the chapel seen here: "Remaining there in prayer for a minute or so," according to Lamar Cecil. After kneeling in prayer, he disdained offers to help him up from his knees, and lifted himself up with the aid of his sheathed sword. (*DH*)

In May 1942, Hitler pointed out: "The behavior of Wilhelm II in society was unworthy of a monarch! Not only did he consistently ridicule the members of his immediate entourage, but also fired a constant stream of ironic remarks at his guests for the amusement of the remainder!"

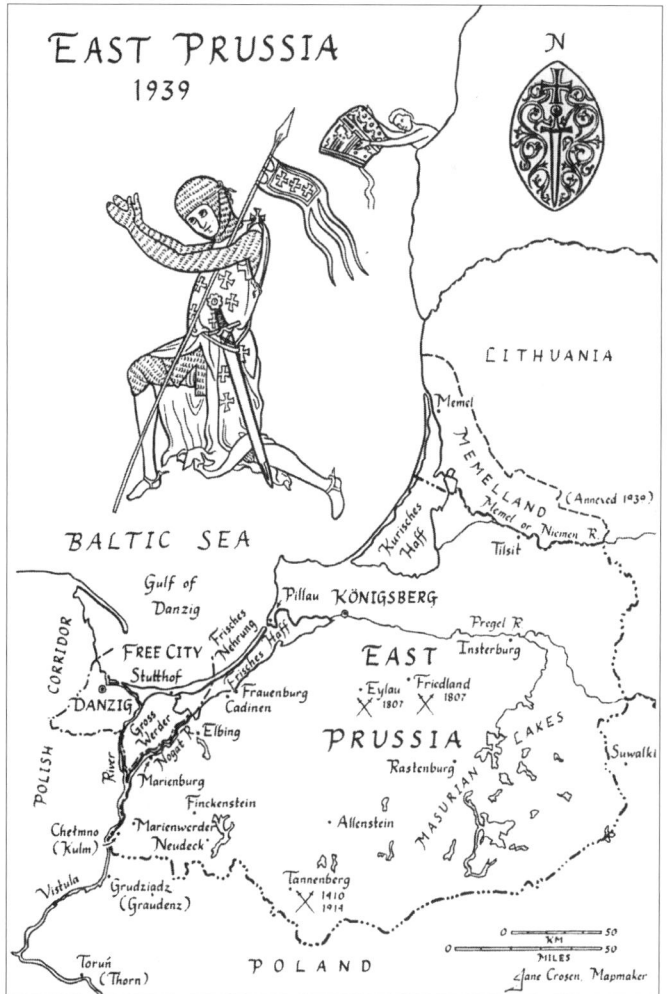

A 1939 map of Prussian battlefields during 1410–1914, including the Napoleonic combats of 1807 at Eylau and Freidland, both French victories, by mapmaker Jane Crosen. (*LC*)

In a series of wartime asides, the field marshal imparted to his civilian painter his maxims on wartime generalship as well: "The general should only lay down the broad lines, leaving details to his subordinates … but all responsibility falls upon the general's shoulders! It is not so easy to manage a battle as you might think!"

The official Sunday, August 23, 1939, poster for the *Jahrfeier* (Annual Celebration) of the Battle of Tannenberg that never was, as Hitler canceled it for two reasons: first, the next day he signed a non-aggression pact with Stalin and second, he was about to invade Poland. Thus, the twenty-fifth anniversary featuring Hindenburg's head over top the memorial remained un-celebrated from that day to this. (*HHA*)

Continued the field marshal to Prof. Vogel: "Nor does it suffice to issue orders like, 'Advance the guns, forward, quick march!' Not a bit of it! You have to maneuver here and there." In this—according to Ludwig Cohn twenty years later—Hindenburg got into character as Blücher by assuming the Berlin dialect for his listener's edification as well.

During the height of his invasion of the Soviet Union in August 1941, Hitler made one final pilgrimage to Hohenstein with his entourage to visit the mighty red brick Tannenberg Memorial. *From left to right*: Colonel General Alfred Jodl; two unknown men; Luftwaffe aide Colonel Gerhard Christian; Foreign Minister Joachim von Ribbentrop; Dr Theodor Morell, the Führer's personal physician; unknown man; German Foreign Office Ambassador Walther Hewel, Ribbentrop's liaison officer with FHQ; Hitler at left center; possibly former German Ambassador to Fascist Italy Georg von Mackensen, second son of the field marshal; SS Führer Escort Physician Dr Karl Brandt; Army Field Marshal Wilhelm Keitel with informal swagger stick baton; Luftwaffe Colonel Nikolaus von Below; Martin Bormann; unknown man; SS General Julius Schaub, chief personal adjutant to the Führer; NSKK liaison Albert Bormann, younger brother of Martin; General Rudolf Schmundt, Chief of Army Personnel; and unidentified other. (*Joachim von Ribbentrop Albums, U.S. National Archives, College Park, MD, USA*)

The married Mackensen couple at right admire the ornate formal field marshal's baton of Wilhelm Keitel—chief of the High Command of the German Wehrmacht—at their country estate of Brüssow on the Black Hussar's ninety-fifth birthday, December 6, 1944, with an oil portrait of their Führer serving as the backdrop. (*HHA*)

Field Marshal August von Mackensen died a month short of the age of ninety-six on November 8, 1945, "in a farmyard near Celle at Schmiedeberg after fleeing to his native Saxony. It was there that this great cavalry leader and true servant of his Kaiser found his final resting place," according to Princess Viktoria Luise of Prussia in her post-World War II memoirs.

On August 2, 1941, Hitler expressed this view of Wilhelm II: "The Kaiser received a delegation of workers just once! He gave them a fine scolding, threatening simply to withdraw the Imperial favor from them! At their local meetings, I suppose the delegates had plenty of time in which to draw their conclusions from the Imperial speech.... The injustice committed by the Kaiser at Bismarck's expense finally recoiled upon him. How could the Kaiser demand loyalty from his subjects when he had treated the founder of the Reich with such ingratitude? The shameful thing is that the German people allowed such an injustice to be committed!"

On November 11, 1941, he added: "Monarchy is an out-of-date form.... The Age of Princes is over."

On March 31, 1942, he added: "In the hereditary monarchies ... there were at least eight kings out of 10 who—if they had been ordinary citizens—would not have been capable of successfully running a grocery!"

The last major event held at the Tannenberg Memorial was the state funeral of slain Luftwaffe Chief of Staff Colonel General of Flyers Günther Korten, killed in the bomb blast meant for Hitler on July 20, 1944. His flag-bedecked coffin rests at right flanked by air force honor guards, his medal cushions displayed in front, with them German Reich Marshal Hermann Goering saluting at left with his interim stab informal swagger stick baton. Behind him, a quartet of Luftwaffe men carry the large funeral wreath forward. (*HHA*)

The very same scene as viewed from behind Goering, with the Iron Cross stand being placed in front of the therefore blocked entry to the Tomb of the Hindenburgs, and situated thus also between the pair of concrete sentries at left and right. Colonel General Korten's helmet is seen atop his casket at center. Note also the pair of photographers at upper left: SS (*left*) and Air Force (right.) (*HHA*)

One time, Hindenburg, "Came with a measuring rod to make sure that the (canvas battle) decorations were to scale. He provided rubber galoshes for his painter of battle scenes, was continually asking about (publisher) Ullstein's color prints of his pictures, and took all his Royal visitors to see them," as well.

The partially destroyed Tannenberg Memorial in January 1945, blown up by German Army Corps of Engineers demolition men at Hitler's orders. (*LC*)

With the Tannenberg scene lit up, "His guests were to parade in front of the canvasses before a row of privates standing at attention, and each holding a lamp." In this regard, one wonders if Pvt. Hitler ever saw any of the illustrious personages described herein during the Great War; in his own postwar memoirs, *Mein Kampf*—he was silent on this point, except for the Austrian Kaiser Karl, for whom he once shoveled snow outside Vienna's Hotel Imperial before the war.

The massive statue honoring Hindenburg with baton and sword inside one of the Tannenberg towers before its overthrow by the Soviets. (*HHA*)

Ludendorff on the other hand could not have cared less about being in wartime paintings, no matter how grand: "I would rather wait to have my portrait done until the job is finished! Popular favor and the fortunes of war are extremely fickle. The Goddess of War is a sorry baggage!"

The colossus beheaded and toppled by the Red Army in January 1945. (*LC*)

"When … Ludendorff gave way and came alone to his first [portrait] sitting, the artist's preliminary sketch infuriated him. Hindenburg … wanted Ludendorff to be looking at him, thereby creating the impression that the younger man was receiving orders from the elder. This was too much!" added Ludwig Cohn.

The Communist KC PZPR in Red Poland postwar had "The stairs of granite tiles from the Tannenberg *Denkmal* [Memorial]."

Post WWI, Vogel wrote: "Ludendorff said that such an arrangement of the two portraits was derogatory to him in respect of his military relationship to Hindenburg.… He became so much excited as to declare that—regarded as an historical document—my picture would be inaccurate. By degrees, I was able to appease him … to let me begin painting, but the atmosphere was somewhat chilly."

Another remnant of Tannenberg went to build *The Monument to a Guerilla* in Warsaw.

Added Ludwig Cohn of this encounter between artist and quartermaster general. "This is the only recorded occasion on which the proud and silent subordinate openly claimed his share in the glory.… It must have been galling to be perpetually spoken to and spoken of by Hindenburg as, 'my loyal assistant."

Yet another part went to build *The Monument of the Liberation of Vermia and Masuria Lands* at Olsztyn, Poland, the square surrounding it being paved with granite tiles from the former Hindenburg Mausoleum in the former Tannenberg *Denkmal*.

Upon seeing his duo epic painting for the first time, Wilhelm II von Hohenzollern commented rather archly: "That Ludendorff's mouth was too tightly closed, but in other respects, I am well pleased! That you have made Hindenburg's figure dominant is most commendable!"

An idyllic view of the Tannenberg National Memorial with stone lion atop the plinth at left. The very same stone lion became a new Polish resident postwar! (*LC*)

"Devoted to the memory of the fallen soldiers of the 147th Infantry Regiment by the Italian sculptor Michelangelo Pietrobelli," according to one modern source.

Le Tissier: "Today, Tannenberg lies in Poland, and has been renamed Olsztynek. All that remains of the Memorial are small vestiges of its walls." German Army engineers blew up the memorial on January 20, 1945.

The Kaiser did have one complaint about Vogel's Tannenberg masterpiece, however: "Ludendorff was too near the field marshal. This gives a false impression, since it was the field marshal who won the battle!" When it was suggested elsewhere that an artillery battery be added, the field marshal put his stamped foot down at last thus: "The picture will be painted in accordance with my wishes!" Finally, as noted by Ludwig Cohn: "Hindenburg's last letter about the Battle of Tannenberg is dated November 7, 1918!" two days before he curtly informed the Kaiser that Holland was to be his new home for the rest of the Kaiser's sojourn upon the planet earth.

In 1992, Le Tissier wrote: "The remains of President Paul von Hindenburg and his wife were removed from their [1935] graves at Tannenberg … [and] taken to Bernterode, 40 kilometers east of Kassel, and walled up in a 2,000-foot-deep salt mine. The US 1st Army overran the area, and seven soldiers inspecting the mine for ammunition noticed fresh mortar in a corridor. They broke down the five-foot-thick wall, and the secret shrine was revealed. The coffins were surrounded by over 200 regimental banners—many dating from the Prussian wars—and other treasures, including the Hohenzollern crown."

Aside from 40,000 tons of explosives and ammunition stored in the 23 kilometers of hidden galleries, Hitler had secreted there two other revered coffins with the von Hindenburgs as well, those of Frederick the Great and his father, the famed "Soldier King" Frederick Wilhelm I. Thus—even to the end—President von Hindenburg's last chancellor did what he could to preserve the mystique of *Der Alte Herr.*

"Walter Hancock explained that, 'To the lid of each coffin a label had been fastened with Scotch tape. Hastily scrawled in red crayon, these read, 'Field Marshal von Hindenburg, Mrs von Hindenburg; Frederick Wilhelm I, the Soldier King.' Hitler's wreath was placed upon this casket—the Führer's tribute to the Soldier King." (*U.S. Army Signal Corps photograph, The Pentagon*)

"The actual work of packing and hoisting consumed four days, and ended on V-E [Victory in Europe Day]. The caskets were the last to be hoisted. We arranged to leave Frederick the Great until the very end, as the great weight and size of his casket might have caused some trouble. His father and Mrs. von Hindenburg—being the lightest—were sent aloft first. I then rode up in the carriage with the field marshal. Meanwhile, a radio installed in the office alongside the shaft entrance poured forth patriotic speeches and music in celebration of the Victory in Europe. Finally, the ready signal came, and we started hoisting as slowly as the engines would turn. By one of the most whimsical of all coincidences ever arranged by the ironic Fates, the radio at this instant began playing 'The Star-Spangled Banner.' And then—just as the casket of the greatest of the Prussian kings rose to the earth's surface—the tune changed to 'God save the King.' Early the next morning, our convoy of eight trucks and two jeeps started on its journey toward a place of safekeeping," Hohenzollern Castle, concluded Hancock.

The nocturnal reburial of the Hindenburgs and the two Prussian kings took place at Marburg's Elizabeth Church in August 1946.

"No one had ever heard Hindenburg or Ludendorff speak of the famous battle in the other's presence.… Each of them was accustomed to open with the words, 'At the time when I won the Battle of Tannenberg.'… Their miffed subordinate General Max Hoffmann felt otherwise, however."

The final resting place of the Hindenburgs postwar at Marburg had slabs below, level with the floor.

Hindenburg counseled, "He who has the best nerves will win the war!"

A generation later, his successor martial as German warlord, Hitler, felt the same way, again wrongly in terms of himself.

Comparing himself later to the great Napoleon, Hindenburg told Prof. Vogel, "At that time [1410], the battlefield where the Teutonic Knights were defeated was the size of my finger nail [on a map], but the battlefield on which I defeated the Slavs is as large as my hand! It is a great joy to me that I was able to wipe out that disgrace!" (*U.S. Army Signal Corps Photograph, The Pentagon*).

Kaiser Wilhelm III (*left*) as a French Army POW (*right*) on May 3, 1945 at Bad, Austria, found living with a young female hairdresser, thus outraging the commander of the French forces, General Jean de Lattre de Tassigny. (*LC*)

Crown Prince Wilhelm died as a French POW six years later. During the Great War, by contrast, "Hindenburg may be regarded as the happiest man in wartime," asserted his 1935 biographer, Ludwig Cohn.

The final resting place of Wilhelm III and his Kaiserin, Cecilie of Germany, Castle Hohenzollern, as seen in 1931. (*DH*)

U.S. Army armored officer William Hancock, U.S. Military Academy West Point graduate, Class of 1971, "The castle has a statue of St Michael Slaying the Dragon, a common German motif."

Outside Warsaw during the Great War, sixty German Army battalions faced off against 224 Russian. While the Battle of Verdun raged in the west, however, Hindenburg hunted in the Polish Forest of Bialowitz, seized in the summer of 1941 as the personal fiefdom of one Hermann Goering.

In October 1918, Hindenburg haughtily vetoed any such notion as equal rations for officers and men, suggested by the final imperial chancellor of the Great War, Prince Maximilian von Baden.

Crown Prince Rupprecht of Bavaria postwar (*right*) with his second wife. (*LC*)

The Battle of Verdun cost 225,000 German Army soldiers their lives.

At the postwar German government Commission of Inquiry, it was asserted by General von Kuhl that "the emperor as a person had retired into the background, and the true Warlord of the German armies was Hindenburg. Although Ludendorff was co-responsible ... in actual fact, Hindenburg was responsible."

Crown Prince Rupprecht—"the uncrowned King of Bavaria"—received a royal state funeral in 1955, and was the very last of Kaiser Wilhelm II's former field marshals of the Great War of 1914–18 to die. (*LC*)

In 1935, Ludwig Kohn asserted that the Kaiser's first of several wartime nervous breakdowns came when he realized that Imperial Germany had, indeed, lost the First Battle of the Marne River, and, thus, the war itself.

Das Eiserne Kreuz 2. Klasse (The Iron Cross 2nd Class), complete with—from top to bottom—black-and-silver ribbon, imperial and royal crown, monogram "W," and 1914 date of first issue. (*LC*)

Bibliography

Great War General Histories

Falls, C., *The Great War* (New York: G.P. Putnam's Sons, 1959)

Hart, P., *The Great War: A Combat History of the First World War* (New York: Oxford University Press, 2013)

Lloyd, N., *Passchendaele: The Lost Victory of World War I* (New York: Basic Books, 2017)

Mozier, J., *The Myth of the Great War: How the Germans Won the Battles & How the Americans Saved the Allies* (New York: Harper, 2001)

Philpott, W., *War of Attrition: Fighting the First World War* (New York: The Overlook Press, 2014)

By and About Hindenburg

Hindenburg, P. von, *The Great War/From Out of My Life*, edited by Charles Messenger, (London: Greenhill Books, 2006)

Hindenburg, L. N. von, *Hindenburg at Home: An Intimate Biography* (New York: Duffield & Green, 1931)

Goltz, A. von der, *Hindenburg: Power, Myth, and the Rise of the Nazis* (New York: Oxford University Press, 2011)

Astore, W. J., and Showalter, D. E., *Hindenburg: Icon of German Militarism*, Washington, DC: Potomac Books, Inc., 2005

Bloem, W., *Hindenburg als Reichsprasident/as Reich President* (Berlin: Fatherland Publishing, 1936)

Asprey, R. B., *The German High Command at War: Hindenburg and Ludendorff Conduct World War I* (New York: William Morrow & Co., Inc., 1991)

Wheeler-Bennett, Sir J. W., *Wooden Titan: Hindenburg in 20 Years of German History, 1914–34* (New York: William Morrow & Co., 1936)

By and About Ludendorff

Ludendorff, E., *Ludendorff's Own Story, August 1914–November 1918: The Great War from the Siege of Liege to the Signing of the Armistice as Viewed from the Grand Headquarters of the German Army* (New York: Harper & Brothers Publishers, 1919)

Ludendorff, M., *My Married Life with Ludendorff* (London: Hutchinson & Co., 1929)

Goodspeed, D. J., *Ludendorff: Genius of World War I* (Boston: Houghton Mifflin Company, 1966)

Brownell, W., and Drace-Brownell, D., *The First Nazi: Erich Ludendorff, the Man Who Made Hitler Possible* (Berkeley, CA: Counterpoint, 2016)

Parkinson, R., *Tormented Warrior: Ludendorff and the Supreme Command* (New York: Stein and Day, Publishers, 1979)

Royals in General

Boff, J., *Haig's Enemy: Crown Prince Rupprecht and Germany's War on the Western Front,* (Oxford, UK: Oxford University Press, 2018)

Fraser, J., *Postcards of Lost Royals,* (Oxford, UK: Bodleian Library, 2009)

Judd, D., *Eclipse of Kings: European Monarchs in the 20th Century* (Briarcliff Manor, NY: Stein & Day Publishers, 1974)

Russell, G., *The Emperors: How Europe's Rulers Were Destroyed by the First World War* (Gloucestershire, UK: Amberley Publishing, 2014)

Sulzberger, C. L., *The Fall of Eagles: The Death of the Great European Dynasties* (New York: Crown Publishers, Inc., 1977)

Van der Kiste, J., *Crowns in a Changing World: The British and European Monarchies 1901–36,* (Stroud, UK: Alan Sutton Publishing, 1993)

The Hohenzollerns

Brimble, E. L., *In the Eyrie of the Hohenzollern Eagle* (London: Hodder and Stoughton, 1917)

Ferdinand, Prince L., *The Rebel Prince: The Memoirs of Prince Louis Ferdinand of Prussia,* (Chicago: Henry Regnery Company, 1952)

Cohn, Emil Ludwig, *Wilhelm Hohenzollern: The Last of the Kaisers* (New York: G.P. Putnam's Sons, 1927)

Gorlitz, W., *The Kaiser and His Court* (New York: Harcourt, Brace and World, 1964)

Hermine, Empress, *An Empress in Exile: My Days in Doorn* (New York: J. H. Sears & Co., Inc., Publishers, 1928)

Jonas, K. W., *The Life of Crown Prince William* (London: Routledge & Kegan Paul, 1961)

Van der Kiste, J., *The Last German Empress: Empress Augusta Victoria, Consort of Emperor William II* (South Devon, England: A & F Publications, 2014)

Van der Kiste, J., *The Prussian Princesses: The Sisters of Kaiser Wilhelm II* (Stroud, UK: Fonthill Media, 2014)

Lochner, L. P., *Always the Unexpected: A Book of Reminiscences* (New York: The Macmillan Company, 1956)

Lochner, L. P., *What About Germany?* (New York: Dodd, Mead & Company, 1942)

Luise, Grand Duchess V., *Bilder der Kaiserzeit [Pictures of the Imperial Time]* (Gottingen-Hannover, West Germany, 1969)

Lockhart, R. H. B., *Comes the Reckoning* (London: Putnam, 1947)

Luise, Grand Duchess V., *The Kaiser's Daughter: The Memoirs of HRH Viktoria Luise, Princess of Prussia* (Englewood Cliff, NJ: Prentice-Hall, Inc., 1977)

Rohl, J. C. G., *Wilhelm II: Into the Abyss of War and Exile, 1900–41,* (Cambridge, NY: Cambridge University Press, 2014)

The Imperial German Army

Brazier, K., *The Complete Blue Max: A Chronological Record of the Holders of the Pour le Mérite, Prussia's Highest Military Order from 1740–1918* (South Yorkshire, UK: Pen & Sword Books, Ltd., 2013)

Fischer, F., *Germany's Aims in the First World War* (New York: W.W. Norton & Co., Inc., 1967)

Gorlitz, W., *History of the German General Staff, 1657–1945* (New York: Praeger Paperbacks, 1962)

Kane, R. B., *Disobedience and Conspiracy in the German Army, 1918–45* (Jefferson, NC: McFarland & Co., Inc., Publishers, 2008)

Pawley, R., *The Kaiser's Warlords: German Commanders of World War I* (New York: Osprey Publishing, 2003)

Thomas, N., *The German Army in World War I (2)* (New York: Osprey Publishing, 2004)

Wheeler-Bennett, Sir J. W., *The Nemesis of Power: The German Army in Politics, 1918–45* (London: Macmillan & Co., Ltd., 1964)

Germany's Eastern & Russia's Western Fronts, 1914–18

Buttar, P., *Collision of Empires: The War on the Eastern Front in 1914* (New York: Osprey Publishing, 2014)

Buttar, P., *Germany Ascendant: The Eastern Front 1915* (New York: Osprey Publishing, 2015)

Buttar, P., *Russia's Last Gasp: The Eastern Front 1916–17* (New York: Osprey Publishing, 2016)

Montefiore, S. S., *The Romanovs: 1613–1918* (New York: Alfred A. Knopf, 2016)

Roy, J. C., *The Vanished Kingdom: Travels Through the History of Prussia* (Oxford, UK: Westview Press, 1999)

Smele, J. D., *The "Russian" Civil Wars 1916–26: 10 Years That Shook the World* (New York: Oxford University Press, 2015)

Stone, D. B., *The Russian Army in the Great War: The Eastern Front, 1914–17* (Lawrence, Kansas: University Press of Kansas, 2015)

Wheeler-Bennett, Sir J. W., *Brest-Litovsk: The Forgotten Peace, March 1918* (New York: W.W. Norton & Co., Inc., 1938)

The Balkans and Romania

Barrett, M. B., *Prelude to Blitzkrieg: The 1916 Austro-German Campaign in Romania* (Bloomington & Indianapolis, IN: Indiana University Press, 2013)

Kaplan, R. D., *Balkan Ghosts: A Journey Through History* (New York: St, Martin's Press, 1993)

Kihntopf, M. P., *(Handcuffed to a Corpse: German Intervention in the Balkans and on the Galician front, 1914–17* (Shippensburg, PA: White Mane Press, 2002)

Marie, Queen of Romania, *The Story of My Life* (New York: Charles Scribner's Sons, 1934)

Torrey, G. E., *The Romanian Battlefront in World War I* (Lawrence, KS: University Press of Kansas, 2011)

Western Europe, 1918

Barnett, C., *The Swordbearers: Supreme Command in the First World War* (New York: Signet Books, 1963)

Best, N., *The Greatest Day in History* (New York: Public Affairs, 2008)

Foch, F., *The Memoirs of Marshal Foch* (Garden City, NY: Doubleday, Doran and Company, Inc., 1921)

Lloyd, N., *Hundred Days: The Campaign That Ended World War I* (New York: Basic Books, 2014)

Paschall, R., *The Defeat of Imperial Germany, 1917–18* (New York: Da Capo Press, 1989)

Pitt, B., *1918: The Last Act* (New York: Ballantine Books, 1962)

Toland, J., *No Man's Land: 1918—The Last Year of the Great War* (Garden City, NY: Doubleday & Co., Inc., 1980)

The Middle East

Crawley, R., *Climax at Gallipoli: The Failure of the August Offensive* (Norman, OK: University of Oklahoma Press, 2014)

Erickson, E. J., *Palestine: The Ottoman Campaigns of 1914–18* (South Yorkshire, UK: Pen & Sword Military, 2016)

Faulkner, N., *Lawrence of Arabia's War: The Arabs, the British, and the Remaking of the Middle East in WW I* (New Haven, CT: Yale University Press, 2016)

Johnson, R., *The Great War in the Middle East* (New York: Oxford University Press, 2016)

McMeekin, S., *The Ottoman Endgame: War, Revolution, and the Making of the Modern Middle East, 1908–23* (New York: Penquin Press, 2015)

Rogan, E., *The Fall of the Ottomans: The Great War in the Middle East* (New York: Basic Books, 2015)

The German Revolution

Watt, R. M., *The Kings Depart—The Tragedy of Germany: Versailles and the German Revolution* (New York: Simon & Schuster, 1968)

The Weimar Republic

Papen, F. von, *Memoirs* (New York: E.P. Dutton & Co., Inc., 1953)

Pietrusza, D., *1932: The Rise of Hitler & FDR: Two Tales of Politics, Betrayal, and Unlikely Destiny* (Guilford, CT: Lyons Press, 2016)

Nazis

Domarus, Max*: Hitler: Speeches and Proclamations 1932-45, Vol. 1 (1932-34)* and *Vol. 2 (1935-38),* (Wauconda, IL, US, 2000-01)

Lepage, J.-D., *Hitler's Stormtroopers: The SA, The Nazis' Brownshirts, 1922–45* (Barnsley, UK: Frontline Books, 2016)

Miller, M. D., and Schulz, A., *Leaders of the Storm Troops, Volume 1* (West Midlands, UK: Helion & Co., Ltd., 2015)

Toland, J., *Adolf Hitler,* (Garden City, NY: Doubleday & Co., Inc., 1976)

Turner, Jr., H. A., *Hitler's 30 Days to Power, January 1933* (London: Addison-Wesley, 1996)

General Reference

François-Poncet, A., *The Fateful Years: Memoirs of a French Ambassador in Berlin, 1931–38* (New York: Harcourt, Brace, & Co, 1949)

Gosling, L., *Brushes & Bayonets: Cartoons, Sketches, and Paintings of World War I* (New York: Osprey Publishing, 2008)

Langenscheidt's German-English, English-German Dictionary (New York: Pocket Books, Inc., 1961)

Mr. Punch's History of the Great War (New York: Frederick A. Stokes Co., Publishers, 1920)

Articles

Dorpalen, A., "Empress Augusta Victoria and the Fall of the German Monarchy," *The American Historical Review,* Vol. 58, #1 (October 1952), pp. 17-38

Gessner, P. K., "Tannenberg: A Monument of German Pride," Internet, January 19, 2017

von der Goltz, A. M., "The Iron Hindenburg: A Popular Icon of Weimar Germany," *German History,* Vol. 26, #3, pp. 357-382, 2008

Kamenir, V., "Showdown at Grunwald (1st Battle of Tannenberg, 15 July 1410)" *Military Heritage* magazine, March 2017, pp. 28-35

Lang, W., "The Case of the Distinguished Corpses: Despite secrecy, ruined castles, US Army finds 'Todesraum' for four famous Germans," *Life* magazine, March 6, 1950

Miranda, J., "Ober Ost: World War I on the Eastern Front, 1914-18," *Strategy & Tactics* magazine, # 301, November–December 2016

Taylor, Pvt. B., "US Army, Der Alte Herr/The Old Gentleman: A Short Life of Field Marshal von Hindenburg," October 10, 1965, Schofield Barracks, HI/USA: previously unpublished manuscript

About the Author

Blaine Taylor (b. 1946) is the American author of twenty-two illustrated histories on war, politics, automotives, biography, engineering, architecture, medicine, photography, and aviation.

The well-read historian is a former Vietnam War soldier and military policeman of the U.S. Army's elite 199th Light Infantry Brigade, which fought under enemy Communist Viet Cong fire during 1966–67 in the now-defunct Republic of South Vietnam. He was awarded twelve medals and decorations, including the coveted Combat Infantryman's Badge (CIB). A later crime and political newspaper reporter, Mr. Taylor is also an award-winning medical journalist, international magazine writer, and the winner of four political campaigns as press secretary for county, state, and U.S. presidential elections.

During 1991–92, he served as a U.S. Congressional aide and press secretary on Capitol Hill, Washington, D.C.

His previously published book titles include:

Guarding the Fuhrer: Sepp Dietrich, Johann Rattenhuber, and the Protection of Adolf Hitler (1993)
Fascist Eagle: Italy's Air Marshal Italo Balbo (1996)
Mercedes-Benz Parade and Staff Cars of the Third Reich (1999)
Volkswagen Military Vehicles of the Third Reich (2004)
Hitler's Headquarters from Beer Hall to Bunker 1920–45 (2006)
Hilerovy Hlavni Stany: Z Oivnice do Dunkru, 1920–45 (Slovak language edition of the above title 2007)
Apex of Glory: Benz, Daimler, & Mercedes-Benz 1885–1955 (2006)
Hitler's Chariots Volume 1: Mercedes-Benz G-4 Cross-Country Touring Car (2009)
Hitler's Chariots Volume 2: Mercedes-Benz 770K Grosser Parade Car (2010)
Hitler's Engineers: Fritz Todt and Albert Speer/Master Builders of the Third Reich (2010)
Inzynierowie tajna armia Hitlera (Polish language edition of the above title, 2011)
Hitler's Chariots Volume 3: Volkswagen from Nazi People's Car to New Beetle (2011)
Mrs Adolf Hitler: The Eva Braun Photograph Albums 1912–45 (2013)
Dallas Fifty Years On: The Murder of John F. Kennedy (2013)

Guarding the Fuhrer: Sepp Dietrich & Adolf Hitler/Upgraded Edition (2014)

Hermann Goering in the First World War: The Personal Photograph Albums of Hermann Goering (2014)

Kaiser Bill! A New Look at Germany's Last Emperor Wilhelm II 1859–1941 (2014)

Hitlerovi Inzenyri: Fritz Todt a Albert Speer/Hlavni stavitele Treti rise (Slovak language edition of *Hitler's Engineers* 2015)

Hermann Goering: Beer Hall Putsch to Nazi Blood Purge 1919–34 (2015)

Reich Rails: Royal Prussia, Imperial Germany and the First World War 1825–1918 (2016)

Hermann Goering: From Secret Luftwaffe to Hossbach War Conference 1935–37 (2016)

Hermann Goering: Blumenkrieg, From Vienna to Prague 1938–39 (2017)